Virginia Pulcini
**The Influence of English on Italian**

# Language Contact
# and Bilingualism

Editor
Yaron Matras

## Volume 23

Virginia Pulcini

# The Influence of English on Italian

Lexical and Cultural Features

Free access to the e-book version of this publication was made possible by the 16 institutions that supported the open access transformation *Purchase to Open Pilot* in collaboration with Jisc.

ISBN 978-3-11-221396-4
e-ISBN (PDF) 978-3-11-075511-4
e-ISBN (EPUB) 978-3-11-075522-0
ISSN 2190-698X
DOI https://doi.org/10.1515/9783110755114

This work is licensed under the Creative Commons Attribution-NoDerivs 4.0 International License. For details go to https://creativecommons.org/licenses/by-nd/4.0.

Creative Commons license terms for re-use do not apply to any content (such as graphs, figures, photos, excerpts, etc.) not original to the Open Access publication and further permission may be required from the rights holder. The obligation to research and clear permission lies solely with the party re-using the material.

**Library of Congress Control Number: 2023930661**

**Bibliographic information published by the Deutsche Nationalbibliothek**
The Deutsche Nationalbibliothek lists this publication in the Deutsche Nationalbibliografie; detailed bibliographic data are available on the internet at http://dnb.dnb.de.

© 2025 the author(s), published by Walter de Gruyter GmbH, Berlin/Boston
This volume is text- and page-identical with the hardback published in 2023.
This book is published open access at www.degruyter.com.

Cover image: Anette Linnea Rasmus/Fotolia
Typesetting: Integra Software Services Pvt. Ltd.
Printing and binding: CPI books GmbH, Leck

www.degruyter.com

[. . .] non si può trovare una lingua, che parli ogni cosa per se senza aver accattato da altri; [it is not possible to find a language which can speak of anything by itself without having taken from others]
Niccolò Machiavelli c. 1524

Contact breeds imitation and imitation breeds linguistic convergence.
André Martinet 1953

In the world trade of lexis, English has – against expectation – never become bankrupt: rather, the Word Bank of England now tends to supply other languages with the necessary loans.
Manfred Görlach 2003

# Contents

**Acknowledgements** — XI

**List of figures** — XIII

**List of tables** — XV

**1 Introducing the study of Anglicisms in Italian** — 1
1.1 The English momentum — 1
1.2 English and Italian in contact — 3
1.3 Research on Anglicisms in Italian — 6
1.4 Loanword lexicography: Collecting and storing Anglicisms — 8
1.5 The reference sources and data — 10
1.6 The structure of this book — 12

**2 English in Italy: History of language contact** — 17
2.1 Chronology of early influences — 17
2.2 Anglomania — 23
2.3 The 19$^{th}$ century — 27
2.4 Neo-purism — 34
2.5 The post-war years — 41
2.6 The new millennium — 46
2.7 Roundup — 50

**3 Direct borrowings** — 51
3.1 Approaches and terminology — 51
3.2 Lexical routes of transmission and mediation — 58
3.3 The Global Anglicism Database — 60
3.3.1 Aims and structure — 60
3.3.2 Methodology — 62
3.4 Loanwords — 64
3.4.1 Non-adapted — 64
3.4.2 Adapted — 83
3.5 False Anglicisms — 85
3.6 Hybrids — 91
3.7 Phraseologisms and pragmatic Anglicisms — 94
3.8 Roundup — 99

| | | |
|---|---|---|
| **4** | **Integration and indirect borrowings —— 101** | |
| 4.1 | Integration —— 101 | |
| 4.1.1 | Orthographic —— 101 | |
| 4.1.2 | Phonological —— 104 | |
| 4.1.3 | Morpho-syntactic —— 107 | |
| 4.1.4 | Semantic —— 116 | |
| 4.2 | Indirect borrowings —— 120 | |
| 4.2.1 | Calques —— 121 | |
| 4.2.2 | Semantic loans —— 125 | |
| 4.3 | Anglicisms in competition with Italian words —— 130 | |
| 4.4 | Anglicisms or internationalisms? —— 132 | |
| 4.5 | Roundup —— 137 | |
| | | |
| **5** | **Dictionaries, newspaper archives and corpora —— 139** | |
| 5.1 | Dictionaries: The quantitative dimension at work —— 139 | |
| 5.2 | A comparison between letter J entries —— 150 | |
| 5.3 | Newspaper archives —— 160 | |
| 5.4 | Corpora: The frequency dimension at work —— 162 | |
| 5.5 | Roundup —— 174 | |
| | | |
| **6** | **Anglicisms in specialized domains —— 175** | |
| 6.1 | The periphery of the lexicon —— 175 | |
| 6.2 | Information and communication technology —— 180 | |
| 6.3 | Economy —— 183 | |
| 6.4 | Sport —— 189 | |
| 6.5 | Obsolescence —— 193 | |
| 6.6 | Ephemera and the Italian linguistic landscape —— 204 | |
| 6.7 | Roundup —— 207 | |
| | | |
| **7** | **English in Italian education —— 209** | |
| 7.1 | An 'English-first' educational system —— 209 | |
| 7.2 | English-medium instruction —— 216 | |
| 7.3 | The cultural debate: From 'Anglomania' to 'Anglophobia' —— 225 | |
| 7.4 | Roundup —— 234 | |

**Conclusions** —— 237

**References** —— 243

**Index of names / subjects** —— 261

**Index of borrowings and quoted words** —— 265

# Acknowledgements

When I first met the German linguist Manfred Görlach in 1995 at the ESSE Conference in Glasgow and was taken on board in his project of the *Dictionary of European Anglicisms*, I did not imagine that the study of Anglicisms in Italian would become the core of my research for almost three decades. To Manfred Görlach goes my utmost gratitude for leading me into the fascinating field of lexicology and lexicography! On the completion of Görlach's trilogy, the dictionary itself and the two companion volumes, I embarked on the compilation of a new dictionary of Anglicisms in Italian, a project that unfortunately was never accomplished, as lack of funding, and partly inexperience, brought the compilation to a stop at letter N. Yet, the lesson that I learned is that good research is not a 'solo' enterprise, but the result of teamwork and of the guidance of a strong leader. Needless to say, working with words requires a good deal of perseverance, as meanings are slippery and neologisms emerge overnight, making the job of the lexicographer a never-ending one, without limiting one's scope. But perhaps this is the most exciting part of the linguist's activity – observe, annotate, evaluate, include, exclude, and back again.

In 2014 I joined a new research team, the Global Anglicism Database (GLAD) network, a group of linguists, some of whom had contributed to Görlach' dictionary. This new joint venture aims at monitoring the spread of Anglicisms and related phenomena in the world's languages, also outside the European context, and compile a database of borrowings. The ultimate goal is the same: measure and compare the way in which English is affecting other languages. This time the A–Z word list of Anglicisms in Italian has been completed and is now available online for consultation and, of course, continuous updating.

This volume brings together my experience and research in the field of English-Italian contact and lexical borrowing over the past decades, and my contribution to the Global Anglicisms Database. As an Italian scholar of English linguistics, my bilingual competence and 'divided soul' have given me, I think, a privileged perspective. My concern is not only focussed on what is happening to Italian under the influence of English, but also on what is happening to English under the pressure of its global diaspora. Monitoring the Anglicization of Italian is only part of a much larger perspective on the Anglicization of the world's languages, a pervasive and far-reaching phenomenon that characterizes the linguistic scenario of the 20$^{th}$ and 21$^{st}$ centuries.

Among the sources of financial support for my research activities over the last decade, I wish to acknowledge the contribution of the *Compagnia di San Paolo* (Torino) for the project "The English language in Italy: linguistic, educational and professional challenges" (2013–2016). An important offspring of this research study was the funded Erasmus+ Strategic Partnership project "Transnational Alignment of

English Competences of Academic Staff" (TAEC) in 2017–2020, which developed a cross-European debate on English-medium instruction.

I would like to express my gratitude to the institution where I work, the Department of Foreign Languages, Literatures and Modern Cultures of the University of Torino, which granted me a sabbatical leave without which this book would never have been written. Many thanks to the members of the GLAD network, especially to the founding steering committee members, with whom so much discussion took place about Anglicisms and loanword lexicography, namely Gisle Andersen, Ulrich Busse, Henrik Gottlieb, Elżbieta Mańczak-Wohlfeld, Elizabeth Peterson, and to the new GLAD members who joined the network and contributed to the making of the database over the last few years. I am greatly undebted to Cristiano Furiassi, John Humbley, Marek Lukasik, Alessio Mattana, Alessandra Molino and Cristina Scarpino, who read parts of this book, pointing out weaknesses and suggesting improvements. Special thanks go to Elana Ochse for the thorough linguistic revision of the whole manuscript and to Christopher Owen for checking translations from Italian into English. Many colleagues, national and international ones, helped me in different ways, in alphabetical order: Sabrina Bonanzinga, Stefania Cicillini, Valeria Fiasco, Jamie Hunt, Matteo Milani, Stefania Nuccorini, Carla Marello, Laura Pinnavaia, Valérie Saugera and Paola Vettorel. A final tribute goes to my family for supporting me during the drafting of this book.

April 2022

# List of figures

**Figure 3.1** Types of lexical borrowings (Pulcini, Furiassi and Rodríguez González 2012: 6) —— **53**
**Figure 3.2** Step-by-step selection of Italian entries in GLAD —— **63**
**Figure 5.1** Number of Anglicisms in the GDU (2007) and *Nuovo Devoto-Oli 2022* —— **141**
**Figure 5.2** The *jeep* entry in Rando (1987) —— **144**
**Figure 5.3** The *jeep* entry in the DEA (2001) —— **146**
**Figure 5.4** The *jeep* entry in De Mauro and Mancini (2003) —— **148**
**Figure 5.5** The *jeep* entry in *Zingarelli 2022* —— **149**
**Figure 5.6** The *jeep* entry in *Nuovo Devoto-Oli 2022* —— **150**
**Figure 7.1** Statistics on language competence to have a conversation (*Special Eurobarometer 386*, 2014) —— **213**
**Figure 7.2** Statistics on attitudes towards multilingualism in the Italian population (*Special Eurobarometer 386*, 2014) —— **215**

# List of tables

**Table 3.1** Eighteenth century Anglicisms still current in the 21st century —— **65**
**Table 3.2** New Anglicisms borrowed in 2012 —— **71**
**Table 3.3** The most productive left-hand elements of compounds —— **74**
**Table 3.4** Anglicisms with neo-classical combining forms —— **76**
**Table 3.5** Anglicisms with English productive prefixes —— **77**
**Table 3.6** False Anglicisms in the form of autonomous compounds (English equivalent in parenthesis) —— **87**
**Table 3.7** False Anglicisms in the form of compound ellipses and semantic shifts —— **88**
**Table 3.8** False Anglicisms in the form of autonomous derivatives, clippings and eponyms —— **91**
**Table 4.1** Orthographic form of Italian Anglicisms and English etymons —— **103**
**Table 4.2** Equivalence of consonant phonemes in English and Italian —— **105**
**Table 4.3** Derivational patterns from English bases —— **114**
**Table 5.1** Criteria of inclusion and exclusion for GLAD —— **151**
**Table 5.2** Comparison of J entries in Rando (1987), the DEA (2001), De Mauro and Mancini (2003), *Zingarelli 2022*, *Nuovo Devoto-Oli 2022* and GLAD —— **151**
**Table 5.3** Absolute frequency (AF) and relative frequency (RF) of letter J candidate Anglicisms retrieved from CORIS (columns 1, 2 and 3) and Italian Web 2020 (columns 4, 5 and 6) —— **165**
**Table 6.1** Most frequent usage domains of Anglicisms in *Zingarelli 2022* (2000–2020) —— **176**
**Table 6.2** The terminology of winter sports in English, Italian, French and German —— **192**
**Table 6.3** 'Archaic' and 'obsolescent' Anglicisms in *Nuovo Devoto Oli 2022*, CORIS and GLAD —— **199**
**Table 7.1** Increase of EMI programmes in Italy (Rugge 2019) —— **219**

# 1 Introducing the study of Anglicisms in Italian

## 1.1 The English momentum

In the early 21$^{st}$ century English is the most widespread and influential language in its diverse geographical and social varieties. The presence of English around the globe, albeit with different degrees of political recognition, socio-cultural integration and nativization, has given it a strategic advantage to become the global lingua franca (Rosenhouse and Kowner 2008). Predictions for the forthcoming decades say that in 2050 English will continue to be a strong language (Graddol 2006; Salomone 2022), and therefore a desirable one to learn for professional purposes and international communication. The influence of English on other languages is therefore likely to intensify and to offer linguists and scholars interested in language contact a productive stock of Anglicisms and a variety of English-induced phenomena to record and describe. At the same time, voices of concern will continue to be raised about growing monolingualism for speakers' intercomprehension in favour of English and at the expense of other languages (Phillipson 2003; 2006; 2008) and the excessive inflow of Anglicisms in world languages (Humbley 2008).

Within Europe, the influence of English has been stronger in countries which have had more intense exchanges with England over the centuries (e.g. France, Germany, Italy, Spain), as explained by Görlach (2002b), and less intense in some Eastern European countries (e.g. Poland and Serbia). Scholars tend to see a geographical divide between the north and the south of Europe, with a greater degree of Anglicization and English language competence in countries like the Netherlands, Denmark and Norway, and a more limited impact and a lower level of competence in Mediterranean countries (Hartmann 1996). As a consequence, some Nordic countries are said to have moved from the status of EFL (English as a foreign language) to ESL (English as a second language), developing a more 'intimate' contact with English, which has led to widespread bilingualism with English and more intense borrowing, beyond the lexical level, affecting phraseological and morpho-syntactic aspects of their national languages. Despite these differences in depth, duration and intensity, the history of language contact between Anglophone countries and Western European ones – France, Italy, Germany and Spain, in particular – can usefully be compared to one another, since these countries have experienced a similar phenomenon, and in the course of time have also acted as mediators for the transmission of English loanwords to their closer neighbours, especially France as far as the Italian peninsula is concerned.

Although the languages and cultures of Europe have intensely circulated across the continent and influenced one another for centuries, the 'Anglicization' of European languages had a great surge after the end of the Second World War, when the English-speaking winners of the two world conflicts established their economic, political and cultural influence on the European continent, whereas beyond the Western European boundaries, English spread to the rest of Europe only in the late 20th century (Furiassi, Pulcini and Rodríguez González 2012). Most European societies were swept by a new wave of modernity, exposed to forms of popular culture, models of business and trade, innovative technology, which were rapidly disseminated by old and new mass media such as the radio, television, cinema, the internet and the social networks. The growing appeal of English has boosted the number of EFL learners and competent non-native speakers – some Europeans are already bilingual with English (Gnutzmann and Intemann 2008; De Houwer and Wilton 2011; MacKenzie 2012). On the one hand, research into pedagogical questions related to teaching and learning English in multilingual Europe has made giant steps ahead, also because of the increase of English-medium instruction in higher education (Dimova, Hultgren and Jensen 2015); on the other hand, the debate about the dangers of 'linguistic imperialism' is continuously breeding upon itself (Phillipson 2003; 2010).

Another key factor contributing to borrowing from one language to another is genetic or typological similarity. Although English is a Germanic language, the Romance component of its vocabulary makes it very similar to the lexicons of Romance languages, with which it also shares a common stock of Latin and Greek terminology. From the Renaissance on, but in particular as of the 18th century first industrial revolution (1760–1840), Greek and Latin elements were extensively exploited for the creation of learned and specialist terminology, from the humanities to science, in all the languages of Europe. As stated by De Mauro and Mancini (2003: viii),

> All'analisi l'inglese si rivela non solo la più latinizzata e neolatinizzata lingua del mondo non neolatino, ma in molti casi è più attivamente neolatina di lingue geneticamente neolatine nello sviluppare con i nuovi derivati il lascito della lingua di Roma.
>
> [Analyzing it, English appears to be not only the most Latinized and Neolatinized language in a non-Neolatin world, but in many cases it is actively more Neolatin than genetically Neolatin languages in the formation of new derivatives from the heritage of the language of Rome.]

It must be added that up to the 18th century most scholarly activity and academic writing was conducted through the medium of Latin. As a consequence, English and Italian share a large stock of matching vocabulary and, when it comes to borrowing, formal similarity is particularly deceitful: an example, out of hundreds, is the Italian polysemous noun *articolo* (from Latin articŭlus), giving rise to the meaning of 'newspaper article' under the influence of English, and to the meaning of 'article of goods' under the influence of French in the 18th century (De Mauro 1999/ 2007).[1] No Italian speaker would ever imagine or accept these two acceptations of the Italian word *articolo* as an Anglicism or a Gallicism. This feature will be discussed and illustrated amply in chapter 3 with reference to the typology of borrowings.

The challenging issues posed by the sociolinguistic status of English today have produced a massive body of research on its native varieties as well as on nativized varieties, or New Englishes, which are used in over 75 countries and territories where English was retained as an additional language in post-colonial times (Fishman, Cooper and Conrad 1977; Crystal 2003). Within the European continent, the English language mainly circulated as a foreign language, studied and promoted for its cultural and technical importance, leaving unchallenged the sovereignty of the national languages. However, the massive increase in the inflow of Anglicisms in the second half of the 20th century marked a turning point for the status of English in Europe and linguists have started to monitor this phenomenon more closely (Linn 2016). Research on Anglicisms in individual languages as well as the compilation of dictionaries of Anglicisms have flourished over the past decades, so that the input of Anglicisms has been recorded and observed on a national basis (for an overview see Pulcini, Furiassi and Rodríguez González 2012). Research articles in collective volumes have explored the sociolinguistic, psycholinguistic and educational aspects of the acquisition of English as a second (and third) language in Europe and beyond (Cenoz and Jessner 2000; Gnutzmann and Intemann 2008; De Houwer and Wilton 2011; Linn, Bermel and Ferguson 2015), the re-conceptualization of English as a lingua franca to comply with the needs of internationalization (people's mobility) and globalization of the world economy (Facchinetti, Crystal and Seidlhofer 2010), and the many facets of English-induced lexical borrowing (Viereck and Bald 1986; Görlach 2001; Anderman and Rogers 2005; Furiassi, Pulcini and Rodríguez González 2012).

## 1.2 English and Italian in contact

This volume offers an up-to-date overview of the influence of the English language on Italian, exploring the historical, social, cultural and linguistic dimensions of the contact between Italy and English-speaking countries. The influence of English on Italian is the outcome of a long-standing relationship between Italian and British

---

**1** This is contradicted by LEI: *Lessico Etimologico Italiano* (Pfister and Schweickard 1979–2012), according to which both these meanings of Italian *articolo* have been transferred from French, respectively in 1690 for 'article of goods' and in 1711 for 'newspaper article'.

and American societies, which dates back to several centuries ago, but intensified in the 18th century and has massively increased since the end of World War II. Narrowing the focus on the European context, among the languages affected by the global wave of 'Anglicization', Italian is considered one of the most open to the influence of English as far as lexical borrowing is concerned, the main reasons being the centuries-old, intense cultural contacts with British and American societies, a strong attraction of Italians towards the Anglo-American cultural models, and only a mild opposition from Italian linguists.

Within the framework of contact linguistics (Haugen 1950; Weinreich 1953; Thomason 2001; Myers-Scotton 2002; Winford 2003; Matras 2009; Darquennes and Salmons 2019; Smith 2020), the type of contact between English and Italian, or better, among Anglophone and Italophone speakers and speech communities, has been a 'casual' or 'distant' one. This means that the mutual influence, from English on Italian, but also the reverse, from Italian on English, has taken place mainly through cultural exchanges and discontinuous social interaction, and the primary outcome has been lexical borrowing. In the past, the transmission of borrowings occurred through physical movements of people for many different reasons, mainly commercial transactions, political relations and travels. This type of contact, leading to the mutual exchange of language and culture, can be described in terms of 'adstratum' influence between geographically close communities, without any imposition of one speech community on the other.

It is evident that the removal of space and time barriers from the 20th century onwards, thanks to global networks of physical movements and diverse mass and social media channels, has led to far more intense contacts across geographical boundaries, and the influence of English has spread to all areas of knowledge, cultural expressions and social behaviours. In the present-day context of globalization, English has taken the leading role as language donor and is exerting a strong influence on other languages in Europe, including Italian, and beyond. Thus, global English functions as a 'cultural adstrate' around the world, exporting culture and language to societies that are only virtually close. In this perspective, in this book the moderate term 'influence' has been preferred to other more intrusive terms such as 'impact' or 'interference', the latter being used in the literature to denote 'deviations from the norm' and contact-induced changes in a language system introduced by bilingual speakers and subsequently integrated into a language (Weinreich 1953). As will be shown in the chapters of this book, Italian has expanded its vocabulary with hundreds of English words, but this has not affected the morpho-syntactic system of the language beyond a natural degree of innovation from an exogenous source, which is a common phenomenon in living languages.

In any language contact situation, several factors are at work, the most decisive one being the higher prestige of one language over the other languages or dialects, determined by the political influence, the economic leadership, the scientific and technological achievements and the cultural contribution carried by the more prestigious languages. The influence of a donor language on a recipient one also depends on its duration and intensity, which may be stronger in some historical periods and mild or absent in others. An example is the 18$^{th}$ century fascination for English society and language, called 'Anglomania' (Graf 1911), a cultural phenomenon that spread from France to many parts of Europe, including the nearby Italian peninsula. In this historical period French was the language of many European courts, of the upper classes and of scientific academies, and therefore it was the most influential language in Europe. Thanks to its dominant role, the French language contributed to the diffusion of Anglomania and also acted as mediator for the transmission of many English loanwords. A completely different scenario was found during the years of the fascist regime in Italy (1922–1945), when the use of foreign words was prohibited for nationalistic reasons and English loanwords were substituted by Italian equivalents. In sum, the influence of a language on another very much depends on social and psychological factors such as a favourable or hostile socio-political setting, language ideology and policy, people's attitudes and motivation for welcoming or opposing foreign influences.

Contact and exchanges among languages and cultures naturally occur in the history of most, if not all, languages in the world. For this reason, the desire to keep a language free from exogenous influences – an ideology that is referred to as 'linguistic purism' – is contradicted by historical evidence, witnessing that languages, as living entities, naturally change in time under the action of internal and external pressures and naturally feed on innovation, creativity, and imitation. This is considered by linguists as a natural way for languages to develop and enrich themselves, especially for the expansion of vocabulary, that is, of their expressive resources. If we consider Italian, a Romance language, we can say that most of its vocabulary derives from learned and popular Latin. Since its initial phases, in the 13$^{th}$ and 14$^{th}$ centuries, Italian absorbed a huge number of French words, which are now fully integrated and assimilated into the texture of Italian vocabulary. Equally unrecognizable as foreignisms are borrowings from Spanish, in turn a mediator of Arabic words, and from German (in addition to Medieval Germanic loans), not to mention as many as 250 languages to which Italian is indebted (De Mauro and Mancini 2003; Zolli 1991; Migliorini 2019; Serianni 2001). In turn, present-day English is the result of centuries of extensive integration of words from various historical layers (Celtic, Anglo-Saxon, Norman-French, Scandinavian, Latin and Greek), together with input of hundreds of other sources. Centuries of Norman-French rule and the overwhelming influence of Latin, the undisputed lingua franca of knowledge and learning, have made English 'the least' Germanic of the Germanic languages, as 65–75% of its vocabulary is composed of non-Germanic words. It follows that English and Italian have a common background of vocabulary based on Latin and Greek, which is a key factor in their linguistic and cultural relationship, with important consequences on the outcomes of borrowing (see 4.4).

The history of language contact between English and Italian, and its social and historical background, which is reviewed in chapter 2 of this volume, is a crucial starting point for understanding the circumstances favouring contact-induced lexical borrowing. Although the directionality of the influence is from English into Italian, it is also important to stress that the influence of the Italian language and culture on English-speaking societies has been equally intense. Italy was the birthplace of the Renaissance and a source of inspiration for fine arts, music, and humanistic studies for many centuries all over Europe. The Italian language and culture enjoyed great prestige in neighbouring countries and transferred to both British and US English more than two thousand words in the fields of music, opera, dance, nature and science, food and drink, arts and learning (Pinnavaia 2001, 2019; Stammerjohann 2008). Thanks to its glorious past and prestige, Italian is today the fourth most studied foreign language in the world, after English, Spanish and Mandarin Chinese.[2] Using an ecological metaphor, Italian is not at risk of 'extinction' under the impact of English, as some linguists may be inclined to believe. Therefore, the scope of this book is to observe and describe the phenomenon of lexical borrowing from English into Italian with no prescriptive intentions, along the lines of previous studies such as that of Klajn (1972), Iamartino (2001) and Dardano (1986, 2020).

## 1.3 Research on Anglicisms in Italian

The study of Anglicisms in Italian is not a neglected area of Italian lexicology and lexicography (Pulcini 2002b). However, a comprehensive monograph on the influence of English on Italian dates back several decades (Klajn 1972) and the only paper dictionary of Anglicisms in Italian is by now outdated (Rando 1973a, 1973b, 1987). Nevertheless, from the beginning of the 20th century, English loanwords have been systematically recorded in general dictionaries of Italian, starting from Panzini's *Dizionario Moderno* (1905 and 10 subsequent editions until 1963), historical

---

2 https://italyuntold.org/en/untold-stories-the-italian-language-is-the-4-th-most-studied-language-in-the-world/ (November, 2022).

dictionaries such as the *Grande dizionario italiano dell'uso* or GDU (De Mauro 1999/ 2007), one of the largest lexicographic sources for Italian, and a dictionary specifically devoted to the description of foreign words (De Mauro and Mancini 2003) based on the GDU. Anglicisms are regularly recorded in many general dictionaries of Italian such as *Il Sabatini Coletti. Dizionario della Lingua Italiana* (Sabatini and Coletti 2004), *Vocabolario Treccani* (2018), *Zingarelli 2022. Vocabolario della lingua italiana* (Cannella and Lazzarini 2021), *Nuovo Devoto-Oli. Il vocabolario dell'italiano contemporaneo* (Devoto et al. 2022) – the latter two are updated yearly. The present work is a synthesis of the numerous publications on different aspects of this phenomenon, relevant to both theoretical and descriptive aspects of English-induced lexical borrowing into Italian.

Research on the influence of English on the Italian language can be grouped into major areas of interest which have mostly attracted Italian scholars. Here below are listed the main research fields and some of the most important reference works:

- Historical accounts of English-Italian contacts in a diachronic perspective: Graf (1911); Dardano (1986; 2020); Zolli (1991); Cartago (1994); Iamartino (2001). Historical information is also contained in volumes on the history of Italian: Migliorini [1960] (2019); Migliorini and Griffith (1966); De Mauro (1970).
- Historical documentation, systematic description of formal adaptation and semantic development of Anglicisms in Italian: Fanfani (1991–1996; 2010, 2020); Bombi (2009a).
- Synchronic description of Anglicisms in Italian and their influence of the lexicon and morphology of present-day Italian: Klajn (1972); Pulcini (2002b, 2017); Carlucci (2018).
- Typology of borrowings: Gusmani (1981, 1986); Furiassi (2010); Bombi (2009a, 2020); Pulcini (2002a); Pulcini et. al. (2012).
- Lexicographic projects focused on the systematic collection and recording of neologisms and foreign words: Quarantotto (1987, 2001); Cortelazzo and Cardinale (1989); Amato, Andreoni and Salvi (1990); Lurati (1990); Bencini and Citernesi (1992); De Mauro and Mancini (2003); Adamo and Della Valle (2003, 2005, 2008, 2018).
- Study of Anglicisms in specialized domains: Pulcini (2008b, 2012a); Pulcini and Andreani (2014); Andreani and Pulcini (2016); Marri (2003); Gianni (1994); Scarpa (2014); Bombi (2019).
- Neo-purism and reactions to Anglicisms: Monelli (1943); Raffaelli (1983); Castellani (1987); Pulcini (1997); Fanfani (2002, 2003); Marazzini and Petralli (2015); Giovanardi, Gualdo and Coco (2008); Pulcini (2019b).

## 1.4 Loanword lexicography: Collecting and storing Anglicisms

Lexical borrowing is the primary outcome of language contact. The most common types of borrowings are single-word items and compounds, but a variety of phraseological units – including phrases and routine expressions – and morpho-syntactic patterns are also observed and described in the literature on Anglicisms, which will be examined in chapter 3 of this volume with reference to the typology that is relevant to the illustration of borrowings in the Italian language.

When it comes to the collection of Anglicisms for lexicographic purposes, the job of the lexicographer consists in the retrieval of candidate Anglicisms from various sources, starting from existing collections (general dictionaries of the language, specialized dictionaries, glossaries, archives and corpora), observing their use in the language and making a decision on whether the items may qualify for inclusion, or otherwise, depending on the criteria set up for a specific lexicographic project, its size, time frame and target audience. This is indeed the first important step in loanword lexicography. A working typology of borrowings is a necessary tool allowing the lexicographer to limit the scope of the dictionary and assign typological labels. These prior decisions constitute the core of the research method, when the actual compilation of any dictionary begins. Different lexicographic sources provide divergent figures on the number of Anglicisms current in Italian, depending on whether only English-looking items are counted, or also calques (loan translations) and derivatives, general words or technical terms (*joule*), or false Anglicisms (Italian *telefilm* / English *tv series*), trademarks or eponyms (*jeep*), foreignisms (*lord*), exoticisms (*bungalow*), hybrids (*ciclocross*), as wells as neoclassical words or internationalisms (English *microphone* / Italian *microfono*, English *telephone* / Italian *telefono*).

As far as currency is concerned, Italian has a stock of well-established single- and multi-word Anglicisms that are familiar to a large number of Italian speakers, such as *film, shopping, baby sitter* and *no problem*. Currency is a usage-oriented concept. It refers to the spread of Anglicisms in newspapers, novels, popular magazines, radio, television and social media, so that it is generally known and accepted by speakers from many layers of society. This process of acceptance and integration of a loanword is referred to in Italian as *acclimatamento* ('acclimatization'). Focusing on specialized domains, currency and frequency (or *representativeness*) vary depending on whether words actually refer to topical themes, such as sport, tourism, internet and the new media, and circulate among common people, against the more peripheral, technical and specialist vocabulary of business, economy and sciences, which may be familiar only to a limited circle of professionals and educated Italians. The degree of technicality of a term is a user-oriented concept. Another dimension is that of *representativeness* of candidate Anglicisms, that is, how frequent they are in general use of the receiving language. Although Anglicisms are low-frequency lexical items, with only a few exceptions (e.g. the discourse marker *okay* and a handful of very frequent Anglicisms in Italian), another crucial factor is their sociolinguistic distribution among categories of speakers and functional contexts (Dardano 2020), an area which has not been systematically explored so far. Finally, the chronological dimension, that is, whether Anglicisms are current (in use) or archaic or obsolescent (falling out of use) also has to be taken into account among the features to consider in order to build the macrostructure of a dictionary or a database of English borrowings.

In sum, any lexicographic project addressed to loanwords requires a series of preliminary decisions on the size of the macrostructure and the time frame, in order to limit the selection of borrowings, which lexical items to include or exclude, considering various types of borrowings, their currency and representativeness in the receiving language as well as the range from core to peripheral lexis. However, the selection of the entries is problematized by the complexity of the borrowing process, and by the fact that many lexical items are casual, short-lived borrowings used in advertising, in the media and in youth speech, or neologisms, buzzwords and creative constructions populating the physical and virtual landscape of today's channels of communication. Some scholars have already noted an acceleration in the circulation of new vocabulary, due to the sociolinguistic conditions of the last decades and the consequent, exponential increase of communication worldwide through the electronic media (Dardano 2020). Moreover, the new economic elites of bilingual speakers, engaged in mobility and international contacts, are inclined to code-switch between English and their mother tongue, adapting and translating English words. New contact settings for the introduction of Anglicisms are the language of the news media, advertising, youth speech and business communication, where the use of Anglicisms has a particularly 'fleeting' nature (Tosi 2006).

Equally important for the selection of candidate Anglicisms is the nature of the donor and recipient languages; in fact, genetic similarity is an important component of interlingual influence. As far as Italian is concerned, whether a loanword has an English-looking form (e.g. *web*) or a Latinate one (e.g. English *celebrity* / Italian *celebrità*) is a key factor, the latter favouring the integration of loanwords and their 'camouflage' in Italian. The formal similarity of the source word and its Italian replica makes it difficult, if not impossible for the lay speaker, to distinguish between English-derived words and phrases from expressions triggered by modern times and virally circulating across languages, especially as far as calques (Italian *tempo pieno* from English *full time*) and semantic loans (Italian *impatto* from English *impact*) are concerned. Moreover, the competition at work between Anglicisms and Italian domestic words (English *tour operator* / Italian *operatore turistico*) and phrases (English *Ladies and Gentlemen* / Italian *Signore e Signori*) poses questions of multiple terminology and pragmatic markedness in discourse (Onysko and Winter-Froemel 2011). This particular aspect may lead the linguist to expand from the traditional systemic, functional perspective (the integration of the loanword into the system of the receiving language) in favour of an 'onomasiological' approach (Zenner and Kristiansen 2014), focusing on both the loanword and on the domestic terms in competition and their usage contexts.

The study of Anglicisms in Italian cannot be approached without considering how this phenomenon has affected other languages (Onysko 2007; Saugera 2017; Gottlieb 2020), in order to compare and measure the influence of English cross-linguistically. A pioneer in the comparative study of English borrowings in European languages was Rudolf Filipović (1974, 1996). He set up the project entitled *The English Elements in European Languages* and identified some guiding principles and a working methodology to study the integration of Anglicisms in selected receiving languages, which were grouped into large European families (Romance, Germanic, Slavic and other minor ones). The aim was to observe regularities of the borrowing process depending on the characteristics of the different language systems and the actual outcomes of integration (phonological, morphological, semantic). This ambitious project was followed up by Manfred Görlach, who compiled the most important work on Anglicisms in Europe so far, the *Dictionary of European Anglicisms* (2001) and some companion articles and volumes (Görlach 1994; 1997; 2002a; 2002b; 2003), in which English-induced lexical borrowing in 16 languages are separately described and the step-by-step methodology for the making of the dictionary is illustrated. Görlach's achievement is unique both for its contribution to loanword lexicography and for the possibility of comparing 3,800 Anglicisms (direct loanwords displaying an English form, 1,600 of which are attested for Italian) across 16 European languages and language families. On the basis of these data, Italian appears to be the most 'Anglicized' language after Dutch, Norwegian and German (Görlach 1997).

## 1.5 The reference sources and data

The data referred to in this volume to illustrate the English borrowings featuring in the Italian language have been retrieved from various sources. To start with, historical accounts of contacts between Italy and English-speaking countries are the sources of early borrowings (Klajn 1972; Cartago 1994; Dardano 1986; 2020; Iamartino 2001), some of which are now obsolete and not recorded in recent dictionaries of general Italian. The Italian dictionaries systematically consulted in our research are the *Dizionario degli Anglicismi nell'italiano postunitario* (Rando 1987), the *Dictionary of European Anglicisms* (Görlach 2001), *Grande dizionario italiano dell'uso*, also called GDU (De Mauro 2007), *Dizionario delle parole straniere nella lingua italiana* (De Mauro and Mancini 2003), *Zingarelli 2022. Vocabolario della lingua italiana* (Cannella and Lazzarini 2021), *Nuovo Devoto-Oli. Il vocabolario dell'italiano contemporaneo 2022* (Devoto et al. 2022). The latter two dictionaries will be referred to as *Zingarelli 2022* and *Nuovo Devoto-Oli 2022*. The quantitative data provided by these reference sources are analyzed in detail in chapter 5. In addition, the online archive of the daily newspaper *la Repubblica* was also used to check orthographic forms, grammatical features and currency of Anglicisms, as they are used in present-day newspaper language (see Section 5.3). The daily press has proved to be an excellent resource for the retrieval of neologisms and Anglicisms, bridging the distance between specialized terms and the general language. Though the topics covered by the daily press tend to focus more on specific news areas – e.g. politics and economy – newspaper language is constantly up-to-date with facts and events, especially international ones, introducing new vocabulary. Anglicisms are also used in the press because of their eye-catching function and stylistic quality, appealing to the readers and attracting their interest.

A further resource for modern lexicography is the use of language corpora, which allows linguists and lexicographers to observe language behaviour through authentic language data (Andersen 2012; Marti-Solano and Ruano San Segundo 2021). Language corpora can be used to check the occurrence and frequency of Anglicisms as well as their use in context (collocations and lexical profile) and morpho-syntactic features, such as gender and number. The results obtained from the query of corpora may offer a useful index of representativeness for candidate Anglicisms – although they are low-frequency words in languages – but the type of corpora chosen for the query may indeed influence the data obtained. Various types of corpora are available for Italian, but only a few of them have proved to be useful for the retrieval of Anglicisms.[3] The two large corpora of Italian used in this work are the CORIS and Italian Web 2020. CORIS (*corpus di Italiano Scritto*) is a general reference corpus of present-day written Italian, consisting of 165 million running words.[4] Italian Web 2020, also known as itTenTen20, is a web-based corpus, consisting of 14.5 billion words and available on the Sketch Engine platform (see 5.4).

The data presented in this volume are the result of a collection and selection of items extracted from the sources listed above and stored in a multilingual database, called Global Anglicism Database (GLAD). A large number of English borrowings

---

[3] See a list of available corpora of Italian at: https://accademiadellacrusca.it/it/contenuti/banche-dati-corpora-e-archivi testuali/6228.
[4] Available at: https://corpora.ficlit.unibo.it/coris_ita.html.

recorded in dictionaries have been filtered through criteria of inclusion and exclusion set for GLAD (see 3.3). GLAD is a project launched by a group of linguists in 2014, some of whom had already contributed to Görlach's *Dictionary of European Anglicisms*, to continue along the lines set by Görlach, extending the number of languages involved, within and beyond the European boundaries, and the typology of English borrowings. The GLAD team's goals are to jointly refine research methods to investigate the various aspects of the influence of English. This research team have created a comprehensive bibliography of studies devoted to the Anglicization of languages, promoted English-related events, setting up a dedicated research area in its own right. The website of GLAD's network of scholars is managed by the Norwegian School of Economics (NHH).[5] The electronic database is hosted by the Instituut voor de Nederlandse Taal (Institute for the Dutch Language) at Leiden.[6] The criteria of inclusion and exclusion set up for GLAD are described in Gottlieb et al. (2018).

The examples quoted and discussed in this book are often accompanied by definitions. In order to avoid an excessive use of references, the sources have been generally omitted. Italian definitions have been taken from the Italian reference sources quoted above (translated into English). As for English definitions, they have been taken (often shortened and adapted) from several English dictionaries, including the *Oxford English Dictionary* (Simpson and Weiner 1989) (henceforth OED), the *Merriam-Webster* (Gove 2022), and the *Collins English Dictionary*. The pronunciation of examples, when needed, is indicated using the International Phonetic Alphabet (IPA) symbols.

## 1.6 The structure of this book

This book has an academic approach which makes it interesting primarily to scholars and university students. Given the topical nature of the debate concerning the excessive inflow of Anglicisms in Italy nowadays and the protection of the national language, the themes and examples presented in this book may also appeal to a lay audience of non-experts, interested in the linguistic and cultural contacts between English and Italian. The analysis of Anglicisms, their typology and the discussion of different lexicographic approaches to the collection, description and recording of Anglicisms, makes this volume appealing to scholars involved in language contact and loanword lexicography. The scope is a synchronic analysis

---

[5] https://www.nhh.no/en/research-centres/global-anglicism-database-network/ (November, 2022).
[6] glad.ivdnt.org (at the moment, access to the database is limited to contributors, but plans are being made to make it available for open and free consultation).

of Italian Anglicisms, but the historical and cultural dimensions are also dealt with. The main focus is on the linguistic outcomes and implications of English-induced lexical borrowing in Italian, so loanwords are treated as markers of cultural, political and economic influence from the donor to the recipient society, signaling closeness and affinity, or distance and hostility, between Italy and English-speaking countries.

Chapter 2 reviews the historical contacts between Italy and the Anglophone world (earlier contacts with Britain and later contacts with the USA) in chronological sequence and provides examples of loanwords imported in the course of time. The goal is to illustrate the historical circumstances that favoured the input of Anglicisms throughout the centuries, highlighting the domains which were more intensely affected by borrowings with reference to the cultural milieu of the time, both on the British and on the Italian sides. Starting from the domains of trade and commerce, many Anglicisms were imported from politics, fashion and social life from the 18$^{th}$ century, and sport from the 19$^{th}$ century. The term Anglomania, introduced in the literature on English-Italian cultural contacts, effectively describes the mental disposition that triggers the imitation of foreign models. This cultural fashion, which would continue in Italy throughout the centuries, was fueled by the stable exchanges between Italy and Britain, and later with north America, when the US appeared on the international scenario. The age of neo-purism during the 30-year regime was the only historical period when resistance to foreign influence was regulated by legislation in Italy. After the end of the Second World War, the real 'Americanization' of Italian society began and the intense input of Anglicisms took place, with an increase of borrowings from the fields of information technology and the internet, together with economy, the domains which mostly influence today's international communication, and in which the English language plays a dominant role.

Chapter 3 introduces the terminology in use in the field of language contact and bilingualism, set up by the scholars who laid the foundations of contact linguistics, language borrowing, loanword lexicography and further developed in the literature produced in the following decades, also in the Italian context. A model typology for lexical borrowing is presented and illustrated, starting from direct Anglicisms. The reference data set on which the typology is based–the Italian entries of the Global Anglicism Database (GLAD)–is presented. The lexicographic criteria set up by the GLAD team is outlined, to delimit the types of borrowings included or excluded from the database, the time frame and the currency of the items that qualify for inclusion. Direct Anglicisms and their subtypes, namely non-adapted and adapted, are discussed and illustrated. Besides Anglicisms displaying different word formation patters such as compounds and abbreviations, further types of borrowings are considered such as Latinisms, eponyms, archaisms and exoticisms, as well as English-inspired coinages (false Anglicisms) and hybrid forms. This chapter ends with the treatment of phraseology, an area of borrowing that is expanding as the influence of English is becoming more pervasive in present-day Italian.

Chapter 4 deals with the integration of Anglicisms into the Italian language system. This process affects the pronunciation of non-adapted Anglicisms (phonological adaptation), spelling (orthographic adaptation), grammatical function (morpho-syntactic adaptation) and form (derivation) in adapted Anglicisms. A very common feature in most Anglicisms is semantic reduction with respect to the English model, both in the case of technical and scientific terms, limiting the borrowing to only one of the original referents, and especially in common words, which may also autonomously develop, as far as meaning is concerned, in order to satisfy the new expressive needs. The genetic similarity that exists between the English and Italian lexicons by virtue of the shared classical origin is constantly raised in this book, since it is considered a crucial factor for the establishment of typological distinctions. On the one hand, it facilitates the transfer of English words and their integration and assimilation into Italian; on the other hand, it makes the description of the two major typologies of indirect borrowings (also called calques), i.e., loan translations and semantic loans, particularly difficult. The category of calques is described and illustrated, drawing especially on the fine-grained typology developed by Italian linguists. The coexistence of Anglicisms side by side with an Italian near-synonym raises stylistic and pragmatic choices that become available to speakers. The historical dimension of language contact is finally addressed with reference to internationalisms, a category of similar lexical items across languages, which may help to refine the typology of lexical borrowings, separating Anglicisms from independent heritage vocabulary and neological creations.

In Chapter 5 the goal is to provide objective figures on the number of Anglicisms imported into Italian on the basis of the chosen sources, namely dictionaries, newspaper archives and language corpora. The number of Anglicisms recorded by dictionaries varies from over a thousand to several thousands, depending on their size and time frame, on divergent criteria of inclusion of technical and scientific terminology and on the types of borrowings considered. To illustrate this difference, a comparison is made between the letter J entries in representative dictionaries and the selection made of GLAD's word list. Subsequently, relevant letter J words are searched for in two corpora of Italian, CORIS and Italian Web 2020, to verify their currency in the language.

Chapter 6 explores the presence of Anglicisms in the specialized domains that today appear to have been more intensely affected by English borrowings, namely ICT, economy and sport. After more than two centuries, the input of Anglicisms in the field of sport has started to decline and many English sports terms have been replaced by Italian equivalents. By contrast, ICT and economy appear to be extremely productive. Both fields possess terminology that is confined only to expert-to-expert communication as well as words that have spread to general vocabulary and are known by common speakers, especially in the rapidly developing domain of computer science and social media. At the other end of the neological spectrum, the neglected area of obsolescence is examined, focusing on words that die out owing to the disappearance of the referents that they denoted or because they are simply replaced by more modern words. Equally peripheral in the Italian lexical repertoire are Anglicisms occasionally used in newspapers, adverts and shop signs because of their eye-catching value, a phenomenon that is culturally noteworthy since it makes the English language 'visible' in the Italian linguistic landscape.

Chapter 7 deals with the growing importance of English in Italian education since the second half of the 20$^{th}$ century and the ensuing cultural debate about its pervasiveness in Italian society and its influence on the Italian language. Since the end of the Second World War Italy has gradually aligned its educational system with the model recommended by the European Union, introducing two foreign languages in the secondary school cycle. However, national reforms have increasingly encouraged the study of English, which has now become the undisputed first foreign language in all school cycles. Attitudes taken by Italians toward English are highly favourable thanks to its positive associations with modernity and because of its importance in the job market. The introduction of English as a medium of instruction in higher education is discussed with reference to a recent controversy about the pros and cons deriving from exclusive use of English in some degree courses in Italian universities, which has led to a legal pronouncement against this policy. A final section reviews the opinions on the popularity of English expressed by Italian scholars, partly in favour and partly against, including the intervention of the Italian *Accademia della Crusca* in support of the use of Italian in education.

# 2 English in Italy: History of language contact

## 2.1 Chronology of early influences

The study of language contact – even when it is carried out from a synchronic perspective – requires a diachronic backdrop against which the mutual linguistic influences between the linguistic communities considered can be explained. A glance at the past is necessary to understand the historical, social and cultural reasons which caused linguistic changes, either in terms of innovation (i.e., neologisms) or obsolescence (i.e., outdated and archaic words) (Iamartino 2001).

Language borrowing is the outcome of social encounters and cultural exchanges among speech communities. This type of lexical innovation in a language is triggered by extralinguistic factors, that is, by the social circumstances in which contacts have taken place. The number of loanwords imported into a language testifies to the amount of contact with the donor language (the cultural impact), which is higher in periods of more intense relations; the nature of this contact, i.e., the affected fields, from commerce to science, lifestyles and arts, which is mirrored in the recorded borrowings; finally, the superiority (in scientific and technological advancement) and prestige of the donor culture in the recipient one is one of the most important drivers of language borrowing. In this chapter the historical, social and cultural background framing language contact between the English-speaking world and the Italian peninsula will be retraced, in order to identify the seamless weaving between cultural contact and lexical borrowing.

The acquisition of new vocabulary from exogenous sources is generally prompted by the need to name new objects and concepts, which originated in the donor culture and are imported from it. In this light, loanwords can function as historical landmarks, and signal the time when new referents were introduced. A simple test is to identify in which century or decade the loanwords *lady, city, rosbif, jazz, big bang,* and *laptop* were imported into Italian. Being well-known Anglicisms, even a lay speaker may be able to guess that the given list is in chronological order: the word *lady* is the oldest loanword (dated 1668) denoting an upper-class, noble woman, a term which filtered into Italian through real or fictional staging of British society; *city* was borrowed in the mid-18th century (1749) to refer to the historical centre of London; the adapted orthography of the word *rosbif* (current spelling in Italian: *roast beef*) indicates that this is an old borrowing too, dating back to the early 19th century (1819); in the early 20th century, *jazz* as a music genre (dated 1919) became very popular; the *big bang* (dated 1963) refers to the current model explaining the beginning of the universe, elaborated in the mid-20th century; finally, *laptop* (dated 1986) was introduced with the diffusion of personal computers, which obviously makes this loanword the most recent one. Each of the hundreds and thousands of Anglicisms have a borrowing history, and this explains the reasons why and the circumstances in which they were introduced in the recipient language. In this paragraphs we will consider the early loanwords borrowed from the 13$^{th}$ to the 17$^{th}$ centuries, which are very few, mostly obsolete, and only familiar to a limited number of users of the time. Our sources are previous historical accounts of English-Italian contacts (Migliorini and Griffith 1984; Dardano 1986, 2020; Zolli 1991; Cartago 1994; Iamartino 2001; Migliorini 2019) and dictionaries of Italian, i.e., *Grande dizionario italiano dell'uso* (De Mauro 2007) (henceforth GDU), *Zingarelli 2022* and *Nuovo Devoto-Oli 2022*.[7] The electronic editions of these dictionaries allow the extraction of Anglicisms by setting the etymon to English and selecting the century of adoption. Dates are taken from all these sources; in case of divergencies, the earliest date is quoted. The *Oxford English Dictionary* (OED) is the reference source for the meaning and the spelling of English lexical items.

Looking back to the Middle Ages, the geographical proximity between the British Isles and the Italian peninsula favoured encounters of various types, mainly commercial transactions,[8] diplomatic relations and personal travels. The loanwords assimilated between the 13$^{th}$ and the 17$^{th}$ century are very few and many of them are now obsolete and no more recorded in dictionaries of Italian. They belong to the fields of commerce, law, politics and administration, and were probably understood by a limited circle of merchants, bankers and diplomats. Thus, the sociolinguistic setting for cultural contact and borrowing is extremely limited by the historical circumstances. It is also important to consider that before the 16$^{th}$ century (i.e., the Renaissance), the Italian peninsula was linguistically fragmented into a great variety of dialects, which had developed from vulgar Latin. The most prestigious Tuscan dialect spoken in Florence is considered the basis from which standard Italian subsequently emerged and established itself as a literary language in the Renaissance (Migliorini and Griffith 1984; Migliorini

---

[7] These are the dictionaries that have been systematically consulted. Information has also been checked in historical and etymological dictionaries such as *Grande dizionario della lingua italiana* (Battaglia and Bàrberi Squarotti 1961–2004), *Il nuovo etimologico. DELI – Dizionario Etimologico della Lingua Italiana* (Cortelazzo and Zolli 1999), LEI: *Lessico etimologico italiano* (Pfister and Schweickard 1979–2012), *L'Etimologico. Vocabolario della lingua italiana* (EVLI) (Nocentini 2010). Lexicographic resources in digital format are available on the website of the *Accademia della Crusca*.

[8] A historical record of business correspondence written by a company of merchants and bankers from Lucca, the Ricciardis, is kept at the Public Record Office in London (Castellani and Del Punta 2005). This company went bankrupt in 1300 and all the documents present in their London offices were confiscated. These letters represent an invaluable testimony for the history of the Italian language and of the economic and political relations between England and Italy.

2019: Serianni 2001). The other 'sister' regional dialects continued to develop in the following centuries, with marked differences between them, and are still nowadays widely used on a regional level (Maiden 2013). Politically, the Italian territory was divided into kingdoms under foreign rule and several city-states (or 'communes') such as Florence and Milan, which were powerful commercial and financial centres, and Genoa and Venice, which were wealthy, independent states thanks to their strategic role in the control of the commercial routes in the Mediterranean sea and to the East. Florence, in particular, was a commune of extreme artistic and cultural vitality, suffice it to name Giotto and Dante among the many artists and writers of this age.[9]

Evidence of 13th century English contacts with the Italian business world is the term *Lombard*, denoting 'A native of Lombardy engaged as a banker, moneychanger, or pawnbroker' (OED), which has given the name to the street known today as Lombard Street in the financial centre of London. The use of early borrowings has been observed in historical correspondence and account books, and are stored in archives; some of these loanwords were reborrowed in later periods for more modern meanings, or became obsolete. Some examples are *sterlino* (sterling) which dates back to 1221 and denoted a wooden or copper coin used in commercial exchanges of goods.[10] In the 14th century scholars mention a few more business terms, i.e., *costuma* (customs); *feo* 'salary' (fee); *chierico* 'employee' (clerk); *cochetto* (receipt for the payment of customs duties). Among the earliest Anglicisms we can find the term *stanforte*, the name of a fabric produced in the English city of Stanford, and sold in Europe by foreign merchants.

In the 15th century, the diplomatic relations between the Republic of Venice and England, to regulate their commercial dealings, were strengthened by the institution of a permanent embassy in London in 1496 (Cartago 1994). The reports drafted by the Venetian ambassadors contain several adaptations, calques and translations from English, testifying the use of terms related to political and social life, administration, law, trade and honorific titles. Some examples of cultural loanwords collected by Rando (1970) are: *alto tradimento* (high treason), *gran cancelliere* (Great Chancellor), *ordine della calattiarra/giarrettiera* (Order of the

---

**9** The three 14th century 'crowns' of Italian literature, Dante, Petrarch and Boccaccio, wrote their masterpieces in the Tuscan dialect, from which standard Italian developed in the following centuries. The use of Latin lasted for a longer time in Italy than anywhere else, up to the early 19th century, for several scholarly and institutional functions, especially in the Catholic Church (Migliorini and Griffith 1984).
**10** The term *sterlina* as a unit of currency (pound sterling) was introduced much later, in 1720 (*Nuovo Devoto-Oli 2022*) (in 1873 according to the GDU).

Garter),[11] *parlamento* (parliament, referring to the Houses of Lords and Commons), *camera/casa* (ellipsis of Chamber / House of Parliament), *serifo* (sheriff 'a high officer of a county in Britain and Ireland').

Other written sources reporting on contacts with English society are writings of Italian expatriates, travellers, geographers and historians. The role of the latter is particularly important for the report of religious controversies, the most serious of which was the schism of the Church of England from the Church of Rome. With reference to this historical event, which had dramatic political repercussions on the relations between the two countries, the term *puritani* (Puritans) is worth quoting, introduced in 1593 by the Italian philosopher, priest and diplomat Giovanni Botero in his censorious description of the Anglican religion. An early contribution to the debate on 'the language question' is that of Niccolò Machiavelli in *Discorso* ovvero *Dialogo intorno alla nostra lingua,* an essay probably drafted around 1524 but published two centuries later, in which the Italian diplomat and philosopher argues in favour of the literary Florentine vulgar, the language used by the celebrated poets Dante Alighieri, Francesco Petrarca (Petrarch) and Giovanni Boccaccio (Inglese 1997). In this essay he also states that borrowing words and ideas from other sources is necessary, useful and a way to enrich a language:

> [. . .] non si può trovare una lingua, che parli ogni cosa per se senza avere accattato da altri; perchè nel conversare gli uomini di varie provincie insieme prendono de' motti l'uno dell'altro. Aggiugnesi a questo, che qualunque volta viene o nuove dottrine in una città o nuove arti, è necessario che vi vengano nuovi vocaboli, e nati in quella lingua, donde quelle dottrine, o quelle arti sono venute; ma riducendosi nel parlare con i modi, con i casi, con le differenze, e con gli accenti fanno una medesima consonanza con i vocaboli di quella lingua che trovano, e così diventano suoi, perchè altrimenti le lingue parrebbono rappezzate, e non tornerebbono bene; e così i vocaboli forestieri si convertono in Fiorentini, non i Fiorentini in forestieri, nè però diventa altro la nostra lingua che Fiorentina; e di quì dipende, che le lingue da principio arricchiscono, e diventano più belle, essendo più copiose: ma è ben vero, che col tempo per la moltitudine di questi nuovi vocaboli imbastardiscono, e diventano un'altra cosa; ma fanno questo in centinaja d'anni; di che altri non s'accorge, se non poichè è rovinato in una estrema barbarie.

> [. . .] it is not possible to find a language which can speak of anything by itself without having taken from others; because in speech men from various provinces take phrases from one another. In addition to this, any time a new doctrine or new art is introduced, it is necessary to add new words, born from that language where these doctrines and arts have arrived; but adapting in speech to the ways, the circumstances, the differences and accents, they conform to the words of the language they find, and become their own, because otherwise languages would sound patched up and would not sound good; and so foreign words

---

11 The Order of the Garter is the oldest Order of Chivalry in Britain, instituted by king Edward III in 1348.

convert into Florentine, not the Florentines into foreigners, no less our Florentine language becomes something else; and from here it depends, as languages are initially enriched and become more beautiful; but it is also true that in time, because of the multititude of these words, they deteriorate and change; but this takes thousands of years; this no one notices, unless reduced to extreme barbarism.

This long quote anticipates the debate on language borrowing and on the defence of the national language which will continue throughout the centuries, up to the present time (see 7.3). Machiavelli's stand, however, sounds quite open-minded and factual for a Renaissance man.

From the examples quoted so far it can be noted that early loanwords belong to the category of "cultural borrowings", i.e., they designate some new entity belonging to another culture. An interesting example is the word *pony* (16th c. from Scottish *powney*, in turn from Old French *poulenet*, 'foal'), which denoted a breed of small horses from Scotland and Ireland. Among the cultural borrowings we can also include units of measument (*acro*, 1498, from acre), terms related to property and administration (*aldrimani*, adapted from *aldermen*, 1551, 'administrative chief'; *enclosures*, 1538, 'pieces of common land converted into private property'; *mayor*, 16th c.); units of money (*scellino* 1667, from shilling; *ghinea*, 1668, from guinea). Many are the terms referring to noble titles such as *baronetto* (1667, from baronet), *lady* and *lord* (1668). The earlier terms *miledi* (1557) and *milordo* (1584) – respectively from English *my lady* and *my lord* – were originally used, especially by the French, to refer to a rich noblewoman or a nobleman, often travelling or temporarily living in Europe. These titles also conveyed a figurative meaning of a person of very refined elegance and aristocratic behaviour.[12] Among English words attested in 16th century writings there are terms related to drinking habits such as *ala* (ale 'English beer', 1498) and *smalto* (malt).

In the 16th and 17th centuries, the most important languages for communication in Europe were Latin, French and Italian. Education was mainly based on proficiency in Latin and Greek, and scholarly activity and academic writing in all disciplinary domains was conducted through the medium of the Latin language. French was the language used by most European courts, the language of the scientific academies, together with Latin, and the lingua franca of the educated elite. Equally influential from a cultural point of view was the flourishing of the Italian Renaissance (where *re-* stands for 'again' and the Latin root *nasc-* means 'be born') which spread all over Europe and raised a new, enthusiastic passion for the classical works in the humanities and in the arts (Pinnavaia 2019). Italy was the cradle of ancient and

---

[12] According to the GDU, the adapted form *milord* (from *milordo*) is attested in later times (1885).

classical culture and learning Italian meant access to a higher level of civilization. The great intellectual and artistic re-birth of the Renaissance, championed by the timeless giants of artistic genius, Leonardo da Vinci and Michelangelo Buonarroti, and of scientific excellence like Galileo Galilei placed Italy in the forefront of the humanities and science. Even Queen Elizabeth I studied Italian and was able to write letters in this language; knowledge of Italian was a sign of distinction and refinement, which could be achieved by reading books in the original language or in translation, travelling to Italy as part of the educational training of a gentleman and learning Italian with the assistance of mother-tongue teachers living in England. A massive input of Italianisms was absorbed by English between the years 1550 and 1650, the highest number in the fields of music, architecture, military activities, mathematics, commerce and finance. In 1583 the *Accademia della Crusca* was founded in Florence, with the aim of preserving the Italian language; the name of the Italian academy (literally, the word 'crusca' in Italian means 'bran') referred to the job of the miller to separate the wheat bran from the flour; analogously the philologist should sort out good usage (14th century Florentine Italian) from corrupted parlance. The Italian dictionary begun by the *Accademia della Crusca* was a model work that inspired other European languages.

By contrast, Early Modern English (late 15th and 16th centuries) was still in search of a standard, and the language was going through a phase of massive borrowing from Latin and Greek. This fueled a debate (referred to as 'inkhorn debate') between Neologisers and Purists, the latter advocating the defense of native (Germanic) vocabulary against the flood of Latinate vocabulary. In Early Modern English society French and Latin were widespread among the upper classes and this fact favoured the circulation of vocabulary in all directions. The dominance of French on the European scenario, linguistically and culturally, which would continue throughout the 18th and 19th centuries, made that language act as a go-between for English loans into Italian. French mediation is evident from the observation of the borrowing path of many Anglicisms, for example in the term *cambric* 'A kind of fine white linen, originally made at Cambray in Flanders' (from English *cambric* 1573; from French *Cambrai*, name of a town in north-west France), and *contraddanza* 'A rural or traditional dance' (Italian 1726, from French *contredance*, 1626; from English *country dance*, 1579). Because of the similarity and the historical links between French and Italian, especially in case of borrowings with neoclassical form, it is difficult or even impossible to establish whether a loanword is from French or from English (more examples from the following centuries will be discussed below).

Among the notable characters featuring in the English-Italian scenario, John Florio, the son of an Italian expatriate, embodies the figure of a teacher, a translator and a lexicographer of the time. He was a reader and teacher of Italian at the court of James I and Queen Anne and the author of the Italian-English dictionary

*A World of Wordes* (1598, extended in a second edition in 1611 under the title of *Queen Anna's New World of Words*). In his preface, Florio explains to the users that his dictionary would serve as a "compass of reading", that is, it would orient English speakers to the reading of Italian texts in their original version. Florio strongly believed in the value of Italian culture for the refinement of a gentleman's or a lady's education. He supported the learning of the Italian language in Renaissance England, and published several books of dialogues in Italian with English translation, for practicing conversation (*First Fruites*, 1578, a collection of "familiar speech, merie prouerbes, wittie sentences, and golden sayings"; *Second Frutes*, 1591, and *Giardino di ricreatione*, 1591). In one of Florio's dialogues, we find an interesting (personal) view of the English language, which may to some extent mirror the limited importance of English in the European Renaissance and is surely in sharp contrast with the role that English would acquire in the centuries to follow:

| | |
|---|---|
| *Certo io non lo harei pensato, che vi pare di questa lingua inglese, ditemi di grazia.* | Certis I would not have thought it: what thinke you of this English, tell me I pray you. |
| *E' la lingua che vi farà bene in Inghilterra, ma passate Dover, la non val niente.* | It is a language that wyl do you good in England but passe Dover, it is woorth nothing. |

## 2.2 Anglomania

From the 18<sup>th</sup> century the relations between the British and Italian societies became direct and stable, and the number of borrowings increased, but now the direction is mainly from English into Italian. The terms Anglicism and Anglomania must be introduced to discuss a phenomenon that from this century on will gradually intensify to reach the pervasiveness that we know today. The term Anglicism (from post-classical Latin *Anglicus* + English suffix *-ism*), meaning 'a characteristically English word, phrase, or idiom, *esp.* one introduced into a sentence in another language' (OED) was already current in English in the mid-17<sup>th</sup> century; the French equivalent *anglicisme* immediately followed, and so did the Italian *anglicismo*, already quoted in 1747 in the Venice translation of Chambers' *Encyclopedia* (Fanfani 2010) and in 1764 by the writer Giuseppe Baretti in his critical journal *La Frusta Letteraria* (The Literary Whip). The term *inglesismo* was introduced in 1757 but enjoyed less success than *anglicismo*. Italian also has the term *anglismo* (in use from the 20<sup>th</sup> century) for the same meaning, which is preferred by those who wish to avoid terminology derived from English. Another word introduced in the 18<sup>th</sup> century is Anglomania, which was first coined in

French (*anglomanie*, 1754) and then transferred to other languages affected by the same phenomenon (*anglomania* in Italian in 1756), with the meaning of 'Mania for what is English (or British); excessive admiration or enthusiasm for England (or Britain), its customs, fashions, etc.' (OED).

The cultural fashion that was named Anglomania started in France and arrived in Italy through the mediation of France in the second half of the 18$^{th}$ century, bringing along a high number of cultural Anglicisms. Anglomania is carefully portrayed by the 20$^{th}$ century Italian poet and scholar Arturo Graf (1911). In his extensive description, Graf analyses both the phenomena of Gallomania – admiration and imitation of the French – and Anglomania – admiration and imitation of the English – with great attention to the cultural debate and to the contribution of 18$^{th}$ century Italian writers and intellectuals. According to Graf, turning to other countries for literary inspiration was a sign of 'decadence' for Italian creative minds, after sharing so generously their art and culture with the rest of Europe during the golden age of the Renaissance. However, the quality of the Italian literary production appeared to be much lower than that of French and English writers. France was already the strongest cultural model and donor language for Italian society, and would continue to be so up to the 20$^{th}$ century, for linguistic closeness and geographical proximity. Instead, the relations with Britain had never been particularly warm, given the few affinities between Britain and the Italian reigns and republics and, above all, because of the religious conflict and subsequent schism of the Anglican Church of England from the Catholic Church of Rome.[13] According to Graf, however, Anglomania spread in Italy anyway, partly as a consequence but also as a reaction to the dominance of French culture and lifestyle, which was further worsened by political tension between Italy and its closer neighbours from the other side of the Alps.

Italy had kept its charm as a destination for the Grand Tour,[14] and its artistic beauties and its glorious past, particularly music and opera, still inspired the British social and cultural elites. Interest in the British world was fostered and popularized by the direct testimony of several men of letters who travelled or lived in England in this century, and reported their experience in this 'free' country in their writings. One of them was Giuseppe Baretti, who lived in England for part of his life, cultivating a friendship with Samuel Johnson and his cultural circle in London. He was a prolific writer, both in Italian and in English, a literary critic, a

---

**13** Graziano (1984) describes a numerous colony of British residents in Rome since the 17$^{th}$ century and a delegation of the Stuart court stationed in Rome since the beginning of the 18$^{th}$ century, causing a negative effect on diplomatic relations, because of spying activity and theft of artwork.

**14** The Grand Tour was a continental trip to France and Italy that upper-class and aristocratic men in early modern Europe would undertake for educational purposes (Tosi 2020).

translator and a lexicographer: he promoted Italian culture in Britain but also championed the English language, literature and civilization (Baretti 1775). Baretti was highly competent in spoken and written English and supported the study of English as a cultural resource for accessing literary and scholarly writings. He was also a teacher of Italian in London ("il maestro italiano") and the author of *A Grammar of the Italian Language, with a copious praxis of moral sentences. To which is added An English Grammar for the Use of Italians* (1762) and a bilingual *Dictionary of the English and Italian Languages* (1760), which was considered the best for at least a century, and reprinted many times in the 18th and 19th centuries. Although only a few English words appear in his Italian works, Baretti wanted Italian writers to develop an interest in the English language, as stated in the often quoted passage from his journal *Frusta letteraria* (no. XXIV, 1764):

> Oh che bella cosa, se mi venisse fatto di svegliare in qualche nostro scrittore la voglia di sapere bene anche la lingua inglese! Allora sì, che si potrebbero sperare de' pasticci sempre più meravigliosi di vocaboli e di modi nostrani e stranieri ne' moderni libri d'Italia! E quanto non crescerebbono questi libri di pregio, se oltre a que' tanti francesismi di cui già riboccano, contenessero anche qualche dozzina d'anglicismi in ogni pagina!
>
> [Oh, how nice, if I could manage to arouse in some of our writers the desire to master the English language as well! Then, surely, one could hope for more and more beautiful mixtures of domestic and foreign words and manners in the modern books of Italy! And how much these books would improve in quality, if, beside so many gallicisms which already abound in them, they also contained a dozen anglicisms on every page!]

During the 18th century, besides Baretti's, other English-Italian dictionaries and grammars were published to support the study of English in Italy, among which Ferdinando Altieri's *Dizionario Italiano ed inglese. A Dictionary Italian and English* (1726–27) is worth quoting;[15] French translations of major literary works of writers such as those of Milton, Pope, Swift and Dryden were often the source of Italian translations, favouring the circulation of English culture (Graziano 1984; Iamartino 2001). Ephraim Chambers' *Cyclopædia: or, An Universal Dictionary of Arts and Sciences*, first published in London in 1728, was translated into Italian in 1748.[16] Translations are the channel of a few loanwords from novels of the time,

---

[15] See Graziano (1984: 376) for details on Italian-English grammars and bilingual dictionaries published in the 18th century and the competence in the English language of a few intellectuals of this age.

[16] Chambers' *Cyclopædia*, one of the first published in English, is the forerunner of modern encyclopedias. The interest that it raised in Italy is witnessed by the several translations, the first promoted by Giovan Battista Pasquali, a Venetian bookseller, and Joseph Smith, an English Consul in Venice. Five subsequent translations were published in Italy between 1747 and 1775: two in Venice (1748–49; 1762), two in Naples (1747–54; 1775), and one in Genoa (1770–1775).

like *silfide* (1739, from English *sylphid*, from Pope's *Rape of the Lock*), *lillipuziano* (1737, from Swift's *Gulliver's travels*) and *rum* (1708) (Zolli 1991).

Anglomania was surely fuelled by direct and indirect information about the English world. The picture of the English society – according to Graf's meticulous analysis of direct testimonies of the time – is that English gentlemen held culture in great esteem and were not as haughty as many Italian noblemen! Recognized qualities were simplicity, rectitude, generosity and good faith. Britain was admired for its writers, scientists and philosophers, but most of all because of its political system, parliamentary institutions and laws, which were considered fair, and the primary source of its economic and political power (Messeri 1957). Both Britain and the United States of America were also considered a political harbour for many Europeans escaping from persecution and conflicts in continental Europe, as in the case of the French writer Voltaire, who was exiled to England between 1726 and 1729 and wrote that English was the language of free people, of 'une nation libre et savante [a free and learned nation]'. Goethe, the great German literary figure, admired the ideals of freedom and independence inspired by the American revolution, and dedicated the much-quoted poem *Den Vereinigten Staaten* (To the United States) containing the famous verse 'Amerika, du hast es besser' [America, you are better off] (Stammerjohann 2003).

The greater number of English loanwords in the 18th century come from the political domain, such as *coalizione* (1778), *comitato* (1749), *commissione* (1780), *convenzione* (1749), *costituzionale* (1768), *legislatura* (1746–48), *maggioranza* (1777), *mozione* (1789), *opposizione* (1773) and *petizione* (1773). As can be noted, all these terms have a Latin origin (see 4.4), some of which already existed before in Italian but acquired a specific, political meaning because of the influence of English. It is highly probable, but not yet ascertained by historical evidence, that these terms were adopted through the mediation of French. Regarding this problem, dictionaries often indicate a double origin (French and English) for many terms. A closer look at the etymology of the political term *mozione* (1789), for example, reveals that its source is both French *motion* and English *motion*, which are homographs, according to *Nuovo Devoto-Oli 2022* and *Zingarelli 2022*, but only from French in the GDU. This is one of the cases in which the origin of the borrowing (semantic, in this case, since the word *mozione* already existed in Italian before the political meaning was taken on) may be ambiguous and may not be detected or established on a purely formal basis.

Other terms worth quoting refer to religion (*conformista*, 1714, 'one who conforms to the usages of the Church of England'), seafaring (*comodoro*, 1749, later *commodoro*, from English *commodore*, from French *commandeur*; *dock*, 1797; *log*, 1751); types of boats (*tender*, 1749; *cutter*, 1779; *schooner*, 1799; *sloop*, 1799), which witness the expertise of Britain in the art and craft of navigation. In the field of fashion we can quote *redingotto* (1748, from French *redingote*, from English *riding-*

*coat*), *fumo di Londra* (1787, from London *smoke*, a colour for fabrics), *plaid* (1757, from Scottish *plaide*) and *tartan* (1788). These examples show that borrowings are partly adapted to Italian forms, especially when they display formal similarity, but were also taken on without any adaptation, presumably for their pronunciation. Moreover, most loanwords are cultural borrowings, i.e., they denote something peculiar to British society, such as the names of the political parties, *Tory* (1718) and *Whig* (1714); *city* (1749), *gentleman* (1788), *speaker* (1748), *penny* (1749, from Old German *pfenning*), but it must be stressed that some established themselves directly in the Italian 'core' vocabulary, like *clan* (1788, from Gaelic *clann*), *club* (1763, early meaning of 'political circle'), *miss* (1764), *toast* (1749), *standard* (1764, originally 'sign', from Old French 'estendart'), *test* (1766), *stock* (1769), *budget* (1799, from French bougette 'small bag'). English also acted as mediator of terms coming from other distant world languages with which Britain came into contact through explorations and colonialism, such as *ketchup* (1712), *opossum* (1771, from American Algonquian), *canguro* (1784, from English kangaroo, from Australian *kängaroo*) and *mogano* (1764, from English mahogany, from Central America). Semantically, it must be noted that the oldest meanings for which these terms were borrowed, would be replaced in later times by new, modern meanings: an example is the term *speaker*, referring to 'the member of the House of commons who is chosen by the House itself to act as its representative and to preside over its debates', which today also refers to 'somebody who speaks' on radio, television, at a conference or meeting, and also through a loudspeaker at a sports event.

## 2.3 The 19th century

During the first half of the 19th century Italy was still socially, politically (and linguistically) divided. The country was troubled by the French invasion of peninsular Italy led by the general Napoleon I, which brought an even stronger Gallicization of Italian, as well as a greater influence on social tastes and habits, and plenty of administrative terms; subsequently, the restoration of Austrian rule of the north of Italy was followed by political uprisings and three wars of independence, leading up to the unification of the kingdom of Italy in 1861 (De Mauro 1970). Having achieved political unity, the aspiration was to have a unified language as a symbol of national identity. To some extent, the use of Italian increased among the ruling classes, politicians and state employees, while the lower classes still used regional dialects. The language controversy – whether or not the Florentine variety should be the model for Italian – was revived, but the social question arising from the lack of a national language was also strongly felt. In a period when the distinction between the written and the spoken language was taking shape, criticism was addressed to unnecessary interference of bureaucratic terminology and foreign words. Yet, a progressive opinion was held by the celebrated Italian poet Giacomo Leopardi, whose authoritative words are often quoted, to remind readers that a national language must not be impoverished of its expressive resources, but, by the same token, foreign words should not be rejected, and a new idea and a new concept should not be "treated as barbarous":

> Rinunziare o sbandire una nuova parola o una sua nuova significazione (per forestiera o barbara ch'ella sia), quando la nostra lingua non abbia l'equivalente, o non l'abbia così precisa, e ricevuta in quel proprio e determinato senso; non è altro, e non può essere meno che rinunziare o sbandire, e trattar da barbara e illecita una nuova idea, e un nuovo concetto dello spirito umano." (Leopardi, 1921: 1558)

> [Giving up or banning a new word or one of its new meanings (however foreign or barbarous this may be), when our language does not have an equivalent one, or it has one that is not as precise, and recorded in that very specific sense; it really means, and it cannot be less than giving up or banning and treating a new idea and a new concept of the human spirit as barbaric and illicit.]

By contrast, 19th century Britain was already the leading nation of the industrial revolution, economically and politically strong, and during the Victorian age it became the most powerful empire in the world. English travellers on the Grand Tour were aristocrats, whereas Italians in England were often exiles or political refugees, like the poet Ugo Foscolo and the political activist Giuseppe Mazzini, a key figure of the Italian *Risorgimento,* and in the USA the patriot and soldier Giuseppe Garibaldi. Linguistically, the English language continued to expand through the formation of specialist terminology by drawing on Greek and Latin elements, thus becoming more and more international. As stated by Migliorini and Griffith (1984: 386), "The great progress of sciences at this period led to more or less parallel growth in their terminologies in most of the languages of Europe." This characteristic of the English language is relevant to the distinction between borrowings and internationalisms which will be discussed in section 4.4.

From a literary perspective, a great number of printed books, newspapers and periodicals circulated in Italy, bringing English culture to the attention of a larger audience, and also contributing to the input of foreign words into the general vocabulary. Among the major English and American authors of the Victorian age whose works were translated into many different Italian versions, we can mention the romantic poet Lord Byron, the Scottish historical novelist Walter Scott, the American adventure novelist James Fenimore Cooper, the novelist Charles Dickens, as well as many essayists in the fields of science, such as Charles Darwin (Zolli 1991). Some of these translations have been examined to identify the Anglicisms which were introduced into the Italian language through the written medium (Benedetti 1974; Sullam Calimani 1995). The word *autobiografia* (1828), for example, takes its origin from

Scott's novels, where the word *autobiography* is often used, and initially translated through the periphrasis 'life written by oneself'. The classical form of the constituent elements (auto + bio + graphy) favoured its input and the immediate integration of many such terms, be they calques, adaptations or Latin-based words, whose English origin can be determined only by historical evidence.

Competence in the English language was now felt to be important not only for accessing knowledge in a foreign, highly valued culture and its literary production, but also for the importance of English in the scientific and technical fields in which Great Britain had achieved ground-breaking results, i.e., means of transport and industrial production. It is worth mentioning that a reform of the Italian educational system (the Casati Law, 1859), which was adopted after the unification of the country, introduced French as the first foreign language, and the study of English was optional in technical schools for its importance in the learning of technical and scientific vocabulary (Schirru 2019). The number of Italian-English grammars, handbooks and bilingual dictionaries for learning English was now very high. Iamartino (2001) claims that over 80 grammars and books were available and continued to be reprinted to support the learning of English in Italy, although education was still an elite phenomenon and nearly 80% of the population was illiterate.

In this century the cultural contacts between Britain and Italy were intense and the number of Anglicisms grew considerably, especially in the second half of the 19th century, which was politically more stable after the unification of Italy. English loanwords of this time were often borrowed without any adaptation, a practice which differed from the preceding centuries. The area of influence extended from the field of politics to other domains of British influence, such as means of transport, fashion and sport, which were used in the periodical press, another source of foreign terms besides translations. The number of words imported from English in this century, although much lower than those imported from French, amounts to several hundreds (320 in *Nuovo Devoto-Oli 2022*; 565 in the GDU; see chapter 5), including Latin-based terms, adaptations, calques and a few non-adapted loanwords, from which a few representative examples will be quoted below.

The field of politics, which had already attracted the interest of Italian in the previous centuries, continues to be a source of loanwords: *assolutismo* (1848, from absolutism); *assenteismo* (1836, from absenteeism); *ostruzionismo* (1894, from obstructionism); *boicottare* (1881, from boycott: this term derives from the name of Captain Charles C. Boycott, an Irish landlord whose tenants refused to work as a protest).[17] Among the non-adapted loanwords, we can quote the term *common law*

---

17 The word *boycott* has been naturalized in many languages of Europe, so that it must be classified as an internationalism (see 4.4). Cf. 'French *boycotter* (1880), German *boycottieren* (1893;

(1892), which characterized the British political system (and subsequently most of Commonwealth countries) versus the civil law of continental Europe; *chairman* (1892); *impeachment* (1895); *leader* (1834); *leadership* (1893); *premier* (1844, originally from French *premier*, 'first').

A new productive field of 19th century loanwords is that of fashion, ushered into Italian society by Anglomania: the term *fashion* itself entered Italian quite early (1808) and has since remained in competition with the domestic term *moda*; in fact, by observing the use of *fashion* in the course of the following centuries, we may verify that it never replaced the Italian word, but today its use is preferred in compounds such as *fashion system, fashion victim, fashion week*. Among the terminology in this field we find quite a few words referring to British menswear, with a few interesting Italian adjustments: the term *tight* (1870) which corresponds to English *tail coat*, 'a dress or swallow-tailed coat', perhaps because of its tight-fitting shape (*tights* was the name of 'tight-fitting breeches, worn by men in the 18th and early 19th centuries, and still forming part of court-dress'; note that the current meaning of *tights* in English and in Italian is completely different, denoting 'Garments of thin elastic material, fitting tight to the skin, worn by dancers, acrobats, and others to facilitate their movements or display the form;[. . .]'). Another curious Italian reshaping of a piece of formal menswear is the term *smoking* (1891), which denotes 'an evening suit worn by men for formal social events', corresponding to English *dinner jacket* or *tuxedo*. Italian *tight* and *smoking* can be classified as false Anglicisms (see 3.5), as they express an Italian meaning with the use of English words. The origin of *smoking* is probably from the term *smoking-jacket*, designed in the 19th century for gentlemen, with a typical shawl collar and turn-up cuffs, made of velvet or other elegant fabric, to wear in cigar rooms.

Other terms belonging to the field of fashion are the names of fabrics, such as *chintz* (1892), *jersey* (1868), *sealskin* (1879) and *tweed* (1878), and types of garments such as *shorts* (1885) and the Scottish *kilt* (1896), which in Italy is worn exclusively by women. Fashion terms are subject to obsolescence, and in fact several terms in this field have gone out of use. Some instances are *knickerbockers* (1865), replaced by *pantaloni alla zuava*, a type of 'Loose-fitting breeches, gathered in at the knee', used in some sports or folk costumes. While the term *knickerbockers* is still recorded in Italian dictionaries, the terms *spencer* 'A kind of close-fitting jacket or bodice commonly worn by women and children early in the 19th century', and *mackintosh*, originally 'garments and other articles made of waterproof

---

now *boykottieren*), Dutch *boycotten* (1904), Russian *bojkotirovat'* (1891), etc.'(OED) The origin of the Italian word *boicottaggio*, usually classified as a calque or an adaptation of English *boycotting*, is considered by some linguists as an adaptation of French *boycottage*, based on the affinity between the Italian suffix *-aggio* and the French suffix *-age* (Bombi 2020: 75).

material', are only recorded in our reference dictionary (GDU) but no more in *Zingarelli 2022* and *Nuovo Devoto-Oli 2022*. The Italian term for *mackintosh* is *impermeabile*, but the actual domestic adjective *impermeabile* (water-resistant) coexists with the Anglicism *waterproof* (1868).

Closely related to fashion is the area of lifestyle, where we find words relating to free-time activities like *picnic* (1820), *five o'clock tea* (1884) and *garden-party* (1895). Societies were still class-conscious, so that the term *sir* (1891) was a form of address reserved to a member of the nobility, and *high life* (1832) was a privilege of a limited circle of people. The term *dandy* (1817) deserves a closer cultural illustration, as dandyism was a fashion which spread in France and in England in the late 18th century and continued in the following century. 'Beau' Brummel, an English gentleman living in London at the turn of the 19th century, is the epitome of the British dandy. He was considered the most elegant man in 18th-century Europe, as he dressed up with meticulous sophistication and greatly influenced the masculine fashion of the time. The term *dandy* was introduced to describe someone behaving like Beau Brummel, i.e., 'one who studies above everything to dress elegantly and fashionably; a beau, fop, exquisite'. In the following century, the Irish writer Oscar Wilde was taken as another example of dandyism: he embodied the stereotypical character of a middle-class man, an artist, who behaved and dressed in an eccentric way and imitated aristocratic manners and lifestyle. Related to *dandyism*, with a different shade of meaning, is the term *snob* (1859), which describes 'one who wishes to be regarded as a person of social importance'.

Several names of liquors and wines were imported through the English language, although not all of them originally British: *brandy* (1829, from Dutch *brandewijn*), *gin* (1823, from Dutch *genever*), *sherry* (1830, from Spanish *Xeres*) and *whisky* (1829, from Gaelic *uisgebeatha*). In the area of food we find *sandwich* (1872), still current today but overtaken in frequency by Italian *panino*, *roast beef* (1819), alternatively spelt *rosbif*, and *bistecca* (1844, adapted from *beef-steak*). The term *cocktail* (1896) seems to have originated from US English (see below) and *budino*, originally a meat sausage (1808, from English *pudding* and from French *boudin*) denotes a sweet dessert in Italian. Among the exotic loanwords we can mention *curry* (1817, from Tamil *kari*).

Echoes from the American world reached the European continent, especially through periodicals and books. The images of the young, new nation fired the readers' imagination and raised enthusiasm and sympathy, both for the historical events of the war of independence and the subsequent civil war, and also for the fictional representation of the adventurous north American world, featuring peculiar flora and fauna, and representing the so-called melting pot of ethnic communities. Examples are *sequoia* (1847, a big tree from the name of native American chief Sequojah), *grizzly* (1875), *Far West* (1892, 'the area of the United States west of the Great Plains'), *cowboy* (1890), and vocabulary referring to the native American world (*tomahawk* 1801, *totem* 1828, *squaw* 1908; *pellerossa* 1848, a calque of *redskin*). New meanings are associated to already existing words, such as *riserva* (1890, from reservation 'An area of land set apart or reserved by the government for occupation by North American Indians'), as well as terms related to the US political system, such as *congresso* (1856, from congress, 'the national legislative body of the United States of America'), *abolizionismo* (1865, from abolitionism 'abolition of the slave trade and the emancipation of African slaves'), *piattaforma* (1890, from *platform* 'the major policy or set of policies on which a political party [. . .] proposes to stand'), *proibizionismo* (1926, from prohibitionism 'the prohibition of alcohol').

Terminology in the fields of business and commerce continues to flow into Italian. Many terms have been completely assimilated into the core vocabulary, such as *banconota* (1849, from *banknote*), *broker* (1892), *business* (1895), *manager* (1895), *self-made man* (1893), whereas others coexist with Italian equivalents, such as *trademark* (1895, coexisting with Italian *marchio di fabbrica* or simply *marchio*), *trade union* (1870, replaced by *sindacato*), *free trade* (1892, replaced by phrases like *libero scambio, libero mercato, libera circolazione delle merci*).

The obsolescence of loanwords after a period of success may be due to several reasons, the most concrete one being the ageing of the referents or cultural products they refer to. In other words, many terms are 'victims of progress' (cf. 6.5). Case in point are means of transport used in the past, such as *tilbury* (1832, a two-wheel carriage), *brougham* (1840, 'a one-horse closed carriage') and *cab* (1842, a horse-drawn type of carriage for public transport), a term which was later rejuvenated in English by assuming the new meaning of *taxi*;[18] means of navigation, like *schooner* (sailing ship, 1799), *steamer* (1837), and *ferry-boat* (1883), which are now all obsolete. By contrast, the sea term *tender* (1749) has resisted obsolescence and is still current with the meaning of 'a small ship used to carry passengers, luggage, mails, goods, stores, etc., to or from a larger vessel (usually a liner), esp. when not otherwise accessible from shore.' The term *tram* for public transport (1878, originally from *tram-car* or *tramway car* or simply *tram*) has been fully integrated into general Italian, through the adaptation *tramvai* or *tranvai* (1956), and equally modernized in time from the early horse-drawn trams. In Italian the old meaning of *trolleybus* no longer exists and has been substituted by *filobus*; the Anglicism *trolley* (1894) is used in general language to denote a modern type of suitcase with wheels (in English, *trolley suitcase*); in technical use, the Italian synonym *pantografo* (pantograph), of French origin, is preferred to *trolley*,

---

**18** *Taxi*, also adapted into *tassì*, is a French borrowing in Italian (1914).

which is recorded by *Nuovo Devoto-Oli 2022*.[19] Britain was in the forefront of the first industrial revolution, which introduced the factory system for manufacturing and new power sources, like the steam engine. The English term *locomotive*, a Latin-based coinage,[20] easily spread to other European languages and into Italian *locomotiva* (1826) (see internationalisms, section 4.4). The unit of mechanic power named *horsepower* (1860) was translated as *cavallo vapore*, but the Italian abbreviation has remained in its English format, i.e., HP. Finally, the eponym *pullman* (1869 from the name of the American industrialist A. G. Pullman, who invented the luxurious Pullman sleeping car for overnight travel) is currently used in Italian for the meaning of bus, together with the near synonyms *autobus* and *bus* (respectively pronounced ['autobus] and [bus]).

The examples quoted so far show that the 19th century was indeed a period of intense contacts and borrowing from English into Italian: in fact, the starting point of continuous input of English loanwords. It was also an age in which tourism developed, and the *Touring Club Italiano* was created, with a partly English name. Special attention must be given to the sphere of influence which has remained one of the most productive in time, namely the field of sport. Historical facts explain the reason why sports terminology is so anglicized. In fact, many modern sports and their terminologies originated in Britain, and consequently also the official regulations were set up in English, in order to provide systematic records of competitive games. The word *sport*, both its generic meaning of free-time recreation and its specific meaning of competitive activity, was adopted by many European languages in the 19th century (by Italian in 1829) and is now a fully integrated word. Football was first introduced in Italy at the end of the 19th century. The *Federazione Italiana Foot-Ball* was created in Torino in 1888, the year recorded for the adoption of the Anglicism *foot-ball* (1888). In his dictionary Panzini adds the following comment to this loanword:

> Qui ricorderemo soltanto come nella patria del *Calcio* e della *Pallacorda* si giochino i detti giuochi con denominazioni inglesi ed i maestri insegnino in inglese, e i vecchi nomi italiani sono obliati. Dicono gli intenditori che il nuovo *foot-ball* non corrisponde all'antico e perciò i nuovi nomi hanno ragione di essere. [. . .]

> Here we will only remind you that in the homeland of *calcio* and *pallacorda*, these games are played with English denominations and coaches train in English, and the old Italian

---

**19** 'A jointed, self-adjusting framework on the top of an electric vehicle for conveying the current from overhead wires.' (OED).
**20** 'The post-classical Latin adjective *locomotivus* is after the phrase *in loco moveri* to move 'locally' or by change of position in space.' (OED).

terms are forgotten. Experts say that the new *football* does not match with the old one and therefore the existence of the new terms is fully justified. [...]

Other popular sports and their names were introduced in the same period, such as *golf* (1825), *tennis* (1828), *cricket* (1831) and *polo* (1895). Other related terminology includes *fair play* (1828), *match* (1873), *ring* (1881), *record* (1884), *derby* (1888, originally 'race for young horses'; the football-related meaning was introduced much later, in 1950) and *rush* 1891. All these terms are still well-established today (see 6.4 for more extended treatment of Anglicisms in sports).

To sum up, the fields of more intense borrowing from English into Italian in the 19th century were politics, business and commerce, fashion, social life and, by far the largest group, sport. A great number of Anglicisms do not fit into these categories, but witness that Anglo-American culture was already filtering into Italian life: a few examples are *clown* (1828), *cockney* (1829), *revolver* (1858), *reporter* (1875), *folklore* (1884), *watt* (1884), *film* (1889), *detective* (1891), *bar* (1892), *college* (1892), *copyright* (1892), *gang* (1892), *flirt* (1895, for the meaning of 'flirtation'), *performance* (1895), *recital* (1897); a good number of dog breeds such as *pointer* (1841), *collie* (1844), *cocker* (1852), *setter* (1875), *retriever* (1883), *terrier* (1895) reveal the British interest in dog breeding and husbandry. Two observations are necessary. First, most Anglicisms belong to the type of non-adapted Anglicisms, that is, they are recognizably English in form. A smaller number of Anglicisms are adapted (e.g., *folklore/folclore*) or translated, such as *giungla* (1828, from jungle), *intervista* (1877, from interview, originally applied to the political field), *romantico* (1824), *turista* (1837), *preistorico* (1871). This latter type of Anglicisms are not recognizably English or clearly from English. In fact, only historical information can shed light on their origin. Further, it may be controversial to consider the word *romantico* and *preistorico* as non-Italian words. Second, in this century the mediation of French as a geographical and social go-between for the transmission of Anglicisms is quite strong. Evidence of this is the orthographic form in which borrowings appear in Italian, both English and French, which is a sign of a double source. Some examples are *choc/shock* (1899), *confort/comfort* (1865), *cachemire* and *cashmere* (1892), where the first instances are from French and the second from English.

## 2.4 Neo-purism

The main historical events which characterize the decades from the end of the 19th century to the first half of the 20th century are the migration of Italians to America, the First World War (1914–18), the fascist regime (1922–1945) and the Second World

War (1939–45). All these circumstances weighed on the relations between Italy, the United Kingdom and the USA, politically, economically, culturally and linguistically. In this section, we will sketch these events and their relevance to culture and language in Italy: the rise of the American myth and the opposition to the use of foreign words, a phenomenon called neo-purism.

Between 1876 and 1930, about 5 million Italians, especially from the southern regions of Italy, migrated to the United States of America, in search of better working conditions (De Mauro 1970). This was the first social event that brought large Italian communities into direct contact with English-speaking societies, settled in many 'little Italies' in the USA (as well as in Australia, South America and Africa). Life in the new world was hard for the first wave of Italian immigrants, engaged in humble jobs, different from the conditions described in guides to emigration published in Italy. Yet, the roots of the 'American myth', which has produced a great deal of historical and sociological debate (Eco 1984, 1992) lie in these years. The USA was considered as a 'promised land' of opportunities, freedom and democracy. Images of the New World had already been popularized by translations of adventure novels set on the north American frontier, a fictional world populated by Indians and cowboys, like the ones by Thomas Mayne Reid and the famous masterpiece by Harriet Beecher-Stowe (*Uncle Tom's Cabin*, published in 1852 and translated into Italian in the same year). Writings about the USA pictured a world that was dangerous and attractive at the same time: on the one hand, the new world had slums and ghettos, gangsters and lynchers; on the other hand, America was perceived as a source of primitive, creative energy and entrepreneurial expertise. A case in point is the European Tour made by Bill Cody, also known as Buffalo Bill, in 1890 and in 1906 (Cottini 2019), which had an amazing impact on Italian audiences. Attitudes towards American society (Pulcini 1997) wavered between admiration and disapproval, despite a campaign of self-promotion through solidarity actions and propaganda in the media launched by the USA during the First World War. The Catholic church, for example, looked down on the material vision of life emanating from the Protestant world. Other events weighed heavily on building distrust toward the USA, such as American legislation for the control of immigration and the death sentence in 1927 of the Italian anarchists Nicola Sacco and Bartolomeo Vanzetti, accused of murder; this controversial case stirred indignation all over Europe.

The Italian immigrant communities that settled in English-speaking countries – in the USA, Canada, Australia and Great Britain – spoke regional dialects. Learning English was important to integrate in the new social environments, but the home dialects were the only means of communication for first generation immigrants and a symbol of ethnic identity for the community members. These contact situations, which resulted in bilingualism in second and following generations of Italians abroad, gave rise to assimilation of English words into the dialects, as adaptations (*giobba* for *job*; *carro* for *car*), false friends (*fattoria* for *factory*) and strongly Italianized pronunciations, like *uozze mera* (What's the matter) (Rando 1967; Haller 1993; Tosi 1991). A case apart is the word *sciuscià* – a word of historical importance – which reproduces the Italian pronunciation of *shoeshine*. After Italy's surrender to the Allied forces in 1943, American troops were stationed in Italy. *Sciuscià* was the name given to homeless boys in Naples living in the streets and earning money by cleaning the shoes of the American soldiers. *Sciuscià* was chosen as the title of an award-winning masterpiece of Italian neorealist cinema, featuring the story of two friends in devastated post-war Rome, who get involved in a gang plot, end up in a spiral of negative circumstances and finally in the accidental death of one of them. The outcomes of language contact between immigrant dialects and English have had little or no influence on standard Italian (Carnevale 2009; Prifti 2013).

The appearance of the USA on the international scene broadened the spectrum of the linguistic and cultural influence of the English language not only for Italy but also for many Western European countries. The growing economic and military power of the USA, in contrast with the decline of the British colonial empire, marked a historical turn from Britain to the USA as a cultural model to admire and imitate, although British society continued to be influential and, in turn, a carrier of American influence. Linguistically, borrowings from American English can be recognized when they are culturally marked, i.e., they denote material and cultural products belonging to the American world. Among the early 20$^{th}$ century loanwords from US English, two terms portray the vision of America in the eyes of Italians, namely *ranch* (1901, 'A large farm or estate for breeding cattle, horses, or sheep', from Spanish *rancho*), the home of the settlers in the wild west, and *grattacielo* (1927, from *skyscraper*, initially translated into *grattanuvole*), the symbol of the magnitude of American urban skylines. As explained by Tosi (2001: 209), "[t]he early borrowings of American origin show a picture of a country perceived as being between life in the wild and a futuristic society."

The political situation of the unified Kingdom of Italy was stable but greater internal mobility and circulation of ideas did not bring economic prosperity. Huge social differences existed between the North, where industries began to expand, and the South of the country, whose conditions were stagnant: from Southern Italy large masses of migrants moved overseas. The introduction of compulsory education for children over six had the beneficial effect of reducing illiteracy from 78% in 1861 to 50% in 1910 (Migliorini and Griffith 1984), and spreading the use of written and spoken Italian, although the definition of a "unified" model for standard Italian – a debate among writers and policymakers, called 'the language question' ('*la questione della lingua*') – continued to be a matter of linguistic and social controversy. The influence of French continued to overshadow that of any other foreign language. English was taught in secondary schools and the first university posts for English were set up in 1918 (Zolli 1991). The First World War brought further social unrest and economic problems, which led to the rise of nationalism, colonial ambitions, and finally totalitarianism. The fascist regime (1922–1945) imposed a series of authoritarian measures to indoctrinate the population and used intimidation and violence to eliminate political opponents. Mussolini's ideology and political ambitions led Italy to ally with Hitler's Germany and enter the Second World War, with disastrous consequences. The Axis powers finally surrendered to the Allied forces and in 1946 the royal family was exiled, and Italy voted to become a republic.

In brief, the historical events sketched above provide the political and ideological setting for matters of language policy in Italy in the first half of the 20$^{th}$ century. First, the strong nationalist ideology imposed the principle that the Italian language should be the symbol of the country and consequently the use of dialects, minority languages[21] and foreign words should be marginalized (Raffaelli 1983, 2010; Klein 1986). A mild form of purism, which was already widespread among the Italian intelligentsia, was transformed by fascism into a xenophobic campaign: this involved the abolition of foreign words and their substitution with Italian ones, the ban of foreign names of towns (and often surnames), the prohibition of foreign words in names of hotels, public signs and advertisements. A first record of 20 non-adapted Anglicisms appeared in Fanfani and Arlìa's dictionary, whose title, *Lessico dell'infima e corrotta italianità* [*The lexicon of the vulgar and corrupted Italian spirit*], re-edited five times between 1877 and 1907, declared the purist intent of the authors, namely to record those words that were considered undesirable, in particular French bureaucratic terms, and proposed Italian substitutes. Hostility was addressed toward the English language because Great Britain and the USA were Italy's enemies (one of the war slogans was "God damn the British"). In the 1930s and 1940s legislative measure were issued to impose fines and even imprisonment for violations of the law; the *Regia Accademia d'Italia* (Italian Royal Academy) was appointed to invigilate the adherence to these impositions and provide Italian substitutes for foreign words. For example, in 1937 the name of the *Touring Club Italiano* was replaced by *Consociazione turistica italiana* (Raffaelli 2010).

---

[21] A campaign against dialects (including their use in schools) was launched in 1931–32. The use or teaching of minority languages were prohibited in state schools (but not by private and religious ones) and in public offices; newspapers written in languages other than Italian were suppressed. These legal measures raised resentment and triggered separatist reactions in the regions involved, which are geographically bordering mixed language areas such as Valle d'Aosta (Franco-Provençal area) and Alto Adige (German area). Other minority languages in Italy are French, Languedocian (Old Provençal), Catalan, Ladin, Sardinian, Greek, Slovenian, Albanian, Croatian and Friulian.

Despite the purist policy, some successfully integrated Anglicisms, such as *sport, bar, film, golf, picnic, poker, tennis, stop, tram*, continued to be used by speakers, also because some of the proposed substitutes sounded quite ridiculous, like *mescita, quisibeve, taberna potatoria* for *bar*, and *elettrosquasso* for *electroshock*! The Commission in charge of language policy would regularly issue a Bulletin with lists of undesirable foreign words and their substitutes. A complete list of 'barbarisms' would eventually be published in a single volume (Monelli 1933). Several Italian replacements were only partially successful and did not replace the foreign words, the majority of which were French, but also English ones: *circolo* (club), *arresto* (stop), *arlecchino* (cocktail), *festivale* (festival).[22]

State purism adopted a rigorous policy against the use of foreign words because the preference for foreign-sounding words was considered as an offence to Italian culture and habits and a disgraceful form of snobbery. In this political climate, linguists and lexicographers in particular felt the pressure of the authoritarian language policy of 'self-sufficiency'. Alfredo Panzini, for example, who was the author of *Dizionario Moderno* (first edition 1905) and a member of the humanities 'class' in the Italian Academy, opened a debate on neology and on the acceptance of foreign words, when necessary. Panzini's dictionary was, in fact, meant to be an addition to general dictionaries, containing especially neologisms, regional and dialectal words and thieves' cant (*gergo furbesco*), which he called '*mostri e mostricini*' (monsters and little monsters). Panzini argued against the use of foreign words when they could easily be substituted by Italian ones, and was indeed in favour of fighting against the irresponsible servitude ('*incosciente servilismo*') towards foreignisms. On the other hand, he also admitted that it would be a mistake to close the frontiers of language ('*barrare le frontiere della lingua*'), that is, to counter the input of borrowings from external sources, which is a natural source of enrichment for languages. He considered his mission as a lexicographer both literary and patriotic, because he meant to monitor the 'health of the Italian language'. Panzini made a clear moderate stance on the matter:

> Dunque io penso che è inutile opporsi all'accettazione tanto dei così detti barbarismi e gallicismi come delle nude voci straniere, giacché la loro forza è maggiore. E né meno penso che per questo soltanto la lingua italiana vada in rovina." (Panzini 1905: xxviii)

---

22 Purist campaigns did not always obtain the desired results. Raffaelli (1983) mentions a competition launched by a daily newspaper in 1932, inviting readers to find substitutes for foreign words (including fifteen Anglicisms). This initiative resulted in the disappearence of *five o'clock tè*, the maintenance of *jazz, smoking, tight, bar, klaxon/clacson, film*, and the survival of *copyright, dancing, raid, flirt, golf, record, sandwich*, with Italian substitutes (Pulcini 2002a).

[In fact, I think that it is useless to counter the acceptance of both the so-called barbarisms and gallicisms and plain foreign words, because their strength is greater. Neither do I believe that the Italian language should deteriorate only for this reason.]

A conflict developed between the *Regia Accademia d'Italia*, the voice of the regime, and the century-old *Accademia della Crusca*, who opted to turn to historical and philological studies and abandon its normative mission. A few years later, in 1942, Bruno Migliorini founded a movement called neo-purism, a mild form of opposition to the excessive 'hospitality' towards foreign words (called 'barbarisms') for the safeguarding of the Italian language; in particular, he was in favour of borrowings that could be structurally harmonized with Italian (adaptations and calques). For example, he accepted *turismo* (from French *tourism*) and *turista* (from Eng. *tourist*) but rejected French *chauffeur* (which was permanently replaced by *autista*).

Thus, academics and lexicographers deemed it necessary to keep track of the constant renewal of Italian through innovation and exploitation of exogenous items, but their attitude was far from objective and 'politically correct', according to today's standards. Although criticism was especially addressed to the undesirable intrusion of French words, also the material and cultural products arriving from the USA were object of scorn and ridicule. Reading through Monelli's entries (1933), an anti-foreign disposition is immediately clear. For example, for the term *vamp*, 'femme fatale' (from *vampire*) Monelli ironically comments that American women are better called 'bloodsuckers' rather than 'vampires'. For *sex-appeal* (*richiamo al sesso*), Monelli comments that there is no Italian equivalent for this term because Italian women do not need to act strangely in order to attract men's attention; instead, American women need to show off excessively to be noted by American gentlemen (who are normally more interested in their own athletic shape than in romance!).

Lexicographic evidence of the purist mindset in the first decades of the 20th century is given by Alfredo Panzini's *Dizionario Moderno* (1905), which had ten subsequent editions up to 1963, and updated appendices edited by Bruno Migliorini (1963). A quantitative study carried out by Rando (1969) on the Anglicisms recorded in this dictionary has shown that the number of Anglicisms recorded is lower in periods of greater political pressure, for example, between the third (1918) and the fourth edition (1923), a period of hostility between Italy and Great Britain in the post-World War I years, and between the seventh (1935) and the eighth (1942), at the peak of the fascist reaction against foreign words. It must be noted that some of the Anglicisms recorded by Panzini are anyway formally integrated into Italian: for example, we find *interferenza* (from the meaning of *interference* in physics), *ultimatum* (Anglo-Latinism), *altoparlante* (a calque from *loudspeaker*), *allenamento* (a calque from *training*), *dissolvenza* (a calque from the cinema term *fade-out*); adaptations like *condizionamento* (from *air conditioning*), *telepatico* (from *telepathic*), *vegetariano* (from *vegetarian*), *pressurizzare* (from *pressurize*), *aggiornare* (a semantic loan of the political term *adjourn*, 'to postpone a session'); but also non-adapted Anglicisms (e.g. *nursery, outsider, ping-pong, tea-room, trainer*) and phraseologisms (*business is business*).

The most productive field of borrowings in the first half of the 20$^{th}$ century continued to be sport. It must be noted that purists considered the term *sport* (1929) acceptable because already deeply entrenched in Italian, a proof of which was the creation of many Italian derivatives like *sportivo, sportivamente*, and *sportività*. Among the sports Anglicisms introduced in this period we can quote the following: *basketball* (1913, replaced by *pallacanestro* in 1935; currently *basket* 1965), *bobsleigh* (1913), *cross-country* (1913, in motor-racing, horse-racing, running, etc.), *curling* (1913), *hockey* (1927), *bob* (1930), and various terminology such as *goal* (1900), *finish* (1905), *game* (1905 in tennis), *net* (1905), *penalty* (1905), *set* (1905), *sprint* (1909), *team* (1909), *corner* (1911), *dribbling* (1911), *knock out* (1911), *smash* (1926, in tennis), *spin* (1920, in tennis), *score* (1923), *cross* (1925 in football, boxing and tennis), and *rally* (1935). Sports terminology, especially connected with the popular game of football, was subject to intense 'Italianization', in contrast with more elitist sports like tennis and golf. The term *football* has been almost completely replaced by *calcio* (literally 'kick'), *goalkeeper* by *portiere* and *foul* by *fallo*; whereas some terms coexist (*goal/rete, corner/angolo, offside/fuori gioco, sprint/scatto, record/primato, match/partita, coach/allenatore*) and some terms can only be named with English loanwords (*dribbling, rally*) (see section 6.4).

Following sport, the next productive fields were those of dances and music, in particular the new styles imported from the USA, such as *foxtrot* (1919) and *charleston* (1926), both obsolescent today, and popular music genres, such as *jazz* (1919), *blues* (1931), *ragtime* (1933), *spiritual* (1936) and *gospel* (1936).

According to the entries in the GDU (Pulcini 2017), the third domain with a considerable number of borrowings is that of seafaring terms (e.g. *racer* 1930, *skipper* 1935), although most of them are not common in the general language, similarly to military (*destroyer* 1913) and technical terms (*detector* 1905 and *timer* 1935). Instead, teminology related to business and commerce circulated more easily in society through the printed press and the media: e.g. *businessman* (1905), *slogan* (1905), *export* (1908), *boom* (1911), *boss* (1913), *holding* (1931), *turnover* (1933), *import* (1938), *partnership* (1950), *antitrust* (1950), and *welfare state* (1950).

The domain of fashion is linguistically less productive than the previous century: some common terms are *pigiama* (1905, from *pyjamas*, or *pajama*, partly from Urdu and partly from Persian *pāy jāma*), *golf* (1915, 'sweater'), *pullover* (1927), *slip* (1935, with the meaning of 'underpants' for both women and men), *trench* (1933, from trench-coat), *blazer* (1942), the eponyms *burberry* (1942) and *tuxedo* (1950). We can mention names of games such as *poker* (1905), *bridge* (1908) and related terminology, e.g. *slam* (1943) and *full* (1948, from full house); *puzzle* (1927); *jolly* (1943, from jolly joker). Some names of means of transport (*spider* 1915 'spider car'; *clacson* 1923, 'car horn'; *container* 1935; *caterpillar* 1936, *cargo* 1942, from Spanish *cargo*; *jeep* 1943; *bulldozer* 1948; *scooter* 1950), and names of dog breeds (*beagle* 1913, *yorkshire* 1930) continue to arrive in Italian.

Finally, it is worth pointing out that more than one third (34.7%) of English borrowings attested in the first half of the 20th century by the GDU belong to general Italian (i.e., are not marked by a specialist label). This means that Anglicisms have started to penetrate many different areas of language use, beyond the specialist ones, related to everyday life and habits of Italian society.

## 2.5 The post-war years

Despite the long list of borrowings found in the first half of the 20th century, the real 'flood' of Anglicisms hit in the years after the end of the Second World War. Numerically, the proportion is three times as many (see 5.1 for the actual figures of Anglicisms recorded in dictionaries). In fact, the historical circumstances were now completely different, indeed, extremely favourable (De Mauro 2014b).

When the Second World War ended in 1945, the US troops that marched through liberated Italy were enthusiastically welcomed as liberators from the long dictatorship, the Nazi occupation and the war. Moreover, the Marshall Plan (European Recovery Program) transferred a huge investment of money in Western Europe for the material reconstruction of devastated regions and for the recovery of European economy. The USA, in fact, were interested in creating stability and peace in war-torn Europe, favouring long-term economic and political bonds across the Atlantic. Thus, as a result of the US military victory, this historical phase is characterized by a global 'Americanization' of Western countries, not without strategic promotion and propaganda.

In the post-war decades, Italy experienced a rapid recovery of its industrial production, an 'economic miracle', and a fast modernization of society, also from a social and cultural point of view. In 1961 the rate of illiteracy dropped to 8.3% and compulsory education was extended to 8 years from elementary to middle secondary school. Several other factors contributed to the diffusion of Italian among the population: first, the mass migration from the south to the industrial north and the consequent inter-regional mixture of the population; second, compulsory military service, moving young men from their regional and linguistic confinement to a national dimension; third, the radio from 1924 and television from 1954, which brought Italian into most Italian homes.

The American myth, which had put down roots at the turn of the 20<sup>th</sup> century, became a social model for Italian society in the post-war years. The pervasive influence of the USA is indeed considered 'the trend of the 20<sup>th</sup> century', as forecasted by the British journalist William Stead (1902), a victim of the Titanic disaster in 1912. The winner of two world wars, the USA forcefully took the political and economic leadership, but also managed to lure people with the glamour of its cultural products – music and entertainment – and set a high profile for the rest of the world with its military superiority and scientific and technical progress. One of the symbols of American marketing success, for example, is the Coca Cola brand, registered in Italy in 1919, the soft drink that became an icon during the 1960 Olympic Games in Rome. Indeed,

> [t]he American way of life infiltrated all social levels through new consumer goods and social behaviours: lotteries and gambling, mail order, coin-operated launderettes, supermarkets, commercial television, and, later, take-away restaurants and fast foods. Skyscrapers, glamour, excess, disposable goods became symbols of modern life for the general public. (Pulcini 1997: 78–79)

The overtones that sparkled from the words America and American are multifarious and contradictory at the same time. The 'American way of life' was pictured in the public imagination as the achievement of material prosperity, such as a comfortable life, a well-paid job, a large house and a car, a happy family, free time at the weekends and holidays. Ideologically, the myth of 'the American Dream' was inspired by principles of equality, democracy and justice for a nation, whereby anybody, irrespective of their social status, would have a chance to move up the social ladder. On the other hand, many aspects of American life looked strange and even ridiculous to the eyes of Italians, after decades of monocultural stagnation. Initially, even divorce was so culturally shocking for traditional Italian customs that it was considered a form of American folklore. The term *'americanata'* was used to define an action that was at the same time bold and sensational but also excessively grandiose and even kitsch (Fanfani 2019).

During the decades leading up to the end and across the new millenium, the economic 'boom' accelerated the transformation of Italy into one of the largest industrialized countries in the world with illiteracy reduced almost to zero. Contacts between English-speaking countries are now both direct and indirect because today 'globalization' has broken down geographical barriers, and people can quickly transfer from one place in the world to another, for business, education or holidays. The cultural exchanges between Italy and the USA are now radically different from the one-way migration of poor Italians in the previous century: over the past decades, many 'New Italians', generally well educated and talented, have temporarily or permanently settled in the USA for professional purposes. An emblematic case is the merger between the Turin-based car firm FIAT and the Detroit-based giant Chrysler in 2014, giving rise to the corporation Fiat Chrysler Automobiles, chaired by the Italian manager Sergio Marchionne as Chief Executive Officer (Bonsaver, Carlucci and Reza 2019).

The impact of the USA in Europe and in Italy should not overshadow the influence of Great Britain, who participated in World War II as a strategic junior partner of the Allied forces. Although decolonization had reduced its worldwide influence, Britain retained its prestige of scholarly excellence thanks to its intellectual and cultural achievements, and top-quality higher education. Multicultural London was a showcase for new styles and new talents in the swinging 1960s, especially in pop and rock music – one need only think of the Beatles and the Rolling Stones dominating the music scene and, in turn, exerting a huge cultural impact on the USA and all over the world. The success of blue jeans as an American fashion icon was equalled by the triumph of the miniskirt, the symbol of women's rebellion and emancipation, of the British designer Mary Quant.

The importance of the English language is closely linked to the power that the USA and the UK achieved in the post-war decades, obtained through their political influence, their economic support and their cultural impact. English is associated with positive values, such as freedom, success, power, modernity, glamour, emancipation, professionalism, not without contradictions and grey areas. Thus, if the importance of a language depends on the number of speakers, its geographical spread, its functional load and the political and economic power of the countries that use this language as a mother tongue, then we can conclude that English has had all these requisites for over a century (Crystal 2003). This is indeed an unprecedented phenomenon in the history of language contact, not free from allegations of linguistic imperialism and cultural hegemony (Phillipson 1992; 2010), which, anyway, explains the 'Anglicization' of European languages (Furiassi, Pulcini and Rodríguez González 2012).

The English language is an asset for both the UK and the USA, and neither of them failed to identify it as an investment on a global scale, worthy of the most advanced marketing strategies. The geographical proximity of the British Isles to mainland Europe has made it the ideal destination for learners of English which, in the 1960s, replaced French as the first foreign language in Italian education. British and American English, despite centuries of independence, have grown more and more similar, having influenced one another in their joint function of international tools for mass communication and intercomprehension, and as model varieties for a growing audience of students. For this reason, it is hard to discern whether a loanword is from British or American English, unless it designates something that is exclusively related to one or the other reality. It follows that the term Anglicism should be preferred to 'Americanism', because the latter would exclude Britain, whereas Anglicisms is an inclusive term for any borrowing from English-speaking countries, including but also beyond Great Britain and the USA.[23]

Considering the Anglicisms imported in the decades described in this section – indeed a phase of sharp rise in borrowing – the most important observation is that the increase regards in particular scientific and technical terms, and the most productive field is information and communication technology or ICT. It must be noted that some terms were initially created for military applications, like *transistor* (1947) and electronic innovations, like *wireless* (1963), *scanner* (1965), *hardware* (1970), *software* (1970), *byte* (1970), *chip* (1972), *modem* (1973); *internet* (introduced in Italian only in 1990) was a network established in 1969 by the U.S. Department of Defense. *Computer* (1964) is a well-integrated term in Italian, despite early attempts to give this new technology an Italian name, e.g *calcolatore* (1963), *ordinatore* (1963) and *elaboratore elettronico* (1963), none of which managed to replace the Anglicism. Because technology develops very quickly, some terms like *floppy disk* (1976) have been displaced by new data storage technology. The leadership of the US computer industry imposed English terminology in this field through technical manuals and guides, which initially circulated only among professionals. Localization of technical terminology introduced Italian equivalents, but the speed of its expansion has made it difficult to keep up with new terms (see 6.2). Since the 1980s personal computers or PCs (1983) have become available to the general public and terms have become familiar to non-specialists, especially to the new generation of digital natives. Among the most common terms in IT, internet and digital technology are: *password* (1972), *mouse* (1978), *database* (1979), *off-line* (1980), *online* (1983), *browser* (1984), *directory* (1985), *hacker* (1985), *hard disk* (1985), *touch screen* (1987), *account* (1988), *backup* (1988), *emoticon* (1988), *font* (1990), *server* (1990), *e-mail* (1991), *upgrade* (1991), *upload* (1992), *desktop* (1992), *set-up* (1992), *tablet* (1993), *mail box* (1994), *tutorial* (1994), *chat* (1995), *download* (1995), *web* (1995), *newsgroup* (1995), *shareware* (1995), *login* (1996), *provider* (1996), *homepage* (1996), *logout* (1997), *laptop* (1997), *banner* (1997), *webcam* (1997), *client* (1998), *router* (1998), *spam* (1998), *username* (1998), *nickname* (1998), *firewall* (1998), *cookie* (1998), *blog* (2000), *blogger* (2000) (Venuta 2004). Digital technology has affected both audio-visual and telecommunications, introducing terms such as *decoder* (1990), *handycam* (1996), DVD

---

**23** In the Italian literature on English-Italian contact, the term '*angloamericano*' is used by many Italian linguists to refer to the English language; this term sounds awkward because '*inglese*' (English) is the name of the language, and its numerous varieties are named by means of premodification, i.e. American English, Canadian English, Australian English etc. The noun Anglo-American refers to 'An American of English or other white European origin' (OED).

(1996) and television also as a form of entertainment, such as *pay-tv* (1990), *reality show* (1992), *format* (1995) and *on-demand* (1996).

The second most productive donor field is that of sport, although the number of borrowings is lower than the first half of the century. Among the new sports recorded in dictionaries, there are *kick-boxing* (1983), *beach volley* (1987), promoted an Olympic discipline in 1992, and *short track* (1992); fitness activities like *jogging* (1978), *spinning* (1993), *aquagym* (1995) and *pilates* (2000); open-air sports like *trekking* (1979), *windsurf* (1979), *mountain bike* (1983), *free climbing* (1985), *bungee jumping* (1995), *sky-diving* (1998) and *kite-surfing* (1999). Motorbike and car racing introduced the terms *pole position* (1978), *pit stop* (1997) and *safety car* (1997). A football-related term denoting violent supporters is *hooligan* (1963).

In third position there are terms related to economics and its sub-disciplines, namely finance, commerce, and business administration. These topics, which are normally used and understood by experts, tend to circulate in the media. Citizens are today more interested in world economy and its effects on their lives, although the specific meanings of some terms is hard to grasp for a lay person. The term *company* (1926) is frequently used in compounds such as *holding company* (1976) and *public company* (1990), but on its own *company* competes with Italian *azienda, società, impresa*. *Commodity* (1989) duplicates the meaning of Italian 'prodotto, bene primario'. Other business terms are *auditor* (1968), *joint venture* (1973), *auditing* (1979), *audit* (1986). In the area of banking there are *home banking* (1983), *money transfer* 1997); in marketing (1957) we find *market leader (1988), marketing manager* (1992), *business to business* (1997), *business angel* (1993). Specialist terms may not be easily translatable, and often need a paraphrase to make their meaning explicit: for example, *non profit* (1992, 'senza scopo di lucro'), *customer care* (2000, 'assistenza alla clientela'), *stakeholder* (1998, 'parte interessata', 'portatore di interesse'), *asset* (1997, 'attività, patrimonio'), *benchmarking* (1989, 'metodo di valutazione delle prestazioni di un dispositivo o dell'efficienza di un servizio fondato sul confronto con i principali standard di riferimento' [evaluation method of the performance of a device or of the efficiency of a service based on the main reference standards]), *core business* (1992, 'attività principale di un'azienda' [main activity of a company]), *start up* (1993, 'nella new economy, azienda, di solito di piccole dimensioni, che si lancia sul mercato sull'onda di un'idea innovativa, spec. nel campo delle nuove tecnologie' [in new economy, usually a small-sized company that enters the marketplace to launch an innovative idea, especially in the field of new technologies]). Closer to the turn of the millenium there are terms relating to the electronic business, starting from *new economy* (1999), *dot com* (1999), and e-compounds such as *e-commerce* (1992), *e-business* (1998) and *e-banking* (1999). Needless to say, from a pragmatic point of view, English loanwords are more concise than their Italian paraphrases and are preferred by journalists for both lack of ready-made Italian equivalents, also because they add international flavour to professional communication.

In the field of entertainment, music and cinema are the main donor fields. New music styles and their names can be quoted as landmarks of each decades of this period: *hot jazz* (1940), *boogie-woogie* (1949), *be-bop* (1950), *cool jazz* (1951), *rock and roll* (1956), *pop* (1964), *soul* (1969), *acid rock* (1970), *funky* (1975), *country-rock* (1980), *ambient* (1980), *easy listening* (1981), *folk music* (1985), *heavy metal* (1983), *new age* (1987), *acid house* (1988), *lounge* (1988), *afro-beat* (1990), *house music* (1990), *grunge* (1992), *gangsta-rap* (1994), *techno* (1994), *acid jazz* (1995), *breakbeat* (1998) and *chill out* (2000).

The expanding cinema industry has introduced the words *flashback* (1959), *colossal* (1986), *location* (1993), and new genres like *black comedy* (1990), combining macabre situations with humour; *beach movie* (1995), a romantic story on beach settings (like California or Florida); *biopic* (1999) a film focused on the biography of a famous character; *docudrama* (1986, documentary+drama), and related terms such as *sequel* (1985, 'a film that continues a previous popular story') and *prequel* (1992, 'a film that is built on episodes taking place in times prior to events of an existing work').

Other productive fields of borrowings are sea transportation and air transport and the automotive sector: from the former there are *cockpit* (1992), *air-show* (1997), *code sharing* (1994), *hub* (1997) and *city airport* (1999); from the latter *full optional* (1986), *airbag* (1989), *cruise control* (1992), *bi-fuel* (1997), *car-sharing* (1999), and *multijet* (1999).

The popularization of science has driven more and more people into developing an interest in personal health and wellbeing: some common medical terms are *pacemaker* (1963), *check-up* (1966), *by-pass* (1974), *screening* (1979), *pet therapy* (1992), *day-care* (1997), *day hospital* (1980) and *day surgery* (2000). Many kinds of dog breeds continue to be imported, such as *bobtail* (1955), *labrador retriever* (1967), *husky* (1973), *pit bull* (1994), *jack russell* (2000) and related training activities, like *agility* (1998).

## 2.6 The new millennium

Over the past two decades of the 21st century some historical and sociolinguistic factors should be considered in order to examine the context in which the English language has continued to spread in Italy. In order of importance, and in line with the suggestions offered by Dardano (1986, 2020) and Tosi (2001, 2004, 2006, 2008), we can identify, first, the effects of intense mass communication through traditional and web-mediated channels; second, increased circulation of neologisms and translations from English; and, third, improved but uneven English competence among the social and professional layers of the Italian population.

From the 1990s the global spread of computer-mediated communication through the internet and social media channels, especially Facebook and Twitter, has exposed users from all over the world to an oversupply of information, most of it in English, and many Anglicisms, many of which irrelevant and ephemeral. As Dardano (2020: 115) points out:

> [s]ince the end of the nineties, social networking has laid the foundation for a new influx of Anglicisms on Italian and, most of all, has fostered new and psychological conditions for the diffusion of this phenomenon.

Social media have been added to the already existing channels for the transmission of high and popular culture – news, entertainment, advertising, fashion, leisure time activities – and facts, ideas, opinions, from useful to bizarre, from dangerous to criminal, and creating a new dimension of 'augmented self' and 'a quantified self', so that we can monitor our own and other people's lives and even empower our perception of reality. Digital communication and its vocabulary have reached out to all social classes, especially younger generations. These factors indicate a crucial difference between the influence of French in the previous centuries (referred to as the first 'Europeanization' of Italian), which was an élite phenomenon spread among intellectuals and aristocrats, while the 'second' Europeanization of Italian brought by English has involved all social classes in society.

The creation of the European Union in 1957, of which Italy is one of the founding countries, has contributed to changing the linguistic scenario. Despite its policy of institutional multilingualism, English in fact predominates as a procedural language (together with French and German), and as a lingua franca for internal communication among delegates (Truchot 2002). The complexity of the translation process of a huge volume of written documents has produced 'Europeanized' versions of national languages, not only because of the non-human intervention of machine translation, but also because of the need to obtain 'visual correspondence' rather than 'textual equivalence'. As Tosi (in Lepsky and Tosi 2006: 165) explains:

> this process is responsible for the establishment of artificial domains of language contacts, where the exchanges between enormous glossaries are accelerated by ad hoc software programs (with little, if any, speaker interaction) that produce unnatural equivalences between different language systems and promote unnatural distortions of meanings in most of the target languages.

Many Italian neologisms, in fact, originate from EU documents translated from English. Tosi provides examples of lexical equivalents which, for the need of visual correspondence, lack precision, such as the pair *equal opportunities / pari opportunità* (instead of more appropriate 'pari trattamento tra uomo e donna'), and *third countries /paesi terzi* (instead of 'paesi esterni all'Unione Europea'). However, besides the administrative terminology of the EU found in the media, the intense circulation of international vocabulary triggers the creation of neologisms. Some instances can be identified as lexical borrowings from English, such as the expression *politically correct* (in Italian *politicamente corretto*), which can be traced back to the 1960s, and *glass ceiling* (in Italian *tetto di cristallo*), introduced in the mid-1980s, both from American English. By contrast, the terms referring to the pandemic in 2020, a global phenomenon, quickly spread in different languages, such as, for example, *social distancing* (*distanziamento sociale*) and *super-spreader* (*super-diffusore*). However, the term *contact tracing* (*tracciamento*) was already recorded in *Nuovo Devoto-Oli 2022*, and *lockdown* was commonly used in Italy, without recourse to a domestic term as happened in other Romance languages (in French *confinement* and in Spanish *confinamiento*). In these cases, there are legitimate doubts about the influence of English, that is, whether a word, phrase or idioms originated in English, or was 'boosted' by English, or is an autonomous neologism. For competent Italian speakers of English, many new expressions may sound 'suspiciously English', like *buone pratiche* (best practices) that can be shared and implemented in the management of research of educational projects or *sfidante* (challenging) with reference to a goal.

A further factor that has caused an increase in the use of Anglicisms is the higher competence in English of Italians, achieved thanks to the teaching of English as a compulsory school subject, in middle school from 1974 (when two foreign languages were introduced), and also from elementary school since 2003. From a French-oriented school system, Italy is now an English-oriented one (Schirru 2019). Also university degree courses have introduced English as a compulsory discipline, and English is also 'tacitly' recommended as a means to increase 'internationalization' by the Ministry of University and Research (Campagna and Pulcini 2014; Pulcini and Campagna 2015).

These factors have modified the sociolinguistic scenario in which English has played its role as contact language for Italian. On the one hand, English has moved away from its historical community of native speakers to be used as a lingua franca in the working lives of Italians in order to communicate beyond the national boundaries. As a consequence, the level of authority of native norms has given way to the adaptation of English to specific needs of intercomprehension and for transactional purposes among speakers with different linguacultural backgrounds and levels of proficiency. On the other hand, the sociolinguistic distribution of competence among the social layers of society is rather uneven, also between spoken and written registers. English loanwords abound in newspaper language, and are frequently found in advertising, young people's slang and in the jargon of some professionals in business communication. Research into these social variables has so far received little attention.

The increase in the number of Anglicisms recorded in dictionaries in the first decades of the 21$^{st}$ century is notable. The trend set in the second half of the previous century has been confirmed, as the three most influenced fields are IT, economy and sport (Pulcini 2017). Information and internet technology provide by far the largest inventory of Anglicisms in the new millennium (73%); economy and sport follow with a much lower incidence, and economy has taken over from sport as the second best donor field. In the domain of IT some terms may be known to a limited circle of experts, with some exceptions. Some examples are: *alert* (2000), *file sharing* (2000), *chatbot* (2001), *touch* (2001, for *touchscreen*), *access point* (2002), *dashboard* (2003), *multitouch* (2003), *pen drive* (2003), *phishing* (2004), *geotag* (2005), *cloud* (2007), *microblog* (2007), *big data* (2010). Internet terminology is more likely to be familiar to non-specialists. Some examples are: *wi-fi* (2000), *cybersecurity* (2001), *digital divide* (2001), *captcha* (2003), *wiki* (2003), *podcast* (2004), *doodle* (2005), *QR code* (2005), *barcamp* (2006), *social media* (2006), *tweet* (2007), *app* (2008), *hashtag* (2009), *hater* (2009), *retweet* (2009), *hangout* (2011), *like* (2011), *social media manager* (2011), *youtuber* (2011), *clickbaiting* (2014) and *fake news* (2016). Some prefixes, suffixes and compound elements are particularly productive, such as e- (electronic), as in *e-health* (2000, *telemedicina*), *e-learning* (2000), *e-mobility* (2005), *e-reader* (2004), *e-ticket* (2000); -ware as in *spyware* (2000), *malware* (1999); video- as in *video-chat* (2000), *videoblog* (2003), *videogallery* (2004): web- as in *dark web* (2000), *web agency* (2000), *web community* (2000), *weblog* (2000), *web radio* (2000), *web-tv* (2000), *webinar* (2007) and *web app* (2011).

The second most productive field of borrowings is that of economy, which includes business, finance, and also terms lying in-between the political and the economic spheres, like *no global* (2001, a pseudo-Anglicism, meaning *anti-globalization*) and marketing, like *viral marketing* (2000). Proper economic terms (business and commerce) are *net company* (2000), *net economy* (2000), *project leader* (2000), *security manager* (2000), *job on call* (2001), *food delivery* (2015), *crowdsourcing* (2006), *crowdfunding* (2009), *sharing economy* (2008), *startupper* (2010) and *jobs act* (2013). In the field of finance: *banking online* (2000, a pseudo-Anglicism, meaning *online banking*), *subprime* (2002), *no tax area* (2000, a pseudo-Anglicism, meaning *tax-free area*), *contactless* (2000), *mobile banking* (2004), *private banking* (2000), *voluntary disclosure* (2009), *bail-in* (2010), *bitcoin* (2011) and *web tax* (2013).

Sport Anglicisms follow with a much lower number of items: *extra-time* (2000), *fitwalking* (2000), *snowboard cross* (2000), *kiteboard* (2001), *power yoga* (2001), *total body* (2003, a pseudo-Anglicism, meaning *total body workout*), *nordic walking* (2003) and *crossfit* (2008). The great number of Anglicisms recorded in the first two decades of the new millenium cover a wide variety of fields, including fashion terms like *dress code* (2004), *peep-toe* (2005), *open-toe* (2007), *jumpsuit* (2008), and an array of domains related to people's lives, habits and society. Here is a short sample: *soft skill* (2000), *Big Pharma* (2001), *personal shopper* (2001), *wedding planner* (2001), *online dating* (2002), *open access* (2002), *red carpet* (2002), *speed date* (2002), *flash mob* (2003), *plug-in* (2006), *stepchild adoption* (2006), *fashion blogger* (2007), *millennial* (2007), *skincare* (2007), *smart city* (2007), *whistleblower* (2007), *show cooking* (2008), *rooftop* (2009), *sexting* (2009), *fashion blog* (2010), *food blogger* (2010), *selfie* (2012), *revenge porn* (2013), *smartwatch* (2013) and *foreign fighter* (2014). Higher competence in English has led to the creation of English-based neologisms with new meanings, such as *smart working* (2013) and *navigator* (2018) (see false Anglicisms in 3.5).

## 2.7 Roundup

In this chapter lexical borrowing from English into Italian has been described and illustrated taking into account the historical and cultural circumstances in which the English language came to influence Italian and the areas of contact which favoured the exchange of vocabulary. Early contacts for commercial and diplomatic relations from the 13th to the 17th centuries brought into Italian a few terms related to political and social life in Britain. Stable exchanges were established in the 18th century, an age in which French, not English, was a strong donor language, but admiration for British society or Anglomania, began to spread in Italian society. Technical advances in industrial production and transport in the 19th century, led by Britain, boosted the input of English vocabulary, but the influence of English involved other fields of social life, besides politics, business and commerce, such as fashion, leisure time and sport. The political settings of both countries – Great Britain and Italy – were drivers or opponents of lexical borrowing. The period of purism in Italy, in the first half of the 20th century, slowed down the input and encouraged the creation of domestic equivalents, which are generally accepted with favour because they do not clash with the morphological characteristics of the receptor language. The USA and the American way of life became a cultural model for Italy in the 20th century, but in the post- World War II years the political, economic and technological impact of the USA transformed the lifestyle of modern Italy. Information and digital technology took the upper hand over all the other fields in term of borrowings, a trend that has continued in the first decades of the new millennium.

# 3 Direct borrowings

## 3.1 Approaches and terminology

The typological model of lexical borrowings presented in this chapter draws on the theoretical thinking and applied research in lexical borrowing produced over the past decades, starting from the mid-20th century. Only some of the key terms and concepts will be introduced, taken from the vast scholarly production, in order to place the influence of English on Italian within the theoretical framework of contact linguistics.

Although derived from the observation of bilingual speech, Haugen's seminal work attributed to the concept of 'borrowing' the linguistic value of "attempted reproduction in one language of patterns previously found in another" (Haugen, 1950: 212). Placing speakers at the core of the borrowing process is particularly important, as it assigns to the bilingual speaker or speech community the task to add loanwords to their language repertoires and exploit their value in interaction and communication, depending on the social context and on the desired pragmatic effects (Matras 2019). Whether speakers make this choice consciously or not, this initial 'leap' from the donor language to the receiving one is crucial for understanding this phenomenon (Haspelmath 2009).

The term 'borrowing' can refer both to the process and to the result of language contact. In the former case, borrowing can be replaced by the synonymic terms importation, transfer or adoption, which all convey the sense of a one-way transaction from the donor (source, or model language) to the recipient (receiving, receptor or borrowing) one. The countable sense of the term 'borrowing' is synonymous of loanword, import word or simply loan, that is, a single borrowed vocabulary item. The term loanword is itself a loan translation of the German term *Lehnwort*, denoting a lexical item which has been assimilated and formally adapted to the recipient language system, from a minor to a greater degree, in pronunciation, grammatical behaviour and meaning. The roles of the languages involved remain basically the same.

The terms 'replication' (Matras 2009) and 'replica' (also used by Haugen) convey a further inference in the process of borrowing, that is, that the foreign word is not merely 'poured' from a lexical container into another; in fact, the borrowing process triggers a remodelling of the source word according to the rules of the receiving language, in one or more of the areas of phonology, grammar and semantics.

The independent creation of lexical 'copies' in the recipient language is emphasized by cognitive approaches to interlingual contacts (Hope 1971; Alexieva 2008), whereby during their transfer foreign words lose their original morphological and semantic motivation, and become free to develop independently, according to the rules of the recipient language. In other words, the donor language limits itself to offer a model, or prototype, to the recipient language, which will creatively reproduce for the purpose of innovating its own lexical stock. Also Gusmani (1986) considers the nature of borrowing as an act of imitation, which may take place with various degrees of adherence to the model, ranging from very close reproduction of the prototype (loanword) to the simple semantic widening of a domestic word under the influence of a foreign model (semantic loan). For example, according to Gusmani, the Italian verb *snobbare* ('to ignore or to treat someone in a patronizing way') is an independent derivation of the English noun *snob*, under the influence of various shades of meanings conveyed by the noun *snob* ('a person acting with an elitist attitude') and the verb *snub* ('humiliate'). For these reasons, the term borrowing has been criticized by many scholars because of its misleading nature, in that it places the focus on the donor language, which provides the source model, rather than on the recipient language, which undertakes an active process of reception and assimilation of the word in its own system.

Despite this criticism, the term borrowing is the most widely used in the literature on language contact. Its metaphorical sense is inaccurate, since nothing is taken away from the donor language or ever returned, except for some occasional cases of reborrowings, i.e., words originally borrowed by the foreign language (English), travelling back to the recipient language (Italian) with a new meaning. Cases of this type are not very numerous, and belong to Italianisms in English such as *portfolio, camera* and *studio* (see 4.2.2).

The linguistic value attributed to the terms borrowing and loanword is particularly useful for the typological classification illustrated in Figure 3.1, where a major distinction is made between direct and indirect borrowings, on the basis of their formal properties. Direct borrowings denote lexical items which keep the formal features of the donor language; in other words, they closely resemble the model word, more or less faithfully, so that a native speaker of the source language would recognize them. In this category, loanwords (see 3.4), false Anglicisms (see 3.5) and hybrids (see 3.6) are included, although false Anglicisms are created in Italian with English elements, and hybrids are only partly made up of an English word, combined with an Italian one. Indirect borrowings, instead, replace the model word with a translation in the case of calques (see 4.2.1), or associates a new imported meaning to an already existing word in the recipient language, in the case of semantic loans (see 4.2.2). Indirect borrowings are formally made up of elements of the receiving language, and are therefore no longer recognizable to native speakers of the donor language. In other words, they appear in domestic 'disguise', so that users are generally not aware of their provenance. The division between direct and indirect borrowings reflects Haugen's distinction between the 'importation' of a

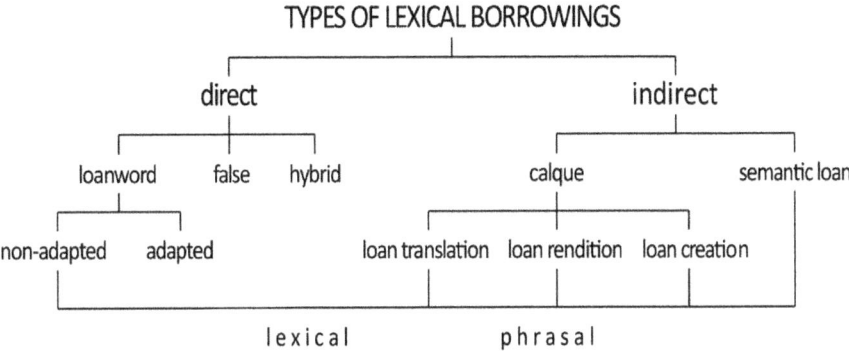

**Figure 3.1:** Types of lexical borrowings (Pulcini, Furiassi and Rodríguez González 2012: 6).

foreign word in contrast with the 'substitution' of a foreign referent with a similar domestic pattern.

Lexical borrowings are normally single-word items and compounds. Yet, larger units composed of two or more elements may be borrowed. These phrasal units include compounds proper – the combination of two or more elements that create a single meaning – or looser combinations, such as collocations or phrase-like patterns (see 3.4.1). Phrasal units may be borrowed directly, keeping their English identity, or be translated into the receiving language, making them more difficult to be recognized as English borrowings rather than independent creations. This feature is indicated in Figure 3.1 by the labels 'lexical' and 'phrasal', encompassing both types of direct and indirect borrowings.

The history of language contact between Italy and English-speaking countries, outlined in chapter 2, showed that the nature of the contact has been mainly a cultural one. The areas of influence, from commerce to politics, from fashion to ICT, brought into Italian the words naming concepts and objects from Anglophone societies and cultures. On the other hand, a situation of 'intimate' borrowing implies a much closer contact among speakers and the rise of bilingual speech communities, a phenomenon which involved migrant Italian communities abroad but did not affect the national language (see 2.3). The cultural nature of borrowing also explains why the large majority of loanwords belong to the grammatical class of nouns, whose primary function is to name concrete and abstract entities existing in the world. Research into borrowing (Haugen 1950; Weinreich 1953; Haspelmath 2009; Matras 2009) has shown that there is in fact a scale of adoptability (also referred to as hierarchy of borrowability) common to all contact situations, with open-class words ranking higher: these include primarily nouns, followed by verbs, adjectives and adverbs. Closed-class words are unlikely to be borrowed, with the exception of derivational morphemes such as *-ing*, *-er*, and *-man*, which may be exploited to create hybrids or false Anglicisms. Furthermore, according to the scale of adoptability, terms belonging to specialized vocabulary are more likely to be borrowed compared to core lexical items. This can easily be explained by the fact that loanwords are generally carriers of new meanings in specific areas of vocabulary. The reason why vocabulary is more prone to transferability than other areas of the donor language is due to the fact that the lexical system of a language is less bound to structural restrictions than other levels of language. Moreover, the lexicon is the most dynamic aspect, which needs to be continuously renewed through processes of lexical innovation, one of them being borrowing from exogenous sources. Lexical transfer may take place directly between languages or through a third language acting as an intermediary or mediating language, which, for Italian, has almost exclusively been French. In 19th century Western European history, English and French were the most active vehicles for the circulation of words, especially of neoclassical terminologies.

A widely discussed dichotomy is the distinction between necessary and luxury loanwords. Necessary loans (also called catachrestic loans or innovations, cf. Onysko and Winter-Frowmel 2011, 2012; Onysko, Winter-Froemel and Calude 2014) denote new referents that need to be given a name. Luxury loanwords (also called non-catachrestic loans or innovations) are imported to name a referent that already exists in the receiving language. The loanword will make the referent sound more modern, and, in the majority of cases, it will continue to be used along with the domesting equivalent. From a pragmatic perspective, necessary loans do not represent speakers' marked choices, since the loanwords would be the only words available (for example, *mouse* for 'computer device' in Italian), whereas the choice between an Anglicism versus a domestic word is pragmatically marked (for example, *cocktail* vs *aperitivo* in Italian), and may be motivated by a range of different expressive reasons.

In his theoretical approach to English-induced lexical borrowing, Filipović distinguishes between primary and secondary Anglicisms (Filipović 2000). A primary Anglicism refers to the transfer of a word directly from the English language, followed by its adaptation to the receiving language at four linguistic levels, namely orthographic (spelling), phonological (pronunciation), morphological (in Italian, gender and number) and semantic (meaning). A secondary Anglicism refers to words that are formed of elements that belong to English but are not English words nor are they found in English vocabulary. This type of borrowings concides with false Anglicisms, which Filipović calls 'pseudoanglicisms'. This scholar lists different types of words that can be transferred from English, namely a) native words of Anglo-Saxon origin, b) loanwords borrowed from French and other European languages, c) words from languages spoken in non-European countries. In the first case, the loanwords take a direct path of transmission. In the second case, French or other European languages act as a mediating route for the transmission of English loanwords. In the third case, 'exotic' words already assimilated into English are subsequently transferred to the receiving language. This distinction leads to a 'broad definition' of Anglicism:

> [. . .] any words borrowed from the English language denoting an object or a concept which is at the moment of borrowing an integral part of English culture and civilization; it need not be of English origin, but it must have been adapted to the linguistic system of English and integrated into the vocabulary of English (Filipović 2000: 206)

This definition seems to resolve the question of whether 'exotic' words like *ketchup* (partly from Chinese *kê-chiap* and partly from Malay *kecap*), *marijuana* (from Spanish *mariguana*), *sherpa* (from Tibetan *shar–pa*) and *pyjamas* (from Urdu *pāy-jāma*; Persian *pāy-jāma)* should be considered English words or not, and consequently potential Anglicisms. According to Filipović, they are indeed potential Anglicisms, since at the moment of their transmission they were fully integrated and assimilated items of English vocabulary. This position is far from uncontroversial and poses quite a few doubts when it comes to the analysis of individual cases (cf. below in 3.4).

In the literature of lexical borrowing, etymology is generally used as synonymous of 'origin' and the etymon is the 'source word'. For example, the etymon of the Anglicism *computer* in Italian is the English word *computer*, because English is the source language from which this word was transmitted (first attestation in Italian in 1966). This acceptation of the meaning of etymology may be in conflict with the traditional view held by speakers of Latin-based languages like Italian, for whom the notion of etymology refers to the historical origin of words from classical roots and their developments of form and meaning in time. Thus, taking a historical path back to its remote etymology, the form of *computer* is built on the Latin verb *computāre* (OED). Yet, its ending in a consonant (unusual for most Italian words, which typically end with a vowel) and especially its pronunciation [kom'pjuter], which is close to the English one confirms the 'Englishness' of this word and its status as a non-adapted Anglicism in Italian. Another uncontroversial example, though only supported by its typically English spelling, is the word *manager*, whose historical etymology is from Italian *maneggiare* (OED). Yet, m*a*nager was borrowed into Italian in 1895 and is considered a bona fide Anglicism. On this question, Filipović's (2000) distinction between primary etymology (historical) and secondary etymology is very useful to separate the diachronic dimension of words, i.e., where they have come from, from the source of borrowing, i.e., the language from which the borrowing has been taken.

The question is not settled for Anglicisms which originated from classical roots, which, once adopted and adapted to Italian, can hardly be distinguished from Italian words. The problem posed by words that come from English-speaking countries but are made up of neo-Latin and neo-Greek elements has been discussed by the German linguist Görlach in his pilot work for the *Dictionary of European Anglicisms* (2001). He points out that there is a stock of words shared by European languages – e.g. *astronaut, automobile, deodorant, holocaust, microphone*, etc. – which are truly international. In other words,

> [. . .] they are not felt to be 'English', and consequently are not subject to the same evaluation that words like *Teenager* or *Babysitter* may well be. Latinate internationalisms should therefore be analysed as a category distinct from Anglicisms, unless they retain clear evidence of their English provenance, as German computer does in its spelling and pronunciation. (Görlach 2003: 22).

According to Görlach, formal evidence is a key factor for the identification of Anglicisms, unless extra-linguistic information can prove the provenance of a term, whether from English or from independent sources (see 4.4). Internationalisms should therefore be dealt with separately from words whose 'Englishness' is clear. These linguistic considerations have led Görlach to formulate a 'narrow' definition of an Anglicism, which he applied to the macrostructure of 3,800 entries recorded in the *Dictionary of European Anglicisms*:

> An anglicism is a word or idiom that is recognizably English in its form (spelling, pronunciation, morphology, or at least one of the three), but is accepted as an item in the vocabulary of the receptor language (Görlach 2003: 7).

This problem will be thoroughly discussed with reference to adapted Anglicisms and calques in Italian. The notion of internationalism is addressed in 4.4.

Moving on to the observation of the outcomes of language contact, another useful concept introduced by Weinreich (1953) is that of interlingual identification, whereby bilingual speakers interpret and realize a feature of a second language in terms of their own first language. A case of English-Italian interlingual identification would be the realization of the English approximant [ɹ] with the Italian dental trill [r], which affects the pronunciation of Anglicisms by Italian speakers. The relevance of interlingual identification for lexical borrowing from English into Italian has been noted and discussed by Klajn (1972), who points out the strong resemblance of Italian and English in quite a few homographs and a large stock of very similar items, especially in learned and scientific vocabulary. The Jewish-American linguist Uriel Weinreich is one of the recognized scholarly pillars of contact linguistics and biligualism. He introduced the concept of interference to describe the introduction of foreign elements into the more highly structured patterns of the receiving language, whereas he found the term borrowing more appropriate for the introduction of a new element in more loosely structured areas of language, although linguistic consequence cannot be excluded even for 'incidental' vocabulary transfers from one language to another. Weinreich believed that the analysis of language contact cannot fail to consider similarities and differences between languages for every domain (phonology, grammar and vocabulary), but also that a purely linguistic approach would not be enough to investigate language contact; it is necessary to integrate it with extra-linguistic considerations, such as, for example, attitudes towards the culture of each language community.

The term Anglicism, since its introduction in the 18$^{th}$ century (see 2.2), seems appropriate to refer to a direct borrowing, which is indeed "a characteristically English word, phrase or idiom", taken in its English form or with minor integration into the structures of the recipient language, leaving it as "recognizably English". The other types of borrowings should be defined with more precision, i.e., false Anglicisms, hybrids, calques and semantic loans. Yet, if a 'broader' definition of Anglicisms is extended to whatever lexical items is triggered by English, then the term Anglicism can be taken as an umbrella label for the wider phenomenon. As shown below, the inclusion policy adopted for GLAD is 'open' to all types of borrowings, broadening the range of contact-induced items, and therefore the label Anglicisms is an inclusive one. Some Italian linguists prefer term *anglismo* to *anglicismo*, because, lo and behold, the latter is considered an Anglicism (!). In this volume, the all-inclusive label of Anglicism is accepted but in the description of different types of loanwords more specific labels will be preferred.

Regarding the adaptation of loanwords to the structures of the recipient language, several different terms are used beside 'adaptation', such as 'integration' (used by Gusmani 1986 and Görlach 2003), and incorporation (Gaudio 2012). Several terms are alternatively, and sometimes in contradiction, applied by scholars to identify two different dimensions of borrowing. The first, called here adaptation, consists in changing the formal appearance of a loanword according to the orthographic and morpho-syntactic rules of the recipient language: in the first case, for example, English *tourism* is adapted to Italian *turismo*; in the second case, the English verb *boycott* is adapted to Italian *boicottare*, adding the inflectional ending in *-are* for the infinitive, as Italian verbs inflect for number, tense and mood. Accordingly, Anglicisms which retain the English form are said to be non-adapted (or unadapted) and the Anglicisms which are modified to comply with the orthographic and grammatical rules of the recipient language are said to be adapted. Nevertheless, a certain amount of integration is involved in borrowing even when the formal aspect remains the same. In fact, once an Anglicism is adopted, the new language system will assign it specific values – for example, masculine or feminine gender, or the word may change grammatical class, and pronunciation will be affected. Thus, integration involves the positioning of the loanword within the new linguistic and semantic environment of the recipient language. Klajn (1972) uses the term 'naturalization' for the substitution of the loanword with a domestic word.

The second dimension, called here assimilation (also called 'acclimatization' by Gusmani 1986), depends on how familiar the word becomes to its users as well as its usage frequency in the language. Given that loanwords are low frequency lexical items, only some of them are particularly successful and in time become totally assimilated. Some examples are the discourse marker *okay* or *OK*, perhaps the most widespread English word not only in Italian but on a global scale, and many others such as *bar*, *film* and *sport*. Many loanwords belonging to specialized fields remain in the periphery of language and are known and used mainly by experts. Yet, newspapers contribute to the circulation of specialized Anglicisms in the general language and the popularization of knowledge has made scientific and technical vocabulary known to a larger number of non-experts. On the other end of the spectrum, several Anglicisms make a brief appearance or are temporarily boosted by a passing fad or the results of bilingual speakers' code-switching. These are called nonce borrowings or casuals. In this group we may include 'foreignisms' (*xénismes* in French and *extranjerismos* in Spanish), i.e., words that describe cultural entities that exist only in Anglophone contexts and are not likely to be assimilated in the recipient culture. As the carrier of a different culture, a foreignism may be exploited for stylistic purposes in speech, to add 'a touch of colour', or simply to quote a word or phrase in its original form (e.g. *ground zero* to refer to the site of a disaster). In speech, competent speakers may resort to code-mixing, inserting single English words or phrases into utterances, a practice that is common among professionals to sound more 'international'. These phenomena may represent a first, initial step for English words to be used or heard in other languages, a testing ground, as it were, for its eventual adoption and final institutionalization in the repertoire of recipient language speakers. The linguistic landscape of modern urban surroundings is populated by shop signs in English and advertisements exploiting English headlines and taglines for their fashionable appeal and playful purposes (cf. 6.6). These Anglicisms belong to a 'fleeting' vocabulary, as pointed out by Görlach (2003), i.e., short-lived, incidental borrowings, bound to be used for the occasion and then disappear. For this reason it is necessary to consider the status of Anglicisms before recording them in dictionaries, to see if they acquire a certain currency in the recipient language to qualify as foreign borrowings in their own right.

## 3.2 Lexical routes of transmission and mediation

The analysis of lexical borrowing would be inaccurate if we looked at it as a straight journey from English into Italian, ignoring the fact that the routes of transmission may be quite intricate. In the first place, the mediation of French, not only for Italy, but for the whole of Europe, has constantly occurred up to very recent times, at least until the end of the Second World War. Klajn (1972) points out that all Italian Anglicisms are found in French, but not all French Anglicisms are found in Italian, which may confirm that the route of transmission from Britain to Italy passed through France, geographically and culturally. As already discussed in the historical overview (see 2.2 in particular), the historical ties and similarities between French and Italian sometimes make it difficult to establish whether a borrowing was actually from French or from English, considering that many words are Gallicisms in Italian – in turn borrowed by the English language – such as *cinema, hotel, routine* (all recorded as French loanwords in Italian by *Nuovo Devoto-Oli 2022*). The word *festival* is attested in Italian as an English loanword from Old French; *pamphlet* as a French word, imported into Italian through English; *tour* and *turismo* were borrowed from French *tour* and *tourism*, but *turista* from English; Italian *supporto* is from French *support*, but the verb *supportare* is a loan translation from English *support*. Contrary to expectations, even *informatica* is not from English *informatics*, but from the French blend *informatique* (information + automatique) (cf. 6.2).[24] Examples of these types are endless, and disagreement between dictionaries are proof of the lexical exchange which went on for centuries among languages in close geographical proximity. For example, Italian *locomotiva* is attested as being from English *locomotive* by *Zingarelli 2022* but from French *locomotive* by *Nuovo Devoto-Oli 2022*. Multiple provenance from English and French is also recorded in Italian dictionaries for *autocarro* (French *autocar* and English *autocar*); *celluloide* (French *celluloid*, English *celluloid*); *partenariato* (English *partnership*, French *partenariat*); *pittografia* (English *pictography*, French *pictographie*); *budino* (English *pudding* and French *boudin*).[25] Italians may be surprised to learn that the word *romantico* derives from

---

**24** The etymology of English *informatics* is the following: < *informat-* (in INFORMATION *n.*) + -IC suffix (see -IC suffix 2), originally after Russian *informatika* (A. I. Mixailov et al. 1966, in *Naučno-texničeskaja informacija* **12** 35). Compare German *Informatik* (K. Steinbuch 1957, in *SEG-Nachrichten* **5** 171), French *informatique* (1962); it is likely that the Russian, German, and French nouns were coined independently of each other.

The three foreign-language nouns were originally semantically distinct: German *Informatik* originally denoted the automated processing of information, French *informatique* the branch of study dealing with information processing in general (although especially by automated means), and Russian *informatika* the theory of scientific information. However, in later use they also came to be used to denote the academic subject which is called computer science in English (see COMPUTER SCIENCE *n.*), and this is now their chief sense. The same semantic development can also be seen in their parallels in most other European languages, except in English. (source: OED).

**25** The meaning of *pudding* may refer to both a sweet dish made of flour and milk and a type of sausage or mixed meat dish, with an endless variety of recipes. Italian *budino* is used only for the meaning of a sweet dish. The etymology of English *pudding* is given as from Anglo-Norman

17th century English *romantic*, meaning 'picturesque, fictional', in turn from French *romantique* (from French *roman* 'novel'), having acquired the main meaning of 'designating, relating to, or characteristic of a movement or style during the late 18th and 19th centuries in Europe marked by an emphasis on feeling, individuality, and passion [. . .]' (OED).

Thus, having established that caution is necessary when dealing with lexical borrowing among languages with long-standing historical relations and genetic similarity, another problem regards the transmission of so-called 'exotic' vocabulary from distant languages. It is likely that vocabulary from North America and from the Far East arrived through the mediation of English, as these populations had contacts with Europeans mainly thorough British and American settlers. Therefore, words like *bungalow* and *curry* (from Tamil), *judo* and *kamikaze* (from Japanese), *sequoia* and *opossum* (from north American languages), *boomerang* and *canguro* (from Australia), *igloo* (from Inuit) and many others reached Italian most likely through the mediation of English. Whether they should be considered Anglicisms is a controversial matter, which should be established on historical and formal characteristics of each of these words (see below in 3.4.1 for more on 'exoticisms').

## 3.3 The Global Anglicism Database

### 3.3.1 Aims and structure

The new data referred to in this volume belong to the Italian entries of the Global Anglicism Database (GLAD), a multilingual project launched in 2014 by a network of linguists, some of whom had already contributed to Görlach's *Dictionary of European Anglicisms* (2001). The research objectives of this international project was to set up a network of scholars and institutions interested in the study of Anglicisms, to share data, language resources, research findings, bibliographical material, and information on Anglicism-related initiatives.[26] A further goal was to update and expand Görlach's lexicographic work on Anglicisms in order to document the lexical input of English into European languages, extending the number of languages involved, also beyond Europe, covering the time span from the 1990s to the present, and widening the types of borrowings, which Görlach had limited to a representative number of

---

*bodeyn, bodin* (sausage), in the plural (*bodeyns*) with reference to animal intestines. See the OED entry for *pudding* for further etymology, which is uncertain and controversial.

[26] https://www.nhh.no/en/research-centres/global-anglicism-database-network/ (November, 2022).

c. 3,800 'recognizably English' words. Since Görlach's pioneering work on Anglicisms and loanword lexicography, research focussing on the influence of English in the European context and beyond has received a new impetus in the new millenium (Fischer and Pułaczewska 2008; Furiassi, Pulcini and Rodríguez González 2012; Zenner and Kristiansen, 2014; Furiassi and Gottlieb 2015; Andersen, Furiassi and Mišić Ilić 2017).

The creation of an electronic database of Anglicisms was considered to be operationally viable. Although the present status of GLAD is in a pilot version, it represents a unique, flexible tool, allowing continuous updates from individual languages, including the addition of new languages willing to join the project.[27] In 2022, the A-Z word lists of Anglicisms had been collected and stored for Albanian, Czech, Danish, Dutch, Italian, Japanese, Korean, Norwegian, Polish, Russian and Spanish, whereas those of French, German and Greek were still in progress and several others were joining the project. The ultimate goal of the database is to allow cross-linguistic comparison among languages and to measure the amount and type of influence brought by the contact with English. The initial lexicographic decisions for the selections of the GLAD entries regarded the time span and the criteria of inclusion and exclusion. As for the time span, GLAD's steering committee decided to focus on items borrowed in the 20$^{th}$ and 21$^{st}$ centuries, exluding obsolete words from the previous centuries, unless still in use. Regarding types of borrowings, the following are potentially included in GLAD:

- Non-adapted borrowings, e.g. *jackpot*
- Adapted borrowings, e.g. *brokeraggio* (English *brokerage*)
- Proper names turned generic nouns, e.g. *kleenex*
- Semantic loans, e.g. *stella* (English *star*, 'celebrity')
- Loan translations, e.g. *tempo pieno* (English *full time*)
- Hybrids, e.g. *clown terapia* (English *clown therapy*)
- Pseudo-Anglicisms, e.g. *mister* (English *coach*)
- Phono-semantic matchings (no examples in Italian)

All these types are represented in Figure 3.1, except for 'proper names turned into generic nouns' (also called eponyms in linguistics), which are treated here within the type of non-adapted borrowings (3.4.1), and phono-semantic matchings (Zucker-

---

[27] glad.ivdnt.org. Nicoline van der Sijs is responsible for the management of the database (see footnote 6).

mann 2003), which are not present in Italian.[28] The category of non-adapted borrowings includes simple words (e.g. *jackpot*), multi-word units (e.g. *bed and breakfast*), acronyms (e.g. SMS), terms originating in non-English speaking communities, e.g. *canyon* (from Spanish), and internationalisms (e.g. *automotive*). Pseudo-Anglicism is another term for false Anglicism. Despite the broad range of borrowing types to be included in GLAD, the following types are potentially excluded:

- Proper names and brand names, e.g. *iPad*
- Proper-name-based adjectives, e.g. Italian *shakespeariano*
- Frequency-boosted domestic words whose increased usage is due to a similarity with the English etymon, e.g. Italian *assolutamente* (by analogy with English *absolutely*)
- Archaisms: items obsolete before c. 1900, e.g. *cakewalk*
- Exoticisms: lexical items from a non-anglophone speech community mediated via English, e.g. *sushi* (from Japanese)
- Specialist terms not used in the general language, e.g. *proxy*
- Internationalisms based on Latin or Greek elements whose English provenance turns out to be impossible to determine, e.g. Italian *telefono*.

As in any lexicographic work, the dilemma between inclusion and exclusion of potential entries is based on objective criteria but, to some extent, also to subjective decisions taken by the compilers on the basis of their own experience and intuition. In actual fact, categories of potential borrowings are far from clear-cut, with particular regard to words that are 'common in the general language', and thus a major dilemma for lexicographers.

### 3.3.2 Methodology

The method of collection to be shared by GLAD's compilers was the selection of candidate Anglicisms from general dictionaries, lexicons of foreign words or dictionaries of English loans, if available in a given language. Furthermore, national text corpora and newspaper archives were used to collect more candidate entries, check their currency, grammatical status and meanings. For the compilation of the Italian wordlist, the workflow illustrated in Figure 3.2 was systematically followed.

---

[28] This type of borrowing seems to be rare in European languages. It implies the matching of a domestic phrase on an English one. An example is the German *Was gibt's?*, coined on the English model 'What gives?' (meaning 'What's going on?'). No similar cases appear to exist in Italian and therefore this category will not be considered here.

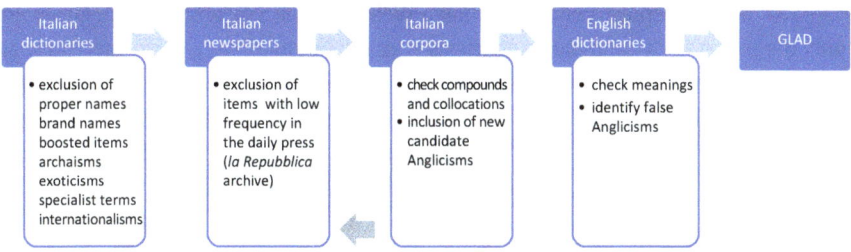

**Figure 3.2:** Step-by-step selection of Italian entries in GLAD.

The first step consisted in collecting candidate Anglicisms from general dictionaries of Italian, in particular from *Zingarelli 2022, Nuovo Devoto-Oli* 2022, *Grande dizionario italiano dell'uso*, also referred to as GDU (De Mauro 2007),[29] *Dizionario delle parole straniere nella lingua italiana* (De Mauro and Mancini 2003), *Dizionario degli Anglicismi nell'italiano postunitario* (Rando 1987), the *Dictionary of European Anglicisms* (Görlach 2001).[30] Medium-sized general dictionaries of Italian have been chosen since new editions are issued every year. This makes it particularly useful for the study of present-day vocabulary and neologisms. Other sources were also consulted such as *Vocabolario Treccani* (2018) and *Dizionario delle Alternative Agli Anglicismi* (Zoppetti 2022). All these sources provided a very high number of candidate Anglicisms, which had to be filtered through the criteria of inclusion and exclusion set for GLAD.

The next step consisted in checking the use of candidate entries in the online archive of the daily newspaper *la Repubblica*, which contains articles published since 1984. The search box allows the query of single words and phrases, and filters results in chronological order or by relevance. This archive was used to check the use of Anglicisms in newspaper articles, their most common orthographic forms and meanings, that is, whether they matched the meaning or meanings quoted by the dictionaries. The *la Repubblica* archive was also useful to track new Anglicisms not recorded in any of the reference dictionaries. Some meaningful cases are the words *lounge bar, limited edition, tribute band* and *killer instinct*, which were considered worthy of inclusion in GLAD.

---

[29] *Grande dizionario italiano dell'uso* (GRADIT), edited by Tullio De Mauro was published in 6 volumes in 1999–2000. Two additional supplements appeared in 2003 and 2007. In this book we relied on the 2007 digital edition, also named GDU.
[30] Collections of foreign words have been published in Italy since the 1980s (Cortelazzo and Cardinale 1989; Quarantotto 1987, 2001; Lurati 1990; Bencini and Citernesi 1992; Adamo and Della Valle (2003, 2005, 2008, 2018).

Two Italian corpora, CORIS and Italian Web 2020 (see 5.4), were used to check not only the presence of candidate Anglicisms – an operation already performed through the newspaper archive – and their frequency, but to extract word combinations, i.e., compounds and collocations. For instance, by doing a Word Sketch of the item 'web' in the Italian Web 2020, it is possible to obtain a frequency list of compounds, such as *web marketing, web design, web designer, webmaster, web radio, web-tv*, etc. Finally, the *Oxford English Dictionary* was used to check the attestation of the English etymon as well as its orthographic form and meaning. Where a word was not attested in the OED, other English dictionaries were consulted, such as the *Collins Dictionary*. In case of necessity, also the online archive of *The Guardian* newspaper was resorted to.

This procedure guaranteed a certain amount of rigour and consistency in the selection, but in fact more often than not, decisions in favour of inclusion or exclusion from GLAD's word list were far from simple. As a matter of fact, there are remarkable differences among dictionaries, not only because of their individual descriptive scope, but also in the way in which 'foreign words' are recorded and, consequently, can be retrieved. This problem will be analyzed in detail in chapter 5.

## 3.4 Loanwords

Loanwords belong to the category of direct borrowings. The word 'direct' implies that a foreign element has been transferred from the donor language to the recipient one, in this case from English into Italian. Loanwords may keep the original English form (non-adapted loanwords) or may be modified according to the orthographic and morphological rules of Italian (adapted loanwords). As far as pronunciation is concerned, a certain degree of adaptation is always present, even when the pronunciation is very close to the English model (cf. 4.1.2).

### 3.4.1 Non-adapted

The form of non-adapted Anglicisms is identical to the one of their English etymons. This category is the easiest to identify and to automatically retrieve from electronic dictionaries through etymology labels. Nowadays, most dictionaries are available in electronic format and allow the extraction of entries on the basis of set criteria through advanced queries. As will be discussed in 5.1, *Zingarelli 2022*, for example, allows the retrieval of entries that are labelled 'ingl.' ('English'), i.e., lexemes that have an English form; it is also possible to select entries that are 'dall'ingl.' ('from English'), i.e., lexemes derived from English, including the ones that do not have an English form because they have been adapted or translated. Instead, *Nuovo Devoto-*

*Oli 2022* allows the retrieval of both direct and indirect Anglicisms by setting the search option on 'language' and 'English'. The extraction of Anglicisms from language corpora can be done though several types of queries containing the search word or part of it. For neological investigation, semi-automatic techniques exploit the combinations of graphemes that are typical of English words (Andersen 2012), but this method has not been used in the present research.

In order to illustrate instances of non-adapted Anglicisms, two sets of Anglicisms have been chosen. The first contains all the Anglicisms borrowed in the 18$^{th}$ century, which are still current today and for this reasons are included in GLAD (Table 3.1). They are accompanied by definitions taken from the general Italian dictionary *Nuovo Devoto-Oli 2022* and translated into English to ease comprehension for non-Italian readers.

**Table 3.1:** Eighteenth century Anglicisms still current in the 21$^{st}$ century.

| | |
|---|---|
| *budget* | **1** fin. Bilancio preventivo di un'azienda<br>Piano finanziario, programma di spesa di un'impresa, di un'istituzione, ecc.<br>**2** Disponibilità economica |
| | **1** fin. Estimated balance of a company<br>Financial plan, programmed expenditure of a business, of an institution, etc.<br>**2** Economic availability |
| *bulldog* | Cane da guardia basso, muscoloso, con pelo raso a tinta unita, e col muso scuro e molto schiacciato |
| | Watchdog, medium-sized, stocky, with short hair of a single colour, and a dark, very flat snout |
| *city* | Il quartiere di una metropoli, spec. quello di Londra, dove si concentrano le principali istituzioni economiche e amministrative<br>come secondo elemento di composti spesso ironici o polemici, città, capitale |
| | The quarter of a metropolis, esp. the one in London, where the main financial and administrative institutions are concentrated<br>As a second element of a compound, often ironical or polemical, city, capital |
| *clan* | **1** antrop. Raggruppamento di famiglie tradizionalmente legate da una stessa discendenza, materna o paterna, da un capostipite mitico e dal culto della stirpe<br>Nei popoli gaelici, il gruppo di famiglie composto dai discendenti in linea maschile da un comune progenitore<br>**2** Gruppo chiuso di persone strette da comuni interessi, spesso al di fuori della legge<br>**3** sport Società sportiva<br>Circolo locale di tifosi |

**Table 3.1** (continued)

| | |
|---|---|
| | **1** anthrop. Group of families traditionally bound by the same lineage, on the mother's or father's side, by a mythical common ancestor or by the cult of ancestry<br>Among Gaelic peoples, group of families composed of the descendants through the male line from a common progenitor<br>**2** Closed circle of people sharing common interests, often against the law<br>**3** sport Sports society<br>Local circle of supporters |
| *club* | **1** Circolo istituito a fini ricreativi, sportivi o culturali che riunisce persone con interessi in comune<br>La sede che lo ospita<br>**2** sport (squadra di) club, la squadra di un luogo, in contrapposizione alla rappresentativa nazionale<br>**3** Ente a carattere nazionale per l'esercizio o il controllo di una determinata attività<br>**4** Gruppo internazionale di rappresentanti di Stati o di enti che si riuniscono periodicamente<br>**5** stor. Durante la Rivoluzione francese, associazione politica<br>**6** sport Bastone per il golf, con spatola rinforzata |
| | **1** Association for recreational, sports or cultural purposes, of people with common interests<br>The place hosting it<br>**2** sport (the team of) a club, the team of a place, as opposed to the national team<br>**3** National institution for the management or the control of a particular activity<br>**4** International group of representatives of States or institutions that meet periodically<br>**5** hist. During the French revolution, political association<br>**6** sport Golf bat, with strong clubhead |
| *cottage* | Casa di campagna, spec. a un solo piano, intonata all'ambiente rustico circostante<br>Country-style house, esp. with a single floor, in character with the rustic surroundings |
| *dock* | mar. Ciascuno dei settori di un grande porto mercantile, fornito di banchine e di tutte le necessarie attrezzature perché le navi possano compiere direttamente le operazioni di carico e scarico |
| | naut. Any of the sectors of a large sea harbour, equipped with quays and all the necessary machines allowing ships to directly undergo loading and unloading operations |
| *gentleman* | **1** Uomo di modi signorili e irreprensibili; gentiluomo<br>**2** stor. In passato, cittadino inglese di buona posizione sociale, intermedia tra l'aristocrazia e la borghesia, garantita dal percepimento di una rendita personale<br>**3** sport Sportivo che partecipi per divertimento a una competizione, in genere automobilistica o ippica |

**Table 3.1** (continued)

| | |
|---|---|
| | 1 A man who has refined and impeccable manners<br>2 hist. In the past, British citizen of good social standing, between aristocracy and middle class, with a guaranteed personal income<br>3 sport A sportsman who takes part in a competition for pleasure, generally in motor racing or horse riding |
| hall | 1 Spazioso ambiente d'ingresso, sosta o disimpegno, tipico spec. dei grandi alberghi; atrio, salone d'ingresso<br>2 mar. Tipo di ancora senza ceppo con marre snodate |
| | 1 Spacious entrance room, landing or hallway, typical esp. of big hotels; lounge, entrance lobby<br>2 nav. Type of anchor with articulated arms and no stock |
| humour | Piacevole senso dell'ironia, tipico degli inglesi<br>Pleasurable sense of irony, typical of the British |
| ketchup | Salsa piccante per condimenti, a base di succo di pomodoro con zucchero, cipolla, aceto, erbe aromatiche |
| | Spicy sauce for seasoning, containing tomato juice with sugar, onion, vinegar and aromatic herbs |
| miss | 1 Appellativo inglese, premesso al nome o al cognome per le donne non sposate, equivalente all'italiano signorina<br>2 La vincitrice di un concorso di bellezza<br>non com. Ragazza molto bella<br>3 Nel linguaggio giornalistico, personaggio femminile di successo<br>4 non com. Istitutrice di origine inglese |
| | 1 English term of address, used before a name or a surname of unmarried women, equivalent of Italian signorina<br>2 The winner of a beauty contest: not common, colloquial beautiful girl<br>3 In journalism, successful female character<br>4 not common Teacher of English origin |
| plaid | Coperta da viaggio o per uso domestico, di lana o di fibre sintetiche, spesso con i tipici disegni scozzesi a grandi quadri vivacemente colorati e con frange alle due estremità |
| | Blanket for travelling or home use, made of woollen or synthetic fibre, often with typical bright-coloured, checked Scottish design and fringes at both ends |
| speaker | 1 polit. Titolo attribuito ai presidenti delle assemblee legislative in vari paesi di lingua inglese<br>2 radio, TV Annunciatore<br>3 sport Chi comunica al pubblico, con un altoparlante, i dati, i particolari tecnici e i risultati di una gara sportiva |

**Table 3.1** (continued)

| | |
|---|---|
| | **1** polit. Title given to presidents of legislative assemblies in various Anglophone countries<br>**2** radio, TV Announcer<br>**3** sport Commentator on data, technical details and results of a sports contest given through a loudspeaker |
| *spleen* | Atteggiamento sentimentale caratterizzato da umore tetro e malinconico, insoddisfazione e noia, frequentemente rappresentato dagli scrittori romantici francesi e inglesi |
| | Sentimental attitude characterized by a gloomy, melancholic mood, dissatisfaction and boredom, frequently represented by French and English Romantic poets |
| *standard* | **A s.m. invar.**<br>**1** Tipo, modello, norma, a cui viene uniformata una data produzione o attività<br>**2** comm. Il complesso dei campioni di una determinata merce, corrispondenti a tipi o gradi della produzione di un dato periodo, su cui ci si basa per le classificazioni di qualità di determinati prodotti; nell'uso tecnico o industriale, modello o tipo di un determinato prodotto, o il complesso di norme fissate per uniformare le caratteristiche del prodotto stesso<br>**3** fig. Rendimento abituale di un individuo<br>**4** TV Standard televisivo, l'insieme degli elementi atti a individuare le caratteristiche di un determinato sistema di televisione<br>**5** biol. L'insieme dei caratteri somatici che contraddistinguono una razza di animali o di piante<br>**6** mus. Nel jazz, brano musicale molto noto, oggetto di numerosi rifacimenti<br>**7** ling. Tipo o livello di linguaggio che, per uniformità e diffusione, è preso come modello nell'insegnamento di una lingua<br>**8** Norma di pianificazione territoriale |
| | **B agg. invar**. (posposto al sost.) conforme a un livello medio assunto come normale orefic., comm. Nel commercio dei metalli preziosi: *oro standard*, *argento standard*, quelli a titolo legale |
| | **A s.m. invar.**<br>**1** Type, model, norm, against which a given production or activity is measured<br>**2** comm. The range of the samples of a given commodity, corresponding to types or degrees of production of a given period, according to which degrees of quality of specific products are classified; in technical or industrial use, model or type of a specific product, or the range of norms fixed to uniform the characteristics of the product itself<br>**3** fig. Habitual performance of an individual<br>**4** TV Television quality, the features that show the characteristics of a particular television system<br>**5** biol. The somatic characteristics that are peculiar to a breed of animals or plants<br>**6** mus. In jazz, popular music track, object of many remakes |

**Table 3.1** (continued)

| | |
|---|---|
| | **A s.m. invar.7** ling. Type or register of a language which, for uniformity and spread, is taken as a model for the teaching of a language<br>**8** Norm of territorial planning |
| | **B adj. inv.** (postponed to the noun) conformed to a medium level chosen as normal goldsmithery, comm. In precious metal trade: *standard gold*, *standard silver*, conforming to the legal title |
| *stock* | **1** comm. Quantità di materia prima, merce o prodotto, specie come giacenza o scorta disponibile per la vendita, oppure immagazzinata in attesa di ulteriori trasformazioni o trattamenti<br>**2** fin. Titolo azionario |
| | **1** comm. Quantity of raw material, goods or product, esp. as unsold goods or supply available for sale, or stored to be further transformed or treated<br>**2** fin. Share |
| *tartan* | tess. Tessuto di lana scozzese a grossi quadri e a colori vivaci e contrastanti fra loro, usato spec. per confezionare i kilt |
| | text. Woollen cloth woven in a chequered pattern and bright, contrasting colours, used esp. to make kilts |
| *tender* | **1** ferr. Il carro unito alle locomotive a vapore, per il trasporto del carbone (o altro combustibile), dell'acqua, ecc.<br>**2** mar. Nave appoggio o nave adibita al trasporto di combustibile, in servizi logistici<br>Nella nautica da diporto, piccola imbarcazione ausiliaria, per lo più un gommone, per lo sbarco dell'equipaggio |
| | **1** rail. A carriage attached to a steam locomotive, for carrying coal (or other fuel), water, etc.<br>**2** naut. A ship or boat employed to carry fuel, in logistical services<br>In sailing, small auxiliary boat, generally a rubber dinghy, for landing the crew |
| *terrier* | Nome di varie razze di cani appartenenti alla categoria dei segugi da tana, di taglia modesta, ma eccezionalmente robusti e coraggiosi |
| | Name of various dog breeds belonging to the category of hunting dogs, of medium size, but exceptionally strong and tough |
| *test* | **1** Esperimento che ha lo scopo di valutare le caratteristiche psicologiche, le capacità intellettive, le inclinazioni attitudinali o aspetti della personalità di un individuo<br>**2** Prova d'esame che prevede una serie di quesiti, ciascuno seguito da diverse risposte, tra le quali il candidato deve indicare quella giusta<br>**3** Prova diretta a verificare il livello di preparazione dello studente in una determinata materia<br>**4** med. Esame clinico per accertamenti diagnostici<br>**5** Prova, saggio, verifica, esperimento |

**Table 3.1** (continued)

|  |  |
|---|---|
|  | **1** Experiment aiming to evaluate the psychological characteristics, the intellective capacities, the attitudinal bents or aspects of an individual's personality<br>**2** Examination consisting of a series of questions, each followed by multiple answers, from which the candidate must choose the correct one<br>**3** Examination to verify a student's level of competence in a specific subject<br>**4** med. Clinical check-up for diagnostic investigation<br>**5** Examination, essay, verification, experiment |
| *whisky* | Acquavite tipica dei paesi anglosassoni, ottenuta per distillazione da mosti fermentati di malto, grano, avena e altri cereali<br>Bicchiere di tale acquavite |
|  | A highly alcoholic liquor typical of Anglo-Saxon countries, obtained from the distillation of fermented must of malt, corn, barley and other cereals<br>A glass of this liquor |

As described in chapter 2 (2.2), 18th century Anglicisms were drawn from different fields of British society, from politics to business, culture and social life. Most of these words have become established in Italian's 'core' vocabulary and familiar to most Italians, even to those who have limited knowledge of English. The only exceptions from this list are the words *spleen* and *tender*: the former belongs to literary language and is unexpectedly quite common in the press, because of its association to Baudelaire and the 'poètes maudits' ('accursed poets'); the latter is confined to the field of navigation (discussed in 6.5 on obsolescence). *Ketchup* is one of the terms imported from distant languages (Chinese and Malay) through the mediation of English, globally popular as a dressing for hamburgers and served in fast food restaurants. A curious fact is the presence of two names of dog breeds (*bulldog* and *terrier*), confirming the British tradition of dog breeding and training, which has given to Italian most of this terminology. The development of a new meaning, or the rejuvination of the older one, is quite common for all words, including Anglicisms. The word *miss*, for example, from a title given to a young lady or an unmarried woman, to a governess or a housekeeper, acquired the meaning of 'winner of a beauty contest', apparently from American English (dated 1895 by Rando 1987). The word *speaker*, from the oldest meaning of 'person in charge of meetings (especially in politics)', developed the technical meaning of 'a piece of electrical equipment through which sound comes out' in the 20th century, and later 'someone providing information in airports and stations through a loudspeaker' and 'sport announcer'. Commercial terms such as *budget* (from French *bougette* 'small bag'), *stock* and *standard* (originally 'sign', from Old French 'estendart') have easily adapted to new, modern uses in the following centuries. The success of these words, which may partly be due to their brevity, has allowed them to develop meanings in different fields (e.g. *test* in science, medicine and education). The word *standard* is perhaps the most successful of all, carrying a meaning that can be easily applied to diverse fields and situations, despite the various Italian synonyms available (*canone, modello, norma, campione, requisito*), which have been unable to displace it.

At the other end of the time line, we have selected another sample of non-adapted Anglicisms, randomly choosing the year 2012 (Table 3.2). These words will certainly be less familiar to the general public than the previous list. Moreover, they have had no time to develop new meanings from the specific ones for which they were imported; they are listed below (definitions from *Nuovo Devoto-Oli 2022*, translated into English).

Table 3.2: New Anglicisms borrowed in 2012.

| | |
|---|---|
| *cash mob* | Raduno di più persone presso un'attività commerciale in difficoltà per sostenerla economicamente tramite l'acquisto collettivo dei suoi prodotti o servizi |
| | Rally of many people at a commercial activity in difficulty, to support it economically by buying its products or services |
| *cashback* | Rimborso parziale della cifra spesa per un acquisto, offerto per lo più come sconto o iniziativa promozionale da venditori o gestori di servizi di pagamento |
| | Partial reimbursement of a sum of money spent for a purchase, offered as a discount or promotional intiative by retailers or managers of payment services |
| *e-cig* | Sigaretta elettronica |
| | Electronic cigarette |
| *fiscal cliff* | Baratro fiscale, politica finanziaria volta a ridurre il deficit di uno stato tramite un consistente aumento delle tasse e una drastica riduzione della spesa pubblica, con conseguente abbassamento del PIL e recessione economica |
| | Fiscal cliff, financial policy aimed at reducing a State's deficit through a substantial increase in taxes and a drastic reduction in public expenditure, with a consequent fall in GDP and economic recession |
| *fiscal compact* | econ., polit. Patto di bilancio, accordo sottoscritto da 25 dei 27 stati membri dell'Unione Europea che, in base ai principi stabiliti nel patto di stabilità e di crescita, vincola gli stati a rispettare una serie di regole per il contenimento del disavanzo pubblico e il conseguimento del pareggio di bilancio |
| | econ. polit. Fiscal compact, agreement signed by 25 of the 27 member states of the European Union which, on the basis of the principles established in the stability and growth pact, binds states to a series of rules for the containment of their public deficit and to achieve a 'balanced budget' |

**Table 3.2** (continued)

| | |
|---|---|
| *gamification* | L'applicazione di tecniche tipiche dei giochi in ambiti professionali o commerciali |
| | The application of techniques typical of games in professional and commercial contexts |
| *selfie* | Autoritratto fotografico realizzato con uno smartphone o con una webcam e pubblicato su un social network |
| | A photograph that one has taken of oneself with a smartphone or webcam and posted on a social network |
| *smartwatch* | telecom., inform. Orologio da polso dotato di un microprocessore che, una volta connesso a uno smartphone, interagisce con esso replicandone le funzioni |
| | telecom. inform. Wrist watch with microprocessor which, once connected to a smartphone, can interact with it and replicate its functions |
| *troll* | **1** mitol. Nelle leggende scandinave, abitante demoniaco di boschi, montagne, luoghi solitari: corrisponde all'orco di altre tradizioni popolari europee |
| | **2** gerg. In Internet, utente di una comunità virtuale, solitamente anonimo, che intralcia il normale svolgimento di una discussione inviando messaggi provocatori, irritanti o fuori tema |
| | **1**. mithol. In Scandinavian legends, fiendish creatures living in the woods, in the mountains and in solitary places: similar to an ogre in other European popular traditions |
| | **2**. slang On the internet, a participant of a virtual community, usually anonymous, who disturbs the normal course of discussions by posting challenging, irritating, and off-the-point messages |
| *upcyling* | ecol. Riutilizzazione creativa, processo di adattamento e trasformazione di un oggetto o di un materiale già usato per poterlo utilizzare ulteriormente prima che entri nel processo di smaltimento dei rifiuti |
| | ecol. Creative recycling, process of adaptation and transformation of an object or of already used material in order to use it again before it undergoes the process of waste disposal |

These items mirror the most common fields affected by English loanwords in the 21$^{st}$ century, namely economy, technology, the internet and the environment. While the word *selfie* is extremely popular, and the meaning of *smartwatch* can easily be inferred as an evolution from the smartphone, the term *troll* (from which the verb *trollare* has been derived) may be known only to younger people and generally to users of the social media. *E-cig*, short for *e-cigarette*, coexists with the Italian *sigaretta elettronica* (and is roughly as frequent). The remaining terms appear rather specific to the field of business and economy, and are likely to be unfamiliar to most Italians. However, they appear to be quite topical nowadays in newspaper discourse. They have been included in GLAD because their use in the archive of *la Repubblica* newspaper is quite high.

Having illustrated the notion of non-adapted Anglicism with old and new examples, we can now focus on the forms and types of non-adapted Anglicisms. Formally, Anglicisms can be simple words, multi-word units (including compounds with English elements, compounds with neoclassical combining forms, and free combinations), and shortenings (clippings, blends and abbreviations). As for types, we will discuss eponyms, specialized terms, archaisms, exoticisms (terms originating in non-English speaking communities), Latinisms and interjections. As for the 'age' of Anglicisms, the focus of GLAD's word list is meant to be on items belonging to modern language as written or spoken in the 20$^{th}$ and 21$^{st}$ centuries, with the exclusion of items obsolete before c. 1900, unless still current (as the items in Table 3.2), and specialist vocabulary not used in the general language.

– Compounds and collocations

Multi-word Anglicisms can be compounds and lexical collocations. Compounds may be one-word units (e.g. *airbag, benchmark, crowdfunding*), two-word units (e.g. *big data, by-pass, open access*) and multi-word units (e.g. *all in one, business to business, duty-free shop*). Opening the word list to frequent collocations has allowed researchers to record units of meaning that are often confined to the bottom of dictionary entries, the place of phraseologisms (see 3.7).

The orthographic form of compounds in Italian Anglicisms may vary with respect to their English etymons. For example, the entry *all inclusive* is recorded as two separate units (*all inclusive*), followed by the hyphenated variant (*all-inclusive*), whereas the English etymon is hyphenated (*all-inclusive*), as recorded by the OED. It is no surprise that spelling displays a good deal of variation already in the English language, and this lack of consistency is also reflected in Italian Anglicisms. For this reason GLAD does not consider hyphenation as a specific type of adaptation. Compounds are the combination of two or more free morphemes to form a lexeme with a new meaning but often they are not distinguishable from noun phrases, i.e., looser combination of separate elements. This type of word formation is very productive in English, especially because of the possibility for a noun to act as modifier of another noun. As a consequence not all two- or more- word combinations are recorded in dictionaries, such as, for example, *baby star, beach tennis, cake designer* or *capsule collection*, though they are plausible and comprehensible combinations, frequently found not only in English but also in Italian. This mechanism of word formation is widely exploited for the creation of neologisms, many of which are not recorded in dictionaries because of their ephemeral nature. The following elements

(Table 3.3) are the most productive in the creation of multi-word units recorded in GLAD; they are also recorded in dictionaries and frequently appear in newspaper articles.

**Table 3.3:** The most productive left-hand elements of compounds.

| | |
|---|---|
| web | web agency, web app, web community, web design, web designer, web developer, web magazine, web marketing, web radio, web series, web tax, webcam, webcast, webcasting, webinar, weblog, webmaster, *webserie*, website, web-tv, webzine[31] |
| baby | baby boom, baby boomer, baby boss, baby club, baby dance, baby doll, baby food, baby gang, baby parking, baby pusher, baby sitter, baby star, babysitteraggio, babysitting |
| free | free access, free climber, free climbing, free flow, free internet, free jazz, freelance, free press, free shop, free software, freemium, freeride, freestyle, freeware |
| new | new age, new company, new dada, new deal, new economy, new entry, new global, new jersey, new look, new media, new romantic, new style, new wave, newco |
| top | top car, top class, top gun, top management, top manager, top model, top player, top price, top rate, top secret, top spin, top ten, top-down |
| black | black bloc, black bottom, black box, black comedy, black Friday, black hole, black jack, black list, black metal, black music, black power, black-out |
| fashion | fashion addict, fashion blog, *fashion* blogger, fashion design, fashion designer, fashion district, fashion scout, fashion show, fashion system, fashion victim, fashion week |

The selection of candidate Anglicisms is greatly facilitated today by the use of electronic resources, such as dictionaries and corpora. However, the size of the textual availability is so vast, that the number of candidate Anglicisms is potentially immense. To give an idea of the actual combinations of the word *web* in the Italian Web 2020 corpus (the second most frequent non-adapted Anglicism in this corpus, after *film*), the number obtained from a Word List query of items starting with *web* gave 1,885 items. Apart from all proper names of software, companies and apps which have a name starting with *Web* and other irrelevant results, the actual potential combinability of *web* with other English or Italian elements is very high. Some plausible examples, excluded from GLAD, are *webmail, webserver, webquest, webservice, webchat, webcomic, webpage, webstore, webwriter,*

---

[31] Adamo and Della Valle (2018) include the following among the neologisms collectied from the press in the years 2008–2018: *web conference, webcrazia* (a blend of *web* and *democrazia*), *web democracy, web-democrazia, web dictionary, web economy, webete* (a blend of *web* and *ebete*), *webetismo, weblearning, webletteratura, webmagazine, web-marketing, web reputation, webserie, webtax.*

*webhosting, webform, webconference, webseminar, webdoc, webview, weblink, webring, webmistress, webpart*, and many others.

The creation of neologisms in language is naturally unstoppable, even with borrowings, leading to the domestic formation of non-English words, or false Anglicisms. The word *baby* offers several instances of compounds which exploit the sense of 'young' expressed by 'baby', as in *baby boss* (juvenile gang leader), *baby dance* (baby discotheque), *baby gang* (teenage gang), *baby parking* (crèche), *baby pusher* (teenage drug dealer). Other interesting hybrid combinations are *pensioni baby* or *baby pensioni*, which refer to pensions issued by the Italian state to workers of the public sectors who retire under the age of 40–50, hence the term *baby pensionato* for the retired person. These neologisms can be considered autonomous creations in Italian with no English model. Moreover, also the sense of 'small size' carried by 'baby' can be used in many English-Italian hybrid combinations such as *moda baby, carote baby, computer baby, sindaco baby* (equally not included in GLAD).

Another productive type are compounds containing combining forms (Iacobini 2015; Bombi 2017). Combining forms are lexical items of Latin and Greek etymology, used to create compound terms in technical and scientific domains. The most productive ones are *multi- video- hydro- micro- auto- tele- bio- mega- photo- bi- mini- porno- cyber- eco- euro- geo- mono- techno-*. These elements differ from affixes in many ways, being closer to free morphemes rather than to bound morphemes, and in particular contexts they may be used as independent words (e.g. *video, cyber, euro*). Their classical origin makes them very familiar to Italian speakers, or better, they are perceived as Italian combining forms, except for the ones that have been adapted to English, like *hydro-* and *cyber-* (in Italian *idro-* and *ciber-*). Research into Anglicisms made up with combining forms has shown that they are more productive in combination with Italian elements rather than English ones. This leads to the observation that in this area of language contact interlinguistic similarity favours the composition with domestic lexical items, which greatly outnumber those of foreign origin (Pulcini and Milani 2017).

The most productive combining form recorded in GLAD is *video*, whose origin is Latin combined with an *-o-* connective (see Table 3.4). It forms 'words relating to the production, transmission, or recording of video images', mostly endocentric. Thus, *video art* is 'art that uses video technology or equipment as a medium'. In Italian *video* is also recorded as a separate word, both an adjective and a noun, with several meanings related to the transmission of images. Its relation to English is also recorded, as a clipping of *videoclip*, and as a substantive derived from the English combining form *video-* (rather paradoxically, as *video-* is more productive in combination with Italian elements than English ones). Some compounds with *video* coexist with translation equivalents, affecting the second elements: *video art* alternates in use with *video arte* (the Italian form is more frequent) and *videogame* with *videogioco* (the English form is more frequent).

**Table 3.4:** Anglicisms with neo-classical combining forms.

| | |
|---|---|
| video- | video art, video arte, video on-demand, video sharing, video tutorial, videoblog, videoblogger, videocamera, videocassetta, videochat, videoclip, videofilm, videogallery, videogame, videogioco, videolottery, videomaker, videomapping, videopoker, videoreporter, videosharing, videostreaming, videotape, videowall |
| cyber- | cyberbullismo, cybercafé, cybercrime, cybercrimine, cybernauta, cyberpunk, cybersecurity, cybersesso, cybersex, cybersicurezza, cyberspace, cyberspazio, cyberterrorismo, cyborg (cyber+organism) |
| super- | superbike, superbowl, superette, superfood, superman, supermanager, supermarket, supermercato, superstar, supertuscan, supervisor, supervisore |
| auto- | autocaravan, autofiction, autofocus, autogol, autogrill, automazione, automotive, autostop, autostoppista |
| mini- | minibar, minibasket, minibus, minicar, miniclub, minicomputer, minidisc, minigang, minigolf |
| multi- | multibrand, multijet, multimedia, multiplayer, multiplex, multiservice, multitasking, multitouch, multiutility |

Besides combining forms, other English prefixes appear to be quite productive (Table 3.5). The prefix *e-* (which stands for electronic) is preposed to nouns to denote the technological equivalent of ordinary referents (*e-book, e-commerce, e-learning, e-mail*). Political orientations are marked by the prefix *no-* and *non-*, often freely alternating in use (e.g. *non stop/no stop, non profit/no profit*) or creatively exploited in false Anglicisms like *no global* (for *anti-globalization*) and *no vax* (for *anti-vax*). The word *out*, used as a noun (in sport, the space outside the court), an adjective and an adverb ('no longer fashionable') and an interjection (in sport, when the ball lands outside the boundary lines of the court), is semantically familiar to Italians (also because of the opposition between 'in' and 'out'); therefore several words beginning with the element *out* have spread, despite their lack of transparency for Romance language speakers (*outlet, output, outsider,* etc.). Finally, the prefix *self-* is quite productive in words expressing a reflexive meaning ('by oneself, independently') and is in competition with the neo-classical combining form *auto-*, generating synonymic calques in Italian like *autocontrollo* (from *self-control*). In this case, the phonetic quality and the evocative power of *self-* have contributed to the success of this English prefix, giving, for example, the word *selfie* a great advantage over the old-fashioned Italian *autoscatto*; the same can be said for *self-service,* which can hardly be rendered with the same semantic impact with an Italian equivalent word or expression.

**Table 3.5:** Anglicisms with English productive prefixes.

| | |
|---|---|
| e- | e-banking, e-bike, e-book, ebook reader, e-business, e-card, e-cig, e-cigarette, e-commerce, e-government, e-health, e-learning, e-mail, e-mobility, e-news, e-procurement, e-reader, e-shop, e-shopping, e-store, e-ticket |
| no- | no comment, no frills, no frost, no gender, no global, no limits, no logo, no problem, no profit, no smoking, no tax area, no vax,[32] no-fly list, no-fly zone, no-show, no stop |
| out- | outbound, outdoor, outfit, outgoing, outlet, outplacement, output, outsider, outsourcing |
| self- | self-control, self storage, self-help, selfie, selfie stick, self-made man, self-made woman, self-promotion, self-publishing, self-service |

– Clippings and blends

The principle of economy in language is extensively exploited nowadays, as the need to save space and encapsulate multiple meanings has become extremely important and necessary, especially when messages are conveyed through the small screen of a smartphone or must be limited to a fixed number of characters in social media posts (Bombi 2015b, 2017). Clipping consists in the cutting of part(s) of a word, to make it shorter. In compounds, only one of the elements may be clipped, as in *op art* (optical art), *showbiz* (show business), and *webcam* (web camera). In addition to brevity, a new meaning can be created for a new referent, as in *chatbot* (chat+robot), *cosplay* (costume+play), *fantathriller* (fantasy+thriller), and *webinar* (web+seminar). In other cases both elements are reduced as in *biopic* (biographical+picture), *bio-tech* (biology+ technology), *hi-fi* (high+fidelity), *Tex-mex* (Texan-Mexican), *sci-fi* (science+fiction), *veejay* (video+jockey) and *wi-fi* (wireless+fidelity).

As a word formation process, blending is the result of the merging of two words, creating a new word with a new blended meaning, as in *blog* (web+log), *Brexit* (Britain+exit), *brunch* (breakfast+lunch), *burkini* (burqa+bikini), *camcorder* (camera+recorder), *edutainment* (education+entertainment), *infotainment* (information+entertainment), *freemium* (free+premium), *glocal* (global+local), *modem* (modulator+demodulator), *prosumer* (producer+consumer) and *vlog*

---

32 In English, *anti-vax.*

(video+blog). Creative combinations of lexical items can engender neologisms such as *nomofobia* (no mobile phobia)[33] and *sexting* (sex+text+ing).[34]

– Abbreviations

The category of abbreviations and acronyms is potentially very long, but only common acronyms frequently heard in everyday speech and frequently used in the press have been included in GLAD. The list of acronyms and abbreviations confirms that the fields which have been mostly enriched by English loanwords is that of Information and Communication Technology (ICT), including terms referring to computers, the internet, mobile and video technology, followed by business and economics (De Cesare 2016).

- Computer technology: ADSL (Asymmetric Digital Subscriber Line), CD (Compact Disc), CD-ROM (Compact Disc – Read Only Memory), PC (Personal Computer), USB (Universal Serial Bus), User ID (User Identification Number), CPU (Central Processing Unit), RAM (Random Access Memory), CAD (Computer Aided Design)
- Internet: cc (carbon copy), IoT (Internet of Things), HTML (HyperText Markup Language), FAQ (Frequently Asked Questions), LAN (Local Area Network), URL (Uniform Resource Locator), WWW (World Wide Web)
- Mobile technology: GPS (Global Positioning System), GSM (Global System for Mobile communications), MMS (Multimedia Messaging Service), PIN (Personal Identification Number), QR code (Quick Response code), SIM (Subscriber Identification Module), SMS (Short Message Service)
- Video technology: DVD (Digital Video Disc), HD (High Definition), HDTV (High Definition Television), LCD (Liquid Crystal Display), LED (Light Emitting Diode), MP3 (Moving Pictures experts group 3), MP4 (Moving Pictures experts group 4)
- Business: B&B (Bed and Breakfast), B2B (Business to Business), B2C (Business to Consumer), CEO (Chief Executive Officer), ISO (International Organization for Standardization), PR (Public Relations), yettie (young, entrepreneurial, and technology-based person), yuppy (young urban or upwardly mobile professional).
- Medicine: AIDS (Acquired Immune Deficiency Syndrome), DNA (Deoxyribonucleic Acid), HIV (Human Immunodeficiency Virus)

---

[33] The first meaning recorded in the OED for *nomophobia* is 'Aversion to or fear of laws or rules.' (from Greek νομός, nomos n. 'law'). The second meaning is 'Anxiety about not having access to a mobile phone or mobile phone services.', which is the one more frequently associated with this word in present-day communication.

[34] *Sexting*: 'The action or practice of sending or exchanging sexually explicit or suggestive messages or images electronically, esp. using a mobile phone.' (OED) .

- Cars: ABS (Antilock Braking System), HP (Horse Power), SUV (Sport Utility Vehicle)
- Sport: BMX (Bicycle Moto-cross), KO (Knockout), VAR (Video Assistant Referee)
- Radio communication: CB (Citizen's Band), FM (Frequency Modulation)
- Music: DJ (deejay, from Disc Jockey), LP (Long Playing)
- Clothes sizes: L (Large), M (Medium), S (Small), XL (Extra Large), XS (Extra Small), XXL (Extra-Extra-Large), XXS (Extra-Extra-Small)
- Mixed: BB cream (Blemish Balm cream), c/o (care of), GMT (Greenwich Mean Time), IQ (Intelligence Quotient), ISBN (International Standard Book Number), IT (Inclusive Tour), laser (light amplification by the stimulated emission of radiation), LOL (Laughing Out Loud), LOL (Lots Of Love), Nimby ('not in my backyard'), OK (okay), Q&A (Questions and Answers), REM (Rapid Eye Movements), UFO (Unidentified Flying Object), W (West), WASP (White Anglo-Saxon Protestant), WC (Water Closet).

The pronunciation of abbreviations in Italian adheres to the English one in some cases, but it is usually adapted to the Italian pronunciation of the letters of the alphabet (see 4.1.2 below). Only in rare cases, the acronym is modified to comply with the Italian translation (e.g. codice RQ for QR code), but in most cases the English pattern is maintained, even when the full form is used (e.g. AIDS, *Sindrome da Immuno Deficienza Acquisita*), differently from other languages.[35]

– Eponyms
A common type of loanword is the category of proper names turned into generic nouns, a lexical process called 'eponymy'. This phenomenon consists in extending a proper name given to an object to all the objects with the same characteristics. A prototypical case is that of *jeep*, the name of the car company Jeep® which has been adopted in common use to denote any 'four-wheel-drive vehicle'. A clue of this formal transition is the loss of the capital letter and of the 'registered trademark' symbol (® or ™) attached to the name, although many cases remain borderline. In old borrowings, this relation with an original proper name is lost in time, or speakers are no more aware of it, as, for example, in the word *tweed*, the name of 'A twilled woollen cloth' made in Scotland, from the name of a river flowing in the area where wool mills were located. Geographical names are frequenty exploited to name fabrics or clothing articles, e.g. *cardigan, jersey, oxford, denim* (from *de Nîmes*, a French city), names of dances (*charleston*), breeds of dogs (*yorkshire terrier*), and other referents, e.g. *limerick* ('non-sense verse') and *derby* ('a sporting contest').

---

35 French has SIDA for *syndrome d'immunodéficience acquise*.

A fairly long list of eponyms derives from commercial names of products. Some are fairly assimilated words, such as *intercity* ('fast train or passenger rail service'), *interrail* (or *interRail*, European rail pass), *kleenex* (paper tissue), *barbie* (a person, esp. a young woman, perceived as blandly attractive and vacuous), *frisbee* ('plastic disc which spins when thrown into the air and is used in a catching game'), *blockbuster* ('a film or book that has a great impact'), *tampax* ('sanitary tampon for women') and *walkman* ('a portable personal music player'). Proper names may produce generic derivatives, like *youtuber* ('A frequent user of the video-sharing website YouTube') and names of events like *Black Friday* ('in the US, the day after Thanksgiving, which traditionally marks the start of the Christmas shopping season') and *Gay Pride* may extend to 'any big sales event' or 'any of various public events intended to promote solidarity among homosexual men and women'. Names of inventors and scientists are traditionally attributed to units of measurements, diseases, technical equipment and the like. GLAD includes the following instances: *colt* ('a type of revolver, pistol, etc.'), *badminton* ('a game played on a court'), *liberty* ('flowery style'),[36] *nobel* (both the prize and the awarded person), and *down* (both the condition and the person affected by this syndrome). The origin of the word *oscar* is uncertain, but possibly from a proper name, denoting the prize itself (the statuette), the Oscar-winner and generically 'any award for excellence'. Some words introduced to denote a specific referent, like Internet (also the Internet, initially a confederation of networks), immediately became generic; the use of the capital letter is losing ground in favour of the small one, and the article is also often dropped.[37] Quite a few eponyms have developed in Italy and are therefore dealt with as false Anglicisms (cf. 3.5 below).

– Specialized terms

As regards specialized vs non-specialized terms, the dividing line between them is often difficult to draw, especially in those technical fields which have become familiar to many speakers, like information and communication technology (cf. 6.2), and also topics that are widely discussed in the daily press, such as economy and finance (cf. 6.3). Therefore, while it is fairly simple to exclude terms belonging to the hard sciences (physics, chemistry, engineering), other scientific disciplines which have been subject to popularization (e.g. medicine) have reached a wider audience of non-specialists. Moreover, even in the most popular field of interest among common people – sport – its terminology embraces 'core' and 'peripheral' terms, which pose

---

36 In France this type of style was called *art nouveau*, and in Great Britain *Modern Style*.

37 Examples of proper names rejected from GLAD because not generic include: Airbus, Boeing, iPad, Jacuzzi, Bloody Mary, Bollywood, Caterpillar, Chinatown, Dolby, I-phone, Interpol, pilates (from the name of the German-born inventor), Playstation, Skylab, Wall Street, Wellington, Worcester (sauce), Skype, Brexit, Twitter, Facebook.

serious problems of selection. Facing this issue, Görlach (2003) carried out a small-scale research about golf terminology, identifying the terms that were most frequently recorded in dictionaries and therefore most widespread and well-known, namely *caddie, birdie, bunker, green, tee, bogey, eagle, fairway, rough* and *dogleg*. A similar investigation was carried out for GLAD, selecting *caddie, birdie, bunker, green, tee, bogey* and *par* (not considered by Görlach), and excluding *eagle, fairway, rough* and *dogleg*. Needless to say, the criteria of inclusion cannot be based on the compiler's familiarity with golf, but on frequency data, which are often difficult to obtain, because of the polysemy of terms (e.g. *bunker*). A specialized corpus of golf in Italian would suit the purpose of establishing an order of representativeness of golf terminology with greater precision.

– Archaisms

Two categories of candidate Anglicisms for exclusion are archaisms and exoticism. Once again, the dividing line between potential inclusions and exclusions is very thin. Archaisms usually refer to cultural products that are no longer in use, have become obsolete or gone out of fashion, although there are many borderline cases of old-fashioned, 'obsolescent', but not completely 'obsolete' words. This area of lexis is dealt with more thoroughly in 6.5.

– Exoticisms

Exotic words imported from distant languages through possible English mediation (mainly Indian and North American) can hardly be considered Anglicisms. In principle, GLAD rejects terms denoting things that belong to a different culture and are clearly not English, such as *curry* (from Tamil), *tandoori* (from Urdu), *chutney* (from Hindi), *pemmican* (from Cree), *sherpa* (from Tibetan), *marijuana* (from Mexican Spanish), *hashish* (from Arabic) and *cannabis* (from Latin). Also the adapted word *pigiama* (partly from Urdu and partly from Persian *pāy-jāma*, via English *pyjamas*) was excluded for not showing any 'Englishness' in form or meaning. Dictionaries can help identify the origin of such exotic words, with some inconsistencies. For example, *curry* (from Tamil) and *lime* (from French and Arabic) are also recorded as 'English' by *Zingarelli 2022*, but they have both been excluded from GLAD. Many names of animals were imported through the mediation of English from distant cultures, starting from the American-Indian one, such as *yak, buffalo,* and *opossum*. A different treatment is offered to words originating in non-English speaking communities, but adopted and integrated into Anglo-American societies, e.g. *canyon* (from Spanish), *kayak* (from Inuit) and *ketchup* (from Chinese and Malay). In these cases, the choice is also corroborated by the presence of derivatives (e.g. *canyoning, kayaking*) and their cultural assimilation (*ketchup* is closely associated with fast food consumption). The cultural dimension is taken into consideration also for 'foreignisms' belonging exclusively to British or American societies, not amenable to transfer into other societies, such as *bobby* (for a policeman) and *public school*, and *totem, tomahawk* and *squaw*, from the world of Native Americans, which are excluded. Yet, some exceptions can be singled out from this category too, for words like *dandy* (and its derivative *dandyismo/dandismo*), *milord, milady, Sir*, which have become well-known to Italians through novels and films.

– Latinisms
Another type worth discussing is that of Latin words which have developed a modern meaning in English and, in turn, transferred it to Italian. A prototypical case is the word *media*, referring to the 'The main means of mass communication, *esp.* newspapers, radio, and television, regarded collectively', as well as 'the reporters, journalists, etc., working for organizations engaged in such communication'. The English etymon *mass media*, in its full form, provides undeniable proof of the status of an Anglicisms for *media* in Italian, as well as its pronunciation which tends to conform to the English one /ˈmiːdɪə/, although many speakers prefer to conform to the Italian spelling pronunciation /ˈmɛdja/, in accordance with the homonymic (and polysemic) Italian word *media*. Another case is that of the word *campus*, carrying the new, modern meaning of university grounds, generally associated with the Anglo-American world, but widely used today in association to other contexts, including Italian academic settings. It may be argued that the gradual assimilation of the word *campus* into non-Anglophone contexts may turn this word into an internationalism, shared by many languages and from a common classical root. A third case of a Latinism, included in GLAD as an Anglicism, is the word *versus*, because of its increased use in scientific and academic writing with the meaning of 'against; in opposition to', also in its abbreviated form *vs*.

Several Latinisms have been temporarily excluded from GLAD, or better, placed under observation. They include *album, aquarium, bonus, forum, premium* and *solarium*, although some of these are recorded as Anglicisms in some of the reference dictionaries. A decisive criterion is the semantic one, as the modern meanings attached to these words do not diverge from the core meanings that they carry, and do not seem to evoke any particular cultural association with the Anglophone world. For example, the word *forum* in Roman times referred to a square where all the important political and economic transactions took place; analogously today a forum is a virtual space for people to exchange ideas on the internet. A *bonus* (from Latin *bonus*, adj. meaning 'good') refers to 'A sum of money or other benefit', expressing a meaning that is very close to the Italian equivalent *buono* (voucher or receipt equivalent to a sum of money), borrowed from French *bon* (from the banking phrase *bon du Trésor*). For this reason, no major semantic innovation seems to be exclusively imported from English. By contrast, when a Latin-derived word is the constituent of a compound, as in *concept album* and *status symbol*, then the lexical item is indeed a fully-fledged component of English vocabulary, and the compounds can be defined as non-adapted borrowings in Italian (not hybrids).

– Interjections

The word class of interjections (including exclamations and onomatopoeia) is quite rich in English items, especially imported through comic books and by the media. They include: *bang, boom, clap, crash, gasp, gulp, sigh, slam, slurp, sniff, sob* and *splash*. Some of these items can also be used as nouns, to denote the action or event that caused the sound or noise. Other interjections have a pragmatic value in discourse, and are used in particular communicative circumstances, e.g. in sport (*break*, in boxing; *out*, in tennis and other sports played on courts); greetings (*bye-bye, goodbye, hello*); various exclamations such as *bingo, cheese* (when taking photographs), *help, hip hip hip urrà, no comment, OK, stop, wow*. Research has recently addressed the phenomenon of pragmatic borrowing, describing multi-word phraseological units like interjections, discourse markers, expletives, vocatives and other constructions which are filtering into European languages (Andersen 2014; Andersen, Furiassi and Mišić 2017), and which are a sign of a more intimate contact between languages and cultures. Some instances of phraseologisms used in Italian are illustrated in 3.7.

## 3.4.2 Adapted

The mechanism of integration of borrowings to the structures of the receiving language becomes formally visible when loanwords are subject to adaptation. This process is an 'active' response of the recipient language to the foreign stimulus. A decisive role is played by speakers – normally unconsciously – and by the system of the recipient language, jointly determining how a given loanwords will be integrated into the domestic environment. In the new language context, the loanword is treated as if it were a domestic element, so that nouns are immediately assigned grammatical gender (masculine or feminine) and class (noun, adjective, verb, etc.) (see 4.1.3). As introduced at the beginning of this chapter, the term integration is used here to refer to the collocation of the loanword in the new linguistic context, and adaptation refers to the actual changes made to the loanword. The two processes are not necessarily an index of assimilation (acceptance) of the Anglicism in the recipient language, that is, a loanword may be very well assimilated into the language without having been adapted at all, as in the case of very common Anglicisms like *film, bar* and *sport*. On the other hand, the Anglicism *serendipità* (from

English *serendipity*)[38] is adapted but not quite assimilated into Italian, as its use is rare and its meaning probably unknown even to educated Italian speakers.

Integration involves several major dimensions, i.e., pronunciation, orthography, morphology and meaning. These dimensions of integration will be dealt with separately in 4.1. In many cases, the degree of formal integration has a strong 'mimetic' power on borrowings, so that their exogenous provenance may no longer be recognizable or even raise doubts about the actual origin of the words, whether borrowings or domestic creations. The Latin factor determines close similarity between the lexicons of English and Italian, thus favouring interlingual identification across vocabularies based on classical etymology and the difficulty to distinguish between borrowings vs autonomous creations. An emblematic example is the Italian word *telefono*, recorded by Rando (1987) as an Anglicism, but it is in fact an international word, made up of neoclassical elements (originally from Greek *tele-* 'afar, far off'+ *phone*, φωνή 'voice, sound'), which could have been created anywhere; in fact, French has *téléphone*, German *Telephon*, Spanish *teléfono*, and so on (see 4.4).

Up to the 19th century, imported Anglicisms were naturally adapted to Italian. Many adapted loanwords dating back to the 18th century belong to old learned vocabulary, and their origin is only traceable on the basis of historical evidence. Examples include Latin-based political terms such as *coalizione, comitato, commissione*, etc. (quoted in 2.2), whose adoption followed a double path from French, via English, or vice versa, from English, via French. As argued before, when Latin etymology is involved, the degree of 'camouflage' into Italian is easily achieved, and the etymon is no longer detectable. A non-Latin root, instead, makes a loanwords recognizable, like for examples the words *scellino* (from shilling), *sterlina* (sterling) and *dollaro* (dollar) as well as *sceriffo* (sheriff), despite their age-old existence in Italian vocabulary as foreignisms.

Another consistent group of adapted loanwords, equally excluded from GLAD because of their high degree of technicality, is the terminology of the hard sciences. In the 18th and 19th century, taxonomies and terminologies of science were created on the basis of Latin and Greek elements, and their spread across European languages was primarily conducted by French and English. This factor has determined large convergence in specialized terminologies and the circulation of 'international words' (cf. 4.4). Selecting the field of 'medicine' and 'English origin' in the electronic

---

**38** Etymology: < *Serendip*, a former name for Sri Lanka + -ITY *suffix*.

A word coined by Horace Walpole, who says (Let. to Mann, 28 Jan. 1754) that he had formed it upon the title of the fairy-tale 'The Three Princes of Serendip', the heroes of which 'were always making discoveries, by accidents and sagacity, of things they were not in quest of'.

'The faculty of making happy and unexpected discoveries by accident. Also, the fact or an instance of such a discovery.' (OED).

edition of the Italian dictionary *Nuovo Devoto-Oli 2022*, 101 lemmas can be extracted, including many adapted terms such as *adrenalina, bruxismo, capacitazione, comorbidità, contraccezione, distale, luetico, motilità, neutracetico, propriocettore, rianimatologia, subliminale*. These examples are characterized by productive suffixes in Italian for the formation of nouns (*-ismo, -azione, -ità, -ologia*) and adjectives (*-ale, -etico*), which create a high degree of 'mimesis' within the Italian language.

Among adapted loanwords dating back to the 19$^{th}$ century and early 20$^{th}$ century, there are *bovindo* (bow window), *bistecca* (beefsteak), *giungla* (jungle), *turista* (tourist), *cip* (chip, in the game of poker), and the obsolescent *tranvia* and *tranvai* (tram, tramway). Modern Anglicisms, borrowed extensively especially as of the second half of the 20$^{th}$ century, tend to keep the same English form. This is due to several factors explored in chapter 2, that is, the prestige of the English language and of the Anglo-American culture, the greater competence in English of Italian speakers, and a tolerant vigilance of Italian linguists and policy-makers. The number of adapted Anglicisms borrowed in recent times is comparatively limited and includes a great variety of derivatives (illustrated in 4.1.3).

Many Anglicisms included in GLAD have Latin-based roots and formal adaptation leaves them practically identical to their etymons. They include: *processore* (processor), *supervisore* (supervisor), *sensore* (sensor), *vegano* (vegan) and *vegetariano* (vegetarian). According to the rules set for GLAD, "internationalisms based on Latin or Greek elements whose English provenance can be determined" should be accepted. In these cases, English-Italian affinity makes it difficult to distinguish adaptations from calques. Klajn argues that words with a classical root or base, also called Anglo-Latinisms (although this term sounds improper, given that these words contain no 'Anglo' elements), should be considered calques (loan translations). By contrast, if words have a root or base that is other than classical, then the words should be classified as adaptations, like the foreignism *dollaro* (dollar). In GLAD's word list the adapted loanword *partenariato* (partnership) complies with this criterion. Given this ambiguity, it is important to underline, once again, that typological distinctions, as well as the origin of borrowings, are complex, controversial matters and often impossible to determine.

## 3.5 False Anglicisms

The category of false Anglicisms reflects a borrowing mechanism whereby the lexical input provided by the donor language (English) is autonomously and creatively reproduced in the recipient language (Italian) for neological purposes. The development of the model, or prototype, gives rise to English-looking words that do not exist in English or, if they do, their meaning is different. In his comprehensive study of false Anglicisms in Italian, Furiassi (2010: 34) defines false Anglicisms as "creations of the Italian language that formally resemble English words but actually do not belong to the English language, e.g. *recordman* instead of *record holder*." For this reason, false Anglicisms are generally not comprehensible to English native speakers and may sound like the result of limited competence in English in the context of the recipient language, creating divergence, instead of convergence, between the two languages in contact. On the other hand, because false Anglicisms formally look like English words, Italian speakers tend to consider them as authentically English. As pointed out in 3.1, Filipović (2000) labelled these items as 'secondary Anglicisms' or 'pseudoanglicism', since they are composed of elements that belong to English but are not part of the English vocabulary.

Delimiting the boundary between real loanwords and pseudo-English ones may depend on different theoretical standpoints and categorizations, as aptly described by Humbley (2015). A comprehensive classification of false Anglicisms in Italian is proposed by Furiassi (2010). In his model, the most productive type of false Anglicism is that of autonomous compounds, consisting of two (or more) English words and generating a new lexical unit with its own independent meaning, which may be more or less transparent with respect to its components. As happens with real compounds, in endocentric ones the meaning is carried by one of the elements, whereas in exocentric ones the meaning is unrelated to its component parts. Thus, the meanings of *infopoint* (information desk) and *pornoshop* (sex shop) can easily be understood by a native speaker of English, even out of context, whereas *bobtail* (old English sheepdog), *hotspot* (carrying two meanings: refugee camp and 'area where a wi-fi connection is available') and *minibar* (trolley service) cannot be understood without a usage context, or even in context. Because in Italian compounds the head element is usually on the left and the modifier on the right (determinatum+determinans), in the creation of false Anglicisms the order of the elements is sometimes reversed, e.g. *agility dog* (dog agility), *film TV* (TV film), *area test* (test area), *banking online* (online banking). The autonomous compounds recorded in GLAD are listed in Table 3.6.

The category of autonomous compounds is considered the 'core' category, as these items do not formally exist in the English language and are indeed independent coinages created in Italian. The term introduced by Humbley (2015) for this particular class of false Anglicisms is 'allogenisms', as they represent neologisms using elements from a different language (from Greek ἄλλος 'different'), as in *babyfoot* ('table football') in French. The new coinage category can indeed be considered 'true' false Anglicisms, since there is no model to be transferred from the donor language, differently from other types that will be described below.

Following Furiassi's classification, the next most numerous types of false Anglicisms are compound ellipses and semantic shifts, whose meaning is much less

**Table 3.6:** False Anglicisms in the form of autonomous compounds (English equivalent in parenthesis).

---

Anti-doping (dope test), aquapark (water park), autocaravan (camper van), autogol (own goal), baby parking (crèche), baby pusher (teenage drug dealer), beauty-farm (beauty centre), block notes (note pad), bobtail (Old English sheepdog), camera car (on-board camera), full optional (fully accessorized), hotspot (refugee camp), infopoint (information desk), job on call (on-call work), luna park (amusement park), minibar (trolley service), no global (anti-globalization), no tax area (tax-free area), no vax (anti-vax), nude-look (see-through), open space (open plan), pornovideo (hard core movie), recordman (record holder), sexy shop (sex shop), skiman (ski coach for professional skiers), smart working (remote work), social card (Italian state welfare benefit), telefilm (tv series), telepass (electronic toll collection system or remote control), telequiz (quiz game).

---

transparent than that of compounds, or totally obscure.[39] In fact, the ellipsis of the compound involves the right-hand element, which is normally the one carrying the core meaning in English, but not in Italian, where the order of the elements is usually the reverse, as pointed out before. Thus, in Italian *dreadlocks* is reduced to *dread*, *camper van* to *camper*, *night club* to *night*, *pole position* to *pole*, and so on, generating misunderstanding for a native speaker of English.

In semantic shifts, a new meaning is attributed to an English word; in other words, a process of resemanticization of an Anglicism is set off. The nature of this shift may be metonymic (the whole meaning is associated to a part), so that, for instance, the term *poker*, besides being the name of a game of cards, is also attributed to the combination of four identical cards (four of a kind), meronymic (the meaning of a part is associated to the whole) in the case of *flipper*[40] (pinball machine), or metaphorical, as in *highlander* (very old, longevous person). The case of *highlander*, popularized by books, television series and films from the 1980s, referring to an immortal warrior, is a recent case of resemanticization, from 'A native or inhabitant of the Scottish Highlands' to jokingly describe an immortal creature (although this acceptation is not yet recorded by any English or Italian dictionary and is thus a potential neologism).

In the category of semantic shifts, the productive success of the words *box* and *ticket* in Italian is worth discussing. Contrary to the fact that Anglicisms undergo semantic narrowing with respect to their etymons, in these two cases there is a productive development of new meanings. *Box*, in fact, is used in Italian to name

---

[39] These three main types of false Anglicisms are also recognized by Gottlieb for Danish, although his terminology is slightly different: clippings (for compound ellipses), recombinations (for autonomous compounds) and neo-semantization (for semantic shifts) (Gottlieb 2015).
[40] Flippers are the wing-shaped mechanisms that are used to push the ball inside a pinball machine.

various things that have a box-like shape, starting from a garage (cf. the hybrid *box auto*), a cubicle in open plan offices, a cage for animals, a container for books, CDs or DVDs, the pits in car racing, an information booth, a playpen for children, and a shower cubicle (cf. the hybrid *box doccia*). None of these meanings is present in the English language, despite the high polysemy of box. The word *ticket* has also enjoyed a particular success in Italian, though its initial association was with 'a tax to pay to access state healthcare services'; *ticket* also denotes 'any receipt that you obtain when paying a toll' (e.g. in car parks) and 'a meal voucher'. Note that Ticket Restaurant® is the name of a company handling meal vouchers; through the process of eponymy, *ticket restaurant* is also used generically to refer to the actual coupon used to pay for one's lunch. So, the origin of ticket with the meaning of 'meal voucher' derives from the ellipsis of ticket restaurant.[41] Compound ellipses and semantic shifts included in GLAD are listed in Table 3.7:

**Table 3.7:** False Anglicisms in the form of compound ellipses and semantic shifts.

| |
| --- |
| Compound ellipses: account (account executive), automotive (automotive industry), basket (basketball), boxer (boxer shorts), camper (camper van), custom (custom bike), disco (disco music), disco (disco dance), discount (discount supermarket), dread (dreadlocks), duty free (duty-free shop), full (poker: full house), holding (holding company), home (home page), junior (junior suite), master (master copy), night (night club), offshore (offshore boat), offshore (offshore racing), optional (optional equipment in cars), oscar (oscar winner), outlet (factory outlet), pole (pole position), scotch (scotch tape), screen (screenshot), social (social media), step (step aerobics), stop-and-go (stop-go penalty), surf (surfboard), talk (talk show), trolley (trolley suitcase), volley (volleyball). |
| Semantic shift: blob (satirical TV programme made up of clips), body (bodysuit), bomber (football: striker), box (garage), box (cubicle in open plan offices), box (cage for animals), box (container for books or CDs), box (playpen for children), box (shower cubicle), corner (corner kick), escort (call-girl), fiction (tv serial), flipper (pinball machine), ginger (soft drink), golf (sweater), highlander (very old, longevous person), mister (coach, trainer), navigator (a worker in the Italian national job finding agency), pile (fleece jacket), poker (poker: four of a kind), residence (apartment hotel), slip (panties), slip (swimming trunks), spider (two-seater), testimonial (the face of an advertising campaign, spokesperson), ticket (tax for healthcare), ticket (meal voucher), ticket (receipt), tilt (temporary mulfunctioning). |

The three types of English-induced neological creations and their formation mechanisms discussed so far are identified in many other European languages (Furiassi and Gottlieb 2015). However, not all linguists agree on their status or wonder

---

**41** Another quite common meaning of *ticket* in Italian, although not yet recorded by dictionaries, is that of 'online request for support to an administration'. In Italian 'aprire un ticket', literally 'to open a ticket', means 'to send a request for support to an administration'.

whether they are real borrowings, in the absense of a model to imitate. Onysko (2007), for example, recognizes as false Anglicisms only the combination of separate English words to create a new word in the recipient languages (e.g. record+man < recordman), but considers morphological and semantic changes, like the clipping of *happy end* from *happy ending* and the new meaning attributed to *handy* (mobile phone in German),[42] as forms of adaptation of already existing Anglicisms. Beside the status of these autonomous creations, also their origin is a matter of debate among linguists. Undoubtedly, false Anglicisms are made up of English words that were previously borrowed. What happens during the process of neological creation is the intriguing side of the question, but we may argue that multiple mechanisms may be responsible. For example, the clipping of *happy end* from *happy ending* may have been caused by analogy with the Italian equivalent *lieto fine*, which verbatim translates *happy end*. Another example is the use of *mister* to refer to a sports coach or trainer. In this case the use of this term of address followed by a surname may have led to the association of *mister* to this professional role when the surname of the person was unknown or not remembered. In other cases, the origin of the false Anglicism may be connected to the boosting effect of the media. For example, the word *blob*, similar to *highlander* described above, arrived through the name of an American science fiction horror film (called 'The Blob'), and gave the name to a satirical tv programme that mixes images, sounds and words, thus creating a chaotic effect; hence the generic use of *blob*. To sum up, from a diachronic perspective, Humbley argues that in the case of clippings and semantic shifts,

> [t]he change has generally taken place in the post integrative phase, either by abbreviating the loanword in some way or through some semantic evolution taking place in the target language or in the source language (or in both). (Humbley 2015: 39)

Although they form a small percentage of all types of borrowings (about 7–10% of direct borrowings in GLAD's Italian word list), false Anglicisms represent a long-standing and particularly interesting phenomenon, attested across European languages (Filipović 1985; Balteiro and Campos 2012; Bagasheva and Renner 2015; Renner & Fernández-Domínguez 2015), which is likely to increase, as the influence of English continues to intensify. In fact, the creation of false Anglicisms is a growing phenomenon, and sometimes the same false Anglicisms circulate across languages, like the word *footing* (jogging), coined in French and then handed over

---

**42** Onysko (2007) argues that *handy* differs from English not only in meaning but also in grammatical class, shifting from adjective to noun (zero-conversion). The origin of *handy* in German is intriguing, as it may be related to the 'handiness' of this device or from the clipping of 'handheld' or 'handset'.

to Italian, and *happy end*, which is also used in German. This fact may ease intercomprehension among non-native speakers, excluding native speakers of English. Nevertheless, some types of deviation from the original etymon is often not so great as to completely obscure the meanings of false Anglicisms to a native speaker of English. For example, *happy end* (happy ending) and *face lifting* (face lift) can easily be understood in the appropriate context. In addition, some false Anglicisms may be successfully re-borrowed by English and turned into real English words. An example is the case of *Slow Food*, the name of a non-profit Italian organization promoting local cuisine and fresh ingredients, which successfully spread to other languages and back to English, as quoted by the OED: 'A movement, originating in Italy, which aims to preserve local culinary traditions and agricultural biodiversity'.[43] Another example is the word *beauty-case*, an often-quoted instance of a prototypical false Anglicism, whose typological status is in fact dubious. Though this object is called *vanity case* in English, an online search of *beauty-case* yields thousands of results, along with a variety of synonyms such as *cosmetic case, beauty box* and *make-up box*. More solid evidence comes from the OED, quoting *beauty case* from Harrods Christmas Catalogue in 1968, and from the Macquaire Dictionary, which has an entry for *beauty case* (cross-referenced to *vanity case*). For these reasons, *beauty-case* is not recorded as a false Anglicism in GLAD (only *beauty* as a clipped form of *beauty-case*). Another interesting example of an Italian creation which could be re-borrowed by English is *smart working*, which spread in Italy during the COVID-19 pandemic in 2020, referring to 'working from home'. This phrase has already been shortened in English into WFH,[44] recorded by the OED both as noun and as verb in April 2020. *Smart working* was criticized by Italian academics and substituted by 'lavoro agile' (agile work), but its success has hardly receded. It also started to be used in the international press, with reference to Italy, at least for the time being, but in the course of time it may be assimilated into English use, being much more expressive than WFH.

The coinage of false Anglicisms can be realized through other word-formation processes, though less productive than the ones described so far. Autonomous derivatives (Table 3.8) are created by the addition of the de-verbal suffix *-ing*, which is exploited in English to describe actions and activities. The suffix *-ing* appears to be semantically loaded for this descriptive function also in Italian, perhaps due to

---

[43] According to Furiassi and Gottlieb (2015: 17) the word *slow food* should be categorized, rather than as an Italianism, as an 'exogenous English coinage', i.e. a neologism created outside the Anglophone world but of wider circulation, including in the Anglophone world.
[44] Work From Home.

its long-standing presence in the warning sign 'No smoking'.[45] Therefore it has been attached to bases for the same purpose, thus yielding the forms *camping* (camp site), *dancing* (dance hall), *parking* (car park), and the more recent neologisms *lifting* (facelift), *living* (living room) and *outing* (coming out). Another English suffix which seems to have acquired currency is *-er*, denoting the agent of an action, not only in bona fide Anglicisms, but also in false Anglicisms such as *bomber* (sport: striker) and *stopper* (sport: sweeper). The reverse happens with clippings, where affixes are eliminated, as in *anti-age* (anti-aging), *fashion* (fashionable), *flirt* (flirtation), *relax* (relaxation), *snob* (snobbish), *mail* (e-mail), also causing a shift of grammatical class, from noun to adjective in *fashion* and in *snob*, and from verb to noun for *relax*. Finally, generic trademarks and brandnames (eponyms) can become false Anglicisms, like *autogrill* (motorway restaurant), *canadair* (water bomber), *k-way* (cagoule or kagool), and *scottex* (paper towel).

**Table 3.8:** False Anglicisms in the form of autonomous derivatives, clippings and eponyms.

| |
|---|
| Autonomous derivatives: bomber (sport: striker), camping (camp site), dancing (dance hall) (also ellipsis of dancing-hall), lifting (facelift), living (living room), outing (coming out), parking (car park), stopper (sport: sweeper). |
| Clippings: anti-age (anti-aging), fashion (fashionable, also change of class), flirt (flirtation, also semantic shift), happy end (happy ending), relax (relaxation), mail (e-mail), snob (snobbish), windsurf (windsurfing). |
| Eponyms: autogrill (motorway restaurant), canadair (water bomber), k-way (cagoule), scottex (paper towel), pullman (bus), montgomery (duffle coat). |

## 3.6 Hybrids

Hybrid creations are made up of an English and an Italian word joined together to form a multi-word unit. This category poses several questions regarding their description and nature as borrowings. Haugen (1950), for example, draws a distinction between loanblends and hybrid creations. A loanblend is a hybrid that reproduces an English model, such as *sito web* in Italian, which is modelled on *website*. By contrast, a hybrid creation is a frequent combination (in corpus linguistics, a collocation) of an English word and an Italian one, independent from an English model. Examples of hybrid creations are the already mentioned false Anglicisms *box doccia*

---

**45** Quite a few Anglicisms with nominal ending *-ing* exist in Italian (*briefing, shopping, messaging, restyling*). They appear to be increasing in the name of sports activities like *pressing, dribbling, jogging, diving, base jumping, bungee jumping*, etc.

and *box auto*, which exploit the loanword *box* to form a brand-new pattern, semantically unrelated to the donor language. It is clear that the latter is indeed an open-ended category, as many English loanwords could be attached to Italian words, if needs be.

The category of hybrids 'proper' or loanblends, which are traceable to an English model, represents the large majority of items collected so far for GLAD's word list and are mostly nouns. The first observation is that from a typological perspective, "a hybrid compound following an English model is not the result of direct lexical transfer (borrowing) but is based on lexical creation by means of partial translation." (Onysko, 2007: 56). In other words, the borrowing process may start from the adoption of the English compound and continue with the translation of one of the constituent elements; if such is the case, then these patterns could be categorized as semi-calques.

Some examples of hybrids are based on the N+N combination, modelled on the Germanic pattern, with the head element on the right, which is very productive in Italian (Grossman and Reiner 2004), such as *clown terapia* and *laserterapia*. It is worth noting that the orthographic form of hybrid borrowings is often unstable, swinging between a solid word or two-word forms, hyphenated or not. Furthermore, the option to translate is sometimes open in the case of look-alike equivalents. In *clown terapia* and *laserterapia* the Italian constituent is preferred, whereas in *pet therapy*, which is a non-adapted Anglicism, the English constituent is preferred (normally with the Italianized pronounciation ['tɛrapi]). A reverse sequence in the order of the compound constituents, with the head on the left (modelled on the Romance pattern), which is equally common, is found in *tennis tavolo* (table tennis), *sito web* (website), *tv color* (colour TV), and *rock duro* (hard rock).

In between compounds and free combinations are the compounds *internet mania* and *web radio*, whose status as hybrids depends on whether *mania* and *radio* are considered Italian or English words, since they are homonymous. In these cases, their pronunciation identifies *mania* [ma'nia] and *radio* ['radjo] as Italian words. A similar problem (mentioned in 3.4.1) arises from the words *concept album*, *status symbol* and *naziskin*, which were initially classified as hybrids, but later moved to the category of non-adapted Anglicisms, despite the fact that *album*, *status* (from Latin) and *nazi* (from German) are considered Italian words and also pronounced accordingly. However, given that these compounds appear to be fully lexicalized in English, they are treated as English lexical units, a criterion that was also adopted for homonymous combining forms like *video-*, *super-*, and *multi-*, when combined with an English element. These examples show how slippery the typological classification of borrowing can be and how necessary it is to examine the historical dimension and the structure of words in order to shed light on the possible steps taken from the donor to the recipient language.

A productive area of compounding is characterized by the use of combining forms, mostly of neo-classical origin (discussed in 3.4.1). Some combining forms are identical in Italian and in English, but a few are borrowed in their anglicized form, like *cyber-*, which coexists with Italian *ciber-*, giving rise to many compounds containing either or both forms (e.g. cybercafé /cibercafé). The pronunciation of *cyber/ciber* may be similar to the English one ['saɪbə(r)] or phonetically adapted to Italian ['tʃiber].[46] In the absence of clear directions from linguists, everyday use in the media swings from one form to another, and from hybrids to loanwords, i.e., *cybercrime* and *cybercrimine, cybersecurity* and *cybersicurezza, cyberspace* and *cyberspazio*. In other cases only the hybrid is preferred, as in *cyber terrorismo* and *cyberbullismo*.[47] Another combining form which appears alternatively in its Italian or English forms is *foto-*, which is prevalent with respect to *photo-*, giving rise to the hybrids *fotoblog, fotofinish* (also foto-finish, foto finish), *fotofit* (also photofit), *fotogallery* (also foto gallery), *fotokit* (also photokit) and *fotoreporter*. Other hybrid borrowings with combining forms are *elettroshock* (electroshock), *termoscanner* (thermal scanner) and *eurobond* (pronounced [ˌɛuroˈbɔnd]).

If we turn to large corpora and search for frequent combinations (collocations), the number of results may indeed be very large, as already pointed out in 3.4.1 with reference to the word *web* in combination with both English and Italian elements. A similar search of *web* as the modifier of an Italian element gives rise to many combinations, such as *pagina web, portale web, spazio web, piattaforma web, applicazione web, indirizzo web, servizio web, interfaccia web* and so on, and can possibly be matched with plausible equivalent English combinations, i.e., *web page, web portal, web space, web platform, web application, web address, web service, web interface*, and so on. Normally, only stable, fully lexicalized compounds are recorded in dictionaries in the cases of such productive combinations. For example, the OED has an entry for *web* in attributive use (with reference to the World Wide Web), listing some combinations like *web address*, and has independent entries for several compounds, including *web app, web page* and *web portal*.

---

[46] In the corpus Italian Web 2020, quite a few compound with both *cyber-* and *ciber-* have been retrieved. With *cyber-* the most frequent ones are: *cyberpunk, cyberbullismo, cyberspazio, cybercrime, cybersecurity, cybercriminali, cyberspace, cybernauti, cybersquatting* [. . .]. With *ciber-* the most frequent compounds are: *cibernetico, ciberspazio, cibernetica, cibernauti, cibernauta, cibercriminalità, ciberneticamente, cibercultura, cibersicurezza* [. . .] (Pulcini 2020b).

[47] The *Accademia della Crusca* recommended that the Italian form *ciber-* should be used in official government documents. With reference to a law on 'cybersicurezza' passed in Italy in 2019, the Accademia pointed out that a hybrid term poses terminological problems and also difficulty in pronunciation. A note in favour of *ciber-* with respect to *cyber-* had already been issued by the Accademia in 2018. In fact, these recommendations have no power to influence political decisions.

Another search for hybrids containing the Italian word *musica* in Italian Web 2016 has yielded a long list of combinations with all the music genres of British and American origin, including *pop, folk, house, techno, rock, jazz, dance, country, reggae, rap, soul, blues, gospel, black, disco, hip hop, swing, funky, ska, fusion, surf, dub, west coast, gypsy,* and *chill out.* These results lead us to conclude that corpora can really offer a huge amount of vocabulary in use, but the retrieval of candidate Anglicisms is only the first step of the lexicographic collection, and accurate verification of the stability and assimilation of a borrowed pattern should follow. As for the category of compounds, it may be advisable to focus only on the patterns that have developed independent meanings, or have achieved stability in general use, leaving out the potentially unlimited stock of independent creations.

## 3.7 Phraseologisms and pragmatic Anglicisms

Both direct and indirect borrowing can be lexical or phrasal, that is, they can be a single word or a multi-word unit (cf. Figure 3.1). As far as multi-word units are concerned, in this chapter the focus has been mainly on types of compounds and lexical collocations, their orthographic form and meaning. In GLAD, grammatical labels are given to lexical units on the basis of the most frequent grammatical functions that they perform in the reference data, irrespective of their pattern, be it simple or phrasal. For example, the compound *self-service* has two separate entries, one for the noun class and the other for the adjective class, since these uses are quite frequent in the archives and corpora referred to for the selection of GLAD's macrostructure. The set of POS (part-of-speech) tags adopted for GLAD is pretty narrow, and includes nouns, adjectives, verbs, adverbs, interjections and 'other', a label that includes types of phraseological units. These can be defined as "ready-made–phrase-like or sentence-like–expressions having semantic and syntactic stability, which play idiomatic, pragmatic and morphosyntactic functions in language" (Pulcini, Furiassi and Rodríguez González 2012: 13). In this section we will look more closely at phrasal types of borrowings, starting from multi-word units (three or more elements) and then moving on to Anglicisms that have a dominant communicative function (pragmatic or discursive) in language use rather than a grammatical (or propositional) one.

According to Granger and Paquot (2008), phraseological units (also called phraseologisms or phrasemes) can be grouped into three main categories, i.e., referential, textual and communicative. Referential phraseologisms denote real objects and phenomena, and include (lexical) collocations, compounds and binomials. Textual phraseologisms have the role of organizing a spoken or written text, providing textual fragments, inserts and formulae. Communicative phraseologisms belong to the expressive side of discourse, allowing speakers to interact with other speakers and perform specific speech acts (Pulcini 2020a).[48]

The class of referential phraseologisms is the largest and includes all the two-word compounds and collocations analyzed in the previous sections. In addition, there are other types of compounding patterns displaying a variety of different forms and orthographic variants (only the most common is given below) which have been grouped into the following types:

– Multi-word compounds, made up of three or more components; they can take different grammatical roles in language use, mainly nouns and adjectives. Examples: *all you can eat* (adjective), *chief executive officer* (noun), *duty-free shop* (noun), *self-made man* (noun), *break even point* (noun), *extra-extra-large* (adjective, noun), *extra-extra-small* (adjective, noun), *fai da te* (noun),[49] *goal line technology* (noun), *management buy-out* (noun), *one-man band* (noun), *one-man show* (noun), *one-woman show* (noun), *print on-demand* (noun), *self-made man* (noun), *self-made woman* (noun), *sense of humour* (noun), *set-top-box* (noun), *social media manager* (noun), *social media marketing* (noun), *video on-demand* (noun), *way of life* (noun)
– Binomials are a fairly large category of phraseological borrowings in Italian. They are made up of two lexical elements belonging to the same word class (usually nouns), linked together by the conjunction 'and', which gives them a rhythmic pattern. The sequence of the constituent elements is normally irreversible. Examples: *bed and breakfast* (noun), *gin tonic* (noun; adapted from *gin and tonic*), *cash-and-carry* (noun), *drum 'n' bass* (adjective, noun), *fly and drive* (adjective, noun; false Anglicism from *fly-drive*), *rhythm and blues* (adjective, noun), *pick and roll* (noun), *plug and play* (adjective, noun), *rock and roll* (adjective, noun), *stop-and-go* (noun) (false Anglicism from s*top-go penalty*)
– x + to + x pattern: *business to business* (B2B) (noun), *door-to-door* (adjective), *faccia a faccia* (adjective, noun),[50] *coast to coast* (adverb), *one-to-one* (adjective)
– x + to + y pattern: *business to consumer* (B2C) (noun), *ready-to-wear* (adjective, noun), *up to date* (adjective)
– Particle+noun: *on the rocks* (adjective, adverb), *on the road* (adjective, adverb, noun)
– x + per + y: *pay per use* (noun, adjective), *pay per view* (noun, adjective)

---

**48** The types of phrasemes identified by Granger and Paquot (2008: 42) are much wider than the ones described in this section, which is limited to the phrasal Anglicisms used in Italian and recorded in GLAD.
**49** Loan translation of *do-it-yourself*.
**50** Loan translation of *face to face*.

- x + by + x: *day by day* (adjective), *step by step* (adverb)
- Possessive patterns: *gentleman's agreement* (noun), *director's cut* (noun)

The category of phraseological units that have a textual function includes a range of textual connectors and sentence stems. Only a few instances of this type can be identified among English borrowings, and this indicates that the influence of English has not (yet) penetrated into the structure of Italian much beyond the lexical level. The examples collected possibly originate from the use of English as an international carrier of popular culture and are spread through the spoken and written channels of communication, nowadays especially through the mass and social media.

- *(the) best of* is a phrase that can be seen in the title of CDs, compilation or other collection of songs or works by a particular artist.
- *(and) the winner is* . . . comes from the world of entertainment. This expression is likely to sound very familiar to any Italian, even with little competence in English. In fact, scenes from international events or awarding prizes like the Oscar Award or the Golden Globe are often broadcast on national televisions or reported in the news media all over the world. This phrase introduces the moment of greatest emotional suspense, followed by the enthusiasm that accompanies the disclosure of the winning artist. It can also be used for events of minor importance, even jokingly, to give an international touch to a public event.
- *last but not least* is a routine expression which can be used with a linking function in spoken discourse, especially on a public occasion, to introduce the last participant in an event, the last name on a list, or the last item in a sequence, and the like. It conveys a light-hearted tone and strategic politeness on the part of the speaker.
- *Welcome (to)* can be used as a direct welcoming expression in a variety of situations but can also feature in adverts, titles and notices of various types. It can also convey sarcasm or pessimism, when used to introduce a negative situation or express disappointment, e.g. *Welcome to Naples* (in an article describing the dreariness of the town in the eyes of tourists – la Repubblica 12 August 2021).
- *made in* . . . is the international wording found on packaged products to indicate their origin and is normally followed by the name of the country of origin. The phrase *made in Italy*, which can be used in subject or modifying function ( i.e., as a noun and an adjective) denotes the Italian domestic products for the export market, especially in the field of fashion.
- *Care of* (shortened into c/o) is an old formula used in written correspondence for the address of a letter or package. The GDU dates its adoption into Italian in 1955.

- *Keep calm and . . .* can be seen on billboards or printed on t-shirts. It is a commonplace expression which was initially launched as a motivational poster by the British government before the Second World War (Keep calm and carry on). The characteristic design of this poster, headed by the British crown, bright colours and large capital letters, was subsequently exploited for commercial purposes, and for a variety of public messages with political, social or humorous intent.

The type of phraseological units that have a communicative function include routine formulae such as greetings, warnings and complete sentences that have become familiar to Italians through various channels of popular culture. Except for *hip hip hip urrà*, which is orthographically integrated, all the quoted examples can be inserted into Italian and therefore they represent instances of code-switching.

- *bye, bye-bye, hello, goodbye* are common greetings in English which are widely known to Italians, because they are elementary expressions and are also repeatedly heard in songs and films.
- *No smoking* is a warning sign internationally used to signal that smoking is prohibited in a particular area.
- *No problem, no comment*: these expressions are fairly transparent to Italians, semantically and pragmatically, given the similarity with equivalent Italian words (*nessun problema, nessun commento*).
- *Game over* is a message in videogames, announcing that all the attempts have been exhausted. The end of the game often corresponds to the death of the player or hero. Figuratively, this expression can be used in any challenging situation which has no way out.
- *Mission impossible* (discussed in 4.1.4) comes from the U.S. television series, first broadcast in 1966. It can be used to comment on any target that is out of reach.
- *Business is business* is a commonplace expressing the popular truth that economic advantage should prevail over personal reasons.
- *The show must go on* is a commonplace expression coined in the world of show business, meaning that an activity must continue as planned not to let anybody down (the audience or the patrons), even in negative circumstances. Figuratively it can be extended to many real-life situations. It is quite current in the common language as the title of famous songs.
- *Dammi un cinque* is a translation of the English expression Give me five or High five!, of African-American origin, which is an invitation to slap somebody's open hand against yours, an act of greeting or a sign of congratulations. Its possible transfer is through situation comedies and films featuring these gestures and accompanying exclamations.

– *hip hip hip urrà* (also *urrah*) is an adapted exclamation (from *hip hip hooray*),[51] used in Italian with the same communicative value of collective cheerfulness, as in English. The degree of partial integration indicates that this expression has been integrated into Italian and is therefore not an instance of code-switching.

The use of lexical items which have a pragmatic function in social interactions is a sign of a more intimate contact between the donor and the recipient language. This phenomenon has started to emerge within speech communities where the status of English has gradually shifted from foreign to second language (e.g. Denmark, Norway and other Nordic countries). A body of research on pragmatic borrowings has shown that this type of influence has taken place for some time in many European languages and is attracting scholarly attention (Andersen 2014; Andersen, Furiassi and Mišić Ilić 2017; Furiassi 2018; Gottlieb 2020). In Italian this phenomenon is still limited but is likely to grow, as the number of competent speakers increases and spoken English becomes available through broadcasting in the original language.

Anglicisms with a pragmatic function does not only include phraseologisms, but also interjections, discourse markers, vocatives and other constructions. The word class of interjections (cf. 3.4.1) includes quite a few English items, which have been popularized especially in comic books for their onomatopeic values (e.g. *gasp, gulp, slurp, sob*), each communicating a particular feeling, and exclamations, e.g. *okay, wow, bingo, help, stop, cheese* (when taking photographs). Other interjections are used in sport (e.g. *break*, in boxing; *out*, in tennis and other sports played in courts).

Research in the field of English-induced phraseology, both as Anglicisms and loan translations, has also focussed on catch-phrases, cliché expressions and proverbs in languages other than Italian, namely French (Marti-Solano 2012), in Spanish (Oncins-Martínez 2012), in German (Fiedler 2012; 2017), in Dutch (Zenner, Speelman and Geeraerts 2012) and in Croatian (Fabijanić and Štrmelj 2016).

---

**51** The etymons of *urrà* are both French *hourra* and English *hurrah* (interjection and noun, also *hurray*), probably adapted from the interjection *huzza*, a cry of British sailors. According to *Nuovo Devoto-Oli 2022*, English *huzza* in turn is an adaptation of *hissa* (issa), of uncertain etymology. In the OED, the etymology of *hurray* is described as follows: 'A later substitute for HUZZA *int.* and *n.* (not in Johnson, Ash, Walker; in Todd 1818), perhaps merely due to onomatopoeic modification, but possibly influenced by some foreign shouts: compare Swedish, Danish, Low German *hurra!*, Dutch *hoera!*, Russian *ura!* whence French *houra*; French *hourra* is from English. Middle High German had *hurr, hurrâ*, as interjections representing rapid whirring motion (compare *hurren* to rush), whence also a shout used in chasing. According to Moriz Heyne in Grimm, *hurrah* was the battle-cry of the Prussian soldiers in the War of Liberation (1812–13), and has since been a favourite cry of soldiers and sailors, and of exultation. In English the form *hurrah* is literary and dignified; *hooray* is usual in popular acclamation.'

Establishing the provenance of phraseological units may be controversial or difficult, as European languages share a large number of phraseologisms which derived from the Bible, classical authors or world literature. For example, the idiomatic expression *essere nella stessa barca* (meaning to be in the same difficult circumstances), which corresponds to English *to be in the same boat*, dates back to the Roman philosopher Cicero and other authors of classical times, but the Spanish translation *estar en el mismo barco* is quoted as from English (example given by Marti-Solano 2012). It follows that accurate historical investigation is necessary to trace the origin of paronymic expressions across European languages, to avoid attributing to English the provenance of international expressions which have originated from other or multiple sources. This is a vast area of cross-linguistic investigation that goes beyond the scope of the present analysis. Yet, nowadays many English slogans and catch-phrases circulate through audio and printed advertisements, television and cinema, and populate the urban landscapes of Italian towns, though their success may last for a short time (cf. 6.6).

## 3.8 Roundup

In this chapter, the goal was to offer a systematic review of the relevant terminology and of the typology of lexical borrowings for the description of Anglicisms in Italian, drawing on the literature of language contact and borrowing between English and European languages. The reference data for the illustration of types of borrowings are the selected entries (and rejected candidates) for the Italian component of GLAD, a multilingual repository of Anglicisms in European and extra-European languages. Contextually, a lexicographic method was introduced for the construction of a specialized database of this kind, with its own criteria of inclusion and exclusion with respect to the many types of lexical outcomes that the influence of English can trigger. An aspect worth considering is that lexical borrowing is not a straight, one-way process, from English into Italian, since words may have been transferred by multiple routes (especially from French in the case of Italian), or have originated in other languages, as in the case of 'anglicized' exoticisms.

The type of borrowings described in this chapter is that of direct borrowings and in particular the largest category of non-adapted loanwords. Formally, loanwords remain recognizably English, whether they are non-adapted or adapted to the system of Italian, and therefore can be easily recognized by Italian speakers. Besides one-word Anglicisms, the category of compounds is very productive (displaying variable orthographic forms), especially the ones containing combining forms. Hybrid neological combinations of Italian and English words are potentially very productive. The category of abbreviations, including acronyms, clippings and blends, is also quite rich. Other types of non-adapted Anglicisms such as eponyms, exoticisms, and archaisms are less numerous and their status as Anglicisms may be controversial. Other phenomena at work within the recipient language is the neological creation of false Anglicisms, whose origin can be the result of formal or semantic exploitation of English models and hybrid forms, which are potentially unlimited. A few instances of phraseologisms are being assimilated into Italian, but their number is still limited and their function seems to be that of code-switchings rather than real borrowings.

# 4 Integration and indirect borrowings

## 4.1 Integration

Integration is defined as the positioning of the loanword within the new linguistic and semantic environment of the recipient language. Adaptation consists in changing the formal appearance of a loanword according to the orthographic, phonological and morpho-syntactic rules of the recipient language. Integration and adaptation are two related phenomena. As explained by Filipović, "an anglicism is a word borrowed from English which in the course of the transfer is adapted to the receiving language in order to be integrated into its linguistic system" (Filipović 2000: 205)

Phonological integration affects the pronunciation of non-adapted Anglicisms, since adapted and indirect loanwords have an Italian form and pronunciation. Orthographic and morphological integration applies to adapted Anglicisms, affecting their formal appearance. Regarding the morphological treatment of borrowings, Klajn (1972) distinguishes between functional and formal integration (which he calls 'assimilation'). Functional integration is limited to the assignment of grammatical class and gender to Anglicisms, both non-adapted and adapted. Formal integration involves the substitution of domestic morphemes (*-ist* into *-ista*, turning *tourist* into *turista*) or addition of domestic morphemes to create derivatives (*-ista* added to *golf*, to obtain *golfista*, i.e., golfer) in order to adapt the Anglicisms to the structures of Italian. Semantic integration has an effect on all types of borrowings, assigning the same or a new meaning or sense to the Anglicism, according to specific denotative or expressive needs. These dimensions of integration of Anglicisms into the Italian language will be analyzed in the following sections (Bisetto 2004).

### 4.1.1 Orthographic

The English alphabet contains graphemes that are not part of the Italian alphabet, i.e., j, k, w, x and y.[52] The spelling of Anglicisms can be adapted to Italian by substituting these foreign graphemes with the nearest Italian ones, as in *iarda* (yard),

---

[52] The graphemes x, k, y existed in Latin, although marginally used, but were gradually abandoned, as well as the digraphs ph, th, ch of Greek origin (substituted by f, t, c). The same happened to j, used in Latin as a graphic variant of i, which was maintained throughout the 17th and 18th centuries for its semivowel value /j/, but then gradually abandoned. Now j is still used in some words such as 'Jugoslavia' (Yugoslavia). The graphemes j, k, w, x, y, which were gradually lost in the course of the centuries, are now used in foreign words. The grapheme j has acquired the English sound value /dʒ/ even in Latin words such as *junior* [ˈdʒuːnjə(r)] instead of [ˈjunjor],

*folclore* (folklore), *vagone* (wagon), *clacson* (klaxon),[53] *ciclocross* (cyclocross). The English spelling may prevail but alternate with the Italian one in *cybernauta /cibernauta* (cybernaut) and *nylon /nailon* (nylon).

Orthographic simplification takes place in *gol* (*goal*, also in *golden gol* for *golden goal*), reflecting the Italian pronunciation with a clear vowel [gɔl] rather than a diphthong [gəʊl]; in *bermuda* (considered in Italian as a single piece of clothing, and therefore a singular noun) for *bermudas* or *bermuda shorts*; and in *gin tonic* for *gin and tonic*. The exclamation *hip hip hip urrà* (hip hip hooray) reproduces the pronunciation of the last element eliminating the <h>, which is in fact never aspirated in Italian; the same happens in *tecnostress* (technostress). The combining element *moto-* (short for Italian *motore*) replaces *motor-* in *motoscooter* (motor scooter), to simplify the pronunciation of three consecutive consonants, unusual for Italian (but not in *motorcaravan, motorhome* and *motoryacht*). The Italian combining form *porno-* replaces English *porn-* in *pornostar* (pornstar) and the prefix *no-* is used (*no profit*) when in English *non-* would be preferred (non profit), generating several domestic creations in Italian (see false Anglicisms in 3.5). The digraph <ph> is realized as the Italian grapheme <f>, following its pronunciation, as in *nomofobia* (nomophobia) and especially in compounds with *photo-* such as *fotofinish, fotofit* (but also *photofit*), *fotogallery*, but not in *phishing, phone banking* and *phone center*.

Other cases of orthographic simplification include derivatives from proper names, e.g. *scespiriano* (also *shakespeariano* for *Shakespearian*), adapted to a form that is more easily read and pronounced by Italian speakers (the adapted form is recorded by the Italian reference dictionaries). A derivative adjective that has undergone a similar type of orthographic simplification to facilitate pronunciation is *claunesco* (also *clownesco*), for *clownish*.

The influence of French mediation for the transfer of Anglicisms is evident both in spelling and in pronunciation, for example, in the words *choc, confort* and *cachemire* (French spelling) and *shock, comfort* and *cashmere* (English spelling), since Italian received these loans from both sources.

---

though the latter is still widely used in Italian. The number of words beginning with h has increased, as well as typically English consonant clusters such as th (*thriller*), sh (*shampoo*), rtn (*partner*), ngst (*gangster*). The grapheme w and y have become fashionable in Christian names like William, Tony, and Mery (spelled with e [ɛ], according to its pronunciation). The grapheme k is often used in adverts and political slogans because of its polarizing power (e.g. *okkupazione* instead of *occupazione*, 'occupation').

53 'Etymology: Name of the manufacturing company. Originally *U.S.* An (electric) horn or warning hooter, originally one on a motor vehicle. Also *klaxon-horn*.' (OED).

As far as hyphenation is concerned, there are no specific rules for the orthography of compound nouns in the English language. As explained by Bauer (1988), two elements are joined together when they are the result of a morphological process, as in *baseball*, which also takes one single stress, whereas the elements remain separate and are individually accented when the compound derives from a syntactic process, that is, a modifying element is joined to a head, as in *base jumping*. No particular rules exist for hyphenation, as confirmed by Bauer (1988: 101)

> [. . .] it is worth making the point that hyphenation in English is totally random, and does not necessarily prove anything at all about the linguistic status of strings of elements.

In GLAD the reference orthography for the English etymons is the first one recorded by the OED. The orthographic form recorded for Italian Anglicisms is the most representative found in the newspaper archive. All candidate compounds are checked in the three possible forms, namely a solid word, a hyphenated word and two separate words, and all frequent variants are recorded. In many cases only one form is prevalent, i.e., there is consensus between the form of the Anglicism and its source word, e.g. *benchmark, check-point* and *social media*. In other cases there is no consensus on the most frequent form, e.g. *selfie stick* (Anglicism) vs *selfie-stick* (English etymon). When frequent, spelling variants are indicated for Anglicisms. Table 4.1 displays some examples of same or different spellings. It can be noted that English tends to hyphenate adjectives (all-inclusive, knock-down) or compact phrases (all-you-can-eat), but this should be taken as a tendency rather than a rule.

**Table 4.1:** Orthographic form of Italian Anglicisms and English etymons.

| Italian Anglicism – main spelling | Italian Anglicism – variant spelling | English etymon (OED) |
|---|---|---|
| benchmark | | benchmark |
| check-point | | check-point |
| social media | | social media |
| selfie stick | selfie-stick | selfie-stick |
| playoff | play-off, play off | play off |
| check-out | | check out |
| e-mail | email | email |
| body building | body-building | bodybuilding |
| all inclusive | all-inclusive | all-inclusive |
| all you can eat | | all-you-can-eat |
| knock down | knock-down, knockdown | knock down (n.) |
| knock down | knock-down, knockdown | knock-down (adj., adv.) |

### 4.1.2 Phonological

The transfer of phonetic features from one's native language to the pronunciation of a foreign language is a rather natural process. As explained by Weinreich (1953: 14), "Interference arises when a bilingual identifies a phoneme of the secondary system with one in the primary system and, in reproducing it, subjects it to the phonetic rules of the primary language." In our analysis Italian is the primary language and English is the secondary one; therefore, the Italian speaker will apply the phonological rules of Italian to pronounce English words. Over the past decades, the pronunciation of Anglicisms has been quite close to the English model, owing to their input through audio channels and a greater competence in spoken English of younger generations of Italians, with minor deviations due to interference with Italian, a language which has a spelling pronunciation. In the past, the input of Anglicisms through written channels caused greater interference, as in the pronunciation of the words *bus* [bus], *tunnel* ['tunnel] and *quiz* [kwitts] (with gemination of the final [tts]), which is pronounced by Italians according to Italian pronunciation rules.

Phonological integration obviously applies to non-adapted Anglicisms which retain an English form. Adapted Anglicisms and indirect borrowings are formally Italian and are naturally pronounced as Italian words. In spelling pronunciation there is a mostly regular spelling-to-sound correspondence. A comparison between the phonological systems of English and Italian reveals many important differences which generally lead to characteristic phonetic adjustments, and adapted or hypercorrected pronunciations on the part of Italian speakers of English.

Because the phonemic inventory of English vowels is more extended than the Italian one (11 vowels in English against 7 vowels in Italian), the most common phenomenon is that of 'underdifferentiation' and 'reinterpretation of distinctions' (Weinreich 1953) leading to the following outcomes:

- underdifferentiation of vowel contrasts, e.g. iː, ɪ > i, so that *bit* [bɪt] and *beat* [biːt] are pronounced in the same way, namely [bit]
- the short and lax vowels ɪ, e, æ, ʌ, ɒ, ʊ are replaced by the closest Italian equivalents i, ɛ, ɛ, a, ɔ, u, which are longer and more tense (length is not a distinctive feature in Italian phonology), e.g. *film* [film], *help* [hɛlp], *trash* [trɛʃ], *hub* [hab], *floppy* ['flɔppi], *full* [ful]
- simplification of diphthongs, especially the central ones: *baby* 'beɪbi > bɛbi; *goal, gol* gəʊl > gɔl (also the spelling of *gol* is simplified)
- substitution of central vowels with closer equivalents: *flirt* [flɜː(r)t] > [flɛrt], or the French pronunciation [flœrt], especially in older speakers; the same applies to *bluff* [blʌf] > [blɛf] and *club* [klʌb] > [klɛb], through the mediation of French [klœb]

The consonant inventory of English and Italian is shown in Table 4.2. Typical phonetic adjustments in the Italian pronunciation of consonants are
- the realization of the grapheme r as a dental trill (Italian is r-full)
- the substitution of fricatives θ and ð with t and d, and the strong pronunciation of weak syllables, so that *thriller* is pronounced ['triller]
- h-dropping; (<h> has no phonetic status in Italian), so that *hip hop* is pronounced [ip 'ɔp]
- pronunciation of final -*ng* as [ng] instead of ŋ
- initial grapheme s followed by voiced consonant is voiced: e.g. *smog* [smɔg] > [zmɔg]
- simplification of consonant clusters, especially in connected speech: e.g. *standard* ['stændə(r)d] > ['standar]
- as a form of hypercorrection, stress placement in initial position: e.g. *self-control* [ˌself kən'trəʊl] > [ˌsɛlf 'kɔntrɔl]
- strong pronunciation of weak syllables: e.g. *mister* ['mister]
- mispronunciation of syllabic consonants: e.g. *jam session* [ˌdʒɛm 'sɛʃon]
- pronunciation of silent graphemes in English, e.g. *stalking* ['stɔlkin(g)], *talk show* ['tolk 'ʃou]
- pronunciation of double consonant graphemes, as geminates, e.g. *college* ['kɔllɛdʒ], *gallery* ['galleri]

**Table 4.2:** Equivalence of consonant phonemes in English and Italian.

| English | Italian | English | Italian |
|---|---|---|---|
| p | p |   | dz |
| b | b | ʒ |   |
| t | t | h |   |
| d | d | tʃ | tʃ |
| k | k | dʒ | dʒ |
| g | g | m | m |
| f | f |   | ɲ |
| v | v | n | n |
| θ |   | ŋ |   |
| ð |   |   | ʎ |
| s | s | l | l |
| z | z | r | r |
| ʃ | ʃ | w | w |
|   | ts | j | j |

American pronunciations are often preferred, as in *privacy* ['praɪvəsi]. Some Anglicisms still retain a French pronunciation, such as *club* [klœb] in the North-Western areas of Italy closer to France, especially among older speakers, but elsewhere it is pronounced [klɛb, klab]. Younger speakers tend to Anglicize loanwords, whatever their origin, incurring mistakes. For example, the French loan *stage* ('traineeship') which should be pronounced [staʒ], is wrongly anglicized into [steɪdʒ], creating a semantic disruption.

The erroneous generalization of the pronuciation of the grapheme <u> and the digraph <ou> in English leads to the deviant pronunciation of *urban* as ['jurban], *journal* as ['dʒurnal] and *open source* as ['open 'surs]. The word *summit* is normally pronounced like the English model ['sammit] and the older spelling pronunciation ['summit] has declined, though still recorded by dictionaries. *Rugby* is pronounced ['rɛgbi] or ['ragbi]. The word *turnover* is normally pronounced [tur'nover] as the central vowel /ɜː/ is alien to Italian and difficult to articulate. The word *tutor* is differently pronounced ['tjutor] or ['tutor], presumably not because of adherence to British or American models, but because of the increased use of the Italian word *tutore* in schools and universities. Variation between British and American English admits alternative pronunciations of *data* as ['deɪtə] or ['dɑːtə] (British) or ['dædə] (American), causing confusion among competent speakers who wish to conform to a native pronunciation.

Stress shift in initial position is another common form of hypercorrection, so that *performance, self-control, report* and *relax* are respectively pronounced ['pɛrformanᵗs], [ˌsɛlf 'kɔntrol], ['rɛport] and ['rɛlaks]. By contrast, *management* is often pronounced [ma'nadʒəment] and *influencer* [influ'ɛnser]. Latinate words may retain the classic pronunciation, as, for example, the word *junior* ['junjor], although the English model ['dʒuːniə(r)] is prevalent but sometimes stigmatized. Conservative-minded speakers may prefer the spelling pronunciation ['mɛdja] instead of the English pronunciation ['miːdiə] in *mass media*.

Apart from the age of the loans, other sociolinguistic variables in the pronunciation of loanwords depend on generational differences in speakers. Older pronunciations may have been brought closer to the English model in younger speakers: for example, *jazz* is pronounced [dʒɛts] by older speakers and [dʒɛz] by younger ones. The tendency towards a pronunciation that is closer to the model has led to the replacement of spelling pronunciations like ['putsle] to ['pazol] for *puzzle*.

The pronunciation of abbreviations and acronyms is normally adapted to Italian. When each grapheme is spelt out in abbreviations, it is read as the Italian letters of the alphabet, e.g. CD [ˌtʃid'di], DNA [ˌdiˌɛnne'a], GPS [ˌdʒipˌpi'ɛsse], HIV [ˌakkaˌi'vu], HTML [ˌakkaˌtiˌɛmme'ɛlle], KO [ˌkappa'ɔ], PC [ˌpit'tʃi], SMS [ˌɛsseˌɛmme'ɛsse]. The pronunciation of acronyms read as words tend to be close to English, e.g. PIN [pin], SIM [sim], CAD [kad], VAR [var]; AIDS ['aids] is Italianized slightly with respect to ['eɪdz] and ISO ['izo] instead of ['aɪsəʊ]. Differences can be noted in abbreviations that are pronounced as acronyms, e.g. LOL ['lɔl] instead of [ˌelˌəʊ'el], CEO ['tʃeo] instead of [ˌsiːˌiː'oʊ], LED ['lɛd] instead of [ˌelˌi'di]. The pronunciation of the letter <v> alternates between [vi] and [vu] in Italian: the word TV (short for *televisione*) is pronounced [ˌti'vu] but in the Anglicism *pay-tv* it is possible to hear a pronunciation closer to the English one, i.e., [ˌpei ˌti'vi]. The abbreviation DVD is alternatively pronounced [ˌdiˌvi'di] or [ˌdiˌvu'di] and WWW is rendered as [ˌvuˌvu'vu] for simplicity. The abbreviation B2B (business to business) is commonly pronounced [ˌbiˌtu'bi] and no interference is caused by the number, which proves that this abbreviation has travelled to Italian through spoken channels.

## 4.1.3 Morpho-syntactic

Following Klajn (1972), morpho-syntactic integration can be functional or formal. Functional integration manages the assignment of grammatical class (noun, adjective, adverb, verb, interjection or phraseological unit), gender (masculine or feminine) and number (singular or plural) to the Anglicism. Formal integration refers to the creation of derivatives from English bases, adapting Anglicisms to the derivational structures of Italian.

The large majority of Anglicisms recorded in GLAD belongs to the category of nouns, which typically denote new objects or concepts, the primary reason for borrowing, followed by adjectives, verbs, phraseological units, interjections and adverbs. The category of phraseological units, which are labelled as 'other', includes phrases carrying a pragmatic value, such as *no comment*, *game over* or *last but not least* (see 3.7). The distribution of grammatical classes in GLAD's pilot word list is as follows (as of November 2022): nouns 81%, adjective 8.1%, verb 6.7%, other 1.9%, adverb 0.9%, interjection 0.9%. This distribution confirms the scale of adoptability common to contact situations (cf. 3.1), which places nouns in top position among the open-class words, and less frequent elements, such as adverbs and interjections at the bottom.

A common feature of Anglicisms is multiple class membership, especially with reference to nouns which can also function as adjectives, or better as 'nouns with modifying function'. The indication of multiple grammatical class is sometimes discordant in dictionaries. For example, the English word *anti-trust* is recorded as an adjective in the OED and the Anglicism *antitrust* is also recorded as an adjective in *Nuovo Devoto-Oli 2022*. *Zingarelli 2022*, instead, has both the adjective and the noun classes for the lemma *antitrust*, the latter normally spelt with capital letter (*Antitrust*) and referring to the 'antitrust authority'. Data from newspaper archives confirm that the noun *Antitrust* is in fact the most frequently used form, and therefore GLAD has *antitrust* both as a noun and as an adjective. In many cases, multiple class membership is further extended: e.g. *on-demand* can be a noun, an adjective and an adverb; *ok* (o.k., OK, O.K., okay) can be a noun, an adjective, an adverb and an interjection; *boom* can be a noun and an interjection; and *online* can be a noun, an adjective and an adverb. The assignment of grammatical class is based on the observation of Anglicisms in the reference tools, in particular in the newspaper archives and corpora, checked against the available lexicographic information.

In some cases, changes in grammatical class may lead to a noticeable semantic shift. For example, the English verb *relax* can be used in Italian as a noun ('relaxation') and as an adjective ('relaxing'), which may indeed cause misunderstanding. Another case is the English noun *snob*, which can be used in Italian as an adjective (in English 'snobbish') and also as a verb (*snobbare*, which in Italian means 'to treat someone in a patronizing way', discussed in 3.1).

In Italian verbs must be adapted to the grammatical system, which has inflectional endings for tense, mood, person, number and gender. The most common category of verb inflection ending in *-are* is applied to loanwords. Many verbs recorded in GLAD are related to the following domains:

- web communication: e.g. *bannare* ('block access to an internet page'), *chattare* (chat), *cliccare* (click), *craccare* ('break the security barriers of a computer system'), *downloadare* (download), *formattare* ('format a computer disk'), *googlare* ('search on google'), *hackerare* ('break into a computer system to steal confidential information'), *linkare* (link), *loggare* ('log into a computer programme'), *postare* ('post something on the internet'), *resettare* ('reset a machine or device'), *retwittare* (retweet), *scannerizzare* (scan), *scrollare* ('scroll on a computer screen'), *spammare* ('to send unwanted emails'), *surfare* ('surf the internet'), *taggare* ('assign an electronic code'), *trollare* ('upset an online discussion by sending offensive or irrelevant messages'), *twittare* ('send a message on Twitter'), *zippare* ('compress a computer file')
- youth speech: *pogare* (pogo), *friendzonare* ('regard someone solely as a friend, despite their unreciprocated romantic or sexual interest'), *flirtare* (flirt)
- the world of drugs: *flashare* ('to lose control or to be shocked by strong emotion'), also used as reflexive *flasharsi* ('to be under the effect of illegal drugs'), *flippare* ('to get high on drugs'), *sniffare* ('inhale a narcotic substance')
- sport: *crossare* ('kick a cross-pass'), *dopare* ('to administer a drug to oneself or another'), also used as reflexive *doparsi* ('take drugs'), *dribblare* (dribble), *liftare* ('to lift the ball in tennis'), *sprintare* (sprint), *stoppare* ('in sports, the action of stopping')
- music: *mixare* (mix), *performare* (perform), *rappare* (rap), *remixare* (remix)
- mixed: *bluffare* (bluff), *bypassare* (bypass), *compostare* (compost), *filmare* (film), *floppare* (flop), *geotaggare* (geotag), *handicappare* (handicap), *liftare* ('to carry

out a face-lift'), *microchippare* ('implant a microchip'), *monitorare* (monitor), *processare* (process), *quotare* (quote), *scioccare* (shock), *settare* (set), *shakerare* ('mix up a drink'), *snobbare* ('to treat s.one in a patronizing way'), *spoilerare* ('anticipate the plot of a TV series, film, or book that could spoil the enjoyment of someone who has not yet seen or read it'), *stoccare* (stock), *stressare* ('stress s.o. out'), *supportare* (support), *testare* (test), and *zoomare* (zoom in).

According to data discussed by Iacobini and Thornton (1992), it is possible to note a progressive productivity of the verbal suffix *-izzare* in 20th century Italian, which is directly related to the formation of the action noun ending in *-zione*, such as, for example, the verb/noun pairs *sponsorizzare* (sponsor) and *sponsorizzazione* (sponsoring), *masterizzare* (master) and *masterizzazione* (mastering), *standardizzare* (standardize) and *standardizzazione* (standardization), *scannerizzare* and *scannerizzazione* (scan), *monitorizzare, monitorare* (monitor) and *monitorizzazione* (monitoring), *customizzare* (customize) and *customizzazione* (customization), *depressurizzare* (depressurize) and *depressurizzazione* (depressurization).

A moot point in the morphological treatment of Anglicisms in Italian is the lack of consensus on the orthographic form of multi-word units, i.e., whether they come as a single or hyphenated unit or separate units, therefore phrases (in Italian *'locuzione'*). This distinction is grammatically relevant to lexicographic practice, because the process of lexicalization, whereby separate elements become one and the same unit, is closely linked to lemmatization, that is, the selection of a unit as entry-word or lemma in a dictionary. This problem may seem unimportant, but in Italian dictionaries this distinction is crucial for the attribution of the correct label (e.g. *sost.* or *loc. sost.*, i.e., 'noun' or 'noun phrase'). Moreover, the unbroken or hyphenated form of a lexical unit is likely to be recorded as an independent entry-word and be assigned a simple grammatical label (e.g. noun, adjective, verb, etc.), whereas a two-word variant may either be recorded as a phrase in its own separate entry or as a run-on within the entry of one of the constituent elements. This is a lexicographic decision which may vary from one dictionary to another. For example, the word *talent show* has an independent entry in *Nuovo Devoto-Oli 2022* but is recorded as a run-on in the entry for the lemma *show* in *Zingarelli 2022*. These lexicographic questions must be taken into consideration when dealing with different dictionaries and lexicographic traditions. As far as GLAD's macrostructure is concerned, this problem has been overcome by the decision to level out the orthographic forms of multi-word units, and assign the same grammatical label according to the values that the units have in authentic use. In other words, the attribution of a grammatical label to compounds is the same, so that *self-control, serial killer* and *security manager* are all labelled as nouns.

Regarding gender assignment, according to Italian grammars (Dardano and Trifone, 1997), foreign borrowings ending in a consonant should be attributed masculine gender, with rare exceptions. By contrast, dictionaries recommend that gender should reflect their closest Italian equivalent's, so that *holding* (in Italian *azienda* f.) should be feminine gender and *cocktail* (in Italian *aperitivo* m.) should be masculine. The prevalent gender assigned to Anglicisms with no specific Italian equivalent is the masculine one, as in *tennis* and *selfie*, which are both masculine and therefore take the masculine determinative article (*il tennis*) or masculine indeterminative article (*un selfie*). Older Anglicisms tend to be treated as masculine (e.g. *il weekend*, m.), causing gender shift in the Italian loan translation (*il fine settimana*), overruling the feminine gender of the word *fine* (end) in Italian. Other criteria can be resorted to, such as, for example, the attribution of feminine gender to all Anglicisms ending in *-ion* and *-ty*, corresponding to Italian *-(z)ione*, and *-tà*, which characterize feminine nouns. Gender assignment is a complex matter owing to the fact that English has no grammatical gender – apart from some cases in which gender is morphologically marked (female gender is normally marked by the suffix *-ess* as in *actress*, *waitress*, and *princess*). GLAD assigns gender according to the one emerging as prevalent from the reference sources. For names of jobs or roles that can be performed by both men and women (e.g. *designer, fan, follower, leader, performer*) both masculine and feminine genders are indicated.

As for the use of articles before nouns, difficulties arise before words beginning with <h> (silent in Italian) and <w> (pronounced as a semi-vowel but perceived as a consonant); normally 'lo' is used for the former (*lo humour*) and 'il' for the latter (*il whisky*). A good deal of variation can be noted in real use for many lexical items, including acronyms used as substantives, like *il CD* (m.), *il DNA* (m.), *l'AIDS* (f.). Variation can be noticed in many cases, among which the case of *email* is particularly interesting, both for its orthographic treatment and gender attribution (discussed in Pulcini and Scarpino, 2017). *Email* is treated differently in general dictionaries, depending on whether the meaning is that of 'mail service' (*l'email*, f.) or that of 'message' (*l'email*, m.), though not evident because of elision in the articles *la* and *lo*.

As far as number is concerned, Italian grammars and dictionaries agree on the invariability of foreign loanwords. The English plural marker *-s* is recorded in dictionaries for the etymon of loanwords. The plural form remains in the loanword for referents that exist mainly in the plural, such as *assets, chips, commodities, corn flakes, news, royalties* or *sneakers*. Data show that the use of the *-s* plural inflection is increasing in more recent borrowings, as a form of hypercorrection, to conform to the English rule, especially in newspaper discourse. Another reason for the increased use of the *-s* plural marker is its use in French, Spanish and Portuguese, so that to indicate the plural of foreignisms is perceived as acceptable (D'Achille 2005; Pulcini and Scarpino 2017).

Moving on to derivation, the word formation mechanism potentially productive through the addition of suffixes to English bases can take advantage of the large inventory of very similar suffixes in English and in Italian, as will be illustrated below. Once again, it is difficult to distinguish the phenomenon of calquing from that of derivation, especially in the case of English bases with a classical origin. As already pointed out in 3.4.2, Klajn suggests that indirect borrowings with a classical root should be considered as calques, whereas borrowings with English roots should be classified as adapted loanwords. Following this rule, *umoristico* is a calque of *humorous* (etymology: French *humor*; Latin *hūmor*), whereas *stoccaggio* (stockage) is an adapted loanword (etymology: Old English *stocc*). Therefore, the following examples should be considered as adapted loanwords, unless they display a classical root, in which case they should be considered as calques. According to Bombi (2020), when the imitation of the foreign model is extended to the whole derivational structure, the typology of the borrowing falls in the category of derivational calques. Thus, when the Italian derivative matches the English model, then we can consider it a derivational calque. If that is not the case, it is a creation of the Italian language, coined from the borrowing of an English base. For example, *leaderismo* does not match with a similar derivational pattern in English (*leaderism); therefore it is an autonomous derivative from the loanword *leader*. The examples quoted below are accompanied by the English model, so that it is evident when a formal resemblance proves the relation between model and replica, or otherwise.

GLAD's data on derivation confirm the trend in 20th century Italian pointed out by Iacobini and Thornton (1992) of an increase in the creation of agent nouns ending in *-ista*, which in fact represents the largest group and generally corresponds to English *-ist*. An agent noun normally denotes a person who does a particular job or activity such as *cartonista* (cartoonist), *hobbista* (hobbyist), *standista* (exhibitor),[54] *umorista* (humourist); it may also refer to a member or supporter of a political movement, practice or ideology such as *lobbista* (lobbyist), *minimalista* (minimalist). The majority of the derivatives recorded as separate entry-words in GLAD are words referring to people taking part in sports: *golfista* (golfer), *hockeista* (hockeyist), *motocrossista* (motocross racer), *rallista* (rallyist), *rugbista* (rugbyist), *scooterista* (scooterist), *surfista* (surfer), *tennista* (tennis player); or engaged in music: *jazzista* (jazzman); or fashion: *stilista* (stylist). The decreasing use in Italian of the suffix *-aro* to denote agent nouns is also confirmed, as the only recorded instance is *rockettaro*

---

[54] The loanword *stand* in Italian refers to 'a promotional display at exhibitions; also the dedicated area'. A *standista* is someone who attends an Expo or exposition representing a particular exhibitor, provides information about products in the dedicated area and hands out brochures and other promotional materials.

(rocker). Similarly, the suffix *-nauta* is confined to creations that have to do with outer space navigation (real or virtual) such as *internauta* and *cybernauta*.

The second most productive suffix is *-ismo*, which corresponds to English *-ism*. This suffix characteristically denotes schools of thought, be they political, philosophical, scientific, artistic, etc. Among the late 19th and early 20th century Anglicisms modelled on this pattern there are several terms that can be traced back to historical facts, fashions or ideas, which have survived in the course of time, e.g. *laburismo* (labourism),[55] *ostruzionismo* (obstructionism),[56] *dandismo* (dandyism),[57] *proibizionismo* (prohibitionism),[58] *populismo* (populism),[59] *pragmatismo* (pragmatism).[60] Along the same pattern, we have terms referring to beliefs or behaviours characteristic of modern society, such as *consumerismo* (consumerism), *cyberbullismo* (cyberbullying), *cyberterrorismo* (cyberterrorism), *escapismo* (escapism), *gangsterismo* (gangsterism), *hooliganismo* (hooliganism), *leaderismo* ('impose oneself as a leader'), *managerialismo* (managerialism), *minimalismo* (minimalism), *scoutismo* (scoutism), *snobismo* (snobbism), *umorismo* (humour), *veganismo* (veganism), *vegetarianismo* (vegetarianism).

Among the suffixes that denote actions or activities in Italian *-aggio* appears to be the most productive, triggered by analogy with the French suffix *-age*, and corresponding to the English ending *-ing*, generating deverbal nouns. Examples include words such as *babysitteraggio* (babysitting), *brokeraggio* (brokering), *compostaggio* (composting), *hackeraggio* (hacking), *missaggio*, also *mixaggio* (mixing), *monitoraggio* (monitoring), *speakeraggio* ('technique used to apply the voice of a "speaker", announcer, actor, radio presenter, to an audio visual product'), *stoccaggio* (stockage), and *tutoraggio* (tutoring). The suffix *-azione* is extremely productive in Italian too (Iacobini and Thornton, 1992) to name actions, and is closely related to the verbal suffix *-izzare* (discussed above); among the instances included in GLAD there are *automazione* (verb: *automatizzare*), *sponsorizzazione* (verb: *sponsorizzare*),

---

[55] *Labourism* is a political movement of socialdemocratic orientation, which emerged at the end of the 19th century in Britain with the large support of labour unions, to protect the workers' rights.
[56] *Obstructionism*, also called filibustering, is a practice generally exploited during parliamentary discussions, aimed at delaying important decisions by requesting long discussions on amendments and delivering long speeches.
[57] Cf. 2.3 on *dandyism*.
[58] *Prohibitionism* was introduced in the United States from 1920 to 1933 to stop the production and the sale of alcoholic drinks.
[59] *Populism*, a loanword from Russian *narodničestvo*, refers to political movements championing the power of ordinary people and their direct relationship with the leaders, against the ruling elites.
[60] *Pragmatism* is a philosophy developed in the United States at the end of the 19th century, supporting the value of practical applications to confirm the validity of theoretical statements.

*standardizzazione* (verb: *standardizzare*), and the blend *stagflazione* (*stagnazione* +*inflazione*, no verbal form).

The formation of adjectives can be obtained through various processes of derivation in Italian (Table 4.3). One is the conversion of the past participle of verbs, as in *glitterato* ('decorated with glitter'), *handicappato* (handicapped) and *stressato* (stressed), expressing a resultative meaning. In the case of *mobbizzato*, the process goes through the creation of the verb from the English base *mob*, the addition of the suffix -*izzare* (*mobbizzare*) and the formation of the past participle *mobbizzato*. The autonomous verbal creation *snobbare* from the English noun snob gives rise to the adjective *snobbato*, meaning 'snubbed' or 'humiliated'. The derivational calque *partenariato* (modelled on *partnership*) reflects the formation of a neologism indicating a 'condition of being partners'. Adjectives can be obtained from the conversion of the present participle of verbs, such as *performante* (performing), *scioccante* (shocking) and *stressante* (stressing). The suffix -*abile*, which corresponds to English -*able*, allows the formation of denominal adjectives such as *compostabile* (compostable), from the loanword *compost* (1986), *dimmerabile* (dimmable) and *filmabile* (filmable).

Among the suffixes that are used to create adjectives expressing a relation, -*ale* has increased significantly in Italian, because of the influence of English, in specialized registers (Grossman and Reiner 2004: 387). Among GLAD's entries we can find the adjectives *computazionale* (computational), *manageriale* (managerial), *mediale* (medial), *minimale* (minimal). The word *editoriale* deserves particular attention, as Italian *editore* (publisher) and English *editor* ('a person who edits written material for publication or use') are false friends. Only recently the English meaning has been assimilated into Italian, so that the word *editore* has been extended to 'the principal person in charge of a newspaper, magazine, or similar publication', normally called 'direttore'. It follows that the adjective *editoriale* in Italian refers to the publishing industry and is an Italian word. The new additional meaning of *editorial* defined as 'an article in a newspaper, magazine, or similar publication that expresses the editor's opinion or the publication's position on a topical issue.', called *articolo di fondo* in Italian, should be considered a 'camouflage' calque developed from the English meaning.

The productivity of derivational processes, which are in fact the primary mechanism of word formation in contemporary Italian (Iacobini and Thornton, 1992), may lead to a variety of patterns starting from the simple Anglicism, which is generally borrowed first, some examples of which are illustrated in Table 4.3. For instance, the word *sponsor*, denoting the agent noun, leads to the name of the activity, usually the infinitive of the verb *sponsorizzare*, to the de-

**Table 4.3:** Derivational patterns from English bases.

| etymon | Agent noun | Activity | De-verbal adjective | Action | Behaviour | Place | Quality |
|---|---|---|---|---|---|---|---|
| hacker | hacker | hackerare hacking | hackerato | hackeraggio (hacking) | | | |
| hamburger | | | | | | hamburgheria | |
| manager | manager | management | | | managerialismo | | manageriale |
| mobbing | | mobbizzare | mobbizzato | mobbing | | | |
| snob | snob | snobbare | snobbato | | snobismo | | snobistico |
| sponsor | sponsor | sponsorizzare | sponsorizzato | sponsorizzazione | | | |
| stop | stopper | stoppare | stoppato | stoppata | | | |
| stress | | stressare | stressato | | | | stressante |
| tennis | tennista | | | | | | tennistico |
| homour | umorista | | | | umorismo | | umoristico |

verbal adjective *sponsorizzato*,⁶¹ and to the name of the action *sponsorizzazione*. The typical ending of agent nouns can be the English *-er* (or *-or*) in non-adapted borrowings (*stopper, sponsor*) or *-ista* (*umorista, tennista*). The name of the activity is usually the infinitive of verbs ending in *-are* but also the English ending *-ing* (*hackerare* or *hacking*), which is quite familiar in Italian, also generating autonomous creations. The name of the single action or state can be expressed by a variety of derivational endings, the most productive being *-aggio* (*hackeraggio*) but also *-azione* (*sponsorizzazione*), *-ata* (*stoppata*). Belief or behaviour is indicated by the suffix *-ismo*. The indication of quality may end in *-ale* (*manageriale*), *-istico* (*tennistico, umoristico*) and *-ante* (*stressante*).

Some other derivational mechanisms that start from English bases are less productive and representative. They include the suffixes *-eria* (*hamburgheria*) and *-teca* (*filmoteca*) to refer to the name of the place, *-istica* for collective nouns (*gadgettistica*, from the loanword *gadget*, 1963; *reportistica* from the loanword *report*, 1987), *-ivo* (*performativo, sportivo*), *-esco* (*clownesco*) and *-ico* (*filmico*) for adjectives expressing quality, the nominal suffix *-ità* (*managerialità*) to express collective value of the quality indicated by the adjective, diminutives with *-ino* (*gingerino* 'aperitif drink') or augmentative with *-one* (*scooterone* 'large scooter'). Finally, the neo-classical combining forms *-grafia* and *-ologia* attached to English bases are not particularly productive (*filmologia, filmografia*).

Beyond the level of word formation, other morphosyntactic phenomena appear to influence present-day Italian: these have been discussed by Carlucci (2018) and have been ascribed to the influence of English, though innovative phenomena are likely to have resulted from multiple causes, both exogenous and endogenous. A case in point regards the use of two coordinated prepositions referring to the same element, as in *da e per l'aeroporto* / 'from and to the airport'. Another innovative pattern is the use of the ordinal number + *più* + adjective, so that 'the second most important' is rendered as *il secondo più importante* instead of *il secondo per importanza* (Berruto 2017; Carlucci 2018; Dardano 2020; Pulcini 2022). The increase of the periphrastic pattern *stare*+gerund (*sto leggendo*) by analogy with the English progressive form (*I'm reading*), has been widely discussed; however, rather than the adoption of an English grammatical structure, it seems as if the exploitation of an old pattern is simply becoming more frequent (Dardano, 2020).

The influence of English is detectable in phrases and patterns which are typical of journalism and advertising. Slogans such as *X is beautiful* has been exploited in

---

[61] In Italian, the past participles of verbs inflect for gender and number, so that *sponsorizzato* (masculine, singular) can be inflected as masculine, plural (*sponsorizzati*), feminine, singular (*sponsorizzata*) and feminine, plural (*sponsorizzate*).

many different circumstances (*X è bello*). The title *Who's Who?* (in Italian *Chi è chi?*), used for biographical handbooks, has been exploited to create new multiple interrogatives (*Chi fa cosa? / Who does what?*). Intransitive verbs are turned into transitive ones, as in *run the hundred meters / correre i cento metri*.

The need for brevity seems to have triggered compact constructions, an increased use of acronyms (CD, DVD), clippings (*sit-com*), blends (*glocal*), and the pattern modifier+modified in compounds (discussed above), although this pattern was already used in classical languages. In fact, this phenomenon is not new but perhaps on the increase, both in specialist terminology, e.g. *immunoterapia* (immunotherapy) and in the general language, e.g. *calciomercato* (transfer market).

### 4.1.4 Semantic

Semantic integration occurs when the meaning of the borrowing deviates from the original one. A close match in meaning between the English model and the loanword can be observed in technical terms, which are borrowed for the purpose of naming something new, for example, to introduce a piece of equipment that did not exist before, e.g. *airbag*. In many other cases the semantic value of the borrowing may be extended, remodelled or enriched with connotative overtones, as a consequence of its assimilation into the new usage context. In this section we will deal with the meaning of Italian Anglicisms with respect to their English models, excluding the maximum semantic shift leading to the creation of a false Anglicism (cf. 3.5).

In order to address the process of semantic integration, it is necessary to return to the term borrowing and to the various synonymic terms adopted in the literature of language contact – importation, transfer or adoption. Some linguists argue that these terms are not satisfactory because they describe this phenomenon as if the loanword travelled from a language to another without being affected in any way. By contrast, the terms copy or replica better interpret the active role of the recipient language in reproducing a foreign model, treating it as a new domestic element, grammatically and semantically, and also remodelling it to answer its own expressive needs. Alexieva (2008: 48–49), for example, highlights two crucial factors at work in contact-induced lexical innovation, namely the loss of motivation and semantic transparency:

> The loss of transparency has far-reaching effects on the behaviour and development of loanwords in the host language: since they are created within the language, they inevitably become part of its structural and semantic networks, which in turn become the source of their

motivation. What is more, being new entities, independent of the words on which they are modelled, these copies are free to develop, especially semantically, in accordance with the socio-cultural needs of the new language community.

Whereas phonological and morpho-syntactic integration is language-specific, lexical meaning can be observed cross-linguistically, so that the meaning of an Anglicism (for example in Italian) can be compared to that of its source model (in English), and also to the meaning that the same Anglicism has developed in other recipient languages (in French, German, Polish, etc.). The semantic profiling of Anglicisms is the primary goal of lexicographic description.

A cognitive approach to the analysis of the semantic integration of Anglicisms into Italian may be very useful, in order to isolate the prototypical characteristics of the object or concept that the word refers to, and compare the semantic traits associated to the source word and its replica. Another useful distinction for the study of meaning is between semasiological and onomasiological approaches (Geeraerts 1997, 2003). A semasiological approach takes the word and the complexity of its various meanings – stylistic, metaphorical, emotional and cultural associations – as a starting point. An onomasiological approach, instead, focuses on concepts and on the lexical items that can be used to express them from a number of alternative options, or near synonyms. It is then clear that the semasiological approach can help to identify the meaning (or more than one) that a loanword has transferred into the recipient language, whereas an onomasiological approch can help to observe the behaviour of an Anglicisms in competition with one or more synonyms, their coexistence or the success of one over the other.

A semasiological analysis of the word *cottage* (Pulcini 2011a, 2011b, 2012b), for example, shows that the semantic traits attached to this referent in its original British context are to some extent different from the same referent in the Italian context. While a British cottage is normally 'a small frame one-family house', usually in the countryside, in Italy it is usually a place for a holiday, not a home, and it is loaded with positive connotations, such as rural charm and an old-time, romantic atmosphere, but it is also equipped with all comforts for a pleasant holiday. This example shows that the same word, displaced from one cultural context to another, even when referring to the same entity, may have similar but nor exactly identical connotations.[62] From an onomasiological perspective, we may compare the denotative and connotative traits of the word *cottage* in Italian in competition with the

---

[62] This discussion on the word *cottage* was inspired by the article of Dunn (2008: 56) in which many examples of semantic deviations of Anglicisms in Russian are illustrated. In particular, the word *cottage* appears to diverge entirely from the English model in post-Soviet times, being defined as 'a private two- or three-storey house with a high standard of comfort, usually located in the suburbs and intended for city-dwellers'.

near synonyms *casetta*, *villetta*, or *bungalow*. In different communicative contexts, usage will require a specific word to denote and connote a specific type of dwelling, the characteristics of which are usually shared by the reference speech community.

Typically, neological innovation takes place especially in the specialized domains of a language, which, in the new millennium, have converged on ICT, economy and finance (Pulcini 2017), but also on many different domains of science, technology, social life and entertainment. As a result of the popularization and increased circulation of technical and scientific knowledge, specialized terminology normally moves into the general vocabulary and circulates among non-specialists. As explained in 3.3.1, GLAD does not include highly technical vocabulary, unless it is used in the general language, but the dividing line between general and specialized vocabulary is difficult to draw and many technical terms have been accepted. From a semantic point of view, specialized terms are monoreferential and normally denote one single referent. For example, in the car industry such technical terms as ABS, *airbag*, *cruise control*, HP, *immobilizer* and *multijet* have become familiar to the general public, and therefore have been included in GLAD. The term *immobilizer* is rather technical, but it is frequently mentioned in newspaper articles dealing with new car models equipped with this anti-theft system, a topic that is of interest to common people. The term *immobilizer* in English has exclusively specialized meanings in the fields of genetics, medicine, botany, and soil science, besides the specific meaning imported into Italian, i.e., 'an electrical anti-theft device which prevents the engine from being started'.

Reduction in the range of meanings is a common feature of borrowing: countless examples show that a word may be polysemic in the source language and monosemic in the recipient language, i.e., only one (or a few) of the original meanings are adopted. Very often, when both a general and a specialized meaning are conveyed by the English word, it is the specialized meaning that is borrowed. An example of a highly polysemic word in English is *round*, which, thanks to the property of conversion, can be a noun, an adjective, an adverb, a verb, and a preposition; as an English noun, *round* has a wide range of meanings, senses and sub-senses. By contrast, as a loanword in Italian, *round* is only used as a noun in boxing to denote 'each of the periods into which a boxing match (or later a match in other combat sports, as wrestling, karate, etc.) is divided'. Nevertheless, specialized terms may easily develop a figurative extension, both in the donor and in the recipient languages: in the case of *round*, in fact, this word can be used to refer to the various phases of a debate, a discussion or a negotiation, by virtue of a cognitive association to conflict. Another example of figurative extension in the field of sport is the compound *pole position*, used in car racing, and whose meaning can be extended to a situation of priority or advantage.

Another interesting example is the word *mission*, which has a complex range of separate meanings and senses in English, having to do with duties or vocation, which can be grouped around the domains of religion, politics, diplomacy, and aerospace. In Italian the word *missione* is normally used for all these meanings and senses, while the Anglicism *mission* is applied to the field of business with the specific meaning of 'a formal summary of the aims and values of a company, organization, or individual'. Incidentally, also the phrase *mission impossible*, from the US television series, first broadcast in 1966, with the meaning of 'a difficult or impossible assignment' is current enough in Italian to be a GLAD entry.

Since polysemy is the rule rather than the exception in the vocabulary of languages, semantic reduction takes place in the borrowing process in most Anglicisms: e.g. *extension* is only referred to a person's hair (hair extension), a *follower* is a person who follows others on a social media website, *guests* and *hosts* only refer to computing, and *intelligence* is a country's secret service, not the faculty of being intelligent, for which Italian has the word *intelligenza*. Reduction and narrowing can also be observed in the class of adjectives, which is not so large as that of nouns: e.g. *dry* is confined to the taste of wine and alcoholic drinks, *cool* is a synonym of 'trendy' in youth speech, *hard* means 'energetic' but also 'pornographic', and *flat* is used in the fields of fashion (flat shoes) and in finance (flat rate). Semantic narrowing consists in limiting the semantic range of a specific meaning: for example, the word *shock* for the meaning of 'a sudden and violent effect' has a narrower range of referents in Italian compared to English, with *shock* being associated to the medical field (*shock anafilattico*), to thermal energy (*shock termico*), to an emotional state (*shock nervoso, shock culturale*), but not to electricity or to an earthquake (in which cases, Italian uses the word *scossa*).

The opposite phenomenon of reduction and narrowing is that of semantic widening of the meaning of an Anglicism, usually through figurative extensions. In some cases, stylistic overtones which are not present in the source language may develop only in the recipient language, towards a more positive or a more unfavourable association. An example popularized in the Italian political scene some years ago is that of the word *escort*, referring to young ladies taking part in parties and mundane events; the term *escort* acquired the negative connotation of *call-girl*, as some of these young ladies turned out to be engaged in prostitution. As a consequence, while in English *escort* covers several senses given to an accompanying person, and the meaning of 'call-girl' is only peripheral, in Italian *escort* is exclusively associated to high-class hookers. Other examples of pejoration are the words *boss* and *connection*. In Italian the Anglicism *boss* is often associated to the mafia, and less frequently to 'the person in charge of you at work'. As negative stereotypes are hard to die, the same criminal association is often attached to the word *connection*, which was introduced in the 1980s with reference to a link between Sicilian and American gangsters involved in drug trafficking, called 'pizza connection'. Conversely, in English 'connections' are 'people you know who may be able to help you' without any negative or illegal implications.

A semantic change in the direction of amelioration is motivated by the taste for exotic, foreign-sounding words, and by the prestige of Anglo-American culture and lifestyle. Accordingly, a *drink* is not just a beverage to quench your thirst, but exclusively an alcoholic drink, normally associated to a mundane situation. *Shopping* does not refer to buying in general, but only to 'buying clothes or other leisure articles', and *look* has overtones of sophistication ('the particular style of clothes or hair'). In fact, the phrase 'rifarsi il look' (reflexive) corresponds to 'restyling' or 'refurbishing', both with reference to a person or to an inanimate referent (furnishings, town areas, or buildings). The word *coffee break* is preferred in academic, international environments, while *pausa caffé* is more common in the workplace. While the term *college* is neutral in English, in Italian *college* has an aura of prestige and exclusiveness. Sometimes Anglicisms are introduced to name a particular job, or make it sound more modern and attractive: so the word *baby sitter* replaced the old-fashioned *bambinaia*, and *accountant*, *area manager*, *barman*, *project manager* are preferred in job postings, to stress the international orientation of a company or simply for image-enhancing reasons (cf. 6.3).

## 4.2 Indirect borrowings

Indirect borrowings are Italian words or multi-word units that reproduce or are influenced by English models. Two broad categories can be distinguished: calques and semantic loans. Calques are new words modelled on English ones both in form and in meaning, e.g. *politicamente corretto*, patterned on *politically correct*. Semantic loans are meaning extensions of already existing words in Italian, triggered by the semantic influence of the foreign model, e.g. *stella*, widening its meaning from 'celestial object' (star) to denote 'A very famous or popular actor, singer, or other entertainer'.

Since indirect borrowings are made up of Italian words, they are characterized by a high degree of 'camouflage' in the recipient language and may be difficult to identify or recognize without historical information. They are also much more acceptable than loanwords by language observers and generally by more conservative language communities, because of their familiarity and compliance with the rules of the national language. The replacement of foreign borrowings with domestic equivalents is not only a spontaneous phenomenon arising from the natural circulation of vocabulary and speakers' use. It is an activity delegated to language academies and commissions in charge of multilingual terminologies for translation purposes, both at national and international levels, such as, for example, the *Translation Centre for the Bodies of the European Union*. On a national level, countries embrace a more or less open attitude to foreign borrowings, and translation is considered the solution to preserve the expressive potential of the national language, especially as far as scientific and technical terminologies are concerned, and its national identity (see 7.3).

Typologies of indirect borrowings reflect the way in which the recipient language accommodates neological creations into the domestic structures. The literature on the typology of borrowings and its outcomes in the Italian language as far as derivation and calquing are concerned is very rich. A key theoretical reference framework was developed by Gusmani (1986). Over the past decades, interlanguage studies and contact linguistics have been widely explored by Italian scholars, in order to detect innovative tendencies in progress in Italian, without neglecting the historical and cultural dimensions of language contact and the multiple directions that neologisms can take (Bombi 2009a, 2019; Giovanardi, Gualdo and Coco 2008; Iacobini 2003; Carlucci 2018; Dardano 2020).

### 4.2.1 Calques

The process that motivates the creation of calques is the substitution of the foreign element (English) with a domestic one (Italian). As shown in Figure 3.1, calques can be divided into three main broad types, namely loan translations, loan renditions and loan creations, following a distinction introduced by Weinreich (1953). For its simplicity, this tripartite division can be applied to cross-linguistic comparisons and was used by Görlach in the *Dictionary of European Anglicisms* (2001) to classify translation replacements for Anglicisms recorded in the 16 languages represented. A loan translation faithfully translates the English pattern, e.g. *alta fedeltà* < *high fidelity*. A loan rendition reproduces the English etymon with morphological changes; most Italian calques, for example, reverse the order of the English components ($N^1+N^2 < N^2+N^1$), e.g. *conferenza stampa* < *press conference* or create an analytic pattern ($N^1+N^2 < N^2+$preposition$+N^1$), e.g. *guardia del corpo* < *bodyguard*. A loan creation is a free coinage that replaces the model word without any formal connection with it, e.g. *pallanuoto* < *waterpolo*.

The distinction between loan translation, loan rendition and loan creation is based on the formal similarity or divergence between the English etymon and its replica. To account for this difference in form and meaning, Haugen (1950) and later Klajn (1972) used the terms loan homonym and loan synonym: *automazione* (automation) and *supermercato* (supermarket) are examples of loan homonyms, being formally quite similar, whereas *appuntamento al buio* (blind date) and *tecnico del suono* (sound designer) are examples of loan synonyms, as their constituent elements do not match. Bombi (2020) uses the terms 'perfect' and 'imperfect' calques with reference to the formal and semantic adherence between the model and the replica.

A fine-grained distinction of the typological classification of English-induced calques in Italian is described in Bombi's work (2009a; 2020), following Gusmani's (1986) theoretical framework, which will be used here to describe some representative categories of calques recorded in GLAD.

– *Syntagmatic calques* reproduce a complex unit both in form and meaning. These are the most common calques, whose forms may show higher or lower formal equivalence with their etymons (corresponding to the distinctions discussed above between homonyms vs synonyms or perfect vs imperfect equivalence). Several patterns are possible:
- Noun+adjective, e.g. *aria condizionata* (air conditioned), *cambiamento climatico* (climate change), *classe capovolta* (flipped classroom), *edizione limitata* (limited edition), *nativo digitale* (digital native), *scatola nera* (black box), *direttore artistico* (art director), *intelligenza artificiale* (artificial intelligence), *realtà aumentata* (augmented reality), *tempo pieno* (full time), *tempo reale* (real time), *assistente virtuale* (virtual assistant);
- Noun+noun, e.g. *pausa caffè* (coffee break), *conferenza stampa* (press conference), *servizio clienti* (customer service), *fine settimana* (weekend), *sito web* (website), *tolleranza zero* (zero tolerance);
- Noun+preposition+Noun: *appuntamento al buio* (blind date), *guardia del corpo* (bodyguard), *carta d'imbarco* (boarding pass), *codice a barre* (barcode), *conferenza al vertice* (summit conference), *carta di credito* (credit card), *conto alla rovescia* (countdown), *faccia a faccia* (face-to-face), *fai da te* (do-it-yourself), *fuga dei cervelli* (brain drain), *gomma da masticare* (chewing-gum), *guancia a guancia* (cheek-to-cheek), *cacciatore di teste* (head hunter), *porta a porta* (door-to-door), *servizio in camera* (room service).
- Other word-classes may be involved in the creation of syntagmatic calques, such as Adj+N in *alta fedeltà* (high fidelity) and Adv+Adj in *politicamente corretto* (politically correct). The order of the constituent of these examples is the same as in the English model, in which case they represent 'perfect' syntagmatic calques. It is worth noticing that some patterns enjoy popularity and become productive, as in the case of 'high' (with the sense of 'high-level'), already present in *alta società* (high society), *alta definizione* (high definition), also used as the acronym HD and HDTV (high-definition television), and in the non-adapted Anglicisms *high school*, *highlander* and *highlight*.

By contrast, some Italian renditions may diverge because of the conflicting word order in English and in Italian, such as, for example, the word *case study*, whose correct equivalent calque should be *studio di caso*, being *study* the head element of the English compound. Interference with Italian word order has generated the word-for-word Italian rendition *caso di studio*, which is in fact more frequently used in Italian, also by experts, than the correct calque *studio di caso*.

– *Compositional calques* consist in the imitation of the English model through a similar compositional pattern in Italian, e.g. *altoparlante* (loudspeaker), *pallacanestro* (basketball), *grattacielo* (skyscraper), *dopobarba* (aftershave), *fuorilegge* (outlaw). This type also includes compounds containing neo-classical combining forms, e.g. *anti-età* (anti-ageing), *autogoverno* (self-government), *minigonna* (miniskirt), *monorotaia* (monorail), *videocassetta* (videotape), *videogioco* (videogame), *post-verità* (post-truth) and *microonde* (microwave).

– *Derivational calques* consist in the imitation of the English model thorough a similar derivational pattern in Italian, e.g. *affidabilità* (reliability), *comportamentismo* (behaviourism), *ostruzionismo* (obstructionism), *partenariato* (partnership), *stilista* (stylist). The words *boicottaggio* (boycotting) and *linciaggio* (lynching), though historically deriving from British and American societies respectively,[63] are likely to have been transferred through French mediation, because of the affinity between the French derivational morpheme *-age* and Italian *-aggio* (cf. 2.2 for the historical background; cf. 4.1.3 for derivation).

A word of caution is in order here. Because of the close affinity between English and Italian lexical and derivational morphemes, due to a common historical heritage of classical languages, in many cases it is difficult to determine whether words are calques or adaptations, such as, for example, *automazione* and *automation*, which share the Greco-Latin base *automat-*.[64] Moreover, it is necessary to verify

---

[63] See chapter 2, footnote 17 for discussion on *boycott*. *Lynching*: 'The action or practice of inflicting extralegal summary punishment on an alleged or convicted offender' (OED). The following information is added: 'Particularly associated with the extrajudicial execution of African Americans, especially that perpetrated in Southern states from the end of the American Civil War (1865) to the Civil Rights movement in the mid-20th cent.'

[64] According to historical dictionaries (Cortelazzo and Zolli 1999; Nocentini 2010), *automazione* is a loan translation of English *automation*. The Italian word *automa* and English *automaton* ('A moving device having a concealed mechanism, so it appears to operate spontaneously.') have originated from the Greek root automat-. Note that the word *automatic* is a post-classical borrowing from Latin *automaticus* (1511 or earlier), from which French *automatique* (1627 or earlier), Spanish *automático* (1736 or earlier), Italian *automatico* (1704 or earlier), German *automatisch* (1763) have derived. Thus, *automatico* falls in the category of internationalisms (cf. 4.4). Instead, *automazione* came directly from English *automation*, in turn from the Greek root automat- to which the Latin suffix *-ion* has been added (which, according to the Italian linguist Migliorini, is 'a little monster', considering that the Latin verbal suffix *-ion* has been added to a Greek adjective!).

whether the base form was borrowed before the derivative: for example, according to the *Nuovo Devoto-Oli 2022* dictionary, the noun *affidabilità* originated from the Italian word *affidabile*, to which the Italian suffix *-ità* was added, and *affidabile* is recorded as a calque of English *reliable*. In other words, the adjective *affidabile* is an indirect borrowing from English, while *affidabilità* is a domestic derivative from Italian *affidabile*. By contrast, in the case of *behaviourism*, Bombi (2020) confirms that the path of adoption started from *behaviorismo*, which was imported first, and was followed later by the creation of the derivative calque *comportamentismo*, where the Italian suffix *-ismo* faithfully matches the English *-ism*.

Typological distinctions are at the core of much research into indirect borrowings. A less explored aspect is the fortune of calques and the relationship with the loanwords from which they originated. For curious reasons, some neologisms start being used immediately as calques, and the English term from which they originated is never integrated or quickly falls into disuse: some examples are *forno a microonde* (microwave oven), *aria condizionata* (air conditioned), *arrampicatore sociale* (social climber) and *disco volante* (flying saucer).[65] The opposite case may occur, when an Anglicism is more successful than its domestic equivalent: for example, the common word *e-mail*, which was introduced in 1992, thus much later than *posta elettronica*, which started being used in 1982, but quickly took over the Italian equivalent.[66] The competition between Anglicisms and translation equivalents is further discussed with reference to the distinction between necessary and luxury loans (cf. 4.3).

Another aspect deserving attention is whether neological creations may be the result of independent national genesis, rather than indirect borrowings from the English language. As argued by Rodriguez Gonzalez and Knospe (2019), in the complex scenario of European cultural history, much vocabulary travels across speech communities, so that multiple origin, or polygenesis, is the rule rather than the exception for things and concepts that emerged in the same historical period (see Anglicisms in specialized domains in chapter 6). Nowadays English is the most active donor language and neologisms are normally considered to come from Anglophone countries (in particular from the United States), but this may not always be the

---

[65] A search in the archive of the Italian daily newspaper *la Repubblica*, covering from 1984 to the present, yielded the following results: *forno a microonde* (419), *microwave oven* (0); *aria condizionata* (10,787), *air conditioned* (7), *air conditioning* (38); *arrampicatore sociale* (102), *social climber* (12); *disco volante* (569), *flying saucer* (10) (search conducted on August 9, 2021). Note that these figures have not been filtered, and occurrences may appear in articles written in English or be used as proper names (brand names, quotations, titles, etc.).

[66] A search in the archive of the Italian daily newspaper *la Repubblica* (cf. footnote 65) yielded the following results: *e-mail* (also spelt email) (50,626), *posta elettronica* (10,419). Note that *e-mail* is normally used when contact data are given or annotated (name, surname, address, email, etc.).

case. The above-mentioned scholars quote the word *superman*, mistakenly associated to English, but which actually came from German *Übermensch* and the Spanish neologism *centro comercial*, borrowed from French *centre commercial*, though in turn adapted from English *shopping centre*. Incidentally, both *superman* (1961) and *shopping center* (also spelt *shopping centre*) (1957) are recorded as Italian Anglicisms in GLAD. Thus, it could be argued that for indirect borrowings, the linguistic and cultural ties with the donor language, if any, are much weaker in comparison with the ones with direct borrowings, and in fact may be lost in time, as was noted for 19th century borrowings, whose British provenance is documented by historical evidence, but it is no longer known to common speakers.

A concluding remark on this question is that the proposal of domestic translation equivalents is systematically made by some Italian academics who are trying to reverse the 'flood' of Anglicisms (Giovanardi, Gualdo and Coco, 2008). This trend is also supported by the latest edition of the Italian dictionary *Nuovo Devoto-Oli 2022*, which has included a new section entitled *"Per dirlo in italiano"* ["To say it in Italian"], suggesting alternative solutions to the use of English loanwords (cf. 7.3).[67] This means that the typological separation between direct and indirect borrowings is crucial not only from a linguistic point of view, but also, and especially, from Italian speakers' perception and attitudes. A further proof of this position coming from a very authoritative lexicographic source (De Mauro and Mancini 2003), is that calques are listed separately from foreign loanwords (non-adapted loanwords) and are labelled as 'multi-word units built on analogous foreign expressions' (*polirematiche costruite su analoghe espressioni straniere*); in other words, calques are separately recorded as Italian creations in their own right.

## 4.2.2 Semantic loans

The typological spectrum of borrowings, at the other end of the formal continuum, is that of semantic loans (also called semantic calques). This process involves the transfer of a meaning from a word of the donor language to an already existing word of the recipient language. As explained by Gusmani (1986), the two words share a common semantic basis and the transfer involves an additional sense developed in the source language which is then taken on by the recipient one. In other words, this phenomenon can be interpreted as "induced polysemy". A protoypical case is represented by the pair *star* and *stella*, sharing the common

---

[67] Another recent, though less authoritative, source is provided by the online *Dizionario delle Alternative agli Anglicismi* (Zoppetti 2022), which is the outcome of a openly purist project.

primary meaning of 'celestial object'. The addition meaning of 'A very famous or popular actor, singer, or other entertainer' developed by *star* in English was taken on by *stella* in Italian. In this case, the semantic extension of the Italian word *stella* dates back to 1856, preceding the actual borrowing of the loanword *star*, which was introduced decades later, in 1929.[68]

The common trait of calques and semantic loans is that it is the new meaning to be transferred from English, which is then reproduced with domestic elements in Italian. The difference is that in the case of calques a new word is created, together with the new meaning, whereas in semantic loans the new meaning is attached, so to say, to an already existing word. Indeed, the phenomenon of semantic loans is the least noticeable one among all types of borrowings, since it does not add any new item to the lexical inventory of the recipient language.

Another case of a semantic loan is the Italian word *navetta*, an old word expressing a range of specific meanings, including that of 'small boat' ('nave' is 'boat' in Italian and *-etta* is a diminutive affix): in the 20th century it extended its meaning to that of 'a means of public transport operating a transfer service to and from a certain destination, like airports and stations, at regular times', for example from an airport to the centre of town. This new meaning in contemporary Italian was borrowed from the English term *shuttle*. It is likely that the process was favoured by the term *navetta spaziale* (a calque of *space shuttle*).

The route from a calque to a semantic loan can be noted in many other cases, as in the sports term *angolo* (corner), which was initially borrowed as *calcio d'angolo*, a calque of *corner kick*, which was then reduced to *angolo*, featuring in Italian side by side with the loanword *corner*. The same borrowing mechanism can be observed in the Italian word *vertice* carrying the meaning of 'A meeting or series of meetings between the heads of state or government of two or more countries, convened for the purpose of discussing matters of international importance.' The route of transmission was probably through the Italian calque *conferenza al vertice*, from English *summit conference*, then reduced to *vertice* (summit).[69]

Semantic loans are subtle phenomena and are even more difficult to detect than calques because of the high degree of 'camouflage' in the recipient language, where they already exist as words. Careful historical investigation can trace their

---

68 *Stella* has multiple meanings in Italian: the core meaning is 'celestial object'; by extension it may refer to 'a star-shaped image or icon' and to several figurative meanings; the more modern meaning is 'a famous person'. The Anglicism *star* only denotes 'an outstandingly successful person' in sports and in society.

69 *Vertice* has several meanings beside 'summit meeting', including 'peak, top', also in a figurative sense; in geometry, *vertice* corresponds to 'vertex' (point of intersection of two sides of a plane figure or angle).

development and ascertain whether they were created autonomously, as the result of independent semantic extension, or under the influence of another language. A confirmation of the latter may be given by the coexistence of both loanword and domestic item, as evidence of an 'overt' connection between them, a criterion that can be applied to both calques and semantic loans. For example, the syntagmatic calque *tempo pieno* and *full time* are both used in Italian, and the same can be said for *angolo* and *corner*, *navetta* and *shuttle*, *stella* and *star*, *vertice* and *summit*, in fact, for all the examples discussed so far. This particular status of 'overt' calques and semantic loans raises interesting questions related to the co-existence of synonymic doublets, and the preference given to the domestic or foreign form, depending on speaker-oriented or usage-oriented criteria.

Italian scholars (Gusmani, 1986; Bombi 2009a, 2020) have drawn further distinctions within the type of indirect borrowings: one of these types is called 'camouflage borrowing', a term that very well expresses the deceiptful nature of these contact phenomena. This type shares the same mechanism as in the creation of semantic loans, with some noteworthy differences. A prototypical case is exemplified by the Italian verb *realizzare*, which developed the new meaning of 'to become aware of' in addition to its basic meaning of 'to make real'. This case cannot be analysed as a simple semantic extension of the verb *realizzare*, but as the creation of a homonymic copy, whose meaning is unrelated to the previous one. In other words, the lexicon of Italian now has two separate verbs, i.e., *realizzare$^1$* 'to make real', and *realizzare$^2$* 'to become aware of', the latter inspired by the additional meaning of the verb *realize* in the English language. The formal affinity between the two words *realizzare* and *realize* plays a key role in the process of interlinguistic identification (Minutella and Pulcini 2014).

According to Italian scholars who have explored these phenomena in depth (e.g. Bombi, 2020), this type of interference is likely to occur across languages sharing a common stock of vocabulary. This is the case of Italian and English, though belonging to different language families, but by virtue of the kinship ties deriving from a common classical stock in their respective lexicons (Pulcini 2019a). Some guiding criteria for the identification of these phenomena are as follows: a) the new meaning must be significantly different from the original one, b) the word generally belongs to a specialized domain, c) the source and the replica must be formally very similar, d) both source word and replica are used in the recipient language. The terms *casuale/casual* and *autorità /authority* fit all these criteria and can therefore be included in the category of 'camouflage' loans. The Italian adjective *casuale*, which carries the basic meaning of 'accidental', has taken on the new meaning of 'informal', with reference to wearables, from English *casual*. The Italian word *autorità*, which denotes 'the right to command and control', has acquired the new political meaning of 'a person or (esp.) body having political or administrative power and control in a particular sphere', under the influence of English *authority*. Bombi (2020: 130–137) discusses several such cases, among which, *applicazione / application* (computing: 'an application programme'), *migrazione / migration* (computing: 'The process of changing from the use of one platform, environment, IT system, etc., to another'), *convenzione / convention* ('political assembly'), and *singolo / single* ('An unmarried or unaccompanied man or woman'). The definitions indicated refer to the new English-induced meanings.

The identical correspondence in the formal appearance of words in English and in Italian plays a major role in lexical borrowing but, on the other hand, creates great difficulties for the understanding of the underlying process, whether a lexical item should be considered a calque, a semantic loan, an adaptation or simply an autonomous creation in the Italian language. Some cases worth discussing are *virtuale* (virtual), *virale* (viral) and *mediale* (medial). If we dismiss the hypothesis of autonomous creations in Italian, complying with the information given by dictionaries, *mediale* (medial) may indeed be considered a derivative from the word *media* (considered as an English word, regardless of its Latin identity). The cases of *virale* (viral) and *virtuale* (virtual) can be analyzed in terms of semantic extensions of already existing Italian words having acquired new modern meanings, referring to information circulating on the internet and quickly spreading like a virus, in the case of *virale*, and situations or activities that are unreal or immaterial, because they were created by electronic technology, in the case of *virtuale*. This hypothesis is confirmed by the fact than none of the reference dictionaries record *virale* and *virtuale* as English semantic loans.

The typological category of semantic loans and the related type of 'camouflage' loans opens up a whole storehouse of similar vocabulary in English and Italian, raising linguistic questions about the way they developed or influenced one another, considering that the English language today is very likely to be responsible for the spread of neologisms. With reference to items displaying similarity, it is important to mention the nearby lexical area of false friends, i.e., words that are etymologically linked and formally similar, but semantically different, which are generally regarded as 'traps' for learners and causes of errors or misunderstandings. An example is the pair *libreria* (in Italian, *bookstore*) and *library* in English. False friends can be considered the gateway to the creation of semantic loans, especially of the separate category of 'camouflage' loans. In fact, words which were considered false friends some decades ago, are now accepted in the language, though perhaps avoided or frowned upon by older speakers. Among the most common instances, we can quote the word *agenda* (in Italian 'diary'), now commonly used by journalists and politicians with the meaning of 'A list of items to be discussed at a formal meeting', *attitudine*, which is often attributed the English meaning of *attitude* (in Italian 'atteggiamento'), *editore* (in Italian 'curatore'), now synonymous of *editor*, *evidenza* (in Italian 'prova') for *evidence*. Several examples of English meanings transferred to Italian words, because of hasty translations have been pointed out by Tosi (2006) (cf. 2.6), giving rise to English-induced interferences such as *cancellare* (cancel) instead of *annullare*, *introdurre* (introduce) instead of *presentare*, *quotare* (quote) instead of *citare*, *processare* (process) instead of *elaborare*, *approcciare* (approach) instead of *affrontare*, *supportare* (support) instead of *sostenere*, *implementare* (implement) instead of *attuare*, and so on. All these examples have either already been accepted in standard Italian, or are on their way to become part of the Italian language, with due sociolinguistic variation among registers and speakers' preferences.

Formal and semantic affinity between English and Italian cannot overlook the existence of several homographs or near homographs of classical origin, posing additional problems in typological distinctions and identification. What at first sight may look like a semantic loan may be the result of a different process. For example, the word *camera*, which comes from Latin *camera (obscura)*, is a case of *reborrowing*. Having developed independently in the two languages, taking the meaning of 'room' in Italian, the word *camera* in English was attributed to 'a device for taking photographs' or 'a device for capturing moving pictures or video signals'. The identical form and the modern meaning of *camera* were then imported into Italian. The independent status of *camera* is proven by the fact that this modern acceptation can also generate derivatives like *cameraman* (Klajn 1972). A similar phenomenon can be detected in the word *studio* (in Italian, 'a room for studying'), which in English came to denote 'a place where motion pictures are made' or 'a company that produces motion pictures', usually in the plural form *studios*. As indicated by the OED, *studio* is a borrowing from Italian,[70] travelling back to it in the early 20th century with a new, modern meaning. A more recent case is that of *portfolio*, borrowed from Italian *portafoglio* and adapted to English, with the meaning of 'a case or stiff folder for holding papers, prints, drawings, maps, etc. Also figurative', which was reborrowed by Italian as a specialist term in the field of economics to denote 'A range of investments', and later on also in education to refer to 'A compilation of academic work and other forms of educational evidence, testifying the academic growth and achievements of a student'.

---

70 Etymology: < Italian *studio* room used for studying (*a*1446), preliminary sketch or design made to refine detail or in preparation for a larger work of art (*a*1574), artist's workroom (*a*1742; *a*1292 in sense 'act of studying'): see STUDY *n*.

## 4.3 Anglicisms in competition with Italian words

In the study of loanwords, a traditional distinction is drawn between 'necessary' (*Bedürfnislehnwörter*) and 'luxury' loans (*Luxuslehnwörter*) (see 3.1), postulated by Hernst Tappolet in the early 20th century (1913). Necessary loans are introduced to name a new referent for which a domestic word is not yet available, whereas luxury loans are imported to name an object or concept already lexicalized in the receiving language, creating a near-synonym. This dichotomy is far too simplistic and describes this phenomenon as a static one, rather than a dynamic and creative flux of lexical resources.

The concept of 'necessary' loan reminds us of an empty slot in the lexical inventory of a language that needs to be filled in order to name a new entity. As Weinreich states (1953: 56), "The need to designate new things, persons, places, and concepts is, obviously, a universal cause of lexical innovation." Nevertheless, it may be argued that all languages are equipped with word formation and stylistic resources allowing them to create new words, if need be. Yet, Weinreich (1953: 57) continues, "[...] using ready-made designations is more economical than describing things afresh. Few users of language are poets." Such "designative inadequacy" may be the result of laziness of the recipient language speakers, but other reasons play a role in the adoption of a foreign word, among which, as already discussed, the prestige of the source language, because the Anglicism sounds better, younger, more modern, professional, international, attractive and successful than the Italian equivalent. As a matter of fact, Anglicisms hardly ever remain the only signifier for new referents. The need for the existence of synonyms in a language naturally triggers the creation of a domestic equivalent, sometimes more than one, which enter in competition with the loanword.

When a loanword stands side by side with a heritage word, it is considered a 'luxury' loan. In other words, it is considered superfluous and redundant. Sometimes Italian words and Anglicisms are both available to speakers because the Italian word has been created simultaneously to its synonymic Anglicism to name something new, or because the referent already existed in the recipient culture, with its own name. The introduction of a luxury loan, though unnecessary, is motivated by diverse reasons, like the stylistic need to replace an old-fashioned term, which has lost its expressive force, with a more conspicuous one, or one offering an inoffensive term for a sensitive or taboo area, like sexual orientations. For example, the light-hearted echo conveyed by the English word *gay* partly motivated its adoption as an alternative of the more explicit Italian term *omosessuale*. A new lexical item tends to specialize semantically with respect to its near synonym, like the Anglicism *survival* which assumed the connotation of a specific ability or training to survive in case of a catastrophe, although the Italian synonym *sopravvivenza,* albeit more general, already existed. In other words, the expressive power of the Anglicism may well justify its adoption and success, even when a substitute equivalent is proposed.

Another example, among hundreds, is the name of the European vaccination certificate introduced during the COVID-19 pandemic in 2020, called *green pass*. In fact, the official name adopted by the European Union was *EU Digital COVID Certificate* (or *Digital Green Certificate*), in Italian *certificato COVID digitale dell'UE*.[71] For unknown reasons, this certificate started to be called *green pass*, despite the fact that several Italian equivalents had been introduced, such as *certificato verde, certificazione verde* or *pass vaccinale*, but the word *green pass* continued to enjoy popularity, because of its brevity and analogy with other words containing the word *pass* in Italian, such as *ski pass, telepass, by-pass, citypass*, or simply *pass* (also the adapted form *passi* exists). News reportings alternated the use of English and the Italian terms, but when the opponents organized mass protests against the introduction of the certificate in the workplace, the rallying cry "no green pass" was shouted out in the streets and shown on banners and placards, proving the greater iconic value and communicative power of this English word. *Green pass* can be classified as a false Anglicisms, being a domestic creation in an English disguise.

The real question is to explain the reasons for the success of an Anglicism over the domestic form or vice versa. New research approaches have tackled this issue from a cognitive and pragmatic perspective. A pragmatic distinction between necessary and luxury loans, renamed as catachrestic and non-catachrestic loans or innovations, has been proposed by Onysko and Winter-Froemel (2011), who argue that the use of a loanword which has no domestic equivalent does not represent a 'marked' choice for speakers, whereas the use of an Anglicism rather than a domestic word, or vice versa, is pragmatically marked. The speaker's choice is motivated by several reasons, which need to be unveiled by accurate research on the use of near-synonymic pairs (see also Winter-Froemel and Onysko 2012). This aspect of loanword research has recently gained new impetus, drawing on cognitive psychology (Laviosa 2012) and cognitive sociolinguistics (Zenner, Speelman and Geeraerts 2012), on the one hand, and corpus linguistics, on the other (Zenner and Kristiansen 2014). Moving beyond the traditional description of Anglicisms in quantitative and frequency terms, this approach considers the success of Anglicisms on the basis of the relative preference for the Anglicism to name a certain concept vis-à-vis synonymic expressions in the recipient language, isolating specific variables which may be responsible for the

---

[71] See Official Journal of the European Union L 211, Volume 64, 15 June 2021. https://eur-lex.europa.eu/legal-content/EN/TXT/PDF/?uri=OJ:L:2021:211:FULL&from=EN (November, 2022).

choice, such as date of adoption, length (number of syllables), phonemic and graphemic features, or the association to a particular lexical field (Onysko, Winter-Froemel and Caldude 2014).

A study on a sample of Anglicisms in competition with equivalent calques used in Italian (Fiasco and Pulcini, forth.) showed that the date of adoption does not influence the preference for either the Anglicism or the domestic word. Being adopted first does not correspond to greater assimilation in the receiving language. For example, *part time* (1963) was borrowed before its Italian equivalent, *tempo parziale* (1978) and is more frequently used, but *e-mail* was borrowed ten years later (in 1992) than the Italian equivalent *posta elettronica* (in 1982), and has been far more successful in the course of time. The same date of adoption shows divergent trends, e.g. *password* is more frequent than *parola d'ordine* (both dated 1966) but *supermarket* is less frequent than *supermercato* (both dated 1956).

Among the reasons which weigh more on the success of Anglicisms over Italian words are brevity, modernity (cf. *pay-tv* vs *tv a pagamento*), and prestige of the donor culture. Specific fields are more likely to transfer terminology, such as information technology, a rapidly growing domain since the 1990s, rich in Anglicisms, which have spread from specialist to general use. Another aspect that plays in favour of Anglicisms is monoreferentiality as in *star* (borrowed into Italian for the specific meaning of 'famous person' or 'celebrity') and *summit* (political meeting), discussed above (cf. 4.2.2).

By contrast, semantic opacity and difficult pronunciation of an Anglicism may induce speakers to opt for the Italian word, as in the case of *passo dopo passo* (preferred to *step by step*) and the nice-sounding Italian *navetta*, which has taken over from English *shuttle* (the Italian suffix –*etto* conveys an affective connotation of something small and pretty). Finally, neoclassical combining forms in compounds are more readily combined with Italian elements rather than with English ones: for example, *autocontrollo* and *supermercato* are more frequently used than *self-control* and *supermarket*, a tendency already found in previous research (Pulcini and Milani 2017).

## 4.4 Anglicisms or internationalisms?

Most languages of Europe share a large amount of cultural history, not only because many Romance languages have developed from a common Latin root but also because Latin was the vehicle of humanistic education from Medieval and Early Modern times, feeding new vocabulary into European vernaculars and acting as a lingua franca for literates, diplomats, lawyers and scientists, and well into the 17th century (Burke, 2004). Later on, classical languages continued to offer a reservoir of linguistic resources for the creation of scientific taxonomies and terminologies in 18th and 19th centuries Europe (Pulcini and Milani 2017), generating a common stock of similar terms across many languages. According to Iacobini (2015: 1661), in Italian "Latin plays a dual role, constituting both the source of the native lexicon and the main source of loanwords and calques, which were absorbed into Italian in the modern age from Latin texts as well as through the mediation of other languages (mainly French and English)."

This historical dimension of language contact in the European context explains the interest of linguists towards lexical items that are similar in form and meaning across unrelated languages, referred to as internationalisms. According to Wexler (1969: 77), "an internationalism is commonly defined as a word attested in a number of unrelated languages or language families, sharing a similar orthographic or phonetic shape and a partial or identical semantic field; most often, 'internationalisms' are of Greek or Latin origin." As an example, Wexler quotes Belarusian электрычнасць (élektryčnasc), Russian электричество (élektričestvo), Polish elektryczność, to which Spanish electricidad, Italian elettricità, French électricité, and Greek ηλεκτρισμός (ilektrismós) can be added (Pulcini 2019a). International words display some characteristics which set apart this lexical category from others, namely: a) they are unmarked as far as cultural ties are concerned; b) they feature in several unrelated languages (i.e., they are not loan translations) and share formal and semantic similarity (i.e., they are not false friends); c) they normally have classical etymology. Another example, among many others, is the Italian word *automatico* (1704 or earlier), and its international counterparts, namely French *automatique* (1627 or earlier), Spanish *automático* (1736 or earlier), German *automatisch* (1763), Russian *автоматический* (*avtomatičeskij*) (end of 18th century), whose remote etymology can be traced back to Latin *automaticus* (1511 or earlier) (cf. footnote 64). Petralli (1992) claims that there exists an established European lexical storehouse of Latin-based internationalisms amounting to 5% of the lexicons of many European languages.

The nature of internationalisms has been thoroughly studied by German scholars, in particular (Braun 1989; Braun, Schaeder and Volmert 1990, 2003). Within the area of language contact, the relevance of international vocabulary to typological distinctions is immediately evident, as a great number of lexical items fall into the blurred boundary between borrowings and internationalisms. This issue was faced and solved by Görlach when he set the criteria of inclusion for the *Dictionary of European Anglicisms* (2001) (cf. 3.1 and 5.1). He excluded international words not only for the need to limit the entries to English-looking forms, but also to prevent dilemmas over neo-Greek and Latin words, which would be included only on the basis of clear evidence of their Anglicisms status. For example, the English pronunciation of the tennis term *ace* [eɪs] in Italian would be a sign of 'Englishness', despite its classical etymology (Old French *as*, classical Latin *as* < coin < Italian *asso*). Historical information may prove that a word was actually coined in an Anglophone cultural context before being borrowed, but it may be argued that in many cases such historical proof rests on shaky grounds, a conceptual stand that is epitomized by the word *telefono*, which is worth discussing at length because of its relevance to the Italian cultural context.

Internationalisms are sometimes informally referred to as 'telephone-words', since *telephone* is a representative example of this class (Pulcini 2019a). Following Bauer, *telephone* belongs to the type of 'neo-classical compounds', i.e., "words formed in the modern European languages from elements of the classical languages, in such a way that there is no native root involved" (Bauer 1988: 248). In other words, *telephone* could be considered as a 'non-English' word from an etymological perspective, because it is composed of the initial combining form *tele-* which derives from Greek *τηλε-*, meaning 'afar, far off', and the final combining form *-phone* (from Greek *φωνή* 'voice, sound'). As far as cultural ties are concerned (criterion a., presented above), the supposed American provenance of this important invention is also questionable. The invention of the telephone was a cause of contention between the Italian Antonio Meucci and the American Alexander Bell. Already in 1871 Meucci had patented a discovery named *telettrofono* for distance communication. He then developed some prototypes of the invention and submitted them to the American company *Western Union* to be financed. Bell managed to get hold of Meucci's prototypes of this ground-breaking invention and won the race to its patent in 1876. A legal controversy followed, not only between Meucci and Bell, but also between Bell and his American rival Elisha Grey, who claimed the recognition of what would be the most valuable patent in history. Only in 2002 did the US congress recognize that Meucci was the inventor of the telephone, more than 100 years after his death.

Understandably, the historical facts behind the invention of the telephone raise sentiments of nationalism in Italians and at the same time prove that the attribution of the origin of a particular innovation or discovery, and of its denomination, cannot be based on the origin of the scientist who supposedly introduced it for the first time. Indeed, scientific discoveries and technological innovations are often the result of joint international efforts rather than the realization of a single scientist. In the case of the telephone, attempts to develop an instrument for receiving and transmitting sound had been made simultaneously by French, Italian and German inventors. Its neo-classical name fits well into all the world languages and can indeed be considered an internationalism, meeting all three criteria presented above.

Examples similar to telephone are manifold. To quote another case from the field of religion and beliefs, the term *agnostic* is indeed present in many different languages in their respective forms: *agnostico* (Italian), *agnostique* (French), *agnóstico* (Spanish and Portuguese), *Agnostiker* n. *agnostizistisch* adj. (German), *agnostyczny* (Polish), etc. with the meaning of 'A person who believes that nothing is known or can be known of immaterial things, especially of the existence or nature of God.' This term was coined by the English biologist Thomas Henry Huxley in 1869 and borrowed into the Italian language in 1870. The remote etymology of *agnostic* is Greek ἄγνωστος, meaning 'unknown'. There is no trace of 'Englishness' in its form or Italian pronunciation [aɲˈɲɔstiko] and few educated speakers are likely to know where this word comes from.

The list of borderline cases could continue with all the 18th century borrowings from English in the political field that were listed in 2.2 (*coalizione, comitato, commissione, convenzione*), assimilated into Italian through the mediation of French, as well as 19th century political terms such as *assolutismo, assenteismo, ostruzionismo, boicottare*. All these terms are fully Italianized and not included in GLAD. This crucial dimension of 'kinship ties' between Italian, English and other European languages (Pulcini 2019a) is well-known by linguists and lexicographers, as it has widespread consequences on the formation of technical and scientific terminologies. Adamo and Della Valle (2018) quote one such example among present-day neologisms, i.e., *nativo digitale*, inspired by English digital native (English) coined in 2001 by the American writer Marc Prensky, and which has spread in other languages, e.g. in French (*natif numérique*), in German (*digital Native*), in Spanish and Portuguese (*nativo digital*). As already discussed in 4.2.1 with reference to calques, whether these neologisms should be recognized as English loan translations or independent creations of modern languages triggered by the process of globalization is open to debate but no definitive word can be given on this question.

The origin of words is controversial also in the attestations provided by dictionaries. A study on a sample of lexical items recorded as 'from English' by the GDU (2007) compared the historical profile given of these items by some general dictionaries of Italian, pointed out differences in their historical provenance, generally from English or French or both, i.e., *assenteismo* (French *absentéisme*, English *absenteeism*), *autocarro* (French *autocar*, English *autocar*), *budino* (English *pudding*, French *boudin*), *celluloide* (French *celluloid*, English *celluloid*), *locomotiva* (English *locomotive*, French *locomotive*), *pittografia* (English *pictography*, French *pictographie*), *romantico* (English *romantic*, French *romantique*, from French *roman* 'novel'), *turismo* and *turista* (from English *tourism* and *tourist*, in turn from French *tour*). Moreover, the 'interlexeme' represented by Italian *aerobica, alchemico, automatizzazione, diorama,* and *psichedelico* and their respective look-alike equivalents,[72]

---

72 - Italian: *aerobica*; English: *aerobics*; French: *aérobie*; Spanish: *aerobic*; German; *Aerobic*; Danish: *aerobic*; Norwegian: *aerobic*; Polish: *aerobik*; Russian: *аэробика* (aerobika).

fully satisfy the requisites for the status of internationalisms, being shared by eight European languages beside Italian (English, French, Spanish, German, Danish, Norwegian, Polish and Russian) of three language families – Romance, Germanic and Slavic (Pulcini 2019a).

An authoritative opinion on this matter was expressed on several occasions by Tullio De Mauro, the author of the *Grande dizionario italiano dell'uso* and the most distinguished Italian linguist and lexicographer in the 20th century. De Mauro (2016) believed that European lexicography was largely hinged on national, if not 'nationalistic', ideals. European languages have been considered autonomous with respect to the other languages. When faced with convergences, that is, similar words across languages, lexicographers busied themselves to trace in which language a particular word had appeared for the first time, and immediately labeled it as Gallicism, Anglicism, Germanism, Italianism, etc. De Mauro concludes by saying that "il ruolo del latino come fonte dei lessici delle diverse lingue è restato a lungo oscurato dalla fallacia nazionalistica" ["the role of Latin as a source of the lexicon of the different languages has long been obfuscated by the nationalistic fallacy"] (De Mauro 2016: 22). This illusion consists in disregarding that a large amount of Latin-based vocabulary actually represents a common linguistic property of Europe. Whether a word emerged for the first time in one language or in another is irrelevant.

To sum up, the classical etymology that characterizes a large share of modern vocabulary across European languages poses major problems when it comes to distinguishing English loanwords from independent creations of international nature. The information provided by dictionaries is often discordant, not because dictionaries are unreliable, but because language contact is a complex phenomenon, taking multiple paths of transmission, and the origin of words is hard or impossible to establish or even irrelevant, following De Mauro's standpoint. In the case of Italian, neologisms were transmitted either from French or from English, but very often from both sources. In most cases, international collaboration and the

---

- Italian: *alchemico*; English: *alchemic*; French: *alchimie*; Spanish: *alquímico*; German: *alchemisch*; Danish: *alkymistisk*; Norwegian: *alchemic*; Polish: *alchemiczny*; Russian: *алхимический* (alkhimichesky).

- Italian: *automatizzazione*; English: *automatization*; French: *automatization*; Spanish: *automatizaciòn*; German: *Automatisierung*; Danish: *automatisering*; Norwegian: *automatisering*; Polish: *automatyzacja*; Russian: *автоматический* (avtomatichesky).

- Italian: *diorama*; English: *diorama*; French: *diorama*; Spanish: *diorama*; German: *Diorama*; Danish: *diorama*; Norwegian: *diorama*; Polish: *diorama*; Russian: *диорама* (diorama).

- Italian: *psichedelico*; English: *psychedelic*; French: *psychédélique*; Spanish: *psicodélico*; German: *psychedelisch*; Danish: *psykedelisk*; Norwegian: *psykedelisk*; Polish: *psychodeliczny*; Russian: *психоделический* (psikhodelichesky).

circulation of scientific findings, discoveries, ideas and social habits has given rise to parallel terminologies.[73] Finally, it is also important not to underestimate the role of speakers' perceptions and attitudes towards words that are formally Italian words, and therefore perceived as familiar and acceptable, as opposed to foreign words, which can be recognized, accepted or rejected. Attitudes to language are a crucial component, acting as 'invisible' social pressures when it comes to language matters (Pulcini 1997). In fact, many speakers are willing to deny the foreign origin of words, when these are formally integrated into the language, that is, when they look and sound Italian.

## 4.5 Roundup

In the post-borrowing phase, loanwords undergo several forms of integration into Italian, to adapt to a new linguistic environment, at the level of pronunciation (in non-adapted loanwords), spelling, grammar (in adapted loanwords) and meaning (potentially, all borrowings). Although most Anglicisms are nouns, grammatical (or morpho-syntactic) integration involves gender attribution, the assignment of grammatical class (mainly noun, adjective, adverb and verb), and formal adaptation (Italian verbs must display inflectional ending for mood, person, number and gender). Semantically, Anglicisms in Italian denote a reduced range and specialization of meanings compared to the English source words, and may deviate from the original meaning to adapt to a new communicative environment and to convey culture-specific concepts or entities.

This chapter dealt with the two main types of indirect borrowings, i.e., calques and semantic loans. The former replace the English model (form and meaning) with an Italian translation equivalent, whereas the latter borrows a new meaning which is attached to an already existing Italian word. The identification of calques and semantic loans is problematic and requires the expertise of a linguist. Their assimilation into the Italian system is extremely easy and therefore they are perceived as Italian words.

A further dimension of the Anglicization of Italian dealt with in this chapter is the coexistence of Anglicisms with Italian equivalents. No definitive conclusion has been reached on the factors that influence speakers' preferences when they are faced with the choice between an Anglicism or an Italian word. Preliminary data

---

[73] Research on philosophical and scientific ideas, and lexical resources to express them, within the European tradition, is the core objective of the *Istituto per il Lessico Intellettuale Europeo e Storia delle Idee* (ILIESI) (Adamo and Della Valle 2019). The historical period considered goes from antiquity to modernity, reaching out to phenomena of present-day Italian.

suggest that brevity and monoreferentiality play in favour of Anglicisms, whereas classical etymology in the composition of words plays in favour of Italian derivatives and calques. Common historical roots in the languages of Europe, standing on a hard core of Latin and Greek, have produced a stock of shared international words, whose lexical status in many cases lies on the border with Anglicisms with neoclassical form. On the one hand, the origin or route of transmission of words should not be underestimated or overlooked; on the other, from a typological point of view, speakers' perceptions are strongly influenced by the formal appearance of words so that words with Italian form and pronunciation are not perceived as borrowings.

A major typological dilemma is caused by the fact that a large portion of English vocabulary has neoclassical origins. Latinisms that are part of the English lexicon may filter into Italian and be immediately assimilated, since Italian is a Latin-based language. English words with a classical root can be matched with identical Italian forms and become indistinguishable. In addition, similar mechanisms of composition (e.g. with neo-classical combining forms) and derivation (similar affixes), makes it hard to tell calques apart from derivatives, and, ultimately, Anglicisms from non-Anglicisms, i.e., internationalisms, independent neological creations or semantic extensions of heritage words. For these reasons, the status of indirect borrowing is indeed much more problematic to analyze than direct Anglicisms.

# 5 Dictionaries, newspaper archives and corpora

## 5.1 Dictionaries: The quantitative dimension at work

Over the past decades, the assimilation of Anglicisms into the Italian language has continuously raised contrasting opinions and attitudes among linguists. The opponents of exogenous influences compare the input of Anglicisms to a 'flood' or an 'invasion' that will distort the identity of Italian. Others downplay the dangers of the Anglicization of Italian, arguing that it is a marginal phenomenon, largely limited to low-frequency, specialized vocabulary. Counting how many Anglicisms are part of the Italian lexicon is a question that many linguists have tried to answer (Klajn 1972; Cartago 1994; Serafini 2001; Bistarelli 2008; De Mauro 2005; Furiassi 2008; Gualdo and Scarpino 2007; Pulcini 2007, 2017). In this chapter, the numerical data provided by some existing dictionaries will be used as a starting point for the quantification of Anglicisms that have been imported and assimilated into Italian and which, as will be shown, can only be indicative but not definitive. Before delving into the analysis of Anglicisms in dictionaries, the composition of the Italian lexicon will be examined in order to get an objective perspective on the share of Italian vocabulary that we are focusing on.

De Mauro (2005) explains that the lexicon of any language can be grouped into three broad categories: a. heritage words; b. exogenous words, borrowed from other languages (non-adapted, adapted and calques); c. endogenous (new) formations, created according to the word formation processes characteristic of a language, especially affixation and composition, starting from lexical bases of groups a. and b.[74] De Mauro (2005: 210) showed that 94.8% of the Italian lexicon is constituted by traditional (heritage) lexis and subsequent formations still in use (categories a. and c.), while the remaining 5% includes words taken from exogenous sources (called 'exoticisms'), including Greek (1.4%) and Latin borrowings (0.8%), and borrowings from modern languages (3%), in the form of both adapted (1.6%) and non-adapted (1.4%) borrowings. Moreover, research into samples of texts which typically contain many foreign words (e.g. texts about sport) proved that the frequency of foreign borrowings amounted to 0.48%. These data justify

---

[74] De Mauro explains (2005: 127) that in the English language this tripartite division is clear-cut: 10% of heritage vocabulary from the Anglo-Saxon stock; 76.5% of borrowings from other languages (42% French, 25% Latin, 4% Spanish, 4% Italian, 1.5% other languages, which makes English the most 'Latinized' and 'Romance' language of the non-Latin languages); 13.5% of endogenous formations, based on heritage or borrowed words. In Romance languages like Italian this distinction is not easy to identify, as both the heritage vocabulary and endogenous formations are Latin-based.

Open Access. © 2023 the author(s), published by De Gruyter. This work is licensed under the Creative Commons Attribution-NoDerivs 4.0 International License.
https://doi.org/10.1515/9783110755114-005

De Mauro's favourable attitude to foreign borrowings, given that, according to his data, their number and frequency rate are low and Italian speakers seem to favour heritage lexis to foreign words. According to De Mauro, foreign words are naturally preferred in advertising and in texts where the foregrounding power of the exotic word is exploited for stylistic reasons, but not in the general language of everyday use, both spoken and written. In addition, he shows that nearly half of the terms marked as 'exoticisms' [ES] in the GDU (De Mauro 2007) are also marked as 'technical and specialized' [TS], that is, they belong to the periphery of the lexicon (see footnote 75 on the layers of the Italian lexicon).

The next important step is to determine the share of English borrowings within the total number of exogenous borrowings. On the basis of the lemmas recorded by De Mauro and Mancini (2003), which is based on the GDU, the number of words originating from foreign languages amounts to 11,104 (4.2%), including 8,196 (3.1%) which are from English. Yet, by focusing on lemmas marked as [ES] (exoticism), i.e., non-adapted borrowings from English, the number goes down to 5,510 (2.1%). Considering the total number of non-adapted borrowings from all languages, it follows that the large majority of all foreign borrowings are from English (73.8%), which makes English the strongest donor language to Italian, albeit not the only one. To sum up, the incidence of Anglicisms in the whole word list of the GDU is 3.1% (of which 2.1% are non-adapted and 1% are adapted).

Similar numerical evaluations have been carried out by other authors, with percentages that are not greatly divergent (Pulcini 2007). Gualdo and Scarpino (2007) provide the same percentage of the input of Anglicisms (3.1%) based on the lemma list of the dictionary *Il Sabatini Coletti* (Sabatini and Coletti 2004). According to older data examined by Klajn (1972), the number of direct Anglicisms discussed in his book is 2,150 (of which 1,600 are non-adapted and 550 are adapted), with an overall incidence of Anglicisms in the whole Italian lexicon amounting to 1.7%. In short, despite numerical differences, there is a consensus among linguists that the share of foreign words attested in Italian and the number of Anglicisms are relatively small.

A different impression of the numerical impact of Anglicisms on Italian is given by their increase over time. Figure 5.1 shows the growth in the number of Anglicisms (non-adapted and adapted) in the GDU (2007) and *Nuovo Devoto-Oli 2022*, which has been remarkable in both dictionaries, even though they differ in size, with the GDU containing 260,709 entries and *Nuovo Devoto-Oli 2022* (digital edition) 110,000 entries. The GDU covers the years up to 2006, whereas *Nuovo Devoto-Oli 2022* is updated every year. What is particularly striking is the rise in the number of Anglicisms in the post-unification years (1851–1900 in Figure 5.1), which is higher than the number of Anglicisms imported in all previous centuries. This makes this period a turning point for the development of the Italian national language. The increase in the 20th century is even more marked, especially in the second half and across the new millennium. Accordingly, these data may justify the alarms raised by some language observers. On the other hand, data need to be interpreted not only in quantitative terms but also in qualitative ones. Following De Mauro's stance on this matter, it is necessary to weigh these numbers against other decisive linguistic factors, such as their sociolinguistic distribution (their currency and usage frequency in the general language or in specialized domains), and their lifetime. In fact, many words may enter a language for a short period and then fall out of use; since many dictionaries are still conservative reference tools, Anglicisms may secure a place in a dictionary and then firmly keep it for a long time, possibly forever, even when their use is extremely limited (cf. 6.5 on obsolescence).[75]

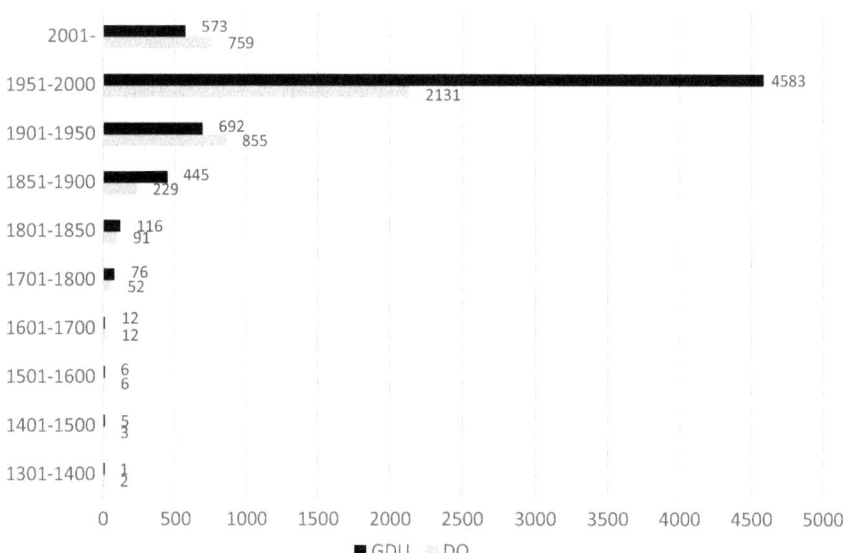

**Figure 5.1:** Number of Anglicisms in the GDU (2007) and *Nuovo Devoto-Oli 2022*.

---

75 De Mauro and Ferreri (2005) provide a wealth of statistical data, based on their own calculations carried out on *Grande dizionario italiano dell'uso* (2007) and studies carried out by other Italian linguists. They show that great variation on the composition of the Italian lexicon can be found depending on which share one focuses on. The Italian fundamental vocabulary (*fondamentali*) includes c. 2,000 words that occur in 90% of all texts. Among the fundamental vocabulary, the only Anglicisms included are *bar*, *film* and *sport*. Another layer of 3,000 words belong to the category of high use ([AU] *alto uso*) (words understood by any user with average education) and 2,300 high availability words ([AD] *alta disponibilità*) (denoting objects, facts and experiences

As shown in Figure 5.1, the number of Anglicisms recorded in the two dictionaries cited above varies greatly, owing to, in the first place, their different sizes, and to other characteristics such as the time frame, their macrostructure and criteria of inclusion of different types of Anglicisms (Pulcini 2008a, 2010). Nevertheless, the numerical data provide a good picture of the strong upward trend of the input of Anglicisms in Italian since the mid-20$^{th}$ century.

The retrieval of Anglicisms for the creation of a new lexicographic tool with its own specific characteristics generally starts from already existing dictionaries. For the creations of GLAD, some reference dictionaries[76] were identified as suitable sources for the collection of candidate Anglicisms. The reasons for this choice lies in the fact that two of these dictionaries are specifically focussed on Anglicisms, namely the *Dizionario degli Anglicismi nell'italiano postunitario* by Rando (1987) and the *Dictionary of European Anglicisms* by Görlach (2001). One of the chosen dictionaries is devoted to foreign borrowings in the Italian language, namely *Parole straniere nella lingua italiana* by De Mauro and Mancini (2003). Finally, two general dictionaries of Italian, available in digital format, yearly updated and rich in neologisms, namely *Nuovo Devoto-Oli 2022* and *Zingarelli 2022* have been systematically consulted. In the following analysis, the chosen dictionaries will be presented in chronological order and their macrostructural characteristics will be briefly described, with the entry for *jeep* as a sample illustration. A comparative analysis of the letter J entries recorded by these dictionaries, illustrated in Section 5.2, will show the diversity in the Anglicisms recorded in these sources and the use of the comparative method adopted for the selection of GLAD's entries.

– *Dizionario degli Anglicismi nell'italiano postunitario* (1987)

The *Dizionario degli Anglicismi nell'italiano postunitario* by Rando (1987) is the first and only paper dictionary of Anglicisms available for Italian. As declared in the preface to the dictionary, the period considered is from the post-unification time (Italy was unified in 1861), when a decline in lexical borrowing from French gave way to an increase of borrowings from English. The actual number of entries is 2,500 but many forms are embedded within the same headword. The

---

that are known by all speakers). The share of 'common vocabulary' includes 45,000 items, which are known by speakers with a medium-high level of education. Other layers of vocabulary are 'technical and scientific terms' [TS], 'regionalisms' [RE], 'low-use words' ([BU *basso uso*), 'obsolete' [OB] and 'foreign words' ([ES] 'exoticism'). It follows that any evaluation on the impact of English (or any other foreign language) must be measured against the layer of the lexicon in which borrowings have penetrated.

76 The lexicographic record of Anglicisms in Italian began towards the end of the 19$^{th}$ century (Fanfani and Arlia 1877; Panzini 1905; Monelli 1943). The purist intentions of these early contributions were discussed in chapter 2 (cf. 2.4).

author states that the total number of Anglicisms recorded is approximately 4,200, including 3,100 direct loanwords (1,503 non-adapted and 1,600 adapted Anglicisms) and calques (1,100). The types of borrowings included in Rando's dictionary reflect his open definition of an Anglicism:

> Per anglicismo (specificatamente *anglicismo italiano*) si intende ogni vocabolo o accezione di vocabolo che sia di origine inglese o che sia giunto nella nostra lingua tramite l'inglese nelle varietà britannica e americana ma anche in quelle dell'Australia, del Canadà e del Sud Africa. (Rando 1987: xvi)

> [By Anglicism (specifically an *Italian Anglicism*) is meant any word or word sense which is of English origin or has arrived in our language through English in its British and American varieties but also in those of Australia, Canada and South Africa.]

As stated by the author himself, the sources for this dictionary are books, magazines and newspapers, but also spoken sources like radio, television and cinema. The most common fields represented in this dictionary are sport, games and entertainment, science and technology, tourism, business and commerce, politics and warfare. Rando discusses the lexicographic problem of identifying indirect Anglicisms when their form is similar to Italian words (e.g. *editoriale*)–a problem discussed at length in this volume, see Section 4.1–and argues that both linguistic and socio-historical information should guide the lexicographer for the selection of Anglicisms. The result of this pioneering dictionary is a collection of non-adapted and adapted Anglicisms, calques, internationalisms, pseudo-Anglicisms, abbreviations and phrases, many of which are common and recognizable Anglicisms, while others appear extremely infrequent, such as names of animals (e.g. *petrello* from *petrel*, sea bird, better known in Italian as *procellaria*; *vonga-vonga* from Australian bird *wonga-wonga*), highly technical terms (*sincrotrone* from *syncrotron*), and many highly specific acronyms (e.g. JATO, Jet Assisted Take-Off). What also strikes the user is the inclusion of items of encyclopedic nature, like proper names of institutions (*Casa Bianca* from *White House*, *Associated Press*, *Lions Club*), trademarks not turned into generic nouns (*Clarks, Gillette, Rolls Royce*), popular and dialectal variants (*casimira* for cashmere; *piccio* for picture) and many scientific terms of international circulation (e.g. *pennicillina* and *antibiotico*).[77] Some entries are questionable and awkward, such as *credere in* (from

---

[77] As discussed in 4.4 many scientific terms can be classified as internationalisms, being made up of neo-classical elements and being attested in many European languages with similar forms and meanings. We argue that basing the attribution of the status of Anglicisms on the nationality of the inventors is a weak criterion. In the examples quoted here, *pennicillina* was discovered by the Scottish scientist Alexander Fleming, and the term *antibiotico* was coined by the biochemist Selman Abraham Waksman, born in Ukraine and naturalized as an American citizen.

*to believe in*), *perdere l'autobus* (from *to miss the bus*), *Rome by night*, *segnorina* (prostitute), and *tisi galoppante* (galloping tuberculosis). The unbalanced selection of this dictionary's word list is also discussed by Fanfani in his review (1991). Besides the criticism addressed to the inclusion of the items listed above, Fanfani points out that this dictionary presents many inaccuracies in the dates of adoption, the inclusion of Gallicisms and Germanisms, as well as words of dubious English provenance, casuals and quotation words, and dialectal forms featuring in non-standard varieties of Italian. A second edition with corrections was never published, so that the *Dizionario degli Anglicismi nell'italiano postunitario*, despite its weaknesses, remains an important reference work for the description of the lexical influence of English on Italian.

Figure 5.2 shows the entry of the Anglicism *jeep*. The microstructure of the entry indicates grammatical class and gender (s.f., substantive, feminine), followed by a definition, the indication of the plural form (invariable or with -*s*). The grammatical information is followed by possible adaptations: in this case, *gippe* in the Tuscan dialect and the rare form *jep* appear irrelevant to standard Italian. Derivatives and compounds are inserted at the end of each entry. In this case, the

**jeep,** *s.f.* (in origine, 1944-46, anche *s.m.*). Camionetta scoperta a 4 o 5 posti, molto robusta e adatta alla marcia su terreni difficili. Plurale: **jeep** (talvolta **jeeps**). Adattamenti: **geep,** *s.f.;* **gip** *s.m.* (a 1945); **gippe** (nel toscano); **jep** *s.f.* (raro). Deriv.: **gippone,** *s.m.* ' camionetta della polizia ' Amer. *jeep* trascrizione secondo le regole fonetiche della sigla G.P. (*general purpose* ' uso generale '); l'autoveicolo, ideato negli Stati Uniti verso il 1936, venne ampiamente usato dagli eserciti alleati durante la II guerra mondiale e fu introdotto in Italia con l'occupazione passando, poi, anche ad uso civile. **Jeep-girl,** *s.f.*, voce dell'occupazione: ragazza che andava volentieri in jeep son soldati alleati; adattata con **gip(p)ista,** *s.f.* ⟨1943: DELI⟩

**Figure 5.2:** The *jeep* entry in Rando (1987).

form *gippone* (vehicle larger than a jeep) appears to be current in present-day Italian, whereas the compound *jeep-girl* sounds obsolete. The entry also contains historical information about the adoption of this word during the American occupation in the post-WW2 years. This type of information is provided only when the author considers it relevant to the lexical profiling of the headword.

– *Dictionary of European Anglicisms* (2001)
Görlach's *Dictionary of European Anglicisms* (DEA) contains 3,800 Anglicisms present in 16 European languages, of which 1,600 are recorded for Italian. The aim of this project was to provide an analytical picture of the impact of the English language in Europe, on the basis of 16 European languages representing many language families: four Germanic (Icelandic, Norwegian, Dutch and German), four Slavic (Polish, Russian, Croatian and Bulgarian), four Romance (French, Italian, Spanish and Romanian) as well as four other languages (Finnish, Hungarian, Albanian and Greek). The time frame encompasses the years 1945–1995, the period of maximum penetration of the English language on a global scale. As for the criteria of inclusion, Görlach preferred to limit his word list by focusing exclusively on words that are "recognizably English", i.e., have an English form, discarding the large number of internationalisms, unless they retain strong evidence of English provenance (a question discussed in Section 3.1). The DEA is an ambitious contribution to comparative loanword lexicography. The method adopted for collecting and assembling the material for each language is meticulously illustrated in Görlach (2003) and the status of English in the selected languages is described in two separate volumes (Görlach 2002a, 2002b), setting the ground for systematic comparison.

Figure 5.3 shows the structure of the entry for *jeep*: the etymon is followed by a part-of-speech label (n. noun) and a definition taken from the *Concise Oxford Dictionary* (if there is more than one entry with the same lemma, a number indicates which one is considered). The definition is followed by a summary paragraph about the history of the lemma (this paragraph is present for some but not all lemmas): in this case, it is explained that *jeep* derives from the abbreviation G.P. meaning 'general purpose' (vehicle). What is interesting is the fact that the word *jeep* has not generated any replacement in the languages considered. What follows is a concise language-by-language presentation of the status of the lemma, in this case the status of *jeep*, including pronunciation, gender, plural formation, date of adoption and degree of acceptance, indicated by symbols and numbers. For instance, number (2) indicates that "the word is fully accepted and found in many styles and registers, but is still marked as English in its spelling, pronunciation, or morphology", whereas number (3) indicates that "the word is not (or no longer) recognized as English;

English origin can only be established etymologically".[78] The acceptance of *jeep* ranges between (2) and (3) in the languages represented. As can be noted, the information provided for *jeep* in Italian is that the pronunciation is close to the English one, gender is feminine, there is no plural (invariable plural), the decade of adoption is the 1940s, and the word is fully accepted.

---

**jeep** *n.* 1 'a small sturdy esp. military motor vehicle with four-wheel drive'

The car and its name (possibly from *G.P.* = *general purpose* [vehicle]) became proverbially popular after 1945 as ↑*jeans* did. The word is used universally and has not sparked off any native replacements.

**Ge** [dʒ-/ʃ-] M, pl. -*s*, 1940s (2) **Du** [=E] C, 1940s (2) **Nw** [jiːp/jep/=E] M, pl. -*er*, 1940s (2) **Ic** *jeppi* [jɛhpɪ] M, pl. -*ar*, 1940s (3) **Fr** [(d)ʒip] F, 1940s (2) **Sp** [=E/jip] M, pl. -*s*, 1940s (2) **It** [=E] F, pl. Ø, 1940s (3) **Rm** <=E>/*jep* [=E/ʒep] N, 1960s, via Fr (2/3) **Rs** *dzhip* M, pl. -*y*, mid20c (3) **Po** [dʒip] M, mid20c (2) **Cr** *džip* M, pl. -*ovi*, mid20c (2) **Bg** *dzhip* M, pl. -*al-ove*, mid20c (2) → -*ka* F **Fi** *jeeppi* mid20c (3) **Hu** *dzsip* [dʒip] pl. -*ek*, mid20c (3) **Al** *xhip* M, pl. -*e*, mid20c (3) **Gr** *tzip* N, mid20c (2) → *tzipaki* N

**Figure 5.3:** The *jeep* entry in the DEA (2001).

---

**– Parole straniere nella lingua italiana (2003)**
*Parole straniere nella lingua italiana* by De Mauro and Mancini (2003; first edition 2001) is an autonomous dictionary of foreign words, based on the unabridged *Grande dizionario italiano dell'uso* or GDU (De Mauro 1999/2007). The macrostructure of this dictionary contains all the words that are marked as 'exoticism' [ES] in the GDU, which amount to 11,104 foreign words. For this reason, the number of Anglicisms recorded in this dictionary is very high, drawing on a wider time frame and an unabridged word list, encompassing all the layers of the lexicon (see footnote 75).

---

[78] The classification scheme for the 'degree of acceptance' is as follows: "- the word is not known but a calque or another native equivalent is provided [. . .]; ° the word is known mainly to bilinguals and is felt to be English [. . .]; ø the word is known but is a foreignism – that is, it is used only with reference to British or American contexts [. . .]; 1 the word is in restricted use in the language [. . .]; 2 the word is fully accepted and found in many styles and registers, but is still marked as English in its spelling, pronunciation, or morphology; 3 the word is not (or no longer) recognized as English; English origin can only be established etymologically; 4 the word is identical or nearly identical to an indigenous item in the receptor language, so that the borrowing takes the form of a semantic loan only [. . .]; 5 the word, as far as the individual language is concerned, comes from a source other than English." (Görlach 2001: xxiv).

As for numbers, non-adapted Anglicisms are 5,510. Some important specifications are applied to the structure of this dictionary. The main A–Z word list contains only non-adapted borrowings, whose orthography or pronunciation make the words recognizably foreign. Two appendices provide lists of Italianized derivatives and words historically connected to foreign languages, and phraseologisms. Appendix I has words mainly of neo-Latin origin such as *anglicismo* (!), *abolizionismo*, c*oalizione*, *conformista, deterrente, editoriale, eurovisione, impatto, manageriale, microfono, omosessuale, placebo, preistorico, realista, romantico, telefono*, etc. but also adapted Anglicisms from a non-Latin English root such as *tabloide, quacchero* and *behaviorismo*. Appendix II contains phraseologisms (*polirematiche*) built on foreign models such as *caccia alle streghe* (witch-hunt), *cane lupo* (wolf dog), *lavaggio del cervello* (brain washing), etc. In sum, De Mauro draws a clear-cut distinction between direct borrowings (the 'real' foreign words, according to the author), on the one hand, and Italianized adaptations, derivations, and phraseological calques, on the other.

Most 'foreign words' recorded in this dictionary belong to the technical-specialized domains and are marked as [TS] (see Table 5.2). However, not all foreign words belong to this share of the lexicon. The words *bar, film* and *sport* are labelled as 'fundamental' [FO], that is, they belong to the core 2,000 words of Italian. The entry *jeep* (Figure 5.4) shows that this word, despite its foreign look, is classified as common [CO], the share of vocabulary known by speakers with a medium-high level of education. The headword is followed by the pronunciation in IPA phonetic transcription, grammatical class (s.f.inv., i.e., substantive, feminine, invariable), the layer of use (common), the date of adoption, the language of origin (ingl.), form and pronunciation. Before the definition, a further specification is given of its origin (from the acronym G.P. meaning 'general purpose' ['vehicle']). Note that the reference to the military field is not openly made explicit here, although the term 'camionetta' refers to vehicles used by the army or by the police, and a generic extension to any off-road vehicle is given. The derivative *jeeppone*, made up of the English base and an Italian suffix (*-one*, expressing large dimension), is given. However, a check in newspaper archives and corpora confirms that the Italianized form *gippone* is more frequent than *jeeppone*. The variant *gip* is still current, but rare.

– *Zingarelli 2022*
*Zingarelli 2022* is a general dictionary of Italian, whose first edition was compiled by Nicola Zingarelli in 1917. It has recently celebrated its 100th anniversary, and 12 editions have been issued over time. The publisher Zanichelli is one of the oldest in Italy, specializing especially in textbooks for school, university and professional books, and is considered the top publisher of monolingual, bilingual and specialized dictionaries. Their sources are diversified and handled by a huge editorial team. Since 1994 *Zingarelli* dictionary has been updated every year and is well-known for

**jeep** /dʒip/ s.f.inv. CO [1943; ingl. *jeep* /dʒiːp/, dalla pronuncia delle lettere *G. P.*, iniziali della loc. *general purpose* "per tutti gli usi", sott. *vehicle* "veicolo", per indicare la versatilità del veicolo] grossa camionetta scoperta a quattro ruote motrici, predisposta per la marcia su terreni impervi | estens., qualunque vettura fuoristrada **Der.** jeeppone **Var.** gip.

**Figure 5.4:** The *jeep* entry in De Mauro and Mancini (2003).

its liberal policy of inclusion of neologisms and foreignisms, in constant competition with other best-selling dictionaries on the market. It also contains literary, archaic and technical vocabulary to help with the comprehension of a wide range of academic, professional and specialized texts. The 2022 edition contains 145,000 entries.

As for Anglicisms, *Zingarelli 2022* allows the extraction of Anglicisms by selecting the option 'Lingua' ('language') and then the English form. In this way all entries marked as 'vc. ingl.' (i.e., English lemma) or 'loc. ingl.' (i.e., English phrase) are displayed. This search yielded 3,990 lemmas. More inclusive searches are also possible: by selecting the abbreviation 'ingl.' in the etymology section, also words related to English such as calques and eponyms are retrieved. This search yields 4,150 lemmas.[79]

Figure 5.5 shows the entry for *jeep*. The first thing to notice is that Jeep is spelled with a capital letter and recorded as a registered trademark,[80] followed by the English phonetic transcription and a link to an audio file. In square brackets the etymological information is indicated, in this case the origin of the word from the initials G. P. and the year of adoption. The grammatical label (s.f.inv., i.e., substantive, feminine, invariable) is followed by the definition, which indicates that this word was originally used in the military field. A cross reference is given to the orthographic variant *gip* (meaning 1), which has a separate entry (including *gippone*).

– *Nuovo Devoto-Oli 2022*

*Nuovo Devoto-Oli 2022* is one of the most definitive general dictionaries of Italian, printed for the first time in 1971. It has had several new editions and revisions

---

[79] The increase in the number of English borrowings in *Zingarelli* dictionary (vc. ingl., i.e. English lemma) has been steady, as is shown by the following figures: 2000 edition (2,055), 2004 edition (2,219), 2006 edition (2,318), 2016 edition (2,761), 2020 edition (2,927). The etymology section yielded 4,080 entries in the 2021 edition and has risen to 4,150 in the 2022 edition (the current one at the time of writing).

[80] Jeep® was registered as a trademark in 1987 by the *Chrysler Group* and is now part of the Dutch multinational company *Stellantis*.

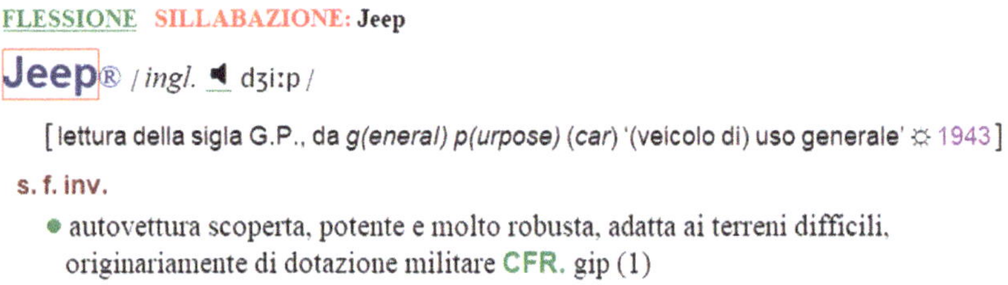

FLESSIONE   SILLABAZIONE: Jeep

Jeep® / ingl. 🔊 dʒiːp /

[ lettura della sigla G.P., da *g(eneral) p(urpose) (car)* '(veicolo di) uso generale' ☼ 1943 ]

**s. f. inv.**
- autovettura scoperta, potente e molto robusta, adatta ai terreni difficili, originariamente di dotazione militare **CFR.** gip (1)

**Figure 5.5:** The *jeep* entry in *Zingarelli 2022*.

under the direction of authoritative linguists, and has been updated yearly since 2006. It is available in paper and digital formats, also for access through mobile devices. This dictionary covers a large variety of registers to allow comprehension of literary, professional, scientific and technical texts. The number of lemmas in the 2022 edition is 110,000. This dictionary is open to neologisms but, at the same time, is vigilant about stylistic correctness. A specific section, named "*Per dirlo in italiano*" ["To say it in Italian"] examines some recorded Anglicisms and their borrowing history, and suggests "Italian equivalents for unnecessary English words, difficult to understand or pronounce" ["alternative italiane alle parole inglesi superflue, difficili da capire o pronunciare"]. The advanced search option allows for the retrieval of lemmas according to category (field), date, etymology, grammatical class and register. Setting the search to 'language' and then to 'English', the database yields 4,140 lemmas, including direct and indirect Anglicisms, the latter consisting of derivatives and scientific vocabulary of international nature.

Figure 5.6 shows the entry for *jeep*. The lemma is printed in lower case lettering, which means that it is considered a common noun. The English pronunciation is given first, followed by both the Italian one in IPA phonetic transcription and both accompanied by an audio file. Grammatical information is 's.f. invar.' (i.e., substantive, feminine, invariable). Additional grammatical information is available after extending the description window (selecting the + symbol). In this case the original English plural is provided. In the etymon section, the lemma is defined as an English word ('voce ingl.') deriving from the abbreviation G.P., which means 'general purpose', a gloss that is also translated into Italian ('per tutti gli usi'). The date of adoption in Italian is 1943.

The analysis of dictionaries carried out so far has shown that the number of Anglicisms recorded in different lexicographic works varies depending on the coverage and the target users that each dictionary has in mind. An unabridged dictionary like the GDU, on which De Mauro and Mancini (2003) was built, is meant to be a comprehensive, national dictionary of modern Italian, whereas *Zingarelli 2022* and *Nuovo Devoto-Oli 2022* are typical 'medium-sized', general purpose dictionaries,

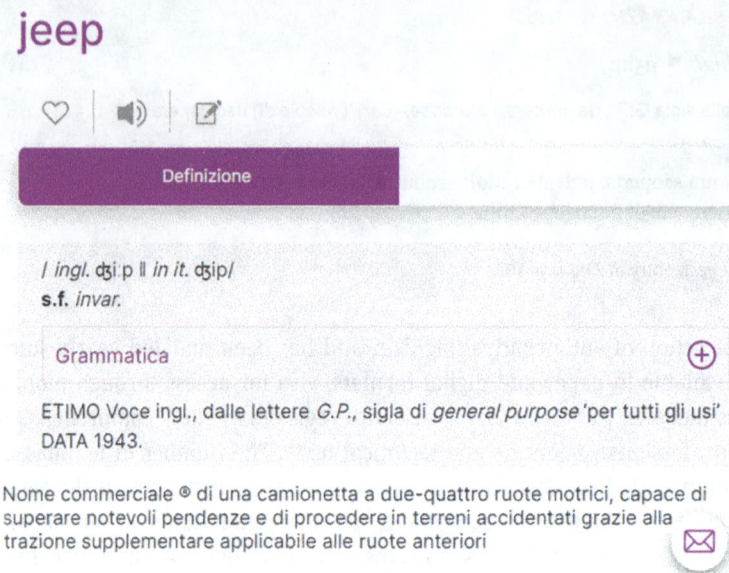

**Figure 5.6:** The *jeep* entry in *Nuovo Devoto-Oli 2022*.

covering the lexicon that college students and educated users may need, and that justifies the inclusion of some technical terminology, proper names and abbreviations. Dictionaries of Anglicisms are focused exclusively on English loanwords, but the macrostructure may be limited to only direct Anglicisms, as in the DEA, or open to both direct and indirect borrowings, as in Rando (1987). Consequently, the number of Anglicisms recorded in different lexicographic works can only be relatively indicative, but not definitive.

## 5.2 A comparison between letter J entries

The method adopted for the selection of Anglicisms to be included in GLAD consisted in an initial step, in which candidate Anglicisms were collected from selected lexicographic sources (see Figure 3.2). Subsequently, these candidate Anglicisms were filtered through the criteria of inclusion and exclusion set by GLAD's compilers, described in Section 3.3.1 and which are briefly reported here as a reminder (Table 5.1).

The entries for letter J in the selected reference dictionaries are displayed in Table 5.2. The final column shows the entries selected for GLAD. The choice fell on the letter J because of its brevity and also to avoid the presence of Anglo-

**Table 5.1:** Criteria of inclusion and exclusion for GLAD.

| INCLUSION | EXCLUSION |
|---|---|
| – Non-adapted borrowings, e.g. *jackpot* | – Proper names and brand names, e.g. iPad |
| – Adapted borrowings, e.g. *brokeraggio* (English *brokerage*) | – Proper-name-based adjectives, e.g. Italian *shakespeariano* |
| – Proper names turned generic nouns, e.g. *kleenex* | – Frequency-boosted domestic words e.g. Italian *assolutamente* (by analogy with English *absolutely*) |
| – Semantic loans, e.g. *stella* (English *star*, 'celebrity') | – Archaisms: items obsolete before c. 1900, e.g. *cakewalk* |
| – Loan translations, e.g. *tempo pieno* (English *full time*) | – Exoticisms: lexical items from a non-anglophone speech community mediated via English, e.g. *sushi* (from Japanese) |
| – Hybrids, e.g. *clown terapia* (English *clown therapy*) | – Specialist terms not used in the general language, e.g. *proxy* |
| – Pseudo-Anglicisms, e.g. *mister* (English *coach*) | – Internationalisms based on Latin or Greek elements, e.g. Italian *telefono*. |

Latinisms, which would add to the complexity of the analysis. The lemmas are accompanied by field labels following the conventions adopted by the individual dictionaries. Further semantic specification is indicated by using numbers of labels in round brackets. Round brackets are also used to indicate that the lemma

**Table 5.2:** Comparison of J entries in Rando (1987), the DEA (2001), De Mauro and Mancini (2003), *Zingarelli* 2022, *Nuovo Devoto-Oli* 2022 and GLAD.

| Rando (1987) | DEA (2001) | De Mauro and Mancini (2003) | *Zingarelli* 2022 | *Nuovo Devoto-Oli* 2022 | GLAD |
|---|---|---|---|---|---|
| | jab (1 tech) | jab [TS] | jab (sport) | jab (sport) | jab |
| | | jabber [TS] | | | |
| jack¹ | jack (1 tech) (playing card) | jack¹ [TS] (playing card) | jack¹ | jack¹ (giochi) | jack¹ (playing card) |
| jack² | jack (1 tech) (elettr.) | jack² [TS] (elettr.) | jack² | jack² (elettr.) | jack² (electr.) |
| jack³ | | jack³ [TS] (mar.) | jack³ | jack³ (mar.) | |

**Table 5.2** (continued)

| Rando (1987) | DEA (2001) | De Mauro and Mancini (2003) | Zingarelli 2022 | Nuovo Devoto-Oli 2022 | GLAD |
|---|---|---|---|---|---|
| | | jack[4] [TS] (bot.) | | | |
| | | jackass [TS] (ornit.) | | | |
| | | jack dempsey [TS] (ittiol.) | | | |
| | | jacket[1] [TS] (abbigl.) | | | |
| | | jacket[2] [TS] (tecn.) | | | |
| | | jack fruit [TS] (bot.) | | | |
| | jackpot (1) | jackpot [TS] (giochi) | jackpot | jackpot (giochi) | jackpot |
| | | jack rabbit [TS] (zool.) | | | |
| | | jack russell [TS] (cinof.) | | | jack russell |
| | | JAL [TS] (aer.) | | | |
| | | | Jacuzzi® | | |
| jam (block) | | | | | |
| | | jam [TS] (mus.) | | | |
| | | jamboree [CO] | jamboree (gerg.) | | |
| | | jambul [TS] (bot.) | | | |
| jamming | jamming (1 tech) | jamming [TS] (telecom.) | jamming | jamming (telecom.) | |
| jam-session | jam session (1 tech) | jam session [TS] (mus.) | jam session | jam session (mus.) | jam session |
| | | jangar [TS] (mar.) | | | |
| | | jansky [TS] (astrofis.) | | | |
| | | | jay (letter j) | | |
| | | | Java (inform.) | java (inform.) | |

**Table 5.2** (continued)

| Rando (1987) | DEA (2001) | De Mauro and Mancini (2003) | *Zingarelli* 2022 | *Nuovo Devoto-Oli* 2022 | GLAD |
|---|---|---|---|---|---|
| jazz | jazz (3) | jazz [CO] | jazz | jazz (mus.) | jazz |
| JATO | | | | | |
| | jazz-band (2) | jazz-band [CO] | jazz-band | jazz-band (mus.) | jazz band |
| (jazzista) | (jazzista) | | (jazzista) | (jazzista) | jazzista |
| (jazzistico) | (jazzistico) | | (jazzistico) | (jazzistico) | (jazzistico) |
| (jazzman) | jazzman (1) | | | | jazzman |
| | | jazz-rap [TS] (mus.) | | | |
| | | jazz-rock [TS] (mus.) | | jazz-rock (mus.) | jazz-rock |
| | | jazzy [TS] (mus.) | | | |
| jean | | | | | |
| jeans | jeans¹ (trousers) (3) | | | | |
| | | jeans¹ [CO] (fabric) | jeans^A (fabric) | jeans (tess.) | jeans (noun) (fabric) |
| | | | jeans^B (agg.) (fabric) | | jeans (agg.) (fabric) |
| | jeans² (denims) (3) | jeans² [CO] (clothing) | jeans^C (pl.) (abbigl.) | jeans (abbigl.) | jeans (noun) (denims) |
| | (jeanseria) | | | | |
| jeep | jeep (3) | jeep [CO] | Jeep® | jeep | jeep |
| | | jenny [TS] (tess.) | | jenny (tess.) | |
| | | jequirity [TS] (bot.) | | jequirity (bot.) | |
| jersey¹ | jersey^{1a} (pullover) (2) | | | | |
| jersey² | jersey^{1b} (fabric) (2) | jersey [TS] (tess.) | jersey | jersey (tess.) | jersey |
| Jesus revolution | | | | | |

**Table 5.2** (continued)

| Rando (1987) | DEA (2001) | De Mauro and Mancini (2003) | *Zingarelli* 2022 | *Nuovo Devoto-Oli* 2022 | GLAD |
|---|---|---|---|---|---|
| jet | jet (aircraft) (2) | jet [TS] (aer.) | jet | jet (aer.) | jet |
| | | jet executive [TS] (aer.) | | | |
| | jet lag (1) | jet lag [TS] (aer.) | jetlag | jet lag | jet lag |
| | jet liner (1) | jet liner [CO] | jet liner | | |
| (jet-set) | jet set (1 mod) | jet set [CO] | jet set | jet set | jet set |
| (jet society) | jet-society (1) | jet society [CO] | jet society | jet society | jet society |
| | | jet stream [TS] (geofis.) | | jet stream | |
| | | jewel box [TS] (inform.) | jewel box | | |
| jigger¹ | jigger (1 tech) | jigger¹ [TS] (tess.) | jigger¹ (appliance) | | |
| jigger² | | jigger² [TS] (tecn.) | | | |
| | | jigger³ | jigger² (measurement unit) | | |
| | | jigsaw [TS] (giochi) | | | |
| jitterbug | | | | | |
| | jingle (1 rare) | jingle [CO] | jingle | jingle (pubbl.) | jingle |
| | | jitter [TS] (elettr.) | | | |
| | | | jive (mus.) | | |
| | job (1 tech) | job¹ [CO] | job¹ | job¹ (econ.) | |
| job (inform.) | | job² [TS] (inform.) | job² (inform.) | job² (inform.) | |
| | | jobber¹ [TS] (fin.) | jobber¹ | jobber (fin.) | |
| | | jobber² [TS] (comm.) | jobber² | | |

Table 5.2 (continued)

| Rando (1987) | DEA (2001) | De Mauro and Mancini (2003) | Zingarelli 2022 | Nuovo Devoto-Oli 2022 | GLAD |
|---|---|---|---|---|---|
| | | | | job center | job center |
| | | job creation [TS] (econ.) | | | |
| | | job description [TS] (ammin. az.) | | | |
| | | job evaluation [TS] (amm. az.) | | | |
| | | job on call [TS] (dir. lav.) | | job on call (econ., dir.) | job on call |
| | | | | | job placement |
| | | | | job rotation (amm. az.) | |
| | job sharing (1 tech) | job sharing [TS] (amm. az.) | | job sharing (econ., dir.) | job sharing |
| | | | | jobs act (polit.) | jobs act |
| | joker (playing-card) | | | | |
| jockey | jockey (1 tech) | jockey [TS] (sport) | jockey[1] (horse riding) | jockey[1] (sport) | |
| | | | jockey[2] (in cards) | jockey[2] (giochi) | |
| | | | jockey[3] (disc-jockey) | | |
| | jockey cap (1 tech) | | | | |
| | jodhpurs (1 tech, rare, obs) | jodhpurs [TS] (abbigl.) | jodhpurs | jodhpurs | jodhpurs |
| | jogger (1) | jogger [TS] (sport) | jogger | jogger | jogger |

**Table 5.2** (continued)

| Rando (1987) | DEA (2001) | De Mauro and Mancini (2003) | *Zingarelli* 2022 | *Nuovo Devoto-Oli* 2022 | GLAD |
|---|---|---|---|---|---|
| jogging | jogging (2) | jogging [TS] (sport) | jogging | jogging | jogging |
| John Bull | | | | | |
| Johnny | | | | | |
| | | join$^1$ [TS] (inform.) | | | |
| | | join$^2$ [TS] (inform.) | | | |
| | joint (1 sla) | joint [CO] | | joint (gerg.) | |
| | | joint-stock [TS] (econ.) | | | |
| joint venture | joint venture (1 tech) | joint-venture [TS] (econ.) | joint venture (econ.) | joint venture (econ.) | joint venture |
| jolly joker | jolly (3) | jolly$^{1a}$ CO (in cards) | jolly$^{A1}$ (jolly joker) | jolly$^{1a}$ (giochi) | jolly (jolly joker) |
| | jolly (3) | jolly$^{2a}$ [CO] (person) | jolly$^{A2}$ (person) | jolly$^{3a}$ (person) | jolly (person) |
| | | jolly$^{2b}$ (in sport) | | jolly$^{2a}$ (sport) | |
| | | | jolly$^B$ (agg.) | jolly$^{1b}$ (agg.) (person) | jolly (adj.) |
| | | | | jolly$^{2b}$ (agg.) (inform.) | |
| | | | Jorkyball® (sport) | | |
| joule | joule (1 tech) | joule [TS] (fis., metrol.) | joule$^A$ (measurement unit) | | |
| | | | joule$^B$ (agg.) | | |
| | | joypad [TS] (inform.) | joypad | joypad (inform.) | joypad |
| | joystick (2) | joystick [TS] (inform.) | joystick (inform.) | joystick (inform.) | joystick |
| | | JPY [TS] (monet.) | | | |
| | | jug [TS] (mus.) | | | |

**Table 5.2** (continued)

| Rando (1987) | DEA (2001) | De Mauro and Mancini (2003) | *Zingarelli* 2022 | *Nuovo Devoto-Oli* 2022 | GLAD |
|---|---|---|---|---|---|
| | | juggernaut[1] [TS] (relig.) | | | |
| | | juggernaut[2] [TS] (polit.) | | | |
| | | | juggling | juggling | juggling |
| | | juju [TS] (mus.) | | | |
| juke-box | jukebox (3) | juke-box [CO] | jukebox[1] | jukebox | jukebox |
| | | | jukebox[2] (inform.) | | |
| | | | jukebox[3] (inform.) | | |
| | | | jumbo[A] | jumbo[1a] (aer.) | jumbo (jet) |
| jumbo | jumbo (agg.) (2) | | jumbo[B] (agg.) | jumbo (agg.) | jumbo |
| | | | jumbo[C] (tram) | | |
| | | | | jumbo[2a] (fin.) | |
| jumbo-jet | jumbo-jet (2) | jumbo jet [CO] | jumbo (jet) | jumbo jet (aer.) | jumbo jet |
| | | jump [TS] (mus.) | jump (mus.) | | |
| | | jumper[1] [TS] (equit.) | | jumper[1] (equit.) | |
| | | jumper[2] [TS] (sport) | | | |
| | | | jumper (elettr.) | jumper[2] (elettron.) | |
| | | jumping [TS] (sport) | | | jumping |
| | | | | jumpsuit (abbigl.) | jumpsuit |
| jungle | giungla/jungla (forest) | | | | |
| | | jungle [TS] (mus.) | | | jungle (mus.) |

**Table 5.2** (continued)

| Rando (1987) | DEA (2001) | De Mauro and Mancini (2003) | *Zingarelli* 2022 | *Nuovo Devoto-Oli* 2022 | GLAD |
|---|---|---|---|---|---|
| | | jungle style [TS] (mus.) | jungle style (mus.) | jungle style (mus.) | |
| junior[1] | | | | | junior (sport) |
| junior[2] | | | | | junior (suite) |
| | | | | | junior suite |
| | | junk bond [TS] (fin.) | (junk bond) | junk bond (fin.) | |
| | | junk food [TS] (alim.) | junk food | junk food | junk food |
| | | junkie [CO] | | | |
| | | junk mail[1] [TS] (pubbl.) | | | |
| | | junk mail[2] [TS] (inform.) | junk mail | junk mail (inform.) | junk mail |
| | | jupiter [TS] (spett.) | | | |
| | | justiciar [TS] (stor.) | | | |
| | | justiciary [TS] (stor.) | | | |
| | | just in time [TS] (industr.) | just in time | just in time (industr.) | |
| | | | Just Pump® | | |
| juta, jute | juta/iuta (3) | | | | |

is quoted within another entry, e.g. (jazzista), (jazzistico) and (jazzman) are included within the entry for *jazz* in Rando's dictionary.

The first noticeable difference is that the number of Anglicisms recorded by De Mauro and Mancini (2003) is much higher than in the other dictionaries. This is mainly due to the extension of the unabridged dictionary on which this word list of Anglicisms is based. The label [TS] is indicated in most of them, except for *jamboree, jazz, jazz-band, jeans, jeep, jet liner, jet set, jet society, jingle, job, joint, jolly, juke-box, jumbo jet* and *junkie*, which are labelled as [CO] 'common' ("words known by speakers with medium-high level of education"). Despite their status of 'common' words, *jamboree, jet liner, job, joint* and *junkie* have been excluded after careful examination of the available data, given that the status of 'common' words was indeed questionable.[81]

Another set of problems concerns polysemy. The lemma *jack*, for example, is recorded by De Mauro and Mancini (2003) for 4 different meanings: jack[1] 'playing card with a man's picture on it, worth less than a queen and more than a ten', *jack*[2] 'electric connection', *jack*[3] 'flag on a ship', *jack*[4] 'jack fruit'; the first three meanings are recorded by *Zingarelli 2022* and *Nuovo Devoto-Oli 2022*, but only two meanings, *jack*[1] and *jack*[2], have been considered current enough to be included in GLAD's word list.

The visualization of entry words and of their meanings in the selected dictionaries is extremely useful for the selection of items to include in a new database of Anglicisms, for which a particular set of criteria have been decided upon (cf. Table 5.1). Accordingly, GLAD excludes brand names such as *Jacuzzi®, Jorkyball®, Just Pump®*, but not *jeep* which has acquired a generic meaning. Highly technical terms representing specialist language registers are not included either, so that terms belonging to fields like botany (*jack*[4], *jack fruit, jambul*), ichthyology (*jack dempsey*), zoology (*jack rabbit*), sailing (*jack*[3], *jangar*), textiles (*jenny, jigger*), astrophysics (*jansky*), geophysics (*jet stream*), religion (*juggernaut*) and history (*justiciar, justiciary*) have been left out, whereas terms of sport, music and business can be considered for inclusion. Very specific acronyms are excluded too, such as JATO (jet assisted take-off), JAL (Japan Air Lines), and JPY (Japanese yen); proper names (*Java*); units of measurement (*joule*), foreignisms like *Johnny* (British or American recruit) or terms of encyclopedic nature like *John Bull* or *Jesus Revolution. Jupiter* (theatre) and *jay* (the pronunciation of letter j) and old-standing, fully Italianized words like *giungla* (*jungle* for the meaning of 'forest') and *juta* (fiber), from non-Anglophone speech communities and mediated via English, were eliminated too.

Careful evaluation was given to words attested in all dictionaries, a status which may confirm the currency of the lemma, unless further checks in corpora and newspaper archives proved otherwise. In the case of the letter j, Anglicisms have been grouped according to the number of dictionaries in which they are recorded. The items that have been accepted are listed first, and then the rejected items follow. In section 5.4 the lexicographic information will be combined with frequency data extracted from corpora, to refine the selection.

---

**81** The attribution of variety labels to dictionary entries may be done on the basis of automatic criteria, sometimes generating dubious results. For example, if a word is recorded in specialized texts, then the label [TS] is attributed, whereas the recording of a specialized term in a general text will determine the assignment of the label [CO] (personal communication with Prof. Tullio De Mauro).

ANGLICISMS INCLUDED:
- Anglicisms recorded in 5 dictionaries: jack[1], jack[2], jam session, jazz, jeep, jersey[2], jet, jet set, jet society, jogging, joint venture, jolly (jolly joker), jukebox[1], jumbo jet;
- Anglicisms recorded in 4 dictionaries: jab, jackpot, jazz-band, jazzista, jazzistico, jeans (noun, denims), jet lag, jingle, jogger, jolly (person, noun), joystick, jumbo (adj.);
- Anglicisms recorded in 3 dictionaries: jeans (noun, fabric), job sharing, joypad, junk food, junk mail[2] (inform.);
- Anglicisms recorded in 2 dictionaries: jazzman, jazz-rock, job on call, jolly (person, adj.), juggling, jumbo (jet);
- Anglicisms recorded in 1 dictionary: jack russell, jeans (agg., fabric), jeanseria, job center, jobs act, jumping, jumpsuit, jungle (mus.), junior[1] (sport), junior (suite).
- Anglicism not recorded in any dictionary: job placement, junior suite.

ANGLICISMS EXCLUDED:
- Anglicisms recorded in 5 dictionaries: jamming, jockey[1];
- Anglicisms recorded in 4 dictionaries: jack[3], jigger[1], job[1], job[2], jodhpurs, joule[A];
- Anglicisms recorded in 3 dictionaries: jet liner, jobber[1], joint, jungle style, junk bond, just in time;
- Anglicisms recorded in 2 dictionaries: jamboree, Java, jeans (trousers), jenny, jequirity, jersey[1], jet stream, jewel box, jigger[2], jigger (measurement unit), jobber[2], jockey[2], jolly (sport), jump, jumper[1], jumper (elettr.), jungle (forest), jute;
- Anglicisms recorded in 1 dictionary: jabber, jack[4], jackass, jack dempsey, jacket[1], jacket[2], jack fruit, jack rabbit, JAL, Jacuzzi®, jam (block), jam (mus.), jambul, jangar, jansky, jay, JATO, jazz-rap, jazzy, jean, Jesus revolution, jet executive, jigsaw, jitterbug, jitter, jive (mus.), job creation, job description, job evaluation, job rotation, joker (playing card), jockey[3], jockey cap, John Bull, Johnny, join[1], join[2], joint-stock, jolly (inform, adj.), Jorkyball®, joule[B] (adj.), JPY, jug, juggernaut (relig., polit.), juju, jukebox[2] (inform.), jukebox[3] (inform.), jumbo (tram), jumbo (fin.), jumper[2], junkie, junk mail[1] (pubbl.), jupiter, justiciar, justiciary, Just Pump®.

## 5.3 Newspaper archives

Useful resources for the study of present-day lexis are newspaper archives, which today are available online and easily searchable. Newspapers are a primary source of information and transmission of current facts, together with other printed, audio-visual and social media channels. The daily and periodical press has been recognized by lexicologists and lexicographers as a rich lexical storehouse for the retrieval of neologisms and Anglicisms, so that newspaper language is today the object of systematic research (Pinnavaia 2005; Rogato 2008; Demata 2014; Adamo and Della Valle 2018). Since the press covers a wide range of topics, from politics and economy to sport and entertainment, newspaper language is constantly updated with new vocabulary. Neologisms and Anglicisms are exploited in journalism because of their eye-catching function, appealing to readers and attracting their interest. Newspaper language has a key function in the process of lexical renewal, especially for specialized terms that spread to the common language and foreign words that circulate internationally and penetrate the national lexicons. Another function played by newspapers is boosting the popularity of certain words in association with particular social events, turning them into real buzzwords for a certain period of time, as, for example, the term *jobs act* discussed below.

At present daily newspapers and magazines have online editions and digital archives that can be searched in order to extract articles containing specific words and phrases and offer the possibility to list extracts in order of relevance or in chronological order, and also to group results according to specific historical timelines. The newspaper archive systematically used in this study for checking Anglicisms is that of the daily newspaper *la Repubblica,* one of the most frequently read newspapers in Italy. This archive contains all the online issues of this newspaper published since 1984. Searching for words and phrases in newspaper archives poses difficulties similar to the ones that will be pointed out with reference to corpora, namely, the need to look up multi-word units in all their possible orthographic forms (two words, hyphenated or solid form) and the impossibility to disambiguate multiple meanings. In addition, English-Italian homographs cannot be automatically distinguished (e.g. mobile, corresponding to the English adjective synonymous of 'portable' and the Italian word 'piece of furniture') (see footnote 89). In addition to polysemy, some items can be proper names of people, bands, public houses (restaurants and discoteques) or titles of songs, such as the word *jack*. In these cases, searches in archives are inconclusive.

In this study, newspaper archives proved very useful to check the currency of doubtful Anglicisms. For example, the word *jab* (in boxing) was initially excluded because it was considered too technical but was subsequently reintegrated because of its use in *la Repubblica* archive (304 articles) and because of the lack of a specific Italian equivalent, which can only be rendered with a paraphrase such as 'short, direct blow'. It is also important to point out that the number of 'hits' obtained from a newspaper archive refers to the number of articles in which the seach item appears. Not being a corpus, the numerical number of 'tokens' for the seach word cannot be retrieved. It follows that the data from the archive are not comparable to the data extracted from the corpora. Nevertheless, the more or less intense circulation of words in newspapers can be indicative of their availability in the repertoire (at least the passive one) of readers. The observation of authentic examples from the archive has contributed to the inclusion of other Anglicisms that were not found in the reference dictionaries or were recorded by only one dictionary (see Section 5.2): for example, *job placement* (117 articles since 1999); *junior suite* (111 articles since 1996); *jack russell* (128 articles since 1992); *jobs act* (6,164 articles since 2004); *jumpsuit* (54 articles since 2008); *jeanseria* (138 articles since 1986); *job center* (193 articles since 1994), *job centre* (55 articles since 1992).[82]

## 5.4 Corpora: The frequency dimension at work

After having explored the quantitative dimension of Anglicisms in Italian, as recorded by different types of dictionaries, we can turn to their actual usage frequency in Italian. As aptly highlighted by De Mauro (2005) the words recorded in dictionaries are only a selection of the vocabulary circulating among speakers and is potentially unlimited in all modern languages. Most importantly, the calculation of the size of a particular lexical set only based on the number of items recorded in dictionaries is not at all meaningful without taking into consideration how frequently these lexical items are used. As for English borrowings, according to De Mauro's data, the most frequent Anglicism in spoken Italian is *okay* and, apart from that, only a few Anglicisms feature among the 5,000 most frequently used words in spoken Italian (*clan, goal, tennis, tram* and *whisky*). This further confirms De Mauro's conclusion that the incidence of Anglicisms is statistically insignificant, a definitive statement based on a corpus of spoken Italian, called *Lessico di frequenza dell'italiano parlato* (LIP) (1993), a collection of texts dating back to 1990–92 (De Mauro et al. 1993).[83] In this section, the role of corpus evidence for linguistic research is dealt with, using two corpora of Italian to assess the frequency of the letter J Anglicisms discussed in Section 5.2.

The use of corpora in linguistic research has revolutionized the way in which data can be gathered and analyzed, allowing linguists to access billion-sized collections of authentic language and perform sophisticated queries that would be manually impossible (Tognini Bonelli 2001) or, if necessary, build one's own *ad hoc* corpora. Corpus-based and corpus-driven investigations have already been carried

---

[82] The last update of figures was done in March 2022.
[83] LIP is available for consultation at http://www.parlaritaliano.it/index.php/it/volip. The VoLIP Corpus contains the transcriptions and the audio file of the LIP corpus.

out for the study of Anglicisms (Pulcini 2006; Furiassi and Hofland 2007; Laviosa 2007; Andersen 2012; Marti-Solano and Ruano San Segundo 2021). In this section, the set of candidate Anglicisms beginning with letter J were searched for in two Italian corpora, i.e., CORIS and Italian Web 2020, to obtain evidence of their currency (degree of assimilation) and representativeness (usage frequency). At present, many corpora of Italian are available,[84] but the two best suited corpora for the observation of Anglicisms are CORIS and Italian Web 2020. CORIS (*Corpus di Italiano Scritto*) was compiled at the Centre for Theoretical and Applied Linguistics of Bologna University starting from 1998. CORIS claims to be a general reference corpus of present-day written Italian, consisting of 165 million running words of texts published from 1980 to 2021. It is freely available online,[85] and is updated every three years by means of an in-built monitor corpus (last update in 2021).[86] Italian Web 2020, also known as itTenTen20, is a web-based corpus, consisting of 14.5 billion words and available on the Sketch Engine platform.[87]

A pilot study on the use of these corpora for the study of Italian Anglicisms was carried out to test their validity and the solidity of the statistical data obtained (Lukasik and Pulcini 2021). The results showed that there was an unexpected match between CORIS and Italian Web 2016 (a previous version of Italian Web 2020, containing 4.9 billion words), despite the great differences in size and content, a result that is partly confirmed by the data on letter J Anglicisms listed in Table 5.3. The major difference between these two corpora is their design, with Italian Web 2016 created by automatic means on the basis of Web-based texts, and CORIS based on specific text genres. The search interface is not very user-friendly in CORIS, relying on its own CQL (corpus query language) and lacking basic tools such as the word list option. By contrast, the Sketch Engine platform, which hosts both Italian Web 2016 and 2020, offers a wide range of easy-to-use tools for word list and concordance search, collocation generation, sorting and filtering options, which are crucial for sense disambiguation of homonyms, as will be explained below. As regards differences in the relative frequency recorded in the two corpora, they were ascribed to the problem of corpus balancing. CORIS is a balanced corpus, i.e., the texts contained represent different textual genres,[88] whereas Italian Web

---

[84] Available at: https://accademiadellacrusca.it/it/contenuti/banche-dati-corpora-e-archivi-testuali/6228.
[85] Available at: http://corpora.dslo.unibo.it/TCORIS.
[86] The sampled texts in CORIS represent six textual varieties, i.e. press, fiction, academic prose (the humanities, science), legal and administrative prose, ephemera (letters, leaflets, instructions) and miscellanea. These six sub-corpora can be queried separately.
[87] Available at: https://www.sketchengine.eu.
[88] https://corpora.ficlit.unibo.it/coris_itaProgett.html (November, 2022).

2016 contains online texts retrieved from the web with no sampling criteria. Another important observation emerging from the pilot study regards the values recorded for absolute frequency and relative frequency, that is, whether these can be considered valuable measures of 'currency' to be used for inclusion or exclusion in the process of lemma selection for a dictionary or a database like GLAD. Whereas relative frequency is indicative of a higher or lower incidence of an Anglicism in the language, it is not advisable to set an arbitrary threshold for inclusion or exclusion. In the data referred to in the present work, for example, the item *job on call*, which scores zero in CORIS and 0.03pmw (per million words) in Italian Web 2020 was included in GLAD on the basis of other linguistic and extra-linguistic criteria (see below).

The most traditional approach to the use of corpora for lexicographic purposes is the corpus-based one, i.e., starting from a list of candidate words, such as Anglicisms, and find out about their frequency and usage context. A preliminary selection of letter J candidates was done, excluding proper names, brand names, archaisms, exoticisms, specialist terms and acronyms (see Table 5.1). The data collected for letter J lemmas are reported in Table 5.3 (frequency pmw from CORIS and from Italian Web 2020), indicating absolute frequency (AF) and relative frequency (RF pmw) side by side, to allow comparisons. The candidate Anglicisms excluded from GLAD are shaded in grey. They are understandably positioned at the bottom of the lists, among the less frequent items. Before single cases of inclusion or exclusion are discussed, two types of obstacles must be mentioned as far as corpus search is concerned. First of all, candidate items having alternative spellings (including capitalization and variant orthography) must be typed in individually in the search box, so that, for example, *job center* must be looked up as two separate words (*job center*), as a solid one (*jobcenter*) or as a hyphenated compound (*job-center*), and also with the alternative spelling *job centre*, *jobcentre* and *job-centre*. At the moment, no tools are available to make alternative spelling searches automatic.

The second type of problem regards word sense disambiguation and homonymy,[89] which was already pointed out for the four different meanings of the Anglicism *jack*. If the number of hits is manageable (e.g. 57 hits for *jack* in CORIS), the desired meaning can be identified manually, so that 25 results of *jack* 'electric connection' were isolated in CORIS. If the number of hits is too high for a manual count (e.g. 202,918 hits for *jack* in Italian Web 2020), the selection of available filters may be a solution. The procedure applied consists in extracting collocations

---

[89] This problem is particularly serious in case of Italian-English homographs, such as, for example, the Italian word *mobile* ['mɔbile] (a piece of furniture, among many other meanings in Italian) and mobile ['məʊbaɪl] in English. Even more demanding and time-consuming would be the identification of new meanings attached to Italian words (semantic loans).

to find possible filters. The lemma filter applied to *jack²* was the inclusion of 'audio' within the span of 15 words in the co-text for the meaning of 'electric connection' (4,303 hits) and for *jack¹* the inclusion of 'carta' (card) for the meaning of 'playing card' (804 hits). Inclusion and exclusion filters are indicated next to items that required it in Table 5.3. In some cases the use of a filter was too complex, as in the lemma *job* (which was excluded, see below) and *junior* (which was included, see below). Moreover, direct borrowings can be easily spotted thanks to their orthographic salience, whereas calques and semantic loans remain hidden in texts and are more difficult to identify.

**Table 5.3:** Absolute frequency (AF) and relative frequency (RF) of letter J candidate Anglicisms retrieved from CORIS (columns 1, 2 and 3) and Italian Web 2020 (columns 4, 5 and 6).

| 1 | 2 | 3 | 4 | 5 | 6 |
|---|---|---|---|---|---|
|   | CORIS AF | CORIS (RF pmw) |   | Italian Web 2020 AF | Italian Web 2020 (RF pmw) |
| jeans | 2,009 | 12.17 | jazz | 359,621 | 24.78 |
| jazz | 1,796 | 10.88 | junior (suite) junior (sport) | 166,573 | 11.48 |
| jeep | 699 | 4.23 | jeans | 103,194 | 7.11 |
| joint venture joint-venture jointventure | 504 173 4 | 4.12 | job¹ | 50,776 | 3.5 |
| jet | 622 | 3.76 | jeep | 50,236 | 3.46 |
| junior (suite) junior (sport) | 506 | 3.06 | jolly (able to do different things, playing different roles) | 46,125 | 3.18 |
| jogging | 243 | 1.47 | jobs act jobs-act jobsact job act job-act jobact | 31,833 159 569 2,616 56 99 | 2.4 |
| juke-box jukebox juke box | 100 46 27 | 1.04 | jam (jam session) | 33,081 | 2.28 |

**Table 5.3** (continued)

| 1 | 2 | 3 | 4 | 5 | 6 |
|---|---|---|---|---|---|
| jolly (able to do different things, playing different roles) | 167 | 1.01 | joint venture<br>joint-venture<br>jointventure | 21,409<br>5,573<br>81 | 1.86 |
| joystick<br>joy-stick<br>joy stick | 132<br>9<br>1 | 0.86 | jackpot<br>jack pot<br>jack-pot | 19,695<br>33<br>14 | 1.36 |
| jet set<br>jet-set<br>jetset | 88<br>34<br>4 | 0.76 | jogging | 19,261 | 1.33 |
| jumbo | 84 | 0.5 | jersey (fabric)<br>(filter: – new) | 15,461 | 1.07 |
| jazzista | 72 | 0.43 | joystick<br>joy stick<br>joy-stick | 13,990<br>57<br>56 | 0.97 |
| jet lag<br>jet-lag<br>jetlag | 43<br>26<br>3 | 0.43 | jazzistico | 13,302 | 0.92 |
| jersey (fabric) | 57 | 0.34 | junior suite<br>juniorsuite<br>junior-suite | 11,356<br>102<br>82 | 0.79 |
| jam session<br>jam-session | 53<br>3 | 0.33 | jazzista | 10,926 | 0.75 |
| jackpot<br>jack-pot | 52<br>3 | 0,33 | jukebox<br>juke box<br>juke-box | 4,556<br>3,080<br>2,484 | 0.69 |
| jingle | 52 | 0.31 | jumbo<br>(filter: – jumbo jet) | 8,764 | 0.60 |
| jungle (music) | 46 | 0.27 | jacket[1] (clothing)<br>(filter: – Full Metal) | 8,579 | 0.59 |
| jobcenter<br>job center<br>job-centre | 36<br>4<br>1 | 0.24 | jam session<br>jam-session<br>jamsession | 8,053<br>478<br>97 | 0.59 |
| jobs act<br>jobsact | 27<br>3 | 0.18 | jet set<br>jet-set<br>jetset | 5,027<br>1,714<br>326 | 0.48 |

**Table 5.3** (continued)

| 1 | 2 | 3 | 4 | 5 | 6 |
|---|---|---|---|---|---|
| jab (boxing) | 27 | 0.16 | jingle (filter: – jingle bells) | 5,876 | 0.40 |
| job sharing<br>job-sharing | 26<br>1 | 0.16 | jet (filter: + privato;<br>+charter) | 5,316 | 0.36 |
| jack² (electr.) | 25 | 0.15 | jet lag<br>jet-lag<br>jetlag | 3,563<br>1,278<br>433 | 0.36 |
| jacket¹ (clothing) | 17 | 0.10 | joypad<br>joy-pad<br>joy pad | 5,284<br>16<br>25 | 0.36 |
| junk bond<br>junk-bond | 15<br>2 | 0.10 | jack² (electr.)<br>(filter: +audio) | 4,303 | 0.29 |
| jazz-band<br>jazz band | 3<br>12 | 0.09 | jumping (filter: base<br>jumping; bungee jumping) | 3,919 | 0.27 |
| jazzistico | 15 | 0.09 | jazz band<br>jazz-band<br>jazzband | 3,555<br>121<br>38 | 0.25 |
| junk food<br>junk-food | 14<br>2 | 0.09 | junk food<br>junk-food<br>junkfood | 3,353<br>240<br>175 | 0.25 |
| jam (jam session) | 13 | 0.07 | jazz-rock<br>jazz rock<br>jazzrock | 1,946<br>1,558<br>104 | 0.24 |
| joint | 11 | 0.06 | jack russell<br>(dog breed)<br>jackrussell<br>jack-russell | 2,430<br>11<br>1 | 0.16 |
| joypad | 10 | 0.06 | job description<br>job-description | 2,406<br>13 | 0.16 |
| jumbo jet<br>jumbojet | 8<br>1 | 0.05 | job placement<br>job-placement<br>jobplacement | 2,354<br>31<br>18 | 0.16 |
| job¹ | 7 | 0.04 | jockey (filter: – disc,<br>– disk, – club) | 2,091 | 0.14 |
| jam (block) | 5 | 0.03 | jab (boxing) | 1,865 | 0.13 |
| jack¹ (cards) | 5 | 0.03 | jazzy | 1,803 | 0.12 |

**Table 5.3** (continued)

| 1 | 2 | 3 | 4 | 5 | 6 |
|---|---|---|---|---|---|
| jack russell (dog breed) | 5 | 0.03 | jive | 1,633 | 0.11 |
| jazzy | 5 | 0.03 | jolly (filter: + *carta*) | 1,338 | 0.09 |
| jolly (card) | 5 | 0.03 | jumpsuit<br>jump-suit<br>jump suit | 1,376<br>4<br>4 | 0.09 |
| jumpsuit | 5 | 0.03 | jamming (interference) | 1,157 | 0.08 |
| junkie (drug dealer) | 5 | 0.03 | job center<br>jobcenter<br>job-center<br>job centre<br>jobcentre<br>job-centre | 435<br>199<br>4<br>401<br>115<br>10 | 0.08 |
| job creation<br>job-creation | 4<br>1 | 0.03 | jack[1] (cards)<br>(filter: +carta) | 804 | 0.06 |
| jazzman<br>jazz man | 3<br>2 | 0.03 | juggling | 886 | 0.06 |
| jazz-rock<br>jazz rock | 5<br>1 | 0.03 | junkie (drug dealer) | 799 | 0.06 |
| jive | 4 | 0.02 | jogger (filter: – baby jogger) | 814 | 0.05 |
| jobber | 4 | 0.02 | juju (music) | 713 | 0.05 |
| junior suite | 4 | 0.02 | job sharing<br>job-sharing<br>jobsharing | 570<br>90<br>6 | 0.04 |
| junk mail<br>junk-mail | 1<br>3 | 0.02 | jazzman<br>jazz man<br>jazz-man | 364<br>52<br>26 | 0.03 |
| jamming (interference) | 3 | 0.01 | job on call<br>job-on-call | 445<br>11 | 0.03 |
| jet executive | 3 | 0.01 | job rotation<br>job-rotation | 470<br>26 | 0.03 |
| jet-society | 3 | 0.01 | jigsaw<br>(filter: – puzzle)<br>jig-saw | 208<br>2 | 0.01 |

**Table 5.3** (continued)

| 1 | 2 | 3 | 4 | 5 | 6 |
|---|---|---|---|---|---|
| jitterbug | 2 | 0.01 | jobber | 430 | 0.03 |
| job placement | 3 | 0.01 | junk bond | 419 | 0.03 |
| | | | junk-bond | 16 | |
| | | | junkbond | 4 | |
| job rotation | 3 | 0.01 | jamboree (rally) | 233 | 0.02 |
| jogger | 3 | 0.01 | jewel box | 286 | 0.02 |
| | | | jewelbox | 74 | |
| | | | jewel-box | 14 | |
| juggling | 3 | 0.01 | jumbo jet | 383 | 0.02 |
| | | | jumbo-jet | 29 | |
| | | | jumbojet | 7 | |
| juju (music) | 3 | 0.01 | jungle (music) (filter: +musica) | 294 | 0.02 |
| jumping | 3 | 0.01 | jacket$^2$ (cover) (filter: +protettivo) | 41 | 0.01 |
| job$^2$ (IT) | 2 | 0.01 | jam (block) (filter: +sistema) | 199 | 0.01 |
| job description | 2 | 0.01 | jazz-rap | 27 | 0.01 |
| | | | jazz rap | 51 | |
| jockey | 2 | 0.01 | jet executive | 122 | 0.01 |
| | | | jet-executive | 1 | |
| joint stock | 2 | 0.01 | jetliner | 60 | 0.01 |
| | | | jet liner | 4 | |
| jump (rhythm) | 2 | 0.01 | jet society | 42 | 0.01 |
| | | | jet-society | 16 | |
| job evaluation | 1 | 0.006 | jitterbug | 133 | 0.01 |
| jazz-rap | 1 | 0.006 | job$^2$ (IT) (filter: +elaborazione) | 151 | 0.01 |
| jetliner | 1 | 0.006 | job creation | 229 | 0.01 |
| | | | jobcreation | 9 | |
| | | | job-creation | 8 | |
| jacket$^2$ (cover) | 0 | 0 | job evaluation | 78 | 0.01 |
| jamboree (rally) | 0 | 0 | joker (filter: +carta) | 6 | 0.01 |
| jewel box | 0 | 0 | jodhpurs | 39 | 0.01 |

**Table 5.3** (continued)

| 1 | 2 | 3 | 4 | 5 | 6 |
|---|---|---|---|---|---|
| jigsaw | 0 | 0 | joint (filter: + canna) | 49 | 0.01 |
| job on call | 0 | 0 | joint stock<br>joint-stock | 128<br>55 | 0.01 |
| jockey cap | 0 | 0 | jump (rhythm) (filter: + musica) | 41 | 0.01 |
| jodhpurs | 0 | 0 | jumper¹ (horse) (filter: + cavallo) | 35 | 0.01 |
| joker | 0 | 0 | jumper (athlete of base jumping) (filter: + atleta) | 9 | 0.01 |
| jumper¹ (horse) | 0 | 0 | jungle style<br>jungle-style | 52<br>2 | 0.01 |
| jumper (athlete of base jumping) | 0 | 0 | junk mail<br>junk-mail<br>junkmail | 206<br>14<br>9 | 0.01 |
| jungle style | 0 | 0 | jockey cap | 0 | 0 |

The data extracted from CORIS and Italian Web 2020 offer a different visualization of candidate Anglicisms, from alphabetical order to frequency rate. Only two lexical items score a value higher than 10pmw in CORIS, namely *jazz* and *jeans*, and only a handful score a frequency above 1pmw in both corpora, confirming that Anglicisms are low-frequency words in the general language. A corpus-based criterion of inclusion does not seem a viable solution. The final decision of inclusion or exclusion was based on all the data collected, i.e., the number of dictionaries in which the Anglicisms were recorded, the frequency score in the two corpora, the number of articles in the archive of the daily newspaper *la Repubblica* (last update done in March 2022) as well as a certain amount of 'native speaker intuition'. Some controversial instances are discussed below.

The following Anglicisms have been considered current in the general language, despite the fact that they were recorded in only 1 or 2 dictionaries (or unrecorded):

– *jazzman*: 'A man who plays jazz; a jazz musician'. CORIS: 0.03pmw. Italian Web 2020: 0.03pmw. Although the frequency of *jazzman* is low in corpora and moderate in the *la Repubblica* archive (*jazzman*: 192 articles; *jazz-man*: 10; *jazz man*: 10), the currency of *jazz* and its Italian derivatives justify the inclusion of *jazzman*. The

Italian word *jazzista* is far more current (*la Repubblica* archive: 3,261 articles) and likely to replace *jazzman* altogether.

– *jazz-rock*: 'type of music which combines elements of jazz and rock'. CORIS: 0.03pmw; Italian Web 2020: 0.24pmw; *la Repubblica* archive: *jazz-rock* (*jazz rock*, *jazzrock*) 4,218. The high frequency of *jazz-rock* in the newspaper archive and in Italian Web 2020 motivates its inclusion, contrary to *jazz-rap*, which was excluded.

– *job on call*: 'working with an intermittent schedule on a needed basis'. CORIS: 0; Italian Web 2020: 0.03pmw. Dated 2001, this false Anglicisms is modelled on the English term *on call work*, which in the USA and in Canada regards the availability of regular employees to be called to work when they are needed. In Italy the meaning is different, as it refers to a temporary form of employment. This new type of contract was introduced in the early 2000s by the Italian parliament to reorganize the job market. The Italian term for this contract is *lavoro a chiamata* or *lavoro intermittente*. *Job on call* is likely to have been coined on the Italian model, which in turn was influenced by the English one, but this is difficult to establish. The data from *la Repubblica* archive indicate that *lavoro a chiamata* is more frequently used in the press (291 articles since 1994) than *lavoro intermittente* (125 articles since 1993) and *job on call* (102 articles since 2000). It was decided to include this term because it is the denomination used in Italian official documents.[90]

– *juggling*: 'the act of throwing and catching several objects continuously so that most are in the air all the time, as an entertainment'. CORIS: 0.01pmw. Italian Web 2020: 0.06pmw. The inclusion of this Anglicisms is controversial. Its frequency is low in both corpora and moderate in *la Repubblica* archive. However, the art of juggling has recently attracted interest as a hobby or a skill for street artists. This neologism has not replaced the older Italian term *giocoleria*, which is far more frequent in *la Repubblica* archive (98 articles for *juggling* since 1987 vs 1,736 articles of *giocoleria* since 2000).

– *jack russell*: 'A variety or breed of small terrier'. CORIS: 0.03pmw; Italian Web 2020: 0.16pmw; *la Repubblica* archive: 128 articles. The decision to include the name of this breed of dogs is that it has become very popular in Italian families since the 1990s (first mentioned in *la Repubblica* archive in 1992).

---

[90] The new types of contracts include *job on call*, *job sharing* and *staff leasing*. In the section "*Per dirlo in italiano*" ("To say it in Italian"), *Nuovo Devoto-Oli 2022* criticizes the use of these English terms in an official, public document of the Italian State, addressed to all citizens, stating that the use of English expressions, whose meaning is not clear to non-experts, has the euphemistic purpose of hiding the negative implications of a job that does not offer long-term perspectives for candidates.

– *job center*: 'An office where a variety of available jobs are advertized'. CORIS: 0.24pmw; Italian Web 2020: 0.08pmw; *la Repubblica* archive: *job center* 193, *job centre* 55; *centro per l'impiego* 747. The economic crisis, unemployment and social security measures taken by the Italian state are topical issues in the daily press. For this reason, quite a few Anglicisms containing the word 'job' are included in GLAD (*job on call, job placement, job sharing* and *jobs act*). Conversely, the word *job* on its own was excluded (see below). *Job center* is frequently found in the newspaper archive, but is likely to give way to the Italian word *centro per l'impiego*, which is far more frequent.

– *jobs act*: 'name of a reform in the job market'. CORIS: 0.18pmw; Italian Web 2020: 2.4pmw. The inclusion of this term is controversial because of its status of a proper noun denoting a specific Italian reform,[91] although it is often written in small letters and partly used in a generic sense. *Jobs act* is a typical term boosted by journalism. In Italian Web 2020 it ranks among the most frequent items, after *jazz, junior, jeans, jeep* and *jolly*, scoring 6,164 articles in *la Repubblica* archive. Its currency is likely to decline in the future or return to a full status of proper noun.

– *jumping*: 'a sport involving the action of jumping from a certain height (such as a bridge, precipice, etc.) while secured by an elasticated rope attached to the ankles'. CORIS: 0.01pmw; Italian Web 2020: 0.27pmw. The frequency of this term is moderate, but the decision to include it is based on the fact the it is generally known by speakers as part of the compounds *bungee jumping* and *base jumping* (both terms included in GLAD), which are very popular sports in Italy. *La Repubblica* archive has 689 articles of *jumping*, as well as 225 of *bungee jumping* (from 1994) and 79 of *base jumping* (from 2000).

– *jumpsuit*: 'a one-piece garment of combined trousers and jacket or shirt'. CORIS: 0.03pmw; Italian Web 2020: 0.09pmw. The name of this garment is little current in corpora and moderately current in *la Repubblica* archive (54 articles since 2008). Anglicisms in the field of fashion are rapidly spreading on the global market, which motivates the inclusion of neologisms like *jumpsuit*, whose success deserves monitoring.

---

**91** A reform of the job market was introduced in Italy in 2014 and was named *Jobs act*. A note on *jobs act* included in the section "*Per dirlo in italiano*" ["To say it in Italian"] of the dictionary *Nuovo Devoto-Oli 2022*, explains that this expression derives from a similar reform introduced in 2012 in the USA by President Barak Obama. JOBS was the acronym of *Jumpstart Our Business Start-ups*. Ignoring the real meaning of this abbreviation, and the wordplay on which it was built, in Italy this expression created some confusion, leading to its modification into *job act* or *job's act*. The equivalent Italian generic phrase 'legge sul lavoro' is proposed by the dictionary, although the impact of the Anglicism conveys a stronger impact and an aura of change and modernity.

– *junior*: (adj.) this Latin word (see 3.4.1) is used as an adjective in different contexts: in sport, 'of athletes between the age of 16 and 21, that are allowed to take part in competitions for this age group', and also in business, 'of less standing or more recent appointment'. *Junior* is the comparative form of Latin *iuvĕnis* 'young' and can be used as a proper name to indicate a younger member in case of homomymy within the same family. This practice is alien to Italian society. In sport the plural *juniores* is often used, in which case the word is a Latinism. The pronunciation of *junior* is anglicized by some speakers–[ˈdʒuːnjə] vs [ˈjunjor]–which reflects an English influence (cf. 4.1.2). *Junior* is nor recorded as an Anglicisms in any dictionary, except for Rando (1987). On the basis of its widespread English pronunciation, *junior* has been included in GLAD in the sports context and as a short form of *junior suite*. The occurrences of *junior* in the corpora and in the newspaper archive are very high and specific senses are difficult to isolate.

– *job placement*: 'a service for finding a suitable job for someone, especially a temporary job for a student or unemployed person'. CORIS: 0.01pmw: Italian Web 2020: 0.16pmw. This compound with *job* has become very common in Italian universities. It is quite frequent in *la Repubblica* archive (117 articles since 1999). Although no dictionary has included this word yet, its recent spread, especially in Italian universities for helping graduates to enter the job market, motivates its inclusion in GLAD.

The following words, though recorded in 5 and 4 dictionaries, have been excluded from GLAD after careful examination of the data available:

– *jamming*: 'interference in a radio or electronic signal which prevents it from being received or heard clearly'. CORIS: 0.01pmw; Italian Web 2020: 0.08pmw; *la Repubblica* archive: 97 articles (but overlap with other meanings). This technical meaning is overridden by other meanings, especially by 'improvising jazz music', but none appears to be frequent enough to be included.

– *jockey*: 'a professional rider in horse-races'. CORIS: 0; Italian Web 2020: 0.14pmw. In horse riding, the Italian word *fantino* is much more frequent compared to the Anglicism, which has been excluded.

– *jigger*: this term is highly polysemic in English; in Italian it is recorded for three technical meanings, namely 'appliance to die textiles', 'high frequency transformer' and 'unit of measurement'. It is difficult to pin down separate meanings in corpora and archives. For this reason it has been excluded from GLAD.

– *job*: this is a highly polysemic word in English, meaning 'a paid position for employment'. This word is hardly ever used in Italian on its own. It occurs as an element of various compounds such as *job description, job placement, job sharing, job on call*, etc. This item's combination with other lexical items makes it difficult to isolate in corpora and archives. For this reason it has been excluded from GLAD.

– *jodhpurs*: 'long breeches for riding'. CORIS: 0; Italian Web 2020: 0.01pmw; *la Repubblica* archive: 0 articles. This word appears to be obsolescent.

## 5.5 Roundup

In this chapter, the aim was to explore the notion of the 'Anglicization' of Italian as an open question rather than a given fact. To measure the influence of English, the observation started from the quantitative evidence provided by dictionaries. The number of Anglicisms recorded in dictionaries varies greatly, depending on size, scope and criteria of inclusion, ranging from approximately 1,600 non-adapted Anglicisms in the DEA to 5,510 non-adapted forms in De Mauro and Mancini (2003). General, medium-sized dictionaries of Italian such as *Zingarelli 2022* and *Nuovo Devoto-Oli 2022* contain about 4,000 lemmas of English origin, including non-adapted and adapted lexical items. A comparative illustration of letter J Anglicisms was carried out, on the basis of which candidate Anglicisms for GLAD were selected. The next step was to look up candidate Anglicisms in a newspaper archive (*la Repubblica*) and in two corpora of Italian, CORIS and Italian Web 2020, to verify their currency, frequency, orthographic forms and meanings, a task that is time-consuming owing to the variable orthographic forms of Anglicisms, which must be individually checked, and the problem of sense disambiguation, which must be done manually. The corpus-based query proved that Anglicisms are low-frequency items in Italian, as only a few Anglicisms of the letter J candidates score a relative frequency that is above 1pmw. Data-based figures suggest that relative frequency alone is not enough to set a benchmark for inclusion or exclusion. What emerges from the research carried out so far is that it would be necessary to compile specialized corpora in order to collect more solid data on Anglicisms in specialized domains. Furthermore, user-oriented register variation in the use of Anglicisms appears to have been totally unexplored so far. If the majority of Anglicisms belong to specialized domains, also their use is confined to certain categories of speakers, such as journalists, economists, scientists and IT experts, when they are engaged in professional communication. New data on the sociolinguistic distribution of Anglicisms in spoken and written registers may indeed contribute to place the supposed 'invasion' of Anglicisms in a more objective perspective.

# 6 Anglicisms in specialized domains

## 6.1 The periphery of the lexicon

The development of new vocabulary in language normally takes place in domains that lie in the periphery of the lexicon, especially in the repertoire of specialized terminologies. As previously discussed, the core vocabulary of a language is rarely affected by neologisms and consequently by Anglicisms. In chapter 2, the fields of Italian vocabulary that were mostly influenced in the various historical periods of contact with the English language were illustrated, starting from trade, commerce, politics, to spread to fields that are closer to people's social interests and leisure activities, such as fashion, sport, and entertainment (Pulcini 2012a; Luján and Pulcini 2018). All these domains are generally grouped under the head term of Social Sciences and Humanities, whereas technical disciplines such as technology, aeronautics and automotive are listed under the head term of Physical Science and Engineering; finally scientific subjects such as medicine, biology and ecology are classified in the category of Life Sciences.[92] Previous research, based on field labels assigned to Anglicisms in dictionaries, has shown that by the end of the 20<sup>th</sup> century the field of Social Sciences and Humanities, which represented the great majority of loanwords, gave way to the area of Physical Science and Engineering, due to the giant steps made by technology. In particular, the impact of information and communication technology (ICT) greatly increased in the second half of the 20<sup>th</sup> century, becoming the top donor field to Italian vocabulary in the new millenium (Petralli 1996; Pulcini 2017). Economy (including commerce, finance and business administration) and sport rank in second and third positions (see 2.6). Actually, the field of sport has drastically declined over the last decades, with respect to previous centuries. These three fields will be dealt with in sections 6.2, 6.3 and 6.4 respectively.

Table 6.1 quotes data on Anglicisms recorded by the general Italian dictionary *Zingarelli 2022* between the years 2000 and 2020. In order to select the items borrowed from English in a specific time span, the 'advanced' search option allows the choice of 'language' and 'time span'. In this case the selected language was 'inglese' (English) and the chronological period was 'XXI secolo' (21<sup>st</sup> century). This query yielded 272 results. Each entry was checked for field label and counted

---

[92] The denomination of these three broad disciplinary domains is adopted by the European Research Council, the funder of research projects in Europe, to cover the wide spectrum of knowledge. https://erc.europa.eu/sites/default/files/document/file/ERC_Panel_structure_2021_2022.pdf (November, 2022).

for the number of meanings, both general and specialized ones. For example, the word *ghosting* was counted twice, for its general meaning and for its specialized one in the field of medicine.[93] The data confirm the leadership of information technology and internet (ICT) as top donors of Anglicisms in Italian. By contrast, the low input of sports Anglicisms (only 5 in 20 years) confirms its continuous decline since the turn of the millenium.

**Table 6.1:** Most frequent usage domains of Anglicisms in *Zingarelli 2022* (2000–2020).

| Field label | Total no. of lemmas: 272 | % of lemmas with field label | examples |
|---|---|---|---|
| ICT | 46 | 40.3 | e.g. advergame, adware, app, captcha, cloud, dashboard, filesharing, freemium, geotag, GIF, hackathon, hangout, peer-to-peer, spyware, tablet, touch, wiki, netbook |
| internet | 30 | 26.3 | e.g. cringe, doodle, hacktivist, hashtag, hater, like, microblog, nanopublishing, paywall, torrent, tweet, videoblog, webinar, websurfer, youtuber |
| economy | 15 | 10.7 | acquiring, anchor investor, bail-in, certificate, crowdfunding, crowdsourcing, double dip, fintech, flessicurezza, gig economy, lock in, patent box, quantitative easing, servicer, subprime |
| sport | 5 | 4.3 | Europa League, kiteboard, nordic walking, ski cross, snow tubing |
| others | 20 | 14.3 | e.g. global warming (ecology), off-label (farm.), droplet (med.), fablab (technol.), revenge porn, stepchild adoption (law) |
| no label | 165 | 60.6 | e.g. bike sharing, bitcoin, bookcrossing, capsule collection, caregiver, cashback, coworking, cybersecurity, driverless, family banker, foreign fighter, gamification, influencer, joypad, millennial, navigator, plastic tax, podcast, selfie, sexting, speed date, ticketless, wedding planner |

---

**93** *Ghosting*: 1 'ending a relationship with someone, suddenly disappearing or not answering messages, telephone calls or emails' 2 in the phrase *ghosting* oculare med. 'visual disturbance as a result of either a misshapen cornea, causing double vision, typical of astigmatism' (translation of definitions provided by *Zingarelli 2022*).

As far as word formation is concerned, the lexical patterns favouring brevity and compactness characterize many new Anglicisms, especially the category of blends. The following list illustrates the patterns of specialized Anglicisms recorded in the years 2000–2020 in *Zingarelli 2022* (many are very technical and rare):
- Blends: *fintech* (financial+technology), *advergame* (adventure + game), *memristore* (memristor > memory+resistor), *moblog* (mobile + blog), *disposofobia* (disposephobia > dispose + fobia), *fablab* (fabrication + laboratory), *flessicurezza* (flexicurity > flexibility + security), *hackathon* (hacker + marathon), *permalink* (permanent + link), *spintronica* (spintronics > spin + electronics)
- Compounds: *copyleft, anchor investor, double dip, geotag, hashtag, multitouch, paywall*
- Derivatives: the most frequent English derivational suffixes are *-ing* to denote activities and sports (*acquiring, crowdfunding, crowdsourcing, deep learning, file sharing, fracking, ghosting, global warming, hydrofracking, loading, microblogging, nanopublishing, nordic walking, quantitative easing, snow tubing*), and *-er* to denote the performer of an action (*servicer, dialer, hater, videoblogger, websurfer, youtuber*).
- Abbreviations: GIF (Graphics Interchange Format)
- Neoclassical coinages: *certificate, cisgenico* (cisgenic), *interattoma* (interactome), *radiomica* (radiomics)
- Neoclassical combinations: *freemium* (free+premium), *quantum bit*

According to Cabré (1999), terms identify a single concept and unambiguously serve the communicative purposes of experts in a specialized field. Indeed, the examples quoted above are all monosemic, and therefore express one single meaning in one of the three represented fields, i.e., ICT, economy and sport. However, the relationship between specialized and general vocabulary is characterized by continuous exchange and semantic cross-fertilization. A well-known characteristic of specialized vocabulary is its capacity to lose its specificity in the course of time, and gradually acquire a generic meaning: for example, the word *follower* refers to 'one that follows the opinions or teachings of another', but in the language of the internet it is 'one who subscribes to a feed especially on social media'. By contrast, common words like *web* or *net* have developed a specific reference to the global computer network or internet, through a mechanism of metaphorical extension, called 'resemanticization'. In addition, as Scarpa (2008) observed, there is a continuous exchange of terms among different disciplines, so that the same term takes on different meanings depending on the domains in which it is used: for example, the term *hub* can be used in a general sense ('core of an activity'), in computing and in aviation,[94] and *administrator* and *client* have been borrowed by computer science from the field of business.[95]

Looking back to the data in Table 6.1, it is worth pointing out that the percentage of word meanings carrying no field label is very high (60.6%), partly contradicting the tenet that neologisms mostly affect the periphery of the lexical spectrum. Indeed, the data show that more than half of new vocabulary circulates in texts addressed to non-specialists. This trend can be interpreted as the result of a widespread appetite for, and curiosity in, specialized knowledge among the Italian population, especially in educated readers. It also explains the shift of a large part of specialized vocabulary, which in the past was exclusively confined to expert-to-expert communication, to texts read by non-specialists, by virtue of a process of popularization of knowledge in newspapers and magazines (scientific journalism) and textbooks and manuals (instruction). This fact seems to be particularly true for ICT, since this discipline has become a subject in Italian education, both secondary and tertiary, since the 1970s.

The principle of monoreferentiality, however, is flouted in specialized discourse, when Anglicisms coexist with native terms and enter into competition with each other (see 4.3). For example, in the field of tourism, *tour operator* coexists with the calque *operatore turistico*, *low cost* with *basso costo*, *all inclusive* with *tutto compreso*. However, research has shown that in business to business communication, tour operators tend to prefer English terms, primarily because English is the lingua franca of international tourism and is dominant in this field of business. Indeed, some professionals in many sectors of the job market make excessive use of Anglicisms for stylistic reasons, because "Anglicisms sound modern, dynamic, fashionable and are thought to convey a higher level of competence and professionalism" (Pulcini 2012: 129).

'Anglicized' speech characterizes the jargon of ICT specialists, owing to the overwhelming influence of the English language in this field. However, there is remarkable 'vertical' variation in the use of Anglicisms by different communities of practice. A study on the use of Anglicisms in the field of computing carried out by Bernardini and Ferraresi (2011) showed that Italian professional translators, when translating specialized texts from English into Italian, tend to avoid calques and adaptations, and opt for 'normalized' lexical solutions. By contrast, Italian technical writers seem to be more in favour of English in their lexical choices, use

---

[94] *Hub*: (computing) 'a central device that connects multiple computers on a single network'; (aviation) 'an airport or city through which an airline routes most of its traffic'.
[95] *Administrator*: (business) 'a person who administers the affairs of an organization', (computer science) 'a person who manages a computer system'.

a higher number of non-adapted Anglicisms, and create English-induced calques and semantic loans.

The influence of English on the terminology of specialized domains is a key aspect in the development of world languages and education, a phenomenon that is nowadays constantly monitored by linguists, lexicographers and terminographers (Ammon 2001; Plo Alastrué and Pérez-Llantada 2015). Many English-Italian bilingual dictionaries are available in all specialized domains, including computer science (Cancila and Mazzanti 2009) and economics and business (Picchi 2017), to quote only a few among the many paper and electronic resources. Some nations have entrusted the job of observing and regulating the neological development of national languages to institutions like the *Délégation générale à la langue française et aux langues de France*[96] in France and the *Real Academia Española*[97] in Spain. Italy has no official body for this purpose, although the *Accademia della Crusca* is committed to the promotion of the Italian language and to the defence of its historical heritage, and several national associations such as the *Associazione italiana di terminologia* (Ass.I. Term.),[98] the already quoted *Istituto per il Lessico Intellettuale Europeo* (ILIESI) and the *Osservatorio neologico della lingua italiana* (ONLI)[99] conduct research on the development of the Italian language and exert an indirect surveillance on its state (Adamo and Della Valle 2019). The right for any language to develop its own lexical resources in any field of knowledge is recognized by the European Union, which supports the principle of linguistic equality amongst its member states and the huge financial cost for translation and interpreting within the EU institutions (Truchot 2002). The *Directorate-General for Translation* deals with translations of written text into and out of the European Union's languages and IATE (Interactive Terminology for Europe), the European Union's terminology database, includes 8 million terms in the 24 official languages. In the face of the growing importance of English as a lingua franca in international communication and business, the role of specialized translation and the training of qualified translators are all the more important in a globalized world in urgent need of sharing knowledge and intercomprehension (Scarpa 2020), although this area of study lies outside the scope of this volume.

What is relevant to the present discussion is the influence of English on Italian (and other languages) in that the creation of neologisms in specialized communication may be the result of multilingual secondary term formation (Cabré 1999; Cabré, Estopà Bagot and Vargas Sierra 2012), whereby a term may be first borrowed from

---

96 https://www.vie-publique.fr/rapport/281330-rapport-2020-de-la-commission-d-enrichissement-de-la-langue-francaise (November, 2022).
97 https://www.rae.es/ (November, 2022).
98 http://www.assiterm91.it/?lang=en (November, 2022).
99 https://www.iliesi.cnr.it/ONLI/BD.php (November, 2022).

English, and then adapted or translated into the receiving language. The coinage of a 'truly' native term may take place almost simultaneously (polygenesis), generating competing synonyms. At present, the production of knowledge takes place and is disseminated through the English language, but in a globalized world this process may be so fast that it may be difficult to establish in which context a term was created first, or, after all, this may become irrelevant for terminographers. This is a recurrent question, already discussed with reference to indirect borrowings (section 4.2) and internationalisms (4.4), which is perennially open to debate.

## 6.2 Information and communication technology

The field of information and communication technology (ICT) represents today the most productive field of English-induced lexical borrowing in Italian vocabulary. In chapter 2 the primacy of ICT in the years following the Second World War (see section 2.5) and in the new millenium (see section 2.6) was already introduced in its historical and cultural dimension, accompanied by examples of Anglicisms adopted in these periods. In this section, the linguistic outcomes of English in contact with Italian in this area of lexis will be described and illustrated. The vocabulary of ICT includes, on the one hand, the specialized discourse of IT, which partly remains the preserve of experts, and, on the other hand, the language used on the new media for synchronous (chat, instant messaging) and asynchronous communication (email and websites), which is widely used by common people, especially by younger people, who have developed their own jargon for communication on social media (Crystal 2001, 2004).

The field of ICT began to develop in Italy around the middle of the 20$^{th}$ century. Influenced by the new terminology of Anglo-American provenance, several terms appeared first as Italian words, such as *calcolatrice* (1948, with feminine gender), and *calcolatore* (*elettronico*) (1959, with masculine gender), *elaboratore* (*elettronico*) (1962), modelled on English (*data*) *processor*, and *ordinatore* (from French *ordinateur*) (1962). None of these terms ever prevailed over *computer*, introduced in 1966, a real Anglicism owing to its pronunciation [kom'pjuter], which is close to the English one, although it is built on the Latin verb *computāre* (calculate). Other neo-Latin coinages are the names of two key disciplines, i.e., *cibernetica* (1950) and *informatica* (1968). *Cibernetica*, possibly modelled on English *cybernetics* (1948), or French *cybernétique* (1948), is also present in German *kybernetik* (1948), Russian *кибернетика*

(1950s), Polish *cybernetyka* (1963) and in many other languages.[100] *Informatica* was created in French as a blend of *information automatique* (*informatique*). It is also attested in English as *informatics* (1967) from Russian информатика (*informatika*), according to the OED, although this discipline is more commonly called computer science or information technology. The existence of German *informatik* and Polish *informatyka* provides support for defining *informatica* as an internationalism. Some earlier terms also include the adaptations *digitale* (1961, from *digital*), taking over the Italian equivalent *numerico,* and *alfanumerico* (1967, from *alphanumerical,* a blend of alphabetic+numerical), and the calques *affidabile* and *affidabilità* (1961, from *reliable* and *reliability*, probably through French *fiabilité*).

The building of ICT terminology can be chronologically divided according to the introduction of innovations. The booming sales of personal computers on the European market in the 1980s introduced computing terminology into the language repertoire of common people, who needed to quickly acquire computer literacy. Terminology was translated in instruction manuals but many English terms were assimilated in their original form. Words like *byte, software, hardware, modem, scanner, file* and *mouse* prevailed over substitutes. The 1990s mark the development of digital communication through the internet for both work and leisure, using 'smart' devices (laptops, tablets, and smartphones). The turn of the millennium ushered in the massive use of social media like Facebook, Twitter, Instagram among most layers of the population, especially young adults and millennials, creating a new generation of digital natives.

Research into the language of IT in Italy began in the early 1990s (Gianni 1994; Marri 1992, 1994, 2003; Lanzarone 1997; Bombi 2009b, 2015a, 2016). As for all specialized domains, bilingual terminological resources for ICT have been compiled for comprehension and translation purposes (e.g. Cancilia and Mazzanti 2009). The language of ICT attracts the attention of Italian linguists because of the richness in the neological mechanisms that are triggered by the influence of English. The expressive register of ICT ranges from the adoption of 'learned' vocabulary, such as *forum* ('an area of a website where users can post comments and have discussions') and *alias* ('An alternative name or identifier that represents an email address'), to informal words, such as *chiocciola* (literally, 'little snail', referring to the '@' sign in an email address), or the diminutive *chiavetta* ('small key', referring to a memory stick). Another peculiar characteristic of ICT language is the richness in the metaphorical extensions that terms can express: the computer is attributed human

---

**100** Cybernetics is a borrowing from ancient Greek κυβερνήτης steersman (< κυβερνᾶν to steer, govern + -της, suffix forming agent nouns) + the English suffix –ic. The Greek root is evident in the Latin word *gubernum,* the steering-wheel of a ship, from the verb *gubernare,* from Greek *kybernao,* steering a ship (see Pulcini 2020).

qualities like *memory* and *artificial intelligence*, as well as the risk of being affected by *viruses*; exploring the internet is compared to 'circulation' in real space (address, link), or 'navigation' (surfing, cyberspace); the internet experience is made more familiar by using words that recall personal space (home, portal/*portale*, window/*finestra*, access key/*chiave d'accesso*, shopping cart/*carrello*, basket/*cestino*, desktop/*scrivania*, tablet, directory, host), edibles (*menu, cookie, breadcrumbs, feed, spam*) or arouse physical sensations (*slideshow, touchscreen*); finally, the names of animals convey an evocative power (*mouse, bug*). It is worth noticing that Italian is the only language that never introduced a substitute for *mouse*, the computer device, differently from other sister languages like French (*souris*) and Spanish (*raton*). Interestingly, the Italian rendition of the Anglicism *bug* ('an error or fault, as in a machine or system, especially in a computer or computer program') is the Italian word *baco*, which in fact corresponds to English 'maggot' ('a small worm that turns into a fly'). The choice of *baco* was probably motivated by the phonetic similarity between the two words (Bombi 2015a).

In the category of indirect borrowings, the largest group is that of semantic loans, whereby a common word acquires a new meaning to denote a new referent in computer science, a phenomenon called 'resemanticization' or 'terminologization'. Some example are: *sito* (site), *icona* (icon), *pacchetto* (package), *cartuccia* (cartridge), *comunità* (community), *migrazione* (migration), *segnalibro* (bookmark). A high number of Italian substitutes are structural calques, such as *tempo reale* (real time), *parola chiave* (keyword), *disco fisso* (hard disk), *sito web* (website) (see calques in 4.2.1). Morpho-syntactic integration involves a large number of verbs such as *cliccare* (click), *downloadare* (download), *processare* (process), *quotare* (quote), *settare* (set), *taggare* (tag) (see more examples in 4.1.3).

Regarding direct borrowings, the number of abbreviations in ICT is much higher than in other specialized domains, as brevity is essential. Some examples are: *app* (application), *bot* (robot), CMC (Computer-Mediated Communication*)*, HTTP (HyperText Transfer Protocol), PC (Personal Computer), XML (Extensible Markup Language); examples of blends are *modem* (modulator+ demodulator), *netiquette* (internet+ etiquette) and *blog* (web+ blog) (see 3.4.1, abbreviations). Among the most productive combining forms are *cyber-* as in *cyberspace* (also in its Italian translation *ciberspazio*), *cybersecurity* (also as the hybrid *cybersicurezza*); *cybercrime; e-,* standing for 'electronic' as in *e-mail, e-learning, e-work; hyper-* as in *hyperlink* and *hypertext* (also in its Italian translation *ipertesto*); *-ware* as in *freeware, hardware, malware, shareware, software* and *spyware* (see 3.4.1 compounds and collocations).

## 6.3 Economy

The first contacts between English and Italian were commercial transactions between merchants and bankers in the Middle Ages and in the Renaissance, transferring some early borrowings (see chapter 2). Evidence of cross-border circulation of economic terms across the British Isles and mainland Europe is provided by several Italianisms such as, among the many, *banca* and *credito*, transferred to French *banque* and *crédit* (mid-15$^{th}$ century), which were adapted into English *bank* (for the meaning of 'financial institution') and *credit*; another interesting case is the term *bankrupt*, which is a borrowing partly from French *bancque roupte* and from Italian *bancarotta*.[101]

Britain has been a business partner for Italy thoughout the centuries, owing to geographical proximity and favourable socio-political relations until the present day. Another crucial phase of intense input of Anglicisms in the field of economy occurred after the Second World War, owing to the expansion of the United States and the economic 'boom' in Italy (Rando 1990; Gaudio 2012; Rosati 2004). The phenomenon of globalization in the 1980s and 1990s, supported by technological innovations, has also raised Italians' interest in international, 'macroeconomic' questions and their consequences on their lives, like the adoption of the European currency in 2002 and the global recession in 2007–2009 (Ventura 2020). New, more profitable forms of investment substituted traditional forms of savings by large-scale and small-scale savers, so that the job of the financial consultant has become indispensable to inform and orient investors. The mass media played a decisive role in the diffusion of economy-related information. Suffice it to recall the record mention of the term *spread*, measuring the different interest rates between the Italian and the German state bonds, going higher and higher during the economic crisis, although the real financial mechanism was not understood by non-experts, but perceived as a worrying signal of incumbent economic recession. The business and financial newspaper *Il Sole 24 Ore* is the third best-selling daily in Italy, which confirms that the lexicon of business and economics has gradually become more accessible to a wider audience, reducing the gap between experts and non-experts, although economic terminology is more resistant to filtering into the common language than other specialized terminologies (e.g. ICT).

---

[101] OED: 'The Italian expression is said to refer to a former custom of breaking the stall of a trader who had become insolvent. The phrase is difficult to trace in Italian, but compare post-classical Latin *banca rupta* (1549 or earlier), *bancae ruptio* (1669 or earlier), both in sense 'bankruptcy', and also Middle French *banque rompue* bankruptcy, *rompre banque* to become bankrupt (both 16th cent.).'

The Italian lexicon of economy started to take shape in the second half of the 18th century, building on the hardcore of international vocabulary which had become established in the previous centuries (Gualdo and Telve 2011). Only in the mid-19th century did French and English begin to exert a significant influence on Italian by transferring loanwords and calques, and the language of economy started to expand its reach to the administrative and bureaucratic system of the country, following its unification. The language of economy has a wide horizontal distribution in terms of related subject fields, spanning from commerce and trade to business administration, marketing, finance, banking, insurance, political economy, law and ICT. Since the introduction of digitalization, professional investors and traders have accessed financial operations through online trading platforms, which requires expertise in the rules of stock market investments, a venture that is open also to lay investors despite evident risks. Non-experts usually engage in simple navigation for browsing, shopping, booking or performing banking transactions on the internet, which can be done from mobile devices. This revolution in handling economic transactions online, which is called new economy, has demanded a great effort to disseminate financial information and develop digital skills among potential users. Needless to say, the field of economy is marked by a strong international character and English is the dominant language.

The number of Anglicisms in the field of economy and its related sub-fields has steadily increased since the second half of the 19th century, when fully assimilated Anglicisms like *business* (1895) and *manager* (1895)[102] were borrowed (see examples in 2.3), but increased significantly in the years following the Second World War, ranking among the top donor fields after ICT and sport (see examples in 2.5) and even more intensely in the new millennium, taking over sport (see examples in 2.6). A comparison between the Italian national press in the 1960s and the 1990s shows that the number of non-adapted Anglicisms in the field of economy has risen by 75% (Gualdo and Telve 2011). In this section, we shall focus our attention on some economic Anglicisms introduced in the 21st century and recorded by *Zingarelli 2022*, and selected for inclusion in GLAD because of their frequent use in the printed press. A rather interesting, but unexplored, phenomenon linked to the internationalization of the job market is the Anglicization of job titles, a topic that will be dealt with at the end of this section on borrowings in the lexicon of economy.

---

**102** As recorded by the OED, *manager* derives from the verb *manage*, a borrowing from Italian *maneggiare*, 'to handle (1298–1309), to be able to use skilfully, to manage, to direct or exercise a horse (14th cent.; > Spanish *manejar* to manage, use, manipulate (1591)), probably < an unattested post-classical Latin verb < classical Latin *manus* hand (see MANUS *n.¹*) + post-classical Latin *-izare* -IZE *suffix*.' (see also Andreani and Pulcini 2016).

– *bail-in* (adopted in Italian in 2010): this term was officially introduced by the European Union in 2016 under the name of 'Bail-in legislation', consisting of laws and regulations for member states, aimed at protecting the financial health of banks, caused by the economic crisis, before instability led to a complete standstill. The bail-in tool allows the reconstitution of the capital base by drawing on the financial resources of the bank's own shareholders and creditors. The *bail-in* tool is different from a *bailout* (this term was adopted in Italian in 1994), which consists in rescuing a bank or business from financial distress by injecting State funds. The dedicated column of the *Nuovo Devoto Oli 2022* dictionary "Per dirlo in italiano" proposes the Italian equivalents *salvataggio interno* (for *bail-in*) and *salvataggio esterno* (for *bailout*), which are semantically more transparent than the Anglicisms, though less concise. In the archive of the newspaper *la Repubblica*, *bail-in* occurs in 824 articles from 2004 to 2021, whereas *salvataggio interno* occurs in 43 articles from 2012, often as a gloss of the Anglicism *bail-in*.

– *crowdfunding* (adopted in Italian in 2009). 'The practice of funding a project or venture by raising money from a large number of people, each of whom contributes a relatively small amount, typically via the internet. Frequently *attributive*.' (OED). It is interesting to point out that the definitions of *crowdfunding* given by our source Italian dictionaries add further semantic specification, i.e., that the funded initiative is addressed to projects that are socially or culturally valuable, or support some innovative idea. No Italian equivalent is available, so that the meaning of *crowdfunding* must be rendered through a paraphrase.[103]

– *crowdsourcing* (adopted in Italian in 2006) 'The practice of obtaining information or services by soliciting input from a large number of people, typically via the internet and often without offering compensation. Also *attributive*.' Also in this case the definitions offered by Italian dictionaries are slightly divergent from the one given by the OED, stressing the advantage offered by collective creativity (ideas, suggestions and opinions) in crowdsourcing.[104]

---

**103** *Zingarelli 2022*: 'econ. finanziamento, in genere di progetti di valore sociale o culturale, al quale partecipa un gran numero di soggetti' [econ. Funding, generally of projects characterized by social or cultural value, in which a high number of subjects participate]. *Nuovo Devoto Oli 2022*: 'Raccolta di fondi, per lo più tramite Internet, attraverso piccoli contributi di gruppi molto numerosi che condividono un medesimo interesse o un progetto comune oppure intendono sostenere un'idea innovativa' [Fund raising, especially through the internet, by means of small donations from a large number of groups sharing the same interest or a common project or wish to support an innovative idea].
**104** *Zingarelli 2022*: 'econ. processo produttivo per la realizzazione di un progetto al quale sono chiamati a collaborare gli utenti della rete, in modo da sfruttare la creatività collettiva e ridurre i costi per l'azienda proponente' [econ. Productive process for the realization of a project for which web users themselves are asked to collaborate, so that the collective creative potential is

– *flessicurezza*: (adopted in Italian in 2000). This is a calque of the English term *flexicurity* (a blend of flexibility and security), an Anglicism in Italian borrowed in 1993. This term is not included in the OED or in the Merriam-Webster, although it has circulated for some time in English. The definition given by the *Collins Dictionary* is: 'a welfare-state model, originating in Denmark in the 1990s, that combines labour-market flexibility, social security, and a proactive labour market'. In sum, *flexicurity* was borrowed first in Italian in 1993, whereas *flessicurezza* was created in Italian in 2000 as a loan translation. *Flexicurity* occurs in 64 articles in *la Repubblica* archive (the oldest in 1997), whereas *flessicurezza* is mentioned in 11 articles (the oldest in 2006). So, this Anglicism appears to have circulated for a longer time and has been used slightly more frequently than the Italian equivalent, though it is important to monitor its use in the next years.

– *subprime*: (adopted in Italian in 2003). 'Of, relating to, or designating a loan, typically having relatively unfavourable terms, made to a borrower who does not qualify for other loans because of a poor credit history or other circumstance; (also) designating the borrower or lender of such finance. Now the most common sense.' This term has occurred in 3,171 articles of the daily newspaper *la Repubblica* archive since 2003. It was introduced following a crisis in the US housing market, due to a sharp increase of subprime mortgages (in Italian, *mutui* subprime), which borrowers were unable to pay, leading to massive sell-offs in the markets and a severe global recession in the following years. The effects of this financial crisis are still discussed today. This term may lead to misunderstanding because the lexical element 'prime' may be confused with the Italian numeral 'primo'. Falling into this trap, the *Nuovo Devoto Oli 2022* dictionary explains that subprime means "propr. 'sotto il primo', cioè sotto chi dà la massima garanzia di essere in grado di pagare le rate" [literally, 'below the first', that is, below those who can provide the highest guarantee of being able to pay the instalments'.[105]

A lexical phenomenon that is closely connected to the internationalization and the Anglicization of the job market is the increasing use of English job titles in job advertisements in non-Anglophone countries such as Finland, the Netherlands (Van

---

exploited and the costs of the proposing business are reduced]. *Nuovo Devoto Oli 2022*: 'Richiesta di idee, suggerimenti, opinioni, rivolta agli utenti di Internet da un'azienda o da un privato in vista della realizzazione di un progetto o della soluzione di un problema' [Request for ideas, suggestions, opinions, addressed to users by a business or a private firm in view of implementing a project or solving a problem].

[105] 'Prime' refers to the rate of interest. *Prime rate* is defined by the Merriam Webster dictionary as follows: '*Banking* (originally *U.S.*) the rate of interest at which money may be borrowed commercially by preferential customers'.

Meurs 2006) and also in Italy (Leonardi 2010; Pulcini and Andreani 2014; Andreani and Pulcini 2016). Many multinational companies have adopted English as a company language, a choice that is deemed necessary to facilitate communication among the managerial staff that operate across different countries. An emblematic case is the merger of Fiat, the historic car company based in Turin, with the American Chrysler in 2014, renamed FCA (Fiat Chrysler Automobiles) and its subsequent merger with the French PSA Group in 2021 to form the multinational automotive manufacturing corporation Stellantis, headquartered in Amsterdam. Perhaps only older-generation Italians recall that the company name Fiat was short for *Fabbrica Italiana Automobili Torino*, and that in the 1960s this company epitomized the glorious age of the economic boom in Italy, socially marked by strong immigration from the south to the Piedmontese capital of the car industry. In the age of globalization, many companies have grown out of their national borders, losing their historical identities. They may exploit the prestige of English to choose a new company name that is distinctive, impactful and memorable so that they can acquire an international profile for branding and product advertising, because English is the lingua franca of global business (Rogerson-Revell 2007; Bergien 2008).

Good competence in English is essential to hold a high-level managerial position, but nowadays a working knowledge of English is often required also to apply for lower-level jobs. Research on the designations and description of job titles retrieved from a corpus of job advertisements and posted online by Italian job finding agencies (Pulcini and Andreani 2014) confirmed the growing habit of using Anglicisms, primarily for pragmatic and stylistic reasons (internationalization and prestige), but also showed the transience of some terms and their decline. Preference for English job titles may be dictated by the nature of the advertisement, in particular when a company advertizes a position for a branch based outside Italy. Some job titles appear to be well-integrated into Italian, with no successful lexical competitors, such as, for example, *deejay*, *baby sitter* and *web designer*. Monoreferentiality and conciseness are features that favour the success of Anglicisms with respect to Italian equivalents, as was already pointed out in 4.3, so that *promoter* in marketing, advertising and entertainment is preferred to the generic Italian term *promotore*. Gender equality issues suggest a change in job designations, so that *barman* is no more realistic to describe a job that is done also by women; therefore *barlady* and *barwoman* have been introduced with modest success in Italian, and *bartender* covers both genders in English. Note that the gender-neutral Italian *barista* has been an Italianism in English for the same meaning since 1982: 'A bartender in an Italian or Italian-style bar. Also *spec.* (originally *U.S.*): a person who makes and serves coffee in a coffee bar.' (OED) Linguistically, English *barista* is a reborrowing, as *barista* is an adapted Anglicism in Italian (from English *bar*+ the suffix *-ista*), returning to

English in its 'Italianized' form. Likewise, for gender-equality reasons, the Anglicism *hostess*, designating an *air-hostess* ('a stewardess on board a passenger aircraft') has been replaced by *flight-attendant* in English and by *assistente di volo* in Italian. The term *hostess* has retained the meaning of 'A woman employed to entertain customers at a night-club' (attested in the OED) and conference assistant (not specifically attested in English dictionaries).[106] In the job market, there is room for creative innovation in the denomination of job titles, like the coinage of false Anglicisms. For example, the term *data entry*, denoting the activity of entering data in a computer, is normally extended to the agent performing this activity (in English, *data entry clerk*).

The unquestionable success of the term *manager*, which has steadily risen from the 1960s and with higher intensity from the 1980s, despite the co-existence of several competing terms in Italian such as *amministratore*, *direttore* and *dirigente*, can partly be explained by its familiarity with Italian (see footnote 102). In its transfer into Italian, *manager* has undergone semantic narrowing and amelioration, turning into an all-purpose word, easily modified by other elements that indicate the specific management area involved. The term *manager* in Italian has proved to be very versatile and productive in the creation of compounds such as *area manager, brand manager, city manager, project manager* and *sales manager*, to quote only a few (Andreani and Pulcini 2016). M*anager* in Italian denotes top-level positions in the fields of business and administration (equivalent to English chief executive or managing director) and conveys an aura of professional prestige, as opposed to manager in English, which may refer to lower-level managerial positions. In recent times, *manager* in Italian has spread to other domains such as banking, national healthcare, and education.

By contrast, the term *engineer* has not been very successful in Italian, being used exclusively in compounds such as *sales engineer* and *sound engineer* (superseded by Italian *tecnico del suono*), despite its familiarity with Italian (from Latin *ingenium/ingeniare* and postclassical Latin *ingeniator*). The difference between English *engineer* and Italian *ingegnere* lies in the educational training that is necessary to acquire this status. In Italy a person qualifies as *ingegnere* only by receiving a degree from a School of Engineering, a very competitive academic programme, leading up to a high-level professional careers. This is not the profile associated with English *engineer*, who may be a technician with specialist competence in the workplace, but not necessarily a graduate, who in Italian would be referred to as

---

**106** Meanings of *hostess* in Italian recorded by *Zingarelli 2022*: 1 assistente di volo a bordo degli aerei di linea 2 est. accompagnatrice, guida turistica / addetta al ricevimento e all'assistenza di chi partecipa a congressi e sim. [1 flight attendant on board of aircrafts 2 ext. hostess, tourist guide / a woman who is responsible for receiving and attending participants at a conference.]

*tecnico*, a difference that is crucial with respect to the salary offered to the prospective worker. Job descriptions normally provide detailed descriptions of the position advertized. Yet, the existence of the Italian partial cognate *ingegnere*, formally similar but semantically different, prevents the assimilation of this Anglicism. When it is used, the Anglicism *engineer* may remind the Italian applicant of a higher level professional status and may generate misunderstanding.

The area of English job titles used in Italian is particularly productive, given the rapid transformation of the job market and the development of new technical and professional profiles. Nevertheless, some job titles that were observed a few years ago have fallen out of use, like *mystery shopper*,[107] featuring in the collected corpus of job titles but only mentioned in one article in 1994 of *la Repubblica* archive, in 4 articles in 2013, in one article in 2015 and in 2 articles in 2018. Thus, its status appears to be that of a casual borrowing.

Two recently added English job titles in Italian are *rider* and *navigator*. *Rider* was introduced in 2015 for the meaning of 'bicycle or motorcycle courier', but achieved popularity around 2018,[108] following the new practice of food delivery in Italy. The bad working conditions of *riders* received wide coverage in the Italian media because of a wave of protest raised by this new category of workers, who are exposed to high risks but are not protected by social security. A previous term used since 1984 for the same type of job is *pony express*, the proper name of a delivery company, turned into a generic noun. The term *navigator* was introduced in 2018 to name workers in the Italian national job finding agency, whose job is to help the recipients of the 'citizen's income' (called *reddito di cittadinanza*) to find a new occupation. The choice of an English name was clearly made for image-enhancing purposes, due to the uncertainty of this intervention to help people who live below the poverty line; unfortunately, the appointed 'navigators' turned out to be of limited use, so that this job position may be eliminated and, as a consequence, its denomination will fall out of use.

## 6.4 Sport

The input of sports terminology began in the 19th century (see 2.3), together with words related to social life, fashion and free-time activities (Beard 1988; Bergh and Ohlander 2012, 2017). The historical circumstances that made the field of

---

[107] *Mystery shopper*: 'a person who is employed, often by the owners, to visit shops, hotels, etc, incognito, and assess the quality of the service offered' (*Collins Dictionary*).
[108] https://accademiadellacrusca.it/it/parole-nuove/rider/18313.

sport the most productive source of Anglicisms for over a century can be traced to the fact that many sports and their regulations were introduced for the first time in Great Britain.[109] The term *sport* spread across European countries in the second half of the 19th century, to become a successful, international loanword. In Italian, *sport* was accepted also by purists and never substituted.[110] In fact, *sport* was considered acceptable because historically linked to Italian *diporto* (dated 1250 in Italian for the meaning of 'free time, entertainment'), through Old French *desport* and later into 16th century English. In other words, *sport* in English can be considered a reborrowing from Italian.[111]

Football was first introduced in Italy at the end of the 19th century with the constitution of the first football clubs (e.g. in Torino in 1888 and in Genoa in 1893). Most of the English sports terminology was replaced by Italian words in the 1930s and 1940s, during the fascist regime, sometimes with no success (Cappuzzo 2008; Pulcini 2017). For example, *football*, *goalkeeper* and *foul* were replaced by *calcio*, *portiere* and *fallo*, but *goal* and *corner* were kept along with *rete* and *angolo*, whereas no viable substitutes for *dribbling*, *pressing* and *derby* were ever introduced. More élitist sports such as tennis and golf largely kept their original English terminology (Caretti 1951a, 1951b; Bascetta 1962).

The lack of normative intervention on language matters in present-day Italy means that it is the use to inform the norm, not vice versa. Corpus evidence is a good starting point to verify usage frequency of selected lexical pairs and preferences between Anglicisms and domestic terms. A search in CORIS, setting the time span in the years 1980–2000, to compare the frequency of *coach*, *match* and *team*, and their Italian equivalents *allenatore*, *partita* and *squadra*, shows that for these pairs the Italian terms are far more frequent than the Anglicisms.[112] For specialized domains, however, the creation of an ad hoc corpus can yield more reliable data. For this purpose, a corpus of articles dealing with the Winter Olympic Games in 2006 was created to analyse Anglicisms in this domain and the specific terminology of winter sports (Pulcini 2008b). As for the three general terms

---

[109] Regulations for many sports were fixed in England for the first time, i.e, the standard distances in running, horse racing, swimming and canoeing. Boxing gloves and other technical equipment such as goals for football were introduced in English-speaking settings and subsequently exported to other countries.

[110] Several substitutes of *sport* were suggested (e.g. *diporto*, *ludo*, *gioco*) but none of them managed to replace it.

[111] However, the OED's etymology of the lemma *sport* is <Anglo-Norman *disport*, Old French *desport*, commonly *deport* 'disport, sport, pastime, recreation, pleasure' .

[112] Results of the query (CORIS): *allenatore* (9.6pmw), *coach* (0.9pmw) – *partita* (46.5pmw), *match* (6.5pmw) – *squadra* (47.2pmw), *team* (5.34pmw).

*allenatore*, *partita* and *squadra*, the results obtained confirm those of CORIS, i.e., the preference for Italian words prevails on the Anglicisms.[113]

Table 6.2 shows the terms of the Olympic winter sports in English, Italian, French and German, as they feature on the official website of the Olympic Games (www.olympics.com). The terminology of Olympic sports is officially established by the international sports bodies. These events are meant to showcase each participant nation's athletic excellence. At the same time, the Olympic environment is characterized by great respect for cultural diversity, including considerable attention to language rights. On the other hand, as happens in many circumstances of international nature, English acts as a lingua franca, so that information gets through to a vast multilingual audience. Looking at the terminology of Olympic winter sports, it is possible to observe the influence of English on the standardization of this terminology. If we exclude the term *biathlon*, which is composed of classical elements (Latin *bi-* 'two' and Greek *-âthlon* 'contest') and French *luge*,[114] we can see that Italian and German appear to be equally receptive to Anglicisms, sharing the names of 7 out of 15 winter sports, namely *bob, curling, freestyle, hockey, short track, skeleton* and *snowboard*, while the rest are domestic terms, while French is more conservative in that it prefers translation equivalents to loans (*ski acrobatique* instead of *freestyle, patinage de vitesse* instead of *short track* and *surf des neiges* instead of *snowboarding*). *Curling*, a very old sport of medieval Scottish origin, was adopted by French, Italian and German in different periods, but never enjoyed wide popularity until it became an official Olympic discipline in 1998. As for the other winter sports, terminologies are likely to have had a parallel development, influencing one another, possibly originating in languages of mainland Europe and then transferring into English, as the geographical references of *Alpine skiing* and *Nordic combined* suggest.

The field of sport continued to transfer many terms in the decades following the Second World War (see 2.5), ranking in second position as a donor field after ICT, now with terms related to personal fitness, and new challenging disciplines and extreme sports. Sport is not only for professional athletes but for common people of all ages. The culture of physical fitness has become a mass phenomenon and many fitness centers (also called fitness clubs or simply 'palestra') have

---

113 The corpus of the Olympic Winter Games was compiled in February 2006, when the Olympic Winter Games were held in the city of Torino (Italy). The size of this corpus was 511,851 tokens (33,536 types; type/token ratio 6.55). The RF of the words *coach, match* and *team*, and their Italian equivalents *allenatore, partita* and *squadra* are as follows: *allenatore* (349.71pmw) / *coach* (113.31pmw) – *partita* (312.59pmw) / *match* (123.08pmw) – *squadra* (1,197.61pmw) / *team* (298.91pmw).
114 *Luge*: 'A sledge, of Swiss origin, of the bob-sleigh type.' In English it is a borrowing from a Swiss dialect (OED).

**Table 6.2:** The terminology of winter sports in English, Italian, French and German.

| English Term | Italian Term | French Term | German Term |
|---|---|---|---|
| Alpine skiing | sci alpino | ski alpin | Ski Alpin |
| biathlon | biathlon | biathlon | Biathlon |
| bobsleigh | bob | bobsleigh | Bobfahren |
| cross-country skiing | sci di fondo | ski de fond | Langlauf |
| curling | curling | curling | Curling |
| figure skating | pattinaggio di figura | patinage artistique | Eiskunstlauf |
| freestyle skiing | sci freestyle | ski acrobatique | Ski Freestyle |
| ice hockey | hockey (su ghiaccio) | hockey (sur glace) | Eishockey |
| luge | slittino | luge | Rodeln |
| Nordic combined | combinata nordica | combiné nordique | Nordische Kombination |
| short track (speed skating) | short track | patinage de vitesse sur piste curte | Shorttrack |
| skeleton | skeleton | skeleton | Skeleton |
| ski jumping | salto (dal trampolino) | saut à ski | Skispringen |
| snowboard | snowboard | surf des neiges | Snowboard |
| speed skating | pattinaggio di velocità | patinage de vitesse longue piste | Eisschnelllauf |

mushroomed everywhere in Italian towns, offering a wide range of workout activities, usually carrying English or pseudo-English names.

The following examples are Anglicisms introduced since the 1980s, grouped according to types. They appear to be quite current in contemporary Italian and in the daily press. Some items are pseudo-Anglicisms, accompanied by the true English terms.

– Indoor physical activities to practice in fitness clubs: *aquagym* (aquafitness), *aquabike* (also called *hydrobike* and *hydrospinning*), *body building, cardiofitness, crossfit, power yoga, spinning, total body* (total body workout)
– Combat sports: *full contact, kick-boxing, wrestling*

- Outdoor physical training: *fitwalking* (power walking), *power walking*
- Cycling sports: *downhill* (downhill cycling), *handbike, mountain bike*
- Snow sports: *bordercross, freestyle, skicross, snowboard, snowboard cross*
- Team sports: *dodgeball, footvolley, handball*
- Beach sports: *beach basket, beach rugby, beach tennis, beach soccer, beach volley, kite-surfing, parasailing, wakeboard*
- Extreme sports: *base jumping, bungee jumping, free climbing, hydrospeed, ice climbing, sky-diving, snow tubing*

The field of sport in Italian has been intensely enriched by Anglicisms for over a century, but the input seems to have slowed down at the turn of the millenium. The reasons for this decline is hard to determine, unless some sort of saturation has occurred or because neological creations enjoy a short-term success.

## 6.5 Obsolescence

The area of neology is one of those 'blurred' peripheries in the vocabulary stock of a language which are particularly prone to rapid changes in terms of innovation and obsolescence.[115] As pointed out by Algeo (1993), the study of neology is historically at the basis of lexicography and, over the last decades, it has developed into a lexicographic industry. To keep up with lexical innovation, a task force of lexicographers is engaged in the compilation of appendices and supplements to major historical dictionaries. Linguists are also constantly keeping the language under scrutiny and periodically produce records of its state – lists of neologisms and other types of glossaries or regular columns in specialized journals and online dictionaries – to document the constant, but often incidental, appearance of new coinages in the language. Today, speakers themselves can contribute to the input of new vocabulary through forums or dedicated sections of publishers' websites, so that their proposals can be placed under observation for possible inclusion.

By contrast, the study of obsolescence, i.e., the discontinued use, the decline, or the fall into disuse of words, is a much less popular field of study because of a general lack of interest and the difficulty in establishing whether a word is no longer used. As Algeo states:

> Gathering evidence for the appearance of a new word is fairly straightforward and relatively easy. And there is a large audience to support studies, both popular and scholarly, of

---

[115] This section is a shorter, updated version of Pulcini (2008c).

the subject. It is much harder to demonstrate lack of survival of a word, and the public finds the death of words a less sexy subject than their begetting. (Algeo 1993: 282)

Biological metaphor is often used to describe language: like any other living entity, it is subject to ageing and mortality. Accordingly, it is reasonable to state that lexical innovation must be balanced out by obsolescence to contrast the excessive growth of the lexicon of a language, which would make it unmanageable by the human mind.

In his fascinating book about the death and birth of languages, Hagège (2000) discusses and illustrates various reasons which in the past have been responsible for the displacement of words from languages: first, language-internal morphological reasons may lead to the disappearance of words or their shifts to different meanings, causing the recession of derivatives from the original roots; second, language-external reasons, such as the breeding of taboos and changes in the socio-economic and cultural realities, may undermine the very existence of words.[116] If applied to contact situations, and to the consequent rise of lexical innovation and obsolescence, these reasons may help to explain: (a) morphological and semantic shifts of the loanwords themselves, which should be considered as forms of innovation; (b) the obsolescence of existing words in the recipient language; and (c) the obsolescence of foreign borrowings in a language after a period of success.

Phenomena included in (a) regard changes of grammatical class (e.g. *snob* from noun to adjective) or meaning (e.g. *mister* < coach) and creative manipulations of loanwords (*smart working* < working from home) which are described as 'false Anglicisms' (cf. 3.5). These processes introduce new lexical items that enrich and expand the lexical repertoire of the language. On the other hand, the success of a word may lead to the decline of another, although the availability of synonyms is at the core of register variation and creativity in language use. The adoption of 'luxury' loans, i.e., loanwords which are borrowed for their modern appeal, characterize phenomena included in (b), whereby old-fashioned Italian words are displaced and replaced by modern-sounding English ones, which are preferred especially by younger speakers. The only case in our data is the term *baby sitter* replacing *bambinaia* (nurse, nanny), the former evoking qualities such as youth, playfulness, creativity, the latter conveying overtones of maturity, austerity and firmness in the child-care job. Finally, phenomena going under (c) include loanwords that become obsolescent because they denote cultural products which have gone out of use, such as means of transport, games, dances and clothes;

---

116 Also see Algeo (1993) for a list of 37 reasons which have been responsible for desuetude in English vocabulary.

in other words, quoting Hagège (2000), these words are 'victims of progress'. This appears to be the case of almost all the items identified in our data.

In this section, obsolescence is discussed on the basis of a sample of 68 Anglicisms labelled as 'archaic' and 'obsolescent' in the *Dictionary of European Anglicisms* (Görlach 2001). Since three Anglicisms are polysemic (*Boston*, *tank* and *tender*), these items denote 71 different meanings (see Table 6.3). The semantic fields to which these items belong are quite indicative of the domains that are likely to renew themselves and generate a dynamic lexical turnover, namely dances, labour and industry, clothes, road transport, sport, lifestyles, military, games, arts, culture and navigation. The fields of food, public places and cosmetics contain only one item but are considered as potentially able to contain more. The field 'miscellaneous' includes stand-alone items which do not fit into any of the other fields.

The Anglicisms listed below are accompanied by some, but not all, information included in the DEA to make consultation more readable. The asterisk attached to some entry words, i.e., *cinemascope\**, *madison\**, *Remington\**, *self-acting\**, *shirting\**, *sweating system\**, *truck (system)\**, indicates that the items derived from English but are not proper English words. In fact, *cinemascope\** and *Remington\** were originally trademarks used as common nouns, and the other terms have fallen into disuse in present-day English too. The entry words are then accompanied by the definitions taken from the DEA, the date, decade or century of adoption, degree of acceptance (a number) and label for usage restriction in brackets. The numbers that indicate the degree of acceptance respectively mean:
– 0 'the word is known mainly to bilinguals and is felt to be English'
– Ø 'the word is known but is a foreignism – that is, it is used only with reference to British or American contexts'
– 1 'the word is in restricted use in the language'
– 2 'the word is fully accepted and found in many styles and registers, but is still marked as English in spelling, pronunciation and morphology'
– 3 'the word is not (or is no longer) recognized as English' (see footnote 78)

The label (5Fr), used only for the word *pamphlet*, indicates that the word comes from a source other than English, in this case from French. The label 'via Fr' indicates the route of transmission. The labels for usage restrictions are 'arch' and 'obs', which mean respectively 'known but no longer used' and 'possibly now going out of use, now rarer than a few years ago'; other labels present in the entries are: 'you' 'usage restricted to the younger generation', 'rare' 'infrequently used'; 'tech' 'used only in specialist vocabularies'. Finally, some entries are accompanied by their Italian equivalent included in the DEA, preceded by a 'wedge' indicating its comparative frequency or acceptability, i.e., more frequent or acceptable (>), less frequent or acceptable (<) or equally frequent or acceptable (=) as the Anglicism

(Görlach 2001: xxiii–xxv). These labels were attributed by the compilers on the basis of personal intuition and comparisons with existing lexicographic sources.

– dances
*Boston* 'a dance', end19c (1 obs) (see games below)
*cakewalk* 'an old dance', beg20c (1 obs)
*country dance* 'a traditional type of dance', (1 obs) = *contraddanza*
*dirty dancing* 'a dance style', 1990s (1 obs)
*foxtrot* 1 'a ballroom dance' 2 'the music for this', 1910s (1 obs)
*hesitation* 'a kind of slow waltz', 1920s (1 tech, obs)
*madison\** 'a type of dance', 1960s (1 obs)
*one-step* 'a vigorous kind of foxtrot in duple time', 1920s (1 arch)
*shake* 'a dance style', 1960s (2 obs)
*shimmy* 'a kind of ragtime dance in which the whole body is shaken, popular in the USA in the 1920s', 1920s (1 obs)
*slowfox* 'a slow foxtrot', 1930s (1 obs)
*twist* 'a dance with a twisting movement of the body', 1960s (2 obs)
*two-step* 'a round dance in march or polka time', 1940s (1 obs)

– labour and industry
*coolie* 'an unskilled native labourer in india, china, etc.', mid19c 1(ø obs)
*farm* 'an agricultural establishment', 1900s (1 obs) < *fattoria*
*groom* 'a person employed to take care of horses', 'a bell-boy', 'an automatic door closer', beg19c (1 arch) < *artiere; valletto*
*lad* 'a stable worker', end19c (1 tech, obs)
*nurse* 'a woman caring for children', beg20c (1 tech, arch) < *bambinaia*
*racketeer* 'a person who operates a dishonest business', 1930s (1 rare, obs)
*run* 'a high general demand (for a commodity, currency, etc.)', 1900s (1 obs)
*self-acting\** 'automatic (esp. in spinning machines)', 1930s (1 arch)
*sweating system\** 'a system of exploiting workers', 1900s (1 tech, obs)
*tank$^1$* 'a large receptacle or storage chamber usu. for liquid or gas', 1910s, (1 obs) (see military below)
*truck (system)\** 'the payment of workers in the form of goods or vouchers', end19c (1 obs)

– clothes
*coating* 'material for making coats', beg19c (1 arch)
*chesterfield* 'a man's plain overcoat', end19c (1 obs)
*clergyman* 'vestments of an anglican minister', 1950s (1 obs)
*jodhpurs* 'long breeches for riding etc.', 1970s (1 tech, rare, obs)

*riding coat, redingote* 'a long coat', 18c, viaFr (3 obs)
*sealskin* 'the skin of a seal, or imitation fur', mid19c (1 arch)
*shirting\** 'a fabric orig. used in making men's shirts', 19c (1 obs)
*spencer* 'a short close-fitting jacket', beg19c (1 obs)
*sweater* 'a pullover', 1920s (1 obs) < *maglione, pullover pesante*
*ulster* 'a long loose overcoat of rough cloth', 1870s (1 arch)
*wellington* 'a waterproof rubber or plastic boot', 1940s (1 obs)

– road transport
*break* 'an estate car with a large rear door, esp. in French cars', 1940s (0>1 tech, obs)
*cab* 'a hackney carriage', mid19c (1 arch)
*easy rider* 'a type of motor-bike (made popular through the US film of the same name, 1969)', 'a person riding this type of motor-bike', 1970s (1 you, obs)
*tanker* 'a ship, aircraft, or road vehicle for carrying liquids, esp. mineral oils, in bulk', 1940s (1 obs) < *nave cisterna*
*tender*[1] 'a special truck closely coupled to a steam locomotive to carry fuel, water, etc.', mid19c (1 tech, obs) < *carro, scrota* (see navigation below)
*trolleybus* 'a bus powered by electricity obtained from an overhead cable by means of a trolley-wheel', end19c (1 obs) < *filobus*
*tramway, tramvai/tranvai/tranvia* 'a tramcar system', 'a tramcar', mid19c (1 obs) < *tram*

– sport
*clinch* 'an action or state in which participants become too closely engaged' (boxing, wrestling), 1910s (1 arch) < *corpo a corpo*
*drive* 'a driving stroke' (tennis, golf)', 1930s (1 tech, obs)
*scull* 'a rowing boat propelled with a scull or pair of sculls for each rower', end19c (1 obs)
*sculler* 'a user of sculls', 'a boat intended for sculling', end19c (1 obs)
*sweepstake* 'a form of gambling on horse races etc.', 'a horse race with betting', end19c (1 tech, obs)

– lifestyles
*flower power* 'the ideas of the hippies regarded as an instrument for changing the world', 1960s (1 you, obs)
*mod* 'a young person (esp. in the 1960s) belonging to a group aiming at sophistication and smart modern dress', 1960s (1 you, obs)
*Teddy boy* 'a youth, esp. in the 1950s, affecting an Edwardian style of dress and manner, usu. a long jacket and drainpipe trousers', 1950s (1 obs)

– military
*Remington\** (orig.™) 'a type of shotgun', beg20c (2 arch) (see miscellaneous below)
*tank²* 'a heavy armoured fighting vehicle carrying guns and moving on a tracked carriage', 1910s, (1 tech, obs) < *carro armato* (see labour and industry above)
*Tommy* 'a nickname for a British private soldier', 1900s, (1 arch)

– games
*backgammon* 'a game for two played on a board', 1930s (1 tech, obs)
*Boston* 'a card game', end19c (1 obs) (see dances above)

– arts
*bagpipe* 'a musical instrument', beg20c (1 obs) < *zampogna, cornamusa*
*cinemascope\** (orig.™) 'a system for showing widescreen-format films' 1950s (2 tech, obs)

– culture
*pamphlet* 'a short text on a political subject', 18c (2 obs)/(5Fr) > *libello satirico*
*teach-in* 'an informal lecture or discussion on a subject of public interest', 1960s (1 obs)

– navigation
*steamer* 'a ship propelled by a steam engine', 1860s (1 arch) < *nave, battello a vapore*
*tender²* 'a vessel attending a larger one to supply stores, convey passengers, orders, etc.', mid19c (1 tech, obs) (see road transport above)

– food
*cake* 'a sweet pastry', mid20c (1 arch)

– public places
*tearoom* 'a small restaurant or café where tea is served', end19c (1 arch)

– cosmetics
*cold cream* 'an ointment for cleansing and softening the skin', end19c (1 arch) < *crema cosmetica*

– miscellaneous
*cromlech* 'a prehistoric stone circle', 1930s (1 tech, obs)
*LSD* 'a synthetic drug', mid20c (1/2 tech, obs)
*pemmican* 'a cake of dried pounded meat mixed with melted fat', 'beef so treated, for use by arctic travellers etc.', end19c (1 rare, obs)

*raid* 'a rally', end19c (2 arch, rare)
*Remington*\* (orig.™) 'a kind of typewriter', beg20c (2 arch) (see military above)
*spleen* 'lowness of spirits', mid18c, (1 obs) < *malinconia, noia*
*toddy* 'the sap of some kinds of palm, fermented to produce arrack', 19/20c, (1 arch)
*turf* 'a layer of grass etc. with earth and matted roots, as the surface of grassland', end19c, (1 obs)

Considering that the chronological cut-off for the DEA entries was approximately 1995, it is interesting to observe how these words have changed after almost three decades. Table 6.3 displays the results of this investigation. Column 1 indicates the recording, or otherwise, of these 'archaic' and 'obsolescent' Anglicisms in the Italian dictionary *Nuovo Devoto-Oli 2022*; column 2 shows their frequency in CORIS; column 3 lists the items selected for inclusion in GLAD, which are highlighted in grey.

Table 6.3: 'Archaic' and 'obsolescent' Anglicisms in *Nuovo Devoto Oli 2022*, CORIS and GLAD.

| Anglicisms | 1 | 2 | 3 |
|---|---|---|---|
| | Nuovo Devoto-Oli 2022 | CORIS | GLAD |
| backgammon 'game' | √ | 0.17 | √ |
| bagpipe 'musical instrument' | √ | – | – |
| Boston 'card game' | √ | – | – |
| Boston 'dance' | √ | – | – |
| break 'carriage' | √ | – | – |
| cab 'carriage' | √ | – | – |
| cake 'sweet pastry' | √ | 0.41 only compounds | √ |
| cakewalk 'dance' | √ | 0.01 | – |
| chesterfield 'overcoat' | – | – | – |
| cinemascope\* 'wide-screen film projection' | √ | 0.15 | √ |
| clergyman 'clergy suit' | √ | 0.14 | √ |
| clinch 'boxing' | √ | 0.03 | – |
| coating 'fabric' | – | – | – |

**Table 6.3** (continued)

| Anglicisms | 1<br>*Nuovo Devoto-Oli 2022* | 2<br>CORIS | 3<br>GLAD |
|---|---|---|---|
| cold cream 'face cream' | √ | 0.006 | – |
| coolie 'Indian labourer' | √ | 0.06 | – |
| contraddanza (country dance) | √ | 0.06 | – |
| cromlech (cromlek) 'pre-historic monument' | √ | 0.06 | – |
| dirty dancing 'dance style' | – | – | – |
| drive 'tennis' | √ | 1.84<br>in IT, fly&drive, tennis | – |
| easy rider 'motor-bike' | – | – | – |
| farm 'country establishment' | – | 0.58<br>esp. beauty farm | – |
| flower power 'beliefs of the hippy movement' | – | 0.01 | – |
| foxtrot 'dance' | √ | 0.07 | √ |
| groom 'boy attending horses' | √ | 0.01 | – |
| hesitation 'dance' | √ | – | – |
| jodhpurs 'riding trousers' | √ | – | – |
| lad 'worker' | – | 0.01 | – |
| LSD 'drug' | – | 0.3 | √ |
| madison* 'dance' | √ | 0.006 | – |
| mod 'follower of modern style' | – | 0.16 | – |
| nurse 'nanny' | √ | 0.08 | – |
| one-step 'dance' | √ | 0.02 | – |
| pamphlet 'political booklet' | √ | 1.4 | – |
| pemmican 'dried meat' | √ | – | – |
| racketeer 'dishonest dealer' | – | – | – |
| raid 'rally' | – | 3.9<br>not for 'rally' | – |

**Table 6.3** (continued)

| Anglicisms | 1<br>*Nuovo Devoto-Oli 2022* | 2<br>CORIS | 3<br>GLAD |
|---|---|---|---|
| Remington* 'typewriter' | – | – | – |
| redingote (riding-coat) | √ | 0.2 | – |
| run 'high demand' | √ | 0.46<br>not for 'high demand' | – |
| sealskin 'fur' | – | – | – |
| self-acting* 'automatic' | – | – | – |
| shake 'dance' | √ | 0.01 | √ |
| shimmy 'dance' | √ | 0.01 | √ |
| shirting* 'fabric' | – | – | – |
| scull 'boat' | – | – | – |
| sculler 'boat' | – | – | – |
| slowfox 'dance' | – | – | – |
| spencer 'tight jacket' | √ | 0.01 | – |
| spleen 'melancholy' | √ | 0.26 | √ |
| steamer 'boat' | √ | 0.01 | – |
| sweater 'jumper' | √ | – | – |
| sweating system* 'workers' exploitation' | – | – | – |
| sweepstake 'gambling' | – | – | – |
| tank$^1$ 'large container' | √ | 0.02 | √ |
| tank$^2$ 'military vehicle' | √ | 0.5 | √ |
| tanker 'ship' | √ | 0.04 | √ |
| teach-in 'teaching method' | √ | – | – |
| tearoom 'small restaurant where tea is served' | √ | – | √ |
| Teddy boy 'a youth dressing in Edwardian style' | √ | 0.03 | √ |

**Table 6.3** (continued)

| Anglicisms | 1 | 2 | 3 |
|---|---|---|---|
| | *Nuovo Devoto-Oli 2022* | CORIS | GLAD |
| tender[1] 'carriage' | √ | 0.01 | – |
| tender[2] 'boat' | √ | 0.12 | √ |
| toddy 'alcoholic drink' | √ | 0.006 | – |
| Tommy 'British soldier' | – | – | – |
| tramway, tramvai, tranvai, tram | √ | 8.67 | √ |
| trolleybus 'public transport vehicle' | – | – | – |
| truck (system)* 'labour payment system' | – | – | – |
| turf 'grassland' | – | 0.01 | – |
| twist 'dance' | √ | 0.3 | √ |
| two-step 'dance' | √ | 0.01 | √ |
| ulster 'overcoat' | – | – | – |
| wellington 'boots' | – | – | – |

The results clearly show that more than half of these Anglicisms (63.4%) are recorded by *Nuovo Devoto Oli 2022*, whereas 36.6% are not. This fact confirms that general dictionaries, even when focussed on contemporary language, record a large stock of technical, obsolescent and rare words, and are unlikely to eliminate them. Readers, in fact, turn to dictionaries to find information about less known words, rather than about common ones, unless these words really belong to the past, in which case a historical dictionary is needed. The data extracted from CORIS, a corpus that covers the period from 1980 to 2021, prove that the large majority of these words display a very low frequency, as expected for Anglicisms. GLAD's entries display an overall convergence with the data extracted from CORIS, resulting in the inclusion of 18 words (25,4% of the total): *backgammon, cake, cinemascope, clergyman, foxtrot, LSD, shake, shimmy, spleen, tank* (container), *tank* (military vehicle), *tanker* (ship), *tearoom, Teddy boy, tender* (boat), *tram, twist, two-step.*

The list of the words that have 'survived' the test of time includes some dances (foxtrot, shake, shimmy, twist, and two-step) which are still mentioned in articles recalling the roaring decades of the early 20th century. The word *tender* has kept its general meaning of 'A ship or boat employed to attend a larger one in various capacities', modernizing its shape and role from 17th century warfare to present-day cruising (contemporary meaning: 'auxiliary boat'). Similarly, the word *cake* is not used in Italian for the meaning of 'sweet pastry', and is rarely used on its own, but is known and used almost exclusively in compounds, especially *cheesecake* and *plumcake*. The game of *backgammon* still seems to be popular, but especially among 'older people', as emerges from several articles in *la Repubblica* newspaper. The only piece of garment that has not become obsolete is *clergyman* (denoting the suit, not the person, in fact), a word that is often an object of appreciation as elegant and even fashionable. The psychedelic substance called LSD is still circulating among drug addicts. The word ta*nk* has kept its currency for both its meanings of 'large container' and 'military vehicle', although the latter meaning is the dominant one in news reports, resisting substitution against the Italian equivalent *carro armato*, which is anyway more frequent than tank. Also *tanker* is being displaced by the Italian word *petroliera*, but still used in the press. *Tearoom* is on the decline, despite its British flavour. *Teddy boy*, which reminds of the teenage subculture in the 1950s, survives because of its association of rock-and-roll music and other types of teenage groups or gangs. The word *spleen*, denoting a state of melancholy, is still a quotable cultural word popularized by the 19th century French poet Baudelaire. Finally, the most frequent word in CORIS is *tram* (8.67pmw), which is widely used in its modern clipped form, while its original form *tramway* and Italian calques *tranvia* and *tranvai* have been completely displaced.

To sum up, lexical obsolescence occurs when material referents or fashions die out. In many cases, however, meanings become obsolete without the loss of the word. *Break*, for example, lost its older meaning of 'estate car' but was re-borrowed in the 1950s as a jazz term, then again in the 1980s as a tennis term and in other sports, and subsequently as a general term to indicate an interruption in a television programme or during work, generating compounds like *coffee break* or hybrids like *palla break* (break point), and so on. Also, the word *drive* and *raid* are current Anglicisms for new meanings, respectively as 'part of a computer where data are stored on a disk' and 'a sudden attack'. conversely, in the cases of *tramway*, *steamer* and *trolleybus*, it is not the referents that have become old-fashioned but the Anglicisms themselves have undergone adaptation and substitution. *Tramway* has been reduced to *tram*, *steamer* has been displaced by Italian *battello a vapore* and *trolleybus* has become the rather outdated but still operative *filobus*.

The status of *pamphlet* and *redingote* as Anglicisms is questionable, or better, to be excluded. *Pamphlet* is an old borrowing, still quite current, as it is freely used without any glosses in the general press, coexisting with *libello*, which is less frequent than *pamphlet* in newspaper archives and corpora. The GDU records *pamphlet* as a borrowing from French, while *Zingarelli 2022* and *Nuovo Devoto Oli 2022* acknowledge the French etymology but indicate that the actual borrowing was from English. Decisive historical information comes from the OED, whereby English *pamphlet* is a borrowing from French (Etymon: Middle French *Pamphilet*), but 'The English word was reborrowed by French (1705; earlier from 1653 in quotations of English texts, see *Trésor de la langue française* at *pamphlet*) and subsequently passed into many other European languages; compare e.g. German *Pamphlet* (18th cent.), Italian *pamphlet* (a1764), Swedish *pamflett* (1775), Dutch *pamflet* (1790).'

A different historical route is the one of the word *redingote*, recorded in the DEA under the English headword *riding coat*. In his dictionary, Görlach explains that the word was originally English, but it spread through the mediation of French; it was actually re-borrowed from French in 1793 by many European languages, which explains the much higher frequency of the French form today. Both spelling and pronunciation indicate a French origin for this loanword in Italian.

## 6.6 Ephemera and the Italian linguistic landscape

Within the dynamic storehouse of words that are used to communicate in society, a large number will never make it to a dictionary. These items are domestic coinages and foreign words, quoted in newspapers, advertisements and signs displayed in public places. We have used the term 'ephemera' to encompass various types of short-lived or 'fleeting vocabulary' (Görlach 2003), including casuals, code-switchings, quotation words and puns. It is no surprise that many of these neologisms are Anglicisms, calques and semantic loans of English origin. The study of 'ephemeral' lexis is far from unimportant, as these words testify the creative vitality of a speech community and the cultural activity therein; some of them may gain currency in the language and turn into 'assimilated' words or loanwords, but the rest will disappear once they have served their communicative purpose. Neologisms and other instances of 'occasionalisms' in written and spoken discourse are recorded in separate dictionaries. For Italian, the observation, collection and storing of neologisms, normally encountered in the written press, is done by linguists and academic institutions, such as the *Osservatorio Neologico della Lingua Italiana* (ONLI), established in 1998 (Adamo and Della Valle 2019) (cf. 6.1).

The daily press is a source of neologisms *par excellence*, as journalists and commentators deal with national and international current affairs, handling a huge amount of information, frequently from English sources. In the latest collection of neologisms authored by Adamo and Della Valle (2018), covering the years 2008–2018, a share of 20.11% out of 3,505 new words retrieved from newspapers are Anglicisms and 5.82% are calques, mainly from English. This rate doubled compared to the previous volume published in 2008. The language of Italian journalism and other media seems to be strongly anglicized (Guţia et al. 1981; Demata 2014). Journalists are inclined to use sensational language, in order to attract interest and emotional response from readers, resorting to code-switchings, quotations and creative puns. Newspapers operate as an echo chamber for neologisms, which may become buzzwords for a certain period of time (Frenguelli 2008). An example of a term that became obsolescent overnight is *millennium bug*: introduced in 1998 to refer to the much feared software disaster forecast for the turn of the millennium, *millennium bug* had no more reason to exist after the event was warded off.[117] Another example is a phrase that was recently boosted by the media, i.e., 'Whatever it takes', uttered by the economist Mario Draghi, former President of the European Central Bank (ECB) (2011–2019). During a forum about the financial crisis in the Eurozone in 2012, Draghi stated that during his mandate the ECB would be ready to do "whatever it takes to preserve the euro", which made him famous in Europe and in the world. This phrase received an extraordinary echo throughout all media channels in Italy when Draghi became Prime Minister in Italy in 2021. Indeed, newspapers have a primary role in the introduction of Anglicisms in the general language, but we may hypothesize that educated native speakers who regularly read newspapers would perhaps recognize many English words but would not use them as active vocabulary.

Another field where English words and phrases play a strong eye-catching function is advertising, an ideal locus of language contact and word play. The use of foreign languages in print and television advertisements is a widely researched field for its strategic role in communication and in marketing (Bathia and Ritchie 2012). Foreign languages carry a symbolic value and are synergically combined by copywriters with other modes (images, colours, sounds) to achieve the desired impact, with diverse indexical projections: the use of a tagline in a foreign language will connect the product or the service to the country or cultures of origin, while a dialect or the language of a minority group will evoke ethnic or local values; the use of English transmits the values that are associated to Anglophone countries, i.e., modernity, innovation, success, and globalness (Hornikx and van Meurs 2019). Code-mixed advertising exploits the connotative power of language, rather than the denotative one, and comprehension is not essential, though implied. For example, the promotion of a brand of sofas accompanied by the slogan *Home soft home* is likely to be understood by the majority of Italian viewers as a pun based on the widely known English proverb *Home sweet home*. This example is taken from a large study on print adverts featuring in Italian newspapers (Vettorel 2013), which

---

[117] Since computers store only the last two digits of years, it was feared that the switch from 1999 to 2000 could produce wrong results or cause a breakdown in the computer softwares, because computers might interpret '00' as 1900. The word *millennium bug* is recorded by GDU but not in *Zingarelli 2022* and *Nuovo Devoto Oli 2022*.

showed that 51% of the sample exploited language mixing with English, 8.32% were only in English, while one third was in Italian and only about 10% involved mixing with other languages (French and German) (see also Vettorel and Franceschi 2019).

The study of the influence of English on the Italian language and culture cannot ignore people's exposure to 'incidental' contact with English words and phrases when they are engaged in their daily routine, leading to the indirect assimilation of language and cultural values. This is a relatively new area of research, which focuses the attention on the 'linguistic landscape', i.e., language used on commercial shop signs, street signs, billboards, notices, graffiti, stickers, and displayed in public spaces, in urban environments, streets, shopping centers, restaurants, museums, airports, parks, means of transport and so on (Shohamy and Gorter 2009; Blackwood and Tufi 2015). The perception of different linguistic landscapes occurs when people travel to another country and a different language or languages are on display in the public environment. The study of linguistic landscapes is particularly meaningful in multilingual societies where languages are strong identity markers and may signal social and political orientations or policies. In a largely monolingual country like Italy,[118] the display of Italian-English notices may have a purely practical function for orienting non-Italian speakers, especially in the areas of towns that are visited by tourists (Griffin 2004; Gorter 2007). Yet, in most circumstances, code-mixing is an intentional practice, and its aims are social, interactional and psychological: the choice of creating a slogan in English for a campaign or for a promotional advert is motivated by sociolinguistic reasons, having to do with the intrinsic positive qualities associated to the English language, the most important one being its cosmopolitan identity (Dardano, Frenguelli and Puoti 2008). Signage on public display include signs and posters produced by designers (so-called top-down signage) or items created by non-professional authors (bottom-up signage), showing a variety of creative patterns, sometimes bending the language rules either intentionally or unintentionally. An example is the brand name of the high-end Italian food store chain *Eataly*, coined by blending the verb 'eat' and 'Italy', and mimicking the way in which Italians would pronounce the word Italy with a long and tense initial vowel. Lexical inventiveness may introduce blended lexical patterns, like the hybrid *ristopub* (ristorante + pub), a restaurant that serves food and beverages typical of pubs, or the derivative *snackeria* (snack+ eria, indicating a shop selling snacks) (examples quoted by Vettorel and Franceschi 2013). Deviation from the norm may affect orthography

---

**118** There are several bilingual areas in the Italian territory, e.g. the French-speaking Valle D'Aosta and the German-speaking South Tyrol as well as large migrant communities in urban contexts (see Dal Negro 2009). However, in 2015, 90.4% of the Italian population had Italian as a mother tongue. www.istat.it/it/archivio/207961 (November, 2022).

and produce a semantic shift from the intended meaning, e.g. the sign *wine testing* displayed on the window of a wine bar (instead of *wine tasting*) or the non-English phrase *next opening* displayed outside a shop being renovated (instead of *opening soon*), sometimes creating unvoluntary hilarious effects, like the tagline *il bum del ribasso* (the boom of discount) in a poster advertising sales in a furniture shop.[119]

To conclude, English is highly visible in Italian society and Italian people generally have a welcoming attitude to it. On the other hand, the information overload to which people are exposed nowadays may indeed generate a sense of saturation towards the ubiquitous presence of English, but this impression can be partly relieved by the fact that many of the words that people read or hear around them belong to the category of ephemera.

## 6.7 Roundup

In this chapter, the attention is focused on the Anglicisms that belong to specialized domains, with particular attention to the three fields that are numerically more productive, i.e., information and communication technology, economy, and sport, although the number of loanwords in sport has been progressively declining over the last decades. Owing to the transfer from specialized to general vocabulary of many technical terms through various media channels, a high number of Anglicisms develop a generic meaning and become familiar to non-specialists. Italian equivalents are regularly introduced through translation or created autonomously within the Italian language itself, as a result of the circulation of neologisms on an international scale. The input of specialized Anglicisms is monitored by linguists and translation bodies; research and training in specialized translation deal with the parallel development of Italian terminologies, although specialists seem to favour the use of 'anglicized' communication. Research into the 'vertical' variation in the use of Anglicisms by different communities of pratice has not been adequately explored in the Italian context.

The theme of the obsolescence of Anglicisms – an aspect that is rarely considered in lexicography, being far less challenging than neology – is dealt with, based on a sample of old-fashioned Anglicisms, many of which have fallen out of use and are no more included in general dictionaries. Obsolescence affects words denoting objects, practices or fashions that disappear or are superseded by modern ones. The last, socially-impactful aspect of the Anglicization of Italian is the

---

**119** Examples collected in the city of Torino.

presence of Anglicisms, mostly ephemeral, in the media and in the linguistic landscape of Italian society (English words and phrases displayed in public spaces), a phenomenon that is caused by the increased volume of information circulating nowadays and the dominance of English as a lingua franca of international communication.

# 7 English in Italian education

## 7.1 An 'English-first' educational system

English is today the first foreign language taught and learned at all levels of education in Italy, followed by French and, to a much lesser extent, German and Spanish (Balboni 2009). The primacy of English is the result of decades of progress in society and reforms of the educational system in Italy, following the end of the Second World War, which led to a progressive rise of EFL (English as a Foreign Language), in particular from the early 1960s. The economic 'miracle' of the post-war years (see 2.5) turned Italy into a modern, industrialized country, politically aligned with the NATO (*North Atlantic Treaty Organization*) since 1949 and a member of the EU (*European Union*) since 1958. These historical circumstances have undoubtedly influenced the educational orientation of the country and the preferences of Italians regarding foreign languages. A quick flashback to the past will explain the turn from a French-oriented to an English-oriented school system in Italy, but the main focus of this section will be on the present-day status of English in Italian education.

Up to the middle of the 20$^{th}$ century, the first foreign language in Italy was French. When Italy was unified in 1861, most of the northern part of the Italian peninsula belonged to the Kingdom of Sardinia, ruled by the House of Savoy, a French-speaking dynasty that reigned in the areas that today are the French Haute Savoie and the Italian Piedmont region from the 15$^{th}$ century to the Italian unification in 1861. French was the language of the court, although the House of Savoy supported the Italian language when the capital was transferred from Chambéry to Torino in 1562, and the Piedmontese dialect was also widespread among the population and the ruling elites.[120]

After the Italian unification, the first reform of the educational system was implemented in 1859 (Casati Law) (Balboni 1988). This reform introduced compulsory education (initially, only for 2 years of elementary school), and elected French as the foreign language to teach in secondary schools: this strategic choice would strike a balance between the existing geopolitical situation, encompassing French-speaking areas across the Alpine regions, and Italian, the language that

---

[120] A paradigmatic example is that of the politician Camillo Benso Count of Cavour, who was prime minister of the kingdom of Sardinia and gave a great diplomatic contribution to the unification of the country. He was known for being more familiar with the Piedmontese dialect and French than with Italian. According to historical accounts, Cavour was worried about his new political role after the unification of Italy and the need to make speeches in fluent Italian.

was to be recognized as the national language of unified Italy. English and German were recommended as optional subjects in technical schools, not as languages of culture, but as a support for the acquisition of technical terminology (Schirru 2019). The situation remained more or less the same after the 1923 educational reform by minister Giovanni Gentile at the onset of the fascist era (1922–1945) but the subsequent radicalization of autarchic policies strengthened the hostility towards foreign languages, especially towards English, the language of the enemies, until the end of the Second World War, when the scenario was totally reversed.

A turning point in education was a reform of the lower secondary school system implemented in 1962. The novelty consisted in opening up the choice of the foreign language to study to the four 'big' European languages, namely English, French, German and Spanish. In addition, the number of hours devoted to foreign languages was increased and the adoption of more learner-centred teaching methods, based on communication rather than grammar and translation, was encouraged. Since then, French has gradually given way to other languages, especially to English, which is now the first choice of most of the Italian school population. Over time, the teaching of foreign languages has been a core theme of special projects, local experimentation, and action research (Balboni 1988, 2009). For example, the 1970s *Progetto Speciale Lingue straniere* (*Special Project on Foreign Languages*), which ran until 1996, promoted in-service training for language teachers. Anglophone associations played a role in promoting the language and its culture; an example is the British Council, which supported EFL teaching conferences, workshops, summer courses and cultural exchanges. For decades the Italian school system was a bustling factory of experimentation and action research, thanks to new language education projects (e.g. *Progetto Lingue 2000*), and the activity of language teachers and their associations, such as GISCEL, *Gruppo di Intervento e Studio nel Campo dell'Educazione Linguistica* (*Intervention and Study Group in the Field of Language Education*). According to Schirru (2019), the Italian educational policy, especially on foreign language matters, gradually aligned with the policies of the European Union, which recommended that each European citizen should become competent in two EU languages besides their mother tongue.[121] In compliance with the Bologna Process (1999),[122] the teaching of two foreign languages was introduced in Italian lower secondary schools already in 2000. However, subsequent reforms gradually oriented the system in favour of

---

[121] *White paper on education and training* (Commission of the European Communities 1996).
[122] The Bologna Declaration was signed on 19 June 1999 by 29 European Ministers of Education. The signatories agreed to harmonize their university systems, establishing comparable degrees, enhancing mobility, promoting employability, and making the European area of higher education attractive world-wide for the richness, diversity and uniqueness of its cultural and scientific traditions.

English: in 2003 a foreign language (with English chosen by the large majority of families) became mandatory for the whole primary school population (*Riforma Moratti*), in 2007 all BA university programmes were required to offer credits in English (*Riforma Mussi*), and in 2009 English was adopted as the primary choice in curricula with only one foreign language, becoming practically a curricular subject when two foreign languages are taught (*Riforma Gelmini*).

To identify competence levels, the common European Framework of Reference for Languages (CEFR) is normally referred to as a benchmark, which is set to B2 (upper intermediate or 'vantage') at the end of the upper secondary school. Cambridge English Qualifications and several other types of certificates (e.g. IELTS, TOEFL, Trinity) are quite popular among the Italian school population and beyond. Following the *Progetto Lingue 2000*, Italian schools may become testing sites for Cambridge English tests for local students, who can take these tests on a voluntary basis at special prices. Also, universities accept language diplomas issued by private organizations, such as the University of Cambridge ESOL and the British Council, to acquire credits or as entry requirements for English-mediated degree programmes (Cicillini 2021). As a results, the number of school-age students who have taken the A2 Key (KET), B1 Preliminary (PET) and B2 First (FCE) has shot up in the last two decades. Since 2010 the CLIL (*Content and Language Integrated Learning*) methodology has been gradually introduced in secondary schools, whereby a non-linguistic discipline is taught through the medium of a foreign language in the last year of the upper secondary schools. Subsequent legislative intervention in 2015 extended CLIL projects to other school levels, from elementary to lower and upper secondary schools.[123] The majority of CLIL experimentations involves the English language (70%), followed by French (21%), German (4%), Spanish (4%) and others (1%) (Cinganotto 2016).

Since the 1990s, the Italian higher education system has also been structurally modified according to the EU model, based on the three-cycle system, namely Bachelor's and Master's degrees (in Italy referred to as "the 3+2 formula"), followed by doctorate programmes, which last three years or longer. The European Credit Transfer System is applied to favour student mobility and implement joint programmes. Most Italian universities are centuries old, like the University of Bologna, founded in 1088 and the oldest in Europe. Originally elitist in character, devoted primarily to the study of the humanities, a radical transformation of the Italian university system took place after the 1968 student movement towards the liberalization of admission and comparatively low fees. Differently from other EU countries, Italian universities grant free admission to all applicants, and only a limited num-

---

[123] https://www.miur.gov.it/web/guest/clil1 (November, 2022).

ber of degree courses are competitive (with *numerus clausus*),[124] and its overall structure is that of a 'mass' university system (Prat Zagrebelsky 1991; Salvi 2009; Solly 2010; Pulcini and Campagna 2015).

These giant leaps in Italian education since the 1960s have indeed changed society for the better. Nowadays, the level of illiteracy in Italy is practically reduced to zero. The portion of the population between the age of 25 and 64 who has completed a secondary school cycle is 62.2% and for tertiary education (university) the rate is 19.6%. Yet, both figures are below the average statistics in EU28 (78.7% for secondary level and 33.2% for the tertiary cycle)[125] (Istat 2020). Compulsory education in Italy lasts 10 years, from the age of 6 to 16. As a result of measures favouring the study of English as a foreign language, at the end of the 10-year period of compulsory education, all Italian school-age population has studied English for at least 10 years. According to the Eurydice data (European Education and Culture Executive Agency 2017: 32), Italy is an 'exceptional' case in Europe, as the learning of a foreign language in school has been compulsory from primary throughout lower and upper secondary levels since 2011. However, like in most European countries "English is the foreign language learnt by most students during primary and secondary education." (European Education and Culture Executive Agency 2017: 13).

Despite the spread of EFL in Italian education and the improvement in teaching time and methods, Italians are generally reported to be less proficient in foreign languages than their European fellows. The data shown in Figure 7.1 (*Special Eurobarometer 386*, 2014) report that only 38% of Italians regard themselves as capable of having a conversation in a foreign language, and 34% think that this foreign language is English. These figures are lower than the EU average, which indicates that 54% of citizens can hold a conversation in a foreign language, and 38% mention English.[126] Another meaningful indicator is the dramatic drop of French (only 16% of Italians declare they are able to have a conversation in this language), which is a particularly negative sign, considering the strong status of French until only a few decades ago. Equally alarming is that 62% of Italian citizens cannot communicate in a language other than their mother tongue (against an average of 46% in EU27).

Attitudes towards the English language are extremely favourable among Italians, to say the least. As shown in Figure 7.2, 70% of Italians consider English the

---

[124] See universitaly.com for an overview of all degree courses offered by Italian universities, including the ones entirely taught in English.
[125] Figures on the achievement of a secondary school diploma are below those of other EU countries such as Germany (86.6%) and France (80.4%). Spain, Malta and Portugal have lower rates of diploma holders than Italy.
[126] The gap is much greater between Italy and Nordic countries, where self-assessed competence in English reaches 86% in Denmark, 86% in Sweden, 70% in Finland, and 90% in the Netherlands.

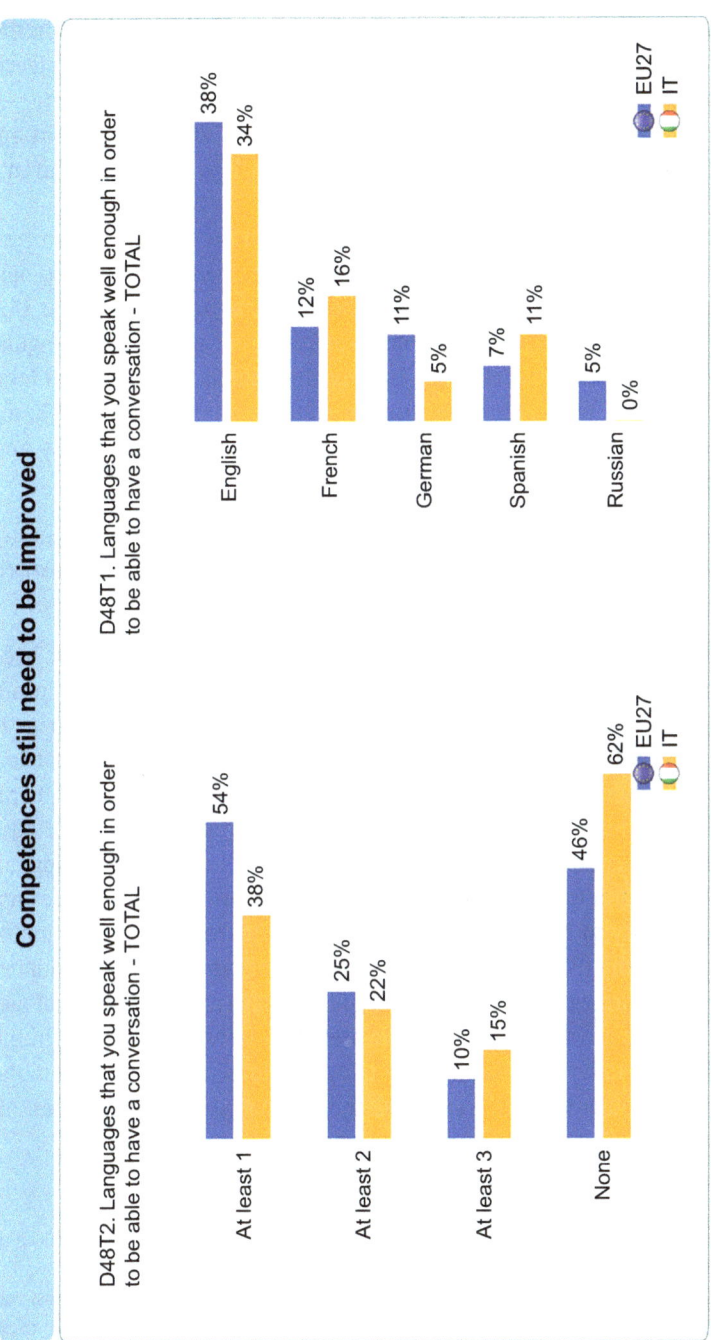

**Figure 7.1:** Statistics on language competence to have a conversation (*Special Eurobarometer 386*, 2014).

most useful foreign language for their personal development (against 67% in the EU27), and 84% consider English the most useful language for children to learn for their future (against 79% in EU27). Surprisingly, as noted above, French (a sister language, geographically close to Italy) appears to have completely lost its appeal, as only 11% consider it useful for themselves and 14% for their children's future (practically at the same level as Chinese).

English is today the most widely spoken language in the world, with an estimated number of native and non-native speakers amounting to 1.45 billion (Eberhard, Simons and Fennig 2021); therefore, the practical advantages that this language offers to communicate with people from different national and linguistic backgrounds are evident to everyone. In Italy, any middle or upper-class family would be ready to invest in English summer courses, especially in the UK, for their children, or English-only education. As explained by Tosi (in Lepsky and Tosi 2006: 165)

> The Italian situation reflects the general picture of the contacts between other European languages and English. This trend began some twenty years ago. Fluency in English was perceived not only as an advantage in one's work but also as a mark of social prestige.

Despite the common intent to create a harmonized *European Education Area* (EEA), evident differences exist across European countries. As far as English proficiency is concerned, a divide between Nordic and Mediterranean countries is well-known and confirmed by data (see footnote 130). In the Nordic countries, people are more intensely exposed to English outside the school environment, through television and other media. In Italy, the long-standing tradition of dubbing films and television shows makes national channels mainly monolingual: while this situation grants general access to audio-visual programmes, it does not offer the opportunity to hear other languages.[127] Arguably, the introduction of Italian television in the 1950s brought the Italian language into everyone's homes, spreading and reinforcing the use of the national language and the decline of dialects. Italian viewers are now accustomed to watching films and tv series in the dubbed version, but today it is also possible to opt for foreign programmes in the original version through satellite transmission and video streaming services. All

---

[127] The dubbing market is a huge and expensive one compared to the subtitling one and is characteristic of populous countries with large audiences, like Italy, Germany, France and Spain. These countries tried to counterbalance the 'flood' of the American film industry in the post-war years by promoting national productions. The practice of dubbing was predominant in these countries also for nationalistic reasons. During the fascist era in Italy (1922–1945), non-dubbed films were prohibited (Minutella 2009; Audissino 2012).

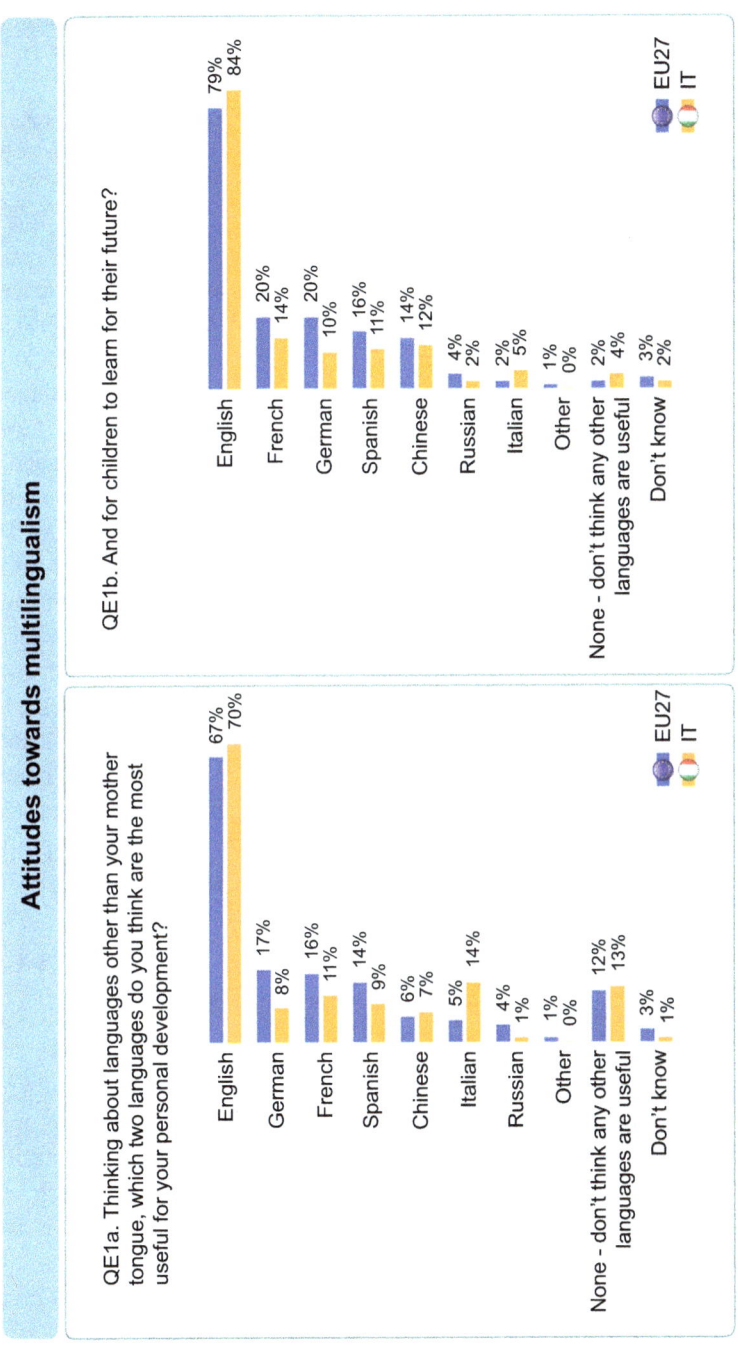

**Figure 7.2:** Statistics on attitudes towards multilingualism in the Italian population (*Special Eurobarometer 386*, 2014).

in all, competence in English of Italians leaves much to be desired, as clearly stated by Carlucci (2018):

> [. . .] direct contact with English speakers is a minority experience within the Italian-speaking community, and [. . .] a confident command of English is beyond reach of many speakers of Italian. Amongst those speakers whose material conditions of life and work make advanced knowledge and usage of English quite detached from everyday practices and priorities, this language is only learnt at a basic level or not learnt at all (Carlucci 2018: 4).

However, the Italian generation of millennials may modify the Italian linguistic scenario. The number of non-native speakers of English (at least 38% of EU citizens) is higher than that of native speakers (about 13% of the EU population before Brexit), which makes English the lingua franca of international communication and, as such, the expression of a 'de-territorialized' culture, at least for many learners (*Special Eurobarometer 386*, 2014). As surveyed by Aiello (2018) in a study of Italian youth learning English in 2012–13, secondary school students have a positive attitude towards the study of English, which they consider 'useful' for their future, as it will enable them to get a good job, to work abroad and travel. Indeed, the motivating driver towards the study of English is largely instrumental, utilitarian and, to some extent, self-centered. It looks as though the 'integrative' motivation which supported the study of English among previous generations, attracted by the British or American cultures and societies, and by the desire to imitate native speakers, is losing ground. Yet, young learners still consider 'native English' (mainly British and American) the best model to aim at as far as pronunciation is concerned. All in all, the widespread view that Italians are not very good at learning foreign languages still endures. However, according to Aiello's data, as far as self-perceived proficiency is concerned, Italian students regard their level of English as not fully satisfactory but have a positive perception of their own potential to learn English.

## 7.2 English-medium instruction

By English-medium instruction (normally abbreviated to EMI) is meant the use of English in tertiary education for the transmission of disciplinary knowledge, and implemented in countries where English is not the first language of the majority of the population (Dearden 2015; Macaro et al. 2018; Pecorari and Malmström 2018). The introduction of English-medium instruction in higher education is another step forward to align Italian education to the EU agenda of internationalization, a guiding principle for the creation of the *European Higher Education Area*

(EHEA).[128] The goals of internationalization, based on the objectives of the Bologna Declaration and extending beyond the EU, are to make higher education programmes more similar and compatible, and encourage transnational alignment and mutual recognition of curricula, so that student and staff mobility can be facilitated. Despite the great variety of languages spoken in the European continent, some 'stronger' languages are more operational than others for cross-border communication, but English is anyway the undisputed supranational lingua franca. Consequently, the goal of internationalization goes hand in hand with the 'Anglicization' of higher education, a strategy that may indeed ease this process, given that on average more than half of the European population is competent enough in English to hold a conversation and English is the most widely studied foreign language in all EU countries, as noted above (Wilkinson and Gabriëls 2021).

This trend towards homogenization across the European educational systems may sound contradictory and even paradoxical, given that linguistic diversity is held as one of the assets for the EU, as expressed by the well-known European motto 'united in diversity' (*in varietate concordia*). In fact, the growing use of English as a medium of instruction in European higher education contradicts the pluralistic approach to languages, traditions and cultures, which has made multilingualism the flagship principle of European identity. The promotion of internationalization, which has become an ever-present buzzword in academic policy-making, is meant to bring the beneficial effects of consolidating cooperation and enhancing mutual understanding among European citizens by subscribing to common key values and contributing to the making of the 'global citizen'. In a more pragmatic vein, once alien to the academic community, increased attraction of international students and staff will contribute to placing universities on the international market as 'brands', make them more competitive, raise their quality standards on international academic rankings, and ultimately increase their budgets (Mautner 2005).

The advantages of EMI have led to a swift surge in the number of programmes offered by universities in non-Anglophone countries (Coleman 2006; Macaro et al. 2018; Molino et al. 2022), giving priority to disciplines that generally attract many students interested in managerial and professional careers, such as economics, business administration, law and engineering. Indeed, from a European perspective, the goal of internationalization is not simply confined to student and staff mobility within the European continent, but, more ambitiously, to reach out much beyond the EU borders and attract students from all over the world.

---

**128** The *European Higher Education Area* (EHEA), launched in 2010, is a collaboration among 49 countries in the European continent and the European Commission. Members of the EHEA agree to gradually transform their educational systems in accordance with the objectives of the Bologna Accord.

The controversial debate on the rise of English as the lingua franca for the development of higher education with a strong international vocation revolves around many arguments, equally valid, in favour or against (Dimova, Hultgren and Jensen 2015). The opportunities offered by the use of a language that is already shared by the majority of scholars and students are likely to bring about positive results in terms of knowledge construction and dissemination. In other words, the English language can be seen as an excellent tool for integration and intercomprehension in a multilingual and plurilinguistic context such as the European one.[129] The positions against English as a European lingua franca include ideological, cultural and educational factors. First, the ideological argument claims that subscribing to English-only education may imply the acceptance of 'English linguistic imperialism', that is, the superiority of the people who speak this language as a mother tongue. Second, the cultural argument maintains that monolingualism conveys the wrong assumption that only Anglophone cultures are relevant for one's future, while the other languages and cultures stand in a diaglossic or ancillary relation with it. Finally, the educational argument stresses the importance of education in one's own native language, which is essential for the full acquisition of expressive means in all knowledge domains, including scientific and technical terminology (Phillipson 2003, 2006, 2008).

Turning now to internationalization and English-medium instruction in Italy, introduced in the 1990s, it must be pointed out that it is a relatively recent phenomenon with respect to other European countries.[130] For this reason, over the last decades many surveys and studies have been devoted to EMI in Italy and to local contexts where EMI has been implemented more or less successfully, with a particular focus on attitudes, implications, advantages and disadvantages for teaching staff and students (Costa and Coleman 2012; Campagna and Pulcini 2014; Molino and Campagna 2014; Pulcini and Campagna 2015; Broggini and Costa 2017; Mastellotto and Zanin 2021). In Italy there are over 90 higher education institutions, mostly State (public) universities, several private ones, and some polytechnics (which have faculties of Architecture and Engineering), as well as other institutions such as the

---

[129] Plurilingualism is a notion that normally refers to individual competence in the use and learning of more than one language, while multilingualism indicates the presence of more than one language in the same geographical area, even though these are not known by all speakers. Plurilingualism and multilingualism are often used as synonyms, but multilingualism is more commonly used in the EU context.

[130] According to Coleman (2006) in the Netherlands and in Sweden English-taught courses were already present in the 1950s, while in Finland, Hungary and Norway they were introduced in the 1980s. The university of Maastricht is considered the pioneer of EMI, since it was the first institution to offer EMI programmes in Europe, starting from 1987.

academies of fine arts, conservatories of music, higher schools of design, fashion and restauration, theological colleges, and military academies (Solly 2010).[131] Since 2010, legislation has given Italian universities an 'autonomous status', according to which institutions are free to decide on their own educational organization, including the introduction of new degree programmes, if they comply with general requirements defined by the Ministry[132] (Solly 2010; Pulcini and Campagna, 2015). As shown in Table 7.1, the increase in English-taught programmes has been noteworthy: according to a national report issued in 2019, the number of programmes (degree courses) in English in the 2013–2014 academic year were 143, rising to 398 in the 2018–19 academic year, registering an increase of 178% (Rugge 2019). At the moment, the number of degree programmes taught entirely in English amounts to just over 10% of all degrees offered in Italian universities (Universitaly).

**Table 7.1:** Increase of EMI programmes in Italy (Rugge 2019).

| A.A. | TOT. CORSI IN INGLESE | AUMENTO % RISPETTO ALL'A.A. 2013/2014 |
|---|---|---|
| 2013/2014 | 143 | |
| 2014/2015 | 193 | +35% |
| 2015/2016 | 248 | +73% |
| 2016/2017 | 279 | +95% |
| 2017/2018 | 341 | +138% |
| 2018/2019 | 398 | +178% |

The data provided by the same report on the distribution of the EMI programmes across cycles and disciplinary areas show that the great majority of EMI programmes are at MA level (91.2%), whereas only 8.8% are at the BA level. Post-graduate, doctoral programmes and winter-summer schools in English have increased by 30% in the

---

[131] Italy has some of the most ancient universities in Europe: the University of Bologna, the oldest, was founded in 1088, the University of Naples "Federico II" in 1321, the University of Rome "La Sapienza" in 1303, the University of Florence in 1321, the University of Turin in 1404 (Solly 2010).
[132] In Italy there are the *Ministero dell'Università e Ricerca* (*Ministry of University and Research*), also known as MUR, and the *Ministero dell'Istruzione e del Merito* (*Ministry of Education and Merit*), whose competence regards all the other school cycles. Until 2020 the two ministries were joined together.

same time span. The most common disciplinary areas are economics, business administration, information science, engineering and medicine. Needless to say, degree programmes in Modern Languages, including the study of English language, literature and civilization as 'curricular' disciplines for the training of teachers and language specialists are a completely different matter, as English in this case is both the focus and the vehicle of disciplinary content.

The importance of English-medium instruction is a priority item on the agenda of the Italian *Ministry of University and Research* (MUR), as a strategic policy to implement internationalization. The *Conference of Italian University Rectors* (*Conferenza dei Rettori delle Università italiane,* also known as CRUI),[133] which holds a consulting role within the Italian university system, regularly conducts national surveys through its dedicated commissions in order to collect data and monitor the implementation of specific actions of academic relevance. The importance of the English language for internationalization has repeatedly been highlighted and discussed in many documents, as the following quote testifies:

> [. . .] l'internazionalizzazione della formazione può realizzarsi attraverso le forme dello scambio (soprattutto con il Programma Erasmus+), della mobilita internazionale strutturata, degli accordi interateneo. La via principale dell'internazionalizzazione rimane comunque l'erogazione dei programmi – di tutti e tre i livelli, ma soprattutto dottorali – in lingua straniera (inglese). (Rugge 2019: 81)

> [the internationalization of education can be realized through forms of exchange (especially through the Erasmus+ Programme), structured international mobility as well as inter-university agreements. The main route to internationalization is anyway the teaching of programmes – of all the three levels, but especially the doctoral ones – in a foreign language (English).]

The various challenges of EMI in Italy are carefully addressed by national documents. As far as competition is concerned, it is fully acknowledged that Italy can hardly stand up to the high-quality programmes in business and economics offered by Anglophone universities, and these particular subject areas normally feature as international EMI programmes all over the world. It follows that Italy needs a tailor-made strategy for implementing internationalization, focusing on its national strong points such as its geographical context, climate, people's welcoming attitude, Italy's strong cultural appeal as well as the Italian language:

> La nostra lingua rappresenta perciò un'opportunità non ancora sfruttata. Così come l'inglese è, ormai, la lingua semi-ufficiale in molte discipline, l'italiano avrebbe le potenzialità

---

[133] CRUI is an association of Italian state and private universities with a co-ordinating and consulting role in the higher education system, linking institution to the Italian parliament and the Ministry of University and Research. Link: www.crui.it

> di essere la lingua-madre in alcune materie di studio come il design, l'architettura, l'arte, il restauro ecc. (Rugge 2018: 70)

> [Thus, our language represents an opportunity not yet exploited. As English is by now the semi-official language in many disciplines, Italian may potentially be the mother tongue of some disciplines such as design, architecture, art and conservation etc.]

On the other hand, the obstacle posed by the Italian language to attract international students cannot be denied. The number of international students attending Italian universities has been relatively low so far, amounting to 5.32% of the whole university population in 2019–20, according to the data issued by the *Ministry of University and Research*.[134] At the moment, the Italian university context is widely monolingual, which may make EMI an artificial operation or, as argued elsewhere, "the cosmetic travesty of internationalisation mandates" (Campagna and Pulcini 2014: 188). In fact, a truly international degree programme should posses specific characteristics, such as being designed for the realization of a joint degree programme, or an international consortium, or have an international orientation, include visiting professors in the teaching staff, and have a congruous number of international attenders. To some extent, given the relatively low number of international students, EMI in the Italian context may be considered as a form of 'internationalization at home', where Italian students have the opportunity of meeting some international students, attending lessons taught by visiting professors, and being fully involved in a 'foreign' academic experience in their home country. Italian reports on internationalization acknowledge this intrinsic drawback of EMI in Italy:

> Con oltre ¾ di una classe composta di italofoni, l'utilizzo, nel corso, della lingua inglese tende a ridursi e a essere percepito come posticcio. Né una così ristretta componente di studenti provenienti da altri Paesi riesce a imprimere al collettivo, oltre alla lingua, quelle prassi di lavoro e studio che rendono l'esperienza di apprendimento effettivamente internazionalizzata. (Rugge 2018: 27)

> [With more than ¾ of a class composed of Italian speakers, the use of the English language in the lessons tends to be reduced and be perceived as a fake. Nor can such a limited component of students coming from abroad transfer to the whole group, besides the language, working and studying styles that make the learning experience truly internationalized.]

---

[134] Data from the *Anagrafe Nazionale degli Studenti* (Osservatorio Studenti Didattica), available at https://anagrafe.miur.it/php5/home.php. The indicators provided by OECD (Organisation for Economic Co-operation and Development) referring to 2021, quote 5% as the share of international and foreign students at all tertiary levels of education (Education at a Glance, available at https://www.oecd-ilibrary.org/education/education-at-a-glance-2021_b35a14e5-en) (November, 2022).

Additional problems may arise in university contexts when a sudden shift to EMI results from a top-down imposition, dictated by political reasons rather than real educational motivations, such as, for example, to attract more students towards a declining degree programme. The teaching staff may not be confident enough to teach in English or not be willing to invest more time in lesson preparation and in the reorganization of the course material. Several professors learned English during their own training or specialization abroad, and feel that they can successfully handle and transfer complex notions in it, but many lecturers may only have a passive knowledge of the language and scarce communicative competence, and be reluctant to take on the extra hurdle of a full course in the EMI mode. Being able to teach in a language other than your own mother tongue, elaborating on complex content with an adequate linguistic richness and interacting with students in class and outside the class requires very high competence. Some Italian lecturers do not have these skills, and their performance in class may result in 'watered-down', simplified presentations of translated slides. Many scholars in the field of EMI argue in favour of adequate in-service methodological training and linguistic support in the transition to EMI, which would in fact reflect the approach referred to as ICLHE (Integrating Content and Language in Higher education)[135] or CLIL at tertiary level (Costa 2016, 2021). In order to encourage EMI, training courses on EMI methodology and linguistic support have been offered to university teaching staff by the British Council in Italy, leading to the acquisition of the ATE diploma (*Academic Teaching Excellence*). Other forms of competence validation are being considered for lecturers in charge of EMI courses to overcome situations of 'forced' recruitment of unenthusiastic lecturers.[136]

A further stumbling block for EMI is the students' level of English. Although universities set entry requirements for local and international students enrolling in EMI programmes, which is usually B2 (upper intermediate), often students' proficiency levels are not up to standard. Thus, it is necessary to provide linguistic support for students too, through the teaching of practical lessons to reinforce their English skills and avoid fossilization of wrong habits. Although EMI does not involve any specific focus on language acquisition, research on students' motivations

---

[135] The Association ICLHE (Integrating Content and Language in Higher Education) was created in 2010 to promote international debate and experience within the university context on the integration of disciplinary content and the language of instruction (not only English).

[136] At the *Center for Internationalization and Parallel Language Use* of the University of Copenhagen the TOEPAS (Test of Oral English Proficiency for Academic Staff), an oral performance test based on a simulated lecture, has been implemented to verify and certify the lecturers' proficiency and teaching skills (Dimova 2017). The advantage of this form of certification, now aligned to the CEFR (Dimova 2018) is international recognition allowing mobility for EMI lecturers.

and expectations from an EMI programme has shown that students choose English-taught programmes also to improve their competence in English by experiencing a 'full academic immersion' in the language. Academic training through the medium of English is considered an additional opportunity of consolidating one's competence in the language that is normally used by professionals, scientists and academics in conferences and in top-class specialized journals to access and disseminate specialist knowledge, especially in the 'hard' sciences, or simply to be more competitive in the global job market (Cicillini 2020).

As for possible drawbacks caused by EMI programmes, difficulties with content recall, note-taking and the learning of specialized terminology have been noted, although these learning problems are not significantly different from those encountered by non-EMI students. As for English competence, it cannot be denied that during an EMI degree programme lasting several years, students are exposed to English through lessons and written course material so that they expand their vocabulary and strengthen their grammar, often in an incidental way. Yet, this may not be enough to make significant progress in English proficiency, especially if the students' entry level is not advanced, without systematic language support and focus on language as well as content. Research into these questions has not yet provided solid evidence on EMI students' language gains. On the other hand, it has also been noted that EMI students are highly motivated to work hard and develop specific socio-affective strategies to achieve good results (Guarda 2018; Molino et al. 2022).

The educational issues related to EMI in Italy has recently provoked fierce debate within the academic community. The increase in the number of English-taught programmes in higher education is a phenomenon that has been criticized for various reasons, particularly because of its legal and cultural implications. The legal question lies in the 'imposition' of English as a medium of instruction on Italian university staff who may not be happy to switch to English. The cultural question, raised by many Italian linguists, is whether an Italian graduate should be trained in a foreign language and miss out on the acquisition of technical and scientific terminology in the national language.

On this particular issue, the case of the Polytechnic of Milan in 2012 is worth mentioning, since it attracted intense media coverage for these legal and cultural implications and is indeed emblematic in the Italian EMI context. The Polytechnic of Milan decided that its MA and PhD programmes would be taught entirely in English starting from the academic year 2014. This decision was opposed by some professors who did not feel or want to teach in English and consequently filed a legal action on the ground that Article 33 of the Italian constitution guarantees freedom of teaching, that is, teachers are free to choose the methods that they consider most suitable and are free to withdraw from a duty that is ideologically incompatible with their own values. The professors won the lawsuit and the appeal brought by the Polytechnic against this sentence was finally ruled out in 2018. This legal controversy, stemming from the adoption of English as a medium of instruction against the will of all the teaching staff involved, brought to the fore some fundamental principles of the Italian constitution, namely, beside the above-mentioned freedom of teaching, the protection of all languages also in matters regarding education. The final sentence of the Italian State Court established that a degree programme taught in any foreign language can be implemented only if a parallel programme taught in Italian is also available. This decision confirmed the principle that the exclusive use of a foreign language—English in this case—creates linguistic discrimination in society, weakens integration among cultures and enforces the superiority of a language over another, and, ultimately, students are denied the opportunity to choose.[137]

The legal implications and the emotional overtones that were brought to the public attention by the case of the Polytecnic of Milan were extensively commented on in the media. The *Accademia della Crusca* organized a conference on this issue and decided to make an open stand against EMI. The question posed by the Academy to society at large was: "Can you abandon your mother tongue altogether in university education? Is it right, is it possible?" Reactions came from academics, legal experts, scientists, linguists, writers and journalists, all eventually gathered in a volume (Maraschio and De Martino 2013). The pro-EMI position taken by the Rector of the Polytechnic of Milan, who was the initiator of this controversy, was that the mission of the university is to train the future managerial classes to operate on a multinational marketplace; therefore, in pragmatic terms, choosing English as a medium of instruction is a rational choice, from an entrepreneurial point of view. In addition, the Rector added, their students never complained about this choice, which confirms that customer satisfaction was fully achieved. Against this pro-English stand, the prevalent opinion that emerged from the debate was that English competence is indispensable nowadays for scientific and professional communication, but imposing this language as the only option is wrong. Moreover, as confirmed by several ministerial documents devoted to internationalization, it is advisable for international students to learn Italian, even if the degree programme is entirely taught in English. Indeed, according to Italian policy-makers, international students cannot live in linguistic isolation during their academic experience in Italy, and it is necessary that the culture of the host country should be transferred and retained to establish a long-lasting cultural bond. As for the benefit of Italian students, the prevailing opinion

---

[137] The case of the Polytechnic of Milan is examined and discussed in detail by Molino and Campagna (2014), Campagna and Pulcini (2014), Santulli (2015) and Costa (2021).

among the Italian linguists that attended the conference about the EMI controversy was that graduates should familiarize with the scientific-technical register in their native language in all knowledge domains and that the exclusion of Italian is undesirable in higher education.

Toning down the myth of English, Beccaria and Graziosi (2015) argued in favour of the importance of one's mother tongue for the emotional and cultural growth of any individual. In their view, it is necessary to oppose "la nuova, grave invadenza" ["the new serious intrusion"] of vehicular English in all educational cycles, since this is the result of a new 'Anglocentric' entrepreneurial culture, the fruit of utilitarianism and consumerism, a negative practice that is motivated by a policy that gives priority to what is useful and not to what is necessary for "la formazione della personalità e la cultura dell'immaginazione" ["the development of personality and the culture of imagination"] (Beccaria and Graziosi 2015: 104).

The overexposure of EMI as an ideological debate in the Italian educational context brought the beneficial effect of making society more aware of the implications that language choices involve. Families normally think that English is a good educational choice for young adults but, on the other hand, monolingualism in favour of English may lead to ignorance in other foreign languages and to the weakening of the Italian language in its specialized registers. In addition, strategic planning, quality assurance, linguistic and methodological support are necessary to avoid 'improvization' in the introduction of educational reforms such as EMI and to beware of a *tout court* 'Anglicization' of knowledge, since future graduates need much more than 'basic English' to become competitive on the marketplace.

## 7.3 The cultural debate: From 'Anglomania' to 'Anglophobia'

Attitudes to language are important sociolinguistic indicators of how a language is perceived by speakers and of the values, positive or negative, that are associated with it (Garret 2010). As an invisible force, speakers' attitudes contribute to building general perceptions in society, which, in turn, may also influence and direct official language policies (Pulcini 1997, 2019b). The appeal of English and its spread in Italy have been boosted by intense echoes of modernity, trendiness, professionalism, innovation, leadership, and success. Yet, the growing presence of English in Italy, which today is favourably welcomed by most Italians, has recently raised a debate in society on whether intervention is needed to protect Italian from the excessive input of Anglicisms and, more generally, to limit the 'Anglicization' of Italian society.

As reviewed in chapter 2, the different historical periods in which the English language and culture were in contact with Italian society were marked by attitudes of acceptance or rejection coming from scholars, thinkers, and ultimately by lay speakers, depending on the prestige that the model culture enjoyed at that particular time, and on the political relations, friendly or hostile, between English-speaking countries and Italy. Anglomania was a cultural fashion that dominated 18th century Italy (cf. 2.2) and lasted for over a century; by contrast, the unification of Italy in 1861 laid the seeds for linguistic patriotism (cf. 2.3). At the turn of the 20th century, America was seen as a promised land, and attracted 5 million Italian migrants, but a new wave of nationalism in Italian society grew into overt opposition to American and British values, including language, during the fascist regime (1922–1945). Neo-purist linguists such as Alfredo Panzini and Paolo Monelli expressed mild disapproval towards Anglicisms, and recorded them in their dictionaries with both descriptive and prescriptive intents (see 2.3). Attitudes to Anglo-American societies and their language changed in time, in the ebb and flow of social events and political relations, swinging back and forth from 'Anglomania' to 'Anglophobia'.

Attitudinal stands towards the influence of English in Italy have come from different voices of society. Italian academics have generally maintained a descriptive attitude, looking at linguistic innovation with curiosity and considering language change as a sign of vitality rather than a pathology (Sabatini 2008). Beccaria's (1988: 240) statement on this matter is worth quoting:

> La lingua è un bene comune, un bene sociale e culturale, ma non è come l'ambiente che va protetto perché vi si scaricano abusivamente liquami e immondezze inquinanti. La lingua non è come il monumento che all'aria si deteriora. Non è come l'Ara Pacis Augustae da tenere sottovetro. Non è un bene da preservare in museo. Va lasciata vivere per le strade, nelle accademie e negli angiporti, nei libri e nelle canzoni, in valli isolate e in tumultuose metropoli. La sua 'babele' rispecchia intensamente la comunità composita di cui è espressione. È stolto parlare di corruzione.
>
> [Language is a common property, a social and cultural asset, but it is not like the environment that must be protected because polluting effluents and garbage are illegally discharged in it. Language is not a monument that deteriorates in contact with air. It is not like the Ara Pacis Augustae to keep in a bell jar. It has to live in the streets, in academies and in narrow lanes, in books and in songs, in isolated valleys and in busy metropoles. Its 'Babelic' spirit forcefully reflects the composite community it is the expression of. To talk of corruption is foolish.]

This 'open' attitude towards exogenous influences that Italy has adopted since the end of the Second World War has granted Italian the fame of a 'democratic' language, in contrast with more 'introvert languages' such as French, German and Spanish, whose language academies exercise the right to decide on linguistic matters.[138] Italian is believed to be the most 'Anglophile' language towards Anglicisms of the Romance languages; according to the number of Anglicisms recorded by Görlach (2001), Italian ranks in fourth position after Dutch, Norwegian and German.

The Italian *Accademia della Crusca*, since its foundation in 1583, has been committed to the preservation of the linguistic heritage of the Italian language, mainly through philological research and lexicographic activity, and was never in favour of active intrusion in national language policy-making. During the fascist regime the Academy was closed down (the compilation of the *Vocabolario degli Accademici della Crusca* was interrupted at letter O) and the *Accademia d'Italia*, the voice of the dictatorship, took over.[139] In contrast to the autarchic ideas of the regime, the scholars and lexicographers of the time had a comparatively moderate attitude to foreign words and dialects, and basically refused to mix language issues with political or racial matters (Marazzini 2015). Neo-purists disapproved of the ecessive borrowing of foreign words, and objected to the 'structural and functional' features of foreign loans which made them inadequate for assimilation into the national language, but did not deny the historical dimension of language and its need to renew itself through contacts and exchanges with other languages. Against the political suppression of liberty, at the end of the regime, Italian dialects reclaimed their status and foreign words banned by legislation emerged again. This confirms that any form of expression of one's self is deeply entrenched in people's identity and any attempt to control or manipulate language is destined to failure.

This position finds support in the insightful writings of the Italian philosopher and labour activist Antonio Gramsci (1891–1937), who was imprisoned during the

---

138 In France, the *Académie française*, founded in 1635, has always invigilated on the purity of the French language and opposed the phenomenon called 'franglais' (anglicized French). Several protectionist measures were introduced to oppose the spread of Anglicisms and create French terminology in specialized domains, imposing quotas in the film industry and in advertising (see Humbley 2008). In Spain, the *Real Academia Española* (RAE), founded in 1713, monitors the development of the Spanish language and its varieties. When foreign words are recorded in the *Diccionario de la lengua española* (DLE), it means that the loanword is admitted and should be typographically marked in italics in case of non-adapted loanwords. Spanish equivalents are suggested but not imposed. The *Verein Deutsche Sprache*, or German Language Association (VDS) is an association, founded in 1997, whose goal is to protect and promote the German language and its development in specialized areas of knowledge, contrasting the excessive use of English words and expressions, a phenomenon called 'Denglisch'. This association regularly issues a list of Anglicisms (Anglicisms Index) used in German and suggests domestic equivalents.
139 The dictionary compiled by the *Accademia d'Italia*, ideologically inspired by the fascist regime, stopped at letter C. The entries contained quotations from Italian authors and from Mussolini's speeches.

Italian regime because of his political dissent. In his contribution to intellectual debate, mainly focused on political relations, Gramsci expressed bright ideas on language and power relations, which may be a source of inspiration for the contemporary debate on the advantages and disadvantages of the spread of English as an international lingua franca (Carlucci 2013, 2018). On the question of language policy, and in the light of the authoritarian policy of his age, Gramsci rejected any form of linguistic imposition, as expressed in the following often-quoted statement:

> Ogni volta che affiora, in un modo o nell'altro, la quistione della lingua, significa che si sta imponendo una serie di altri problemi: la formazione e l'allargamento della classe dirigente, la necessità di stabilire rapporti più intimi e sicuri tra i gruppi dirigenti e la massa popolare-nazionale, cioè di riorganizzare l'egemonia culturale (*Quaderni del carcere*, Quaderno 29, § 3)

> [Every time that a language question arises, in one way or another, it means that a series of other problems are being imposed: the formation and widening of the ruling classes, the necessity to establish more intimate and safe relations between the establishment and the national-popular mass, that is, to reorganize the cultural hegemony (*Prison Notebooks*, Book 29, § 3)]

In Gramsci's view, multilingualism is a positive measure as it enriches the linguistic repertoire and expressive means of all speakers and language competence is indispensable to enable citizens to participate in social and political life. This also means that the exclusion from the 'standard' language or from the mainstream code of communication may bring the negative consequence of people's social marginalization and frustration.

According to some linguists, looking closely at the presence of English loanwords in the common language and the repertoires of specialized vocabularies, the growing use of Anglicisms is not an alarm and will not spoil the integrity of Italian. Among the most authoritative scholars, Tullio De Mauro has always toned down the preoccupations concerning the 'invasion' of Anglicisms. As pointed out in Section 5.1, De Mauro's data on absolute numbers and frequency of Anglicisms show that their overall incidence is very low, and the presence of foreign words can be recorded outside the core vocabulary, that is, in specialized domains. Moreover, Italians seem to prefer heritage lexis to foreign words for everyday use. In one of De Mauro's books, whose title echoes a line from Mozart's *Don Giovanni* (*In Europa son già 103. Troppe lingue per una democrazia?* [In Europe there are already 103. Too many languages for a democracy?]), he traces the linguistic history of the European continent and its plurilingual roots–a large inventory of transnational and regional languages–held as symbols of local identities. The genetic roots of Latin and Greek, which have contributed to the formation of the intellectual, philosophical and scientific lexicons of European languages, is a common heritage that is stronger than differences. Given that Europe needs a common language for communication, not only to simplify communication at institutional level, but especially to build a strong democratic community, English can be chosen for this role of transnational or supra-national language, being the most 'Latinized' language in Europe. In sum, according to De Mauro, the linguistic and cultural identity of national languages would not be jeopardized if European citizens adopted English as a common language, that is, "Più inglese non comporta necessariamente meno altre lingue." ['More' English does not necessarily imply 'fewer' other languages.] (De Mauro 2014a: 67).

This tendency has also been noted by Fanfani (2001) who argues that the use of Anglicisms has declined in some key fields such as sport and computing, compared to some decades ago. He also presents the opinions of other authoritative scholars in Italian linguistics and literature, whose arguments are in line with De Mauro's, i.e., that the 'intellectual lexicon' of Italian and the language used by educated speakers for daily communication have not been influenced by English to such an extent as to undermine its integrity. Forms of linguistic hybridization occured in the past between languages; for example, the French language penetrated into the structures of Italian much more forcefully than English is doing today. The English language is indeed taking over many areas of knowledge, so that it would be short-sighted to deny its importance for contemporary scientists or for whoever wants to operate in any field on an international level.

The reactions to the influence of English described so far come from linguists who have a liberal attitude to language borrowing. By contrast, many scholars observe this phenomenon with preoccupation and open hostility. A well-known position is that of Arrigo Castellani, expressed in an article entitled *Morbus Anglicus* (1987), in which he compared the eccessive input of English loanwords into Italian to a deadly disease. The title of this article was particularly impactful, and raised echoes of agreement and solidarity in Italian academia, though the author himself was not so strongly prejudiced against the English language, and the title meant to introduce the argument with a light-hearted tone, as can be gathered from the opening lines:

> Nome del paziente: Italiano. Professione: Lingua letteraria. Età: quattordici secoli, o sette, secondo i punti di vista. Carriera scolastica: ritardata, ma con risultati particolarmente brillanti fin dall'inizio.
> Diagnosi: sintomi chiarissimi di *morbus anglicus*, con complicazioni (fase acuta).
> Prognosi: favorevole, purché (puntini di sospensione). Già, purché: dato che il *virus*, nel caso che c'interessa, agisce in profondità, attaccando gli organi essenziali. Un medico prudente parlerebbe piuttosto di prognosi riservata.
>
> [Name of the patient: Italian. Job: Literary language. Age: fourteen centuries, or seven, depending on viewpoints. Education: late, but with particularly brilliant results from the beginning.

Diagnosis: very clear symptoms of *morbus anglicus*, with complications (acute phase). Prognosis: favourable, as long as. . . Right, as long as. . .: since the *virus*, in this specific case, acts in depth, attacking the vital organs. A careful practitioner would rather talk about a critical condition.]

Castellani acknowledges the limited incidence of Anglicisms, proved by the data presented by other eminent linguists who have taken a tolerant position, but claims that the structures of Italian may anyway be seriously jeopardized by alien lexical models. He rejects Anglicisms that are unnecessary and argues in favour of systematic adaptation and substitution of non-adapted loanwords. Since the Italian language derived from the Florentine model, syllable-final consonants (except for rare cases of liquids and nasals) and complex consonant clusters are not admitted. Therefore, words like *bar* and *bum* (*boom*) may be accepted, but *film, sport, bluff* and *boomerang* should be adapted to '*filme*', '*sporte*', '*bluffo*' and '*bumerango*'; the word *bestseller*, containing the complex cluster <sts>, should be replaced by the very Italian creation *vendissimo* (which never caught on after Castellani's proposal). In short, loanwords that clash with the orthographic and morpho-syntactic rules of the Italian language challenge its linguistic stability, create perplexity and cause distress, like 'a pebble in your shoe'. Many proposals put forward by Castellani are often quoted as anecdotal examples generated by a stubbornly purist mind: *intredima* for *weekend*, *fubbia* (*fumo+nebbia*) for *smog* (*smoke+ fog*), *velopattino* for *windsurf*, *ubino* for *hobby*, *abbuio* for *blackout*, *trotterello* for *jogging*, and *guardabimbi* for *baby sitter*. In any case, some Italian equivalents mentioned by Castellani as acceptable substitutes, such as *bilancio* for *budget* and *allibratore* for *bookmaker*, have been naturally assimilated into Italian without any academic imposition.

An analogous line of intervention to contrast the allegedly 'superfluous' use of Anglicisms in Italian and make them structurally acceptable for assimilation is the work done by Giovanardi and Gualdo (2008), who claim for themselves a neutral position between the opposing views of 'Anglo-skepticals' and 'Anglo-enthusiasts'. Following the new wave of concern among the Italian intelligentsia about the presence of Anglicisms in Italian, they propose 14 sociolinguistic parameters that may measure the strength of an Anglicisms or the possibility/probability of their replacement by Italian substitutes. These criteria are briefly illustrated below:

1) Type of equivalence: this parameter indicates whether the Italian equivalent is an adaptation or a substitution of the Anglicism. Adaptation is preferable when a fully Italian word is obtained, and it is particularly favourable when the words share a neo-Latin base (e.g. *community / comunità*; *devolution / devoluzione*; *extension – estensione*). Conversely, the substitution of an Italian equivalent may be an unfavourable solution; in fact, *auto da città* and *pagina iniziale* are less popular than *city car* and *homepage*.

2) Age (old or recent borrowing): older borrowings tend to be fully assimilated and harder to replace; recent borrowings can be replaced more easily.

3) Degree of assimilation: this parameter is measured on the attestation, or otherwise, of the Anglicisms in dictionaries; the more dictionaries record an Anglicism, the less this item is amenable to replacement.

4) Presence in French and Spanish: the attestation of an Anglicism in other Romance languages may strengthen or weaken its chances of success.

5) Domain of use (general or specialized): if an Anglicism belongs to a specialized domain, its spread may be limited within a small community of users and replacement is more difficult; however, many terms transfer from specialist to common use.

6) Register: this parameter refers to the use of Anglicisms according to social classes (educated vs general vs widely available); a distinction is made between Anglicisms that are typically used by educated speakers (e.g. *e-commerce* / *commercio elettronico*), which are more likely to be substituted), general words whose currency may vary depending on the age of speakers (e.g. *e-mail* / *posta elettronica*) and words that have wide circulation, through not yet assimilated in general speech (e.g. *exit poll* / *sondaggio a caldo*). The two latter categories are more resistant to substitution.

7) Spoken vs written medium: Anglicisms spreading through the written medium are more likely to become assimilated, whereas Anglicisms entering the language through spoken or broadcast media have a more transient nature.

8) Degree of technicality: highly technical Anglicisms are difficult to replace with Italian equivalents, whereas a lower degree of technicality may favour adaptation or substitution.

9) Expressive value: the connotative power of an Anglicism is a strong driver for its preference with respect to an Italian equivalent. Several aspects come into play, namely brevity, evocative power, sound, status symbol. Words like *blog*, *cookie* and *tag* do not offer much chance to Italian competitors.

10) Spelling and pronunciation: complexity in the orthographic form and the pronunciation of an Anglicisms may contribute to the preference for an Italian equivalent.

11) Number of possible Italian substitutes: when the possible Italian substitutes are more than one, the strength of the Anglicisms may be increased and its replacement becomes more difficult.

12) Combinability: Anglicisms may be particularly successful when they replicate similar already existing patterns (the element *-day* in *election day, tax-day*, etc.); this property also applies to derivation such as, for example, the creation of verbs from a base noun (e.g. *format / formattare*)

13) Semantic divergence (false Anglicisms): when Anglicisms are Italian autonomous creations, with little correspondence in equivalent English models, their strength is reduced and therefore they are likely to give in to Italian substitutes.

14) Semantic status (monosemic, polysemic): monosemy represents an advantage for the success of an Anglicism, whereas polysemy may lead to the creation of successful multiple translation equivalents.

The selection of 150 Anglicisms that are analyzed and discussed in this work includes exclusively non-adapted Anglicisms, which confirms once again that purist concerns are addressed to 'foreign-looking' items, whereas adaptations and calques are not formally in conflict with Italian structures and therefore perceived as natural additions to the lexical resources of the language. The parameters singled out by the authors are indeed very interesting for understanding lexical borrowing, and the attempt to propose Italian substitutes is a legitimate policy, albeit prone to failure in most cases. As happened to Castellani's awkward proposals, also in Giovanardi and Gualdo's study there are several cases of humorous or improbable renditions such as *giallino* for *post-it, pensatoio* for *think tank, rullovaligia* (or *valigia a rotelle*) for *trolley* or *fusopatia* for *jet lag*. The proposal to substitute *slow food* with the Italian phrase *mangiar bene* sounds rather unconvincing, given that this word is an Italian creation (from proper name to common noun); in fact, it is the brand name of the movement founded in the Piedmont region of Italy. On the other hand, the fact that every selected items is analyzed through linguistic parameters and accompanied not only by the comments of the authors but also by common people's opinions makes this approach particularly worthy of attention.

The cultural debate on the dominance of English in Italian society has also been fuelled by journalists and commentators, whose viewpoints are often much more subjective, direct and often disrespectful than the objective ones expressed by academics. For example, the journalist Indro Montanelli cried out against the overuse of English words in the press and defined this habit as 'a mental vice inherited by centuries of servitude'. On the opposite front, the Italian scientist and media-man Piero Angela stated that the modern 'illiterate' is the person who knows no English, because they have no access to scientific culture. Opinion-makers often feel that the excessive use of Anglicisms is irritating when speakers intentionally sprinkle their speech with English words as a form of 'snobbery' and 'exhibitionism', especially some categories of speakers such as managers, economists, and ICT experts. Newspaper language is full of English (Dardano, Frenguelli and Puoti 2008; Caimotto & Molino 2011), not only for their eye-catching power in headlines but also as a result of sloppiness, laziness, lack of time or effort to transfer news from English sources into Italian, according to some commentators. In political discourse, politicians are criticized for using Anglicisms as a rhetorical strategy to give an attractive name to an unpleasant measure (e.g. *spending review*, with the meaning of 'cuts to expenses') or to make small allowances sound like benefits (e.g. *social card*).

By analogy with *franglais and Denglisch*, the term '*itangliano*' was coined some decades ago to denote "the overuse or misuse of English terms for the purpose of adding a touch of class to Italian discourses" (Pulcini, 2019: 40). The word 'itangliano' was used for the first time by the Italian-American author Giacomo Elliot, who published a book containing a list of 400 English words that are necessary to work your way up in professional careers, highlighting the function of English as a 'status symbol' (Elliot 1977; Dunlop 1989; Botticella 2007). Criticism towards the superfluous use of English is addressed to speakers who try to communicate in business transactions with limited competence, producing an ungrammatical 'Italianized' form of 'bad simple English' or 'macaroni' English that would sound incomprehensible to competent speakers (Caimotto 2013, 2015; Incelli 2013; Furiassi 2018).

Following the mediatic protest against the introduction of English-medium instruction in higher education in 2012, several actions were undertaken to sensitize public attention to 'the language question'. In 2015 an online petition was launched, pleading politicians, public administrators, the media and companies for a more 'respectful' use of the Italian language in public discourse. The petition #dilloinitaliano (#say it in Italian)[140] received the support of the *Accademia della Crusca*, who organized a conference on the impact of Anglicisms on Italian and on other Romance languages in times of globalization. The themes discussed among international experts were the much debated attraction of Italians towards English at the expense of Italian, the overuse of unnecessary Anglicisms and the importance of the historical and cultural heritage of one's native language. This occasion, and the positions expressed by linguists and recorded in the proceedings of this symposium (Marazzini and Petralli 2015), testified a widespread preoccupation about the welfare of Italian but, at the same time, the rejection of direct intervention through national language policies. The memory of the fascist regime is a constant reminder for Italian academics to avoid radical stands and assume a consultative role in language

---

[140] https://www.internazionale.it/opinione/annamaria-testa/2015/02/17/dillo-in-italiano (November, 2022).

matters, on the basis of data acquired from 'unbiased' observation. To counter the irresistible appeal of Anglicisms, the position that emerged from the academic community was that it is important to foster a greater sense of identity and raise the awareness of Italian speakers of their own historical heritage and national culture.

Despite the soft-spoken support of the Italian academy, crusades in the defence of Italian and against the 'invasion' of Anglicisms are made by journalists and independent scholars (Zoppetti 2017, 2022). For example, a portal officially dedicated to the promotion of the Italian language is actually primarily focused on the insidious flood of Anglicisms and hosts an online dictionary with Anglicisms and Italian substitutes.[141] In 2021, this group of self-appointed 'activists of Italian' presented an appeal to the government for a series of legislative measures that they deem necessary to protect the Italian language: to abolish the use of Anglicisms in job contracts, to eliminate the requirement of English as a foreign language to work in the the public admnistration, to cancel the compulsory use of English to submit proposals for research projects of national interest, to waive the exclusive use of English as a medium of instruction in higher education (this was already ruled out by Italian legislation in 2018), and to write in the Italian constitution that Italian is the official national language. Actually, these requests may never obtain serious consideration by the Italian parliament but may contribute to bring the discussion on language matters to the public opinion.

To conclude, although the majority of Italians consider knowing English a great opportunity, the steady rise of English in Italy over the past decades, both as a language donor and as a cultural model, has bred sentiments of soft but proud 'purism' among some scholars and external observers, nurturing a useful and legitimate debate on the health and future developments of the Italian language (Beccaria 2006; Marazzini 2018; Marello 2020).

## 7.4 Roundup

Since the post-WW2 period, the Italian educational system has been transformed following on from national reforms and activism in foreign language teaching, gradually giving greater priority to the study of English as a foreign language mainly to the detriment of French. Although the level of English competence in Italians is not up to the standards reached by speakers in other European countries, Italian learners are favourably motivated to study English owing to its importance in any walk of life. The prestige of English and its association with modernity, success and professionalism is not free from criticism coming from linguists and

---

[141] https://aaa.italofonia.info/ (November, 2022).

observers who condemn an 'Anglocentric' vision in education and consider the dominance of English as a threat for the Italian culture and language. Italy appears to be changing its welcoming attitude towards English into a moderate acceptance, which is consistent with protectionist sentiments expressed by other Romance languages such as French and Spanish. The stand made by academics is anyway tolerant, generally more inclined to the creation of Italian substitutes of Anglicisms and to fostering a greater sense of respect and pride for Italian, rather than resentment towards English. Despite protectionist reactions, the spread of English in Italy is generally perceived as an opportunity rather than a threat, and efforts are being made in education to raise the competence of Italian learners of English up to the standards of their more advanced European peers.

# Conclusions

This book has offered an updated overview of lexical borrowing from English into Italian, filling a gap in the literature on English-Italian studies available to English-speaking readers. Although the focus has been exclusively on the Italian language, the phenomenon of language contact has been explored with a wider sociolinguistic perspective in mind, placing the English language at the core of an unprecedented phenomenon, that is, its spread as a lingua franca for international communication on a global scale and the continuous and pervasive outflow of Anglicisms in many world languages.

Focusing on Europe, the influence of the English language in all its varieties followed similar pathways across the Western European countries which experienced a comparable social history, often taking complex routes of transmission. France is the most conspicuous example of a country geographically close to Italy that greatly influenced Italian society culturally and linguistically until the 20$^{th}$ century, both for the shaping of the Italian language and for the transmission of English loanwords. An important step in the research of English-induced lexical borrowing is to continue comparing the outcomes of this influence across different languages and language families, both within and outside the European continent, taking into account the historical and sociolinguistic conditions that have made the assimilation of English more or less welcome.

A founding principle in the study of lexical borrowing is that the influence of any donor language depends on the relationship between the languages and cultures involved as well as the status and prestige of the model language in the recipient social context. The starting point of the study of language contact is the historical backdrop against which the speech communities involved established and fostered mutual exchanges. English-Italian contacts throughout the centuries were motivated by commercial reasons, political relations and interest in each other's culture, besides being favoured by geographical proximity (with Britain) and political consonance (with North America and the Western bloc). Thus, the status of English in Italy has always been that of a foreign language, taught and learned in the national school system since the mid-20$^{th}$ century. This means that the influence of English on Italian can be described in terms of an 'adstratum' relation, whereby a speech community transfers cultural products, primarily lexical items, onto another without any imposition and not leading to situations of bilingualism (but see below on 'bilingual elites').

A crucial question raised in various quarters of the Italian educational and academic environments is whether these social conditions will change in the new millenium. As a consequence of the importance of English in the job market, its popularity as a foreign language in the school system and the increase of English-medium instruction in higher education, linguists and observers believe that English may gain a dominant role so that Italians may not acquire adequate competence in their own national language, especially as far as specialized and professional knowledge is concerned. A cultural debate is at work in present-day Italy, featuring, on the one hand, those who consider the use of Anglicisms in journalism, digital communication and advertising as a strategy to capture people's attention and convey a positive message of modernity, and those who are afraid that the Anglicization of the Italian language and culture will lead to a decline of the Italian national identity. It is feared that the shift of English from foreign to second language in some Nordic countries may take place in Italy too. Purist sentiments and alarmed attitudes towards the spread of English pervade popular and scholarly debates on the cultural hegemony of English. This phenomenon is still limited but is likely to increase, as the number of Italian competent speakers in English grows and new Italian-English 'bilingual elites' of professional groups, businessmen, economists and politicians emerge in Italian society.

A large part of this book has focused on the typology of lexical borrowings and the description of English-induced borrowing into Italian. Some linguists consider this area of studies less 'worthy' of attention than other phenomena that have deeper and more long-lasting consequences on the structures of a language, such as innovations in morpho-syntactic patterns, which are rarer and more resistant to integration. In fact, only a few instances of English-induced morpho-syntactic change have been identified in 'neo-standard Italian' (Berruto 2017), which signals that the influence of English has not (yet) penetrated the Italian language much beyond the lexical level. By contrast, the lexicon of a language is, by its very nature, extremely dynamic and volatile. New words or senses – about 20% of which are from English, as has been calculated (Adamo and Della Valle 2018) –are introduced in newspapers daily; yet most of them are bound to disappear once they have served their communicative goals. In short, neologisms testify to the creative vitality of a language, without affecting the structural pillars of the language.

The typology of lexical borrowings adopted in this book (Figure 3.1) is meant to apply to the analysis of borrowings in all languages, besides Italian. Reading through the list of borrowings and quoted words appended at the end of this volume, it is immediately clear that borrowings take many different varieties of formal 'disguise', the most evident of which is undoubtedly when the word has the same form as the English etymon (loanwords or Anglicisms 'proper') or remains 'recognizable English' despite some degree of orthographic, phonological or morphological integration.

The formal appearance of words greatly influences speakers' perceptions, which means that calques and semantic loans may no longer be recognized as borrowings, being made up of Italian elements and pronounced as Italian words. The degree of 'camouflage' of calques and semantic loans can be extended to derivatives from English bases with neo-classical etymology, which adds to the familiarity of the words to speakers of Latin-based languages. The neo-classical component is relevant not only to Italian but also to all European languages that were influenced by Latin and Greek in the formation of their lexicons, especially for the creation of specialist terminologies. The common classical substratum is directly responsible for the creation of internationalisms across European languages, which makes it very difficult to discern whether a word has come from English or not, a debate that has been exemplified by the Italian word *telefono*. Besides speakers' perceptions, from a linguistic point of view it is not irrelevant to tell apart borrowings from autonomous neological creations or semantic extensions of heritage words, a question with no definitive answer.

The alphabetical order of the final word list in this volume levels out two important dimensions of borrowings, namely age and currency (usage-oriented), and degree of technicality (user-oriented). The age of borrowings plays a major role, since lexical items that were borrowed before the 20$^{th}$ century are either fully assimilated into Italian (formally and semantically) or obsolete. We may argue that very old borrowings like *ostruzionismo* (from English *obstructionism*, 1894) have historically come from English but have become fully-fledged Italian words. Put differently, when a long-standing borrowing has been completely integrated and assimilated into the recipient language in form and meaning, it can be considered as part of Italian vocabulary and no more an Anglicism, since its remote origin is only historically relevant. The characteristic of currency is partly related to the age of the borrowing but especially to the degree of familiarity that a word has acquired for common speakers: the most current Anglicisms in Italian, and possibly in all the world's languages is *okay*. Despite this, its 'foreign-looking' form reveals its Englishness. A large number of 'core' Anglicisms have achieved a high level of currency. We may place borrowings along a continuum from very well-known to less-known items, depending on speakers' education and exposure to current facts and to the mass media. Finally, the dimension of technicality separates general Anglicisms from technical ones, which may be familiar only to specialists, although this distinction, like all the other dimensions of borrowings, is better described as a continuum rather than a clear-cut distinction.

The difficulties posed by such slippery typology of borrowings and their usage-related (currency) and user-related (technicality) characteristics must be considered and transposed into criteria of inclusion or exclusion by linguists dealing with the selection of borrowing for lexicographic purposes. In order to show differences between various types of dictionaries, a comparative illustration of letter J entries recorded in general, medium-sized and specialized dictionaries of Anglicisms was carried out. This represents the first step of the methodology of loanword lexicography presented for the creation of GLAD (Figure 3.2), i.e., collecting candidate Anglicisms from already existing lexicographic sources and then applying the criteria of inclusion and exclusion set for this database (Table 5.1). The following step consists in checking their currency in archives of daily newspapers (e.g. *la Repubblica*), which, in our experience, is the most powerful index of inclusion. The frequency of the candidate Anglicism is subsequently looked up in corpora (CORIS and Italian Web 2020) and the Italian form and meaning is compared to the original English etymon in a general English dictionary. In this process, new Anglicisms, unrecorded by dictionaries, emerge and the analysis of candidate items starts again.

The method implemented for the compilation of the Italian component of GLAD has brought to light old and new problems that are relevant to loanword lexicography. The first regards the continuous inflow of borrowings into Italian and the need to keep collecting and evaluating candidate items to update the database. Nowadays the channel of transmission of neologisms is primarily the language of journalism, a key vehicle of linguistic innovation, through printed, audio-visual and social media sources. This makes the job of the lexicographer particularly hard and often frustrating, since a large number of collected potential Anglicisms are short-lived and bound to end up in the lexicographer's reject list. The expert eye may be able to discern Anglicisms that are likely to settle in the recipient language from potential Anglicisms related to transient fashions and events but amenable to obsolescence, and fleeting vocabulary that is used 'incidentally' for eye- and ear-catching purposes like casuals and code-switchings. On the other hand, the continuous inflow of neologisms causes a rapid ageing of a word list – a problem pointed out by Manfred Görlach for the compilation of the DEA, the closest precursor of GLAD. However, whereas the DEA was 'manually' compiled, GLAD is a dynamic database that can be updated by its compilers in real time. Digital technology has given modern lexicography the great advantage of allowing the storage and the retrieval of data with a mouse click and making data immediately available to users.

Another advantage of digital technology for modern lexicography is the open access to a great number of online resources, including dictionaries, newspaper archives and language corpora. As previously mentioned, the archives of daily newspapers that are freely querable online have proved to be extremely useful and flexible for checking spelling, currency, meaning and usage contexts of candidate Anglicisms. However, the problems posed by searches in newspaper archives are the need to look up words in all their possible orthographic forms, the difficulty to distinguish multiple meanings of polysemic words, to disambiguate English-Italian homographs and to identify semantic loans. The same obstacle arises in the query of candidate Anglicisms in language corpora. Unless sophisticated techniques are applied to carry out corpus-driven searches (which was not done in the present study), corpora can be used for corpus-based investigations in order to check the frequency of search items. A pilot study conducted on CORIS and Italian Web 2020 on the same letter J entries looked up in the reference dictionaries proved that Anglicisms are indeed low-frequency items in Italian, as only a few Anglicisms of the letter J candidates scored a relative frequency above 1pmw. The unexpected match in the relative frequencies of Anglicisms obtained in the reference corpora, despite their great difference in size, suggests that relative frequency alone is not enough to set a benchmark for inclusion in dictionaries or even provide a convincing index of currency in the language. Our pilot study confirmed that a corpus-based study of Anglicisms, the majority of which belong to specialized domains, would yield more solid data with the use of specialized corpora (at the moment not yet available for Italian), giving priority to the most productive domains, namely ICT, economy and sport. Another dimension that appears to be unexplored so far is variation in the use of Anglicisms across different language registers. The majority of Anglicisms are characteristic of specialized communication among specific categories of speakers, such as journalists, economists, scientists and ICT experts. Therefore, we may envisage further progress in corpus compilation, which may assist linguists in the identification of the sociolinguistic and register distribution of Anglicisms.

By way of conclusion, we may try and provide a sufficiently satisfactory answer to the key question in English-induced lexical borrowing in Italian, i.e., the number of Anglicisms now present in the Italian language. Given the argumentation on typology, currency and technicality conducted at length in this volume, a partial answer may be that the number of Anglicisms in Italian ranges from 1,600 (DEA), 4,000 (*Nuovo Devoto-Oli 2022*) to 5,510 (GDU). At the moment the GLAD-Italian word list contains ca. 3,500 items. Although these figures are different, we may conclude that the overall 'impact' of English is not as high as it is normally argued, not only in the number of Anglicisms recorded in dictionaries but especially as far as the frequency of the Anglicisms circulating in Italian is concerned.

The methodology for research on lexical borrowing presented here seems to be viable, given the lexicographic and digital resources available for the Italian language. GLAD represents a strong tool for comparative research on English-induced lexical borrowing into the European and non-European languages that are already part of this project and will hopefully join in future. With the aid of digital technology and the commitment of expert lexicographers, more answers will be given to the many questions raised by research into lexical borrowing.

# References

*Accademia della Crusca*. https://accademiadellacrusca.it (November, 2022).
Adamo, Giovanni & Valeria Della Valle. 2003. *Neologismi quotidiani. Un dizionario a cavallo del millennio (1998–2003)*. Firenze: Leo S. Olschki.
Adamo, Giovanni & Valeria Della Valle. 2005. *2006 parole nuove. Un dizionario di neologismi dai giornali*. Milano: Sperling & Kupfer.
Adamo, Giovanni & Valeria Della Valle. 2008. *Il Vocabolario Treccani. Neologismi. Parole nuove dai giornali*. Roma: Istituto della Enciclopedia italiana.
Adamo, Giovanni & Valeria Della Valle. 2018. *Il Vocabolario Treccani. Neologismi. Parole nuove dai giornali 2008–2018*. Roma: Istituto della Enciclopedia Italiana.
Adamo, Giovanni & Valeria Della Valle. 2019. *Osservatorio neologico della lingua italiana. Lessico e parole nuove dell'italiano*. Istituto per il Lessico Intellettuale Europeo e Storia delle Idee. ILIESI-CNR. Roma. https://www.iliesi.cnr.it/pubblicazioni/Temi-01-Adamo_DellaValle.pdf (November, 2022).
Aiello, Jacqueline. 2018. *Negotiating Englishes and English-speaking identities: A study of youth learning English in Italy*. London: Routledge.
Alexieva, Nevena. 2008. How and Why are Anglicisms often Lexically Different from their English Etymons? In Roswitha Fischer & Hanna Pułaczewska (eds.), *Anglicisms in Europe. Linguistic Diversity in a Global Context*, 42–51. Newcastle: Cambridge Scholars Publishing.
Algeo, John. 1993. Desuetude among new English words. *International Journal of Lexicography* 6(4). 281–293.
Altieri, Ferdinando. 1726. *Dizionario Italiano ed inglese. A Dictionary Italian and English*. London: William and John Innys.
Amato, Antonio, Maria Francesca Andreoni & Rita Salvi. 1990. *Prestiti Linguistici dal mondo anglofono: una tassonomia*. Roma: Bulzoni.
Ammon, Ulrich (ed.). 2001. *The Dominance of English as a Language of Science: Effects on Other Languages and Language Communities*. Berlin & New York: Mouton de Gruyter.
Anderman, Gunilla & Margaret Rogers (eds.). 2005. *In and Out of English: For Better, For Worse?* Clevedon: Multilingual Matters.
Andersen, Gisle. 2012. Semi-automatic approaches to Anglicism detection in Norwegian corpus data. In Cristiano Furiassi, Virginia Pulcini & Félix Rodríguez González (eds.). *The Anglicization of European Lexis*, 111–130. Amsterdam / Philadelphia: John Benjamins.
Andersen, Gisle. 2014. Pragmatic borrowing, *Journal of Pragmatics* 67: 17–33.
Andersen, Gisle, Cristiano Furiassi & Biljana Mišić Ilić. 2017. Special Section: The Pragmatics of Borrowing: Investigating the Role of Discourse and Social Context in Language Contact. [Special issue]. *Journal of Pragmatics* 113.
Andreani, Angela & Virginia Pulcini. 2016 . English job titles in Italian: The case of *manager* and *engineer*. *Lingue e Linguaggi*, 17. 73–87.
Audissino, Emilio. 2012. Italian "Doppiaggio". Dubbing in Italy: Some notes and (in) famous examples. *Italian Americana* 30(1). 22–32.
Bagasheva, Alexandra & Vincent Renner. 2015. False Anglicisms in French and Bulgarian. *Съпоставително езикознание/Сопоставительное языкознание/Contrastive Linguistics* XL(3). 77–89.
Balboni, Paolo E. 1988. *Gli insegnamenti linguistici nella scuola italiana*. Padova: Liviana.

Balboni, Paolo E. 2009. *Storia dell'educazione linguistica in Italia. Dalla Legge Casati alla Riforma Gelmini*. Torino: UTET.

Balteiro, Isabel & Miguel Ángel Campos. 2012. False anglicisms in the Spanish language of fashion and beauty. *Ibérica* 24. 233–260.

Baretti, Giuseppe. 1760. *Dictionary of the English and Italian Languages*. London: Printed for J. Nourse [et al.].

Baretti, Giuseppe. 1762. *A Grammar of the Italian Language, with a copious praxis of moral sentences. To which is added An English Grammar for the use of Italians*. London: Printed for C. Hitch and L. Hawes [et al.].

Baretti, Giuseppe. 1775 . *Easy Phraseology, for the use of young ladies, who intend to learn the colloquial part of the Italian language*. London: Printed for G. Robinson in Pater noster row: and T. Cadell in the Strand.

Bascetta, Carlo. 1962. *Il linguaggio sportivo italiano*. Firenze: Sansoni.

Bathia, Tej K. & William C. Ritchie. 2012. Bilingualism and Multilingualism in the Global Media and Advertising. In Tej K. Bathia & William C. Ritchie, *The Handbook of Bilingualism and Multilingualism*, Second Edition, 563–597. Chichester, West Sussex, UK; Malden, MA: Wiley-Blackwell.

Battaglia, Salvatore & Giorgio Bàrberi Squarotti (eds.). 1961–2004. 21 Volls. *Grande dizionario della lingua italiana* (GDLI). Torino: UTET.

Bauer, Laurie. 1988. *Introducing Linguistic Morphology*. Edinburgh: Edinburgh University Press.

Beard, Adrian. 1988. *The language of sport*. London: Routledge.

Beccaria, Gian Luigi. 2002 [1988]. *Italiano antico e nuovo*. Milano: Garzanti.

Beccaria, Gian Luigi. 2006. *Per difesa e per amore. La lingua italiana oggi*. Milano: Garzanti.

Beccaria, Gian Luigi & Andrea Graziosi. 2015. *Lingua Madre. Italiano e inglese nel mondo globale*. Bologna: Il Mulino.

Bencini, Andrea & Eugenia Citernesi. 1992. *Parole degli anni Novanta*. Firenze: Le Monnier.

Benedetti, Anna. 1974. *Le traduzioni italiane da Walter Scott e i loro anglicismi*. Firenze: Olschki.

Berg, Gunnar & Sölve Ohlander. 2012. English direct loans in European football lexis. In Cristiano Furiassi, Virginia Pulcini & Félix Rodríguez González (eds.), *The Anglicization of European Lexis*, 281–304. Amsterdam & Philadelphia: John Benjamins.

Bergh, Gunnar & Sölve Ohlander. 2017. Loan translations versus direct loans: The impact of English on European football lexis. *Nordic Journal of Linguistics* 40(1). 5–35.

Bergien, Angelika. 2008. English elements in company names: Global and regional considerations. In Roswitha Fischer & Hanna Pułaczewska (eds.), *Anglicisms in Europe. Linguistic Diversity in a Global context*, 183–204. Newcastle, Cambridge Scholars Publishing.

Bernardini, Silvia & Adriano Ferraresi. 2011. Practice, Description and Theory come Together: Normalization or Interference in Italian Technical Translation? *Meta* 56(2). 226–246.

Berruto, Gaetano. 2017. What is changing in Italian today? Phenomena of restandardization in syntax and morphology: an overview. In Massimo Cerruti, Claudia Crocco & Stefania Marzo (eds.), *Towards a New Standard. Theoretical and Empirical Studies on the Restandardization of Italian*, 31–60. Berlin: De Gruyter Mouton.

Bisetto, Antonietta. 2004. L'influsso dell'inglese sul lessico e la morfologia dell'italiano: osservazioni teoriche. In Giuliana Garzone & Anna Cardinaletti (eds), *Lingua, mediazione linguistica e interferenza*, 49–64. Milano: Franco Angeli.

Bistarelli, Andrea. 2008. L'interferenza dell'inglese sull'italiano. Un'analisi quantitativa e qualitativa. *inTRAlinea* 10. https://www.intralinea.org/index.php/archive/article/1644 (November, 2022).

Blackwood, Robert J. & Stefania Tufi. 2015. *The Linguistic Landscape of the Mediterranean: French and Italian Coastal Cities*. New York: Palgrave Macmillan.

Bombi, Raffaella. 2009a. 2nd edn. [2005]. *La linguistica del contatto: tipologie di anglicismi nell'italiano contemporaneo e riflessi metalinguistici*. Roma: Il Calamo.

Bombi, Raffaella. 2009b. Riflessioni sul rimodellamento semantico di alcuni anglicismi informatici. In Raffaella Bombi, *La linguistica del contatto. Tipologie di anglicismi nell'italiano contemporaneo e riflessi metalinguistici*, 409–430. Roma, Il Calamo.

Bombi, Raffaella. 2015a. Inaspettati percorsi di parole dell'informatica: da migrazione a open source. In Alessandra Ferraro (ed.), *Dal Friuli alle Americhe. Studi di amici e allievi udinesi per Silvana Serafin*, 93–102. Udine: Forum.

Bombi, Raffaella. 2015b. Il contatto anglo-italiano e i riflessi nel lessico e nei processi di "formazione delle parole". In Carlo Consani (ed.), *Contatti interlinguistici fra presente e passato*, 379–396. Milano: LED.

Bombi, Raffaella. 2016. Su alcune voci della lingua dell'informatica: da shibboleth a cookie. In Fabiana di Brazzà, Ilvano Caliaro, Roberto Norbedo, Renzo Rabboni & Matteo Venier (eds.), *Le carte e i discepoli. Studi in onore di Claudio Griggio*, 475–482. Udine: Forum.

Bombi, Raffaella. 2017. Anglicisms in Italian. Typologies of language contact phenomena with particular reference to word-formation processes. In Massimo Cerruti, Claudia Crocco & Stefania Marzo (eds.), *Towards a New Standard. Theoretical and Empirical Studies on the Restandardization of Italian*, 269–292. Berlin: De Gruyter Mouton.

Bombi, Raffaella. 2019. *Anglicismi e comunicazione istituzionale*. Roma: Il Calamo.

Bombi, Raffaella. 2020. *Interferenze linguistiche. Tra anglicismi e italianismi*. Alessandria: Edizioni dell'Orso.

Bonsaver, Guido, Alessandro Carlucci & Matthew Reza (eds.). 2019. *Italy and the USA. Cultural Change Through Language and Narrative*. Oxford: Legenda.

Botticella, Tania. 2007. Si, Parliamo Itangliano, Baby! Italian English Revisited. http://homes.chass.utoronto.ca/~cpercy/courses/eng6365-botticella.htm (November, 2022).

Braun, Peter. 1989. Internationalisms: identical vocabularies in European languages. In Florian Coulmas (ed.), *Language Adaptation*, 158–167. Cambridge: Cambridge University Press.

Braun, Peter, Burkhard Schaeder & Johannes Volmert (eds.). 1990. *Internationalismen. Studien zur interlingualen Lexikologie und Lexikographie*. Tübingen: Niemeyer.

Braun, Peter, Burkhard Schaeder & Johannes Volmert (eds.). 2003. *Internationalismen II. Studien zur interlingualen Lexikologie und Lexikographie*. Tübingen: Niemeyer.

Broggini, Susanna & Francesca Costa. 2017. A survey of English-medium instruction in Italian higher education: An updated perspective from 2012 to 2015. *Journal of Immersion and Content-Based Language Education* 5(2). 238–264.

Burke, Peter. 2004. *Language and Communities in Early Modern Europe*. Cambridge: Cambridge University Press.

Cabré, Maria Teresa. 1999. *Terminology: Theory, Methods and Applications*. Amsterdam/Philadelphia: John Benjamins.

Cabré Castellví, Teresa, Rosa Estopà Bagot & Chelo Vargas Sierra (eds.). 2012. Neology in specialized communication. [Special Issue]. *Terminology* 18(1). 1–8.

Caimotto, Maria Cristina. 2013. The unsustainable Anglicization of sustainability discourse in Italian green companies. In Rita Salvi & Winnie Cheng (eds.), *Textus. English Studies in Italy* XXVI(1). 115–126. Roma: Carocci.

Caimotto, Maria Cristina. 2015. Gli stakeholder contro il climate change per un mondo più green versus parla come mangi. L'uso degli anglicismi nei testi promozionali a sfondo ambientalista:

un'analisi discorsiva. In Daniela Fargione & Serenella Iovino (eds.), *ContaminAzioni ecologiche: Cibi, nature, culture*, 37–48. Milano: LED.

Caimotto, Maria Cristina & Alessandra Molino. 2011. Anglicisms in Italian as alerts to greenwashing: a case study. *Critical Approaches to Discourse Analysis across Disciplines* 5(1). 1–16. https://www.lancaster.ac.uk/fass/journals/cadaad/wp-content/uploads/2015/01/Volume-5_Caimotto-Molino.pdf (November, 2022).

Campagna, Sandra & Virginia Pulcini. 2014. English as a medium of instruction in Italian universities: linguistic policies, pedagogical implications. In Mariagrazia Guido & Barbara Seidlhofer (eds.), *Textus. English Studies in Italy. Perspectives on English as a Lingua Franca*. XXVII(1). 173–190.

Cancila, Daniela & Stefano Mazzanti. 2009. *Dizionario Enciclopedico di informatica: inglese-italiano, italiano-inglese*. Bologna: Zanichelli.

Cannella, Mario & Beata Lazzarini (eds.) 2021. *Lo Zingarelli 2022. Vocabolario della lingua italiana*. Bologna: Zanichelli.

Cappuzzo, Barbara. 2008. Calques and loanwords from English in Italian specialized press. An investigation on the names of sports. *Rivista della Facoltà di Scienze Motorie dell'Università degli Studi di Palermo* 1(1). 129–139.

Caretti, Lanfranco. 1951a. Noterelle calcistiche. *Lingua Nostra* 13. 14–8.

Caretti, Lanfranco. 1951b. Noterelle tennistiche. *Lingua Nostra* 13. 77–80.

Carlucci, Alessandro. 2018. *The Impact of the English Language in Italy*. Muenchen: Lincom GmbH.

Carnevale, Nancy C. 2009. *A New Language, A New World: Italian Immigrants in the United States 1890–1945*. Urbana: University of Illinois Press.

Cartago, Gabriella. 1994. L'apporto inglese. In Luca Serianni & Pietro Trifone (eds.), *Storia della lingua italiana*, 721–750. Torino: Einaudi.

Castellani, Arrigo. 1987. Morbus Anglicus. *Studi linguistici italiani* 13(1). 137–157.

Castellani, Arrigo & Ignazio Del Punta (eds.). *Lettere dei Ricciardi di Lucca*. Salerno: Salerno Editrice.

Cenoz, Jasone & Ulrike Jessner. 2000. *English in Europe: The Acquisition of a Third Language*. Clevedon [UK]: Multilingual Matters.

Chambers, Ephraim. 1728. *Cyclopædia: or, An Universal dictionary of Arts and Sciences*, 2 vols. London: James & John Knapton; John Darby; and others.

Cicillini, Stefania. 2020. Studying in an English-Medium Instruction (EMI) Medical Degree Program in Italy: Students' Perspective – Ongoing Research. In *ESC 2020 Proceedings (1st Educational Sciences Conference)*. 51–66. https://eujournal.org/files/journals/1/books/december_online_proceedings_2020.pdf (November, 2022).

Cicillini, Stefania. 2021. English language entry requirements in EMI degree programmes at Bachelor level in Italy. *Lingue e Linguaggi* 44. 53–66.

Cinganotto, Letizia. 2016. CLIL in Italy: A general overview. *Latin American Journal of Content and Language Integrated Learning* 9(2). 374–400.

Coleman, James A. 2006. English-medium teaching in European higher education. *Language Teaching* 39(1). 1–14.

*Collins English Dictionary*. 2022. www.collinsdictionary.com (January, 2022).

Commission of the European Communities. 1996. *White Paper On Education and Training*. Luxembourg: Office for Official Publications of the European Communities. https://op.europa.eu/s/xekG (November, 2022).

CORIS – *Corpus di italiano scritto*. http://corpora.dslo.unibo.it/TCORIS/ (November, 2022).

Cortelazzo, Manlio & Paolo Zolli. 1999. *Il nuovo etimologico. DELI – Dizionario Etimologico della Lingua Italiana*, 2nd ed. + cd rom. Bologna: Zanichelli.

Cortelazzo, Manlio & Ugo Cardinale. 1989. *Dizionario di parole nuove. 1964–1987*. Torino: Loescher.

Costa, Francesca. 2016. *CLIL (Content and Language Integrated Learning) through English in Italian Higher Education*. Milano: LED.
Costa, Francesca & James A. Coleman. 2012. A survey of English-medium instruction in Italian higher Education. *International Journal of Bilingual Education and Bilingualism* 16(1). 3–19.
Costa, Francesca. 2021. EMI Stakeholders and Research in the Italian Context. Moving Towards ICLHE? In Lynn Mastellotto & Renata Zanin (eds.), *EMI and Beyond: Internationalising Higher Education Curricula in Italy*, 1–16. Bozen-Bolzano University Press.
Cottini, Luca. 2019. Buffalo Bill and the Italian Myth of the American West. In Guido Bonsaver, Alessandro Carlucci & Matthew Reza (eds.), *Italy and the USA. Cultural Change Through Language and Narrative*, 89–102. Oxford: Legenda.
CRUI. *Conferenza dei Rettori delle Università italiane*. www.crui.it (November, 2022).
Crystal, David. 2001. *Language and the Internet*. Cambridge: Cambridge University Press.
Crystal, David. 2003. *English as a global language*. Cambridge: Cambridge University Press.
Crystal, David. 2004. *A Glossary of Netspeak and Textspeak*. Edinburgh: Edinburgh University Press.
D'Achille, Paolo. 2005, L'invariabilità dei nomi nell'italiano contemporaneo. *Studi di Grammatica Italiana* 24. 189–209.
Dal Negro, Silvia. 2009. Local policy modelling the linguistic landscape. In Elana Shohamy & Durk Gorter (eds.), *Linguistic Landscape. Expanding the Scenary*, 206–218. New York & London: Routledge.
Dardano, Maurizio. 1986. The influence of English on Italian. In Wolfgang Viereck & Wolf-Dieter Bald (eds.), *English in Contact with Other Languages. Studies in Honour of Broder Carstensen on the Occasion of his $60^{th}$ Birthday*, 231–252. Budapest: Akadémiai Kiadó.
Dardano, Maurizio. 2020. Notes on Anglicisms. *La Lingua Italiana. Storia, strutture, testi* XVI. 113–141.
Dardano, Maurizio & Pietro Trifone. 1997. *La nuova grammatica della lingua italiana*. Bologna: Zanichelli.
Dardano, Maurizio, Gianluca Frenguelli & Alberto Puoti. 2008. Anglofilia nascosta. In Maurizio Dardano & Gianluca Frenguelli (eds), *L'italiano di oggi. Fenomeni, problemi, prospettive*, 75–98. Aracne: Roma.
Darquennes, Jeroen, Joseph C. Salmons & Wim Vandenbussche. 2019. *Language Contact: An International Handbook*. Berlin: Mouton de Gruyter.
De Cesare, Anna-Maria. 2016. Assessing the impact of English abbreviations on the Italian language: A discussion based on the forms, frequency and functions of USA in written texts. *The Italianist* 36(1). 128–145.
De Houwer, Annick & Antje Wilton (eds.). 2011. *English in Europe Today. Sociocultural and educational perspectives*. Amsterdam & Philadelphia: John Benjamins.
De Mauro, Tullio. 1970. *Storia linguistica dell'Italia unita*. Bari: Laterza.
De Mauro, Tullio (ed.) 1999, $2007^2$. *Grande dizionario italiano dell'uso* (GDU), ideato e diretto da Tullio De Mauro, con la collaborazione di G. C. Lepschy e E. Sanguineti. Torino: UTET, 6 vols. Supplements: *Nuove parole italiane dell'uso*, 2003; *Nuove parole italiane dell'uso*. 2, 2007. Torino: UTET.
De Mauro, Tullio. 2005. *La fabbrica delle parole. Il lessico e problemi di lessicologia*. Torino: Utet Libreria.
De Mauro, Tullio. 2014a. *In Europa son già 103. Troppe lingue per una democrazia?* Bari-Roma: Laterza.
De Mauro, Tullio. 2014b. *Storia linguistica dell'Italia repubblicana: dal 1946 ai nostri giorni*. Roma/Bari: Laterza.
De Mauro, Tullio. 2016. Antiquam exquirite matrem (Virgilio Aen.III 96). In Raffaella Bombi & Vincenzo Orioles (ed.), *Lingue in contatto/Contact linguistics*, 19–26. Roma: Bulzoni.

De Mauro, Tullio & Silvana Ferreri. 2005. Quantità dei lemmi nei dizionari. In Tullio De Mauro & Isabella Chiari (eds.), *Parole e numeri. Analisi quantitative dei fatti di lingua*, 297–306. Roma: Aracne.

De Mauro, Tullio & Marco Mancini. 2nd edn. 2003. *Dizionario delle parole straniere nella lingua italiana*. Milano: Garzanti.

De Mauro, Tullio, Federico Mancini, Massimo Vedovelli & Miriam Voghera. 1993. *Lessico di frequenza dell'italiano parlato*. Milano: Etas. www.parlaritaliano.it/index.php/it/volip (November, 2022).

Dearden, Julie. 2015. *English as a medium of instruction–a growing global phenomenon*. London: British Council.

Demata, Massimiliano. 2014. English Interferences in Italian Journalism: the Use of Anglicisms in *Il Fatto Quotidiano*. In Domenico Torretta (ed.), *Contacts. Studies in Intralinguistic, Interlinguistic and Intersemiotic Relationships*, 137–157. Bari: Edizioni dal Sud.

Devoto, Giacomo, Gian Carlo Oli, Luca Serianni & Maurizio Trifone. 2022. *Nuovo Devoto-Oli. Il vocabolario dell'italiano contemporaneo*. Firenze: Le Monnier.

Dimova, Slobodanka, Anna Kristina Hultgren & Christian Jensen. 2015. *English-Medium Instruction in European Higher Education*. Berlin: Mouton De Gruyter.

Dimova, Slobodanka. 2017. Life after oral English certification: The consequences of the Test of Oral English Proficiency for Academic Staff for EMI lecturers. *English for Academic Purposes* 46. 45–58.

Dimova, Slobodanka. 2018. Linking the TOEPAS with the CEFR: Technical report. TAEC Erasmus+ project (2017–2020). https://cip.ku.dk/english/documents/Alignment_of_TOEPAS_with_the_CEFR.pdf (November, 2022).

Dunlop, Anna. 1989. Parliamo Itangliano. *English Today* 5(2). 32–35.

Dunn, John. 2008. Face Control, Electronic Soap and the Four-storey Cottage with a Jacuzzi: Anglicisation, Globalisation and the Creation of Linguistic Difference. In Roswitha Fischer & Hanna Pułaczewska (eds.), *Anglicisms in Europe. Linguistic Diversity in a Global Context*, 52–70. Newcastle upon Tyne: Cambridge Scholars Publishing.

Eberhard, David M., Gary F. Simons & Charles D. Fennig (eds.). 2021. *Ethnologue: Languages of the World*, Twenty-fourth edition. Dallas, Texas: SIL International. http://www.ethnologue.com (November, 2022).

Eco, Umberto. 1984. Il modello americano. In Umberto Eco, Gian Paolo Cesarani & Beniamino Placido, *La riscoperta dell'America*. Bari: Laterza.

Eco, Umberto. 1992. Il mito americano di tre generazioni antiamericane. In Carlo Chiarenza & William L. Vance (eds.), *Immaginari a confronto. I rapporti culturali tra Italia e Stati Uniti. La percezione della realtà fra stereotipo e mito*, 15–28. Venezia: Marsilio.

Elliot, Giacomo. 1977. *Parliamo itang'liano, ovvero le 400 parole inglesi che deve sapere chi vuole fare carriera*. Milano: Rizzoli.

European Education and Culture Executive Agency, Eurydice, Baïdak, N., Motiejunaite, A., Balcon, M., *Key data on teaching languages at school in Europe: 2017 edition*, Publications Office, 2017. https://data.europa.eu/doi/10.2797/828497 (November, 2022).

Fabijanić, Ivo & Lidija Štrmelj. 2016. The Adaptation of Anglicisms – Phraseological Units in Croatian Economic Terminology. In Gloria Corpas Pastor (ed.), *Computerised and Corpus-based Approaches to Phraseology: Monolingual and Multilingual Perspectives*, 487–494. Geneva: Editions Tradulex.

Facchinetti, Roberta, David Crystal & Barbara Seidlhofer (eds). 2010. *From International to Local English – and Back Again*. Frankfurt: Peter Lang.

Fanfani, Massimo. 1991-1996. Sugli anglicismi nell'italiano contemporaneo, *Lingua Nostra* (1991) LII: 11–24, 73–89, 113–118; LIII (1992): 18–25, 79–86, 120–121; LIV (1993): 13–20, 63–71, 122–124; LV (1994): 19–25, 76–77, 117–120; LVI (1995): 14–17; LVII (1996): 72–92.

Fanfani, Massimo. 2002. Reazioni italiane agli anglicismi. In Félix San Vicente (ed.), *L'inglese e le altre lingue europee. Studi sull'interferenza linguistica*, 215–35. Bologna: CLUEB.
Fanfani, Massimo. 2003. Per un repertorio di anglicismi in italiano. In Anna-Vera Sullam Calimani (ed.), *Italiano e inglese a confronto*, 151–176. Firenze: Franco Cesati Editore.
Fanfani, Massimo. 2010. Anglicismi. In Raffaele Simone (ed.), *Enciclopedia dell'Italiano*, Vol. 1: A–L. Roma: Istituto della Enciclopedia italiana.
Fanfani, Massimo. 2020. A century of Americanisms. In Guido Bonsaver, Alessandro Carlucci & Matthew Reza (eds.), *Understanding Cultural Change: Language and Narrative between Italy and the USA*, 232–245. Oxford, Legenda.
Fanfani, Pietro & Costantino Arlìa. 1877. *Lessico dell'infima e corrotta italianità*. Milano: Libreria d'Educazione e d'Istruzione di Paolo Carrara.
Fiasco, Valeria & Virginia Pulcini (forthcoming). Overt calques from English and their currency in Italian.
Fiedler, Sabine. 2017. Phraseological borrowing from English into German: cultural and pragmatic implications. *Journal of Pragmatics* 113. 89–102.
Filipović, Rudolph. 1974. A contribution to the method of studying Anglicisms in European languages. *Studia Romanica et Anglica Zagrebiensia* 37. 135–148.
Filipović, Rudolf. 1985. Pseudoanglicisms in European Languages. In Ursula Pieper & Gerhard Stickel (eds.), *Studia Linguistica Diachronica et Synchronica*, Werner Winter Sexagenario, 249–255. Berlin & New York: Mouton de Gruyter.
Filipović, Rudolf. 1996. English as a word donor to other languages of Europe. In Reinhard R. K. Hartmann (ed.), *The English Language in Europe*, 37–46. Oxford: Intellect.
Filipović, Rudolph. 2000. Historical-Primary Etymology vs. Secondary Etymology of Anglicisms in European Languages. In Olga Mišeska Tomić & Milorad Radovanović (eds.), *History and Perspectives of Language Study*, 205–216. Amsterdam/Philadelphia: John Benjamins.
Fischer, Roswitha & Hanna Pułaczewska (eds.). 2008. *Anglicisms in Europe. Linguistic Diversity in a Global Context*. Newcastle upon Tyne: Cambridge Scholars Publishing.
Fishman, Joshua A., Robert L. Cooper & Andrew W. Conrad (eds.). 1977. *The Spread of English: The Sociology of English as an Additional Language*. Rowley, MA: Newbury House Publishers.
Florio, John. 1611. 2nd edn. *Queen Anna's new World of words, or dictionarie of the Italian and English tongues*. London: Printed by Melch. Bradwood, for Edw. Blount and William Barret.
Frenguelli, Gianluca. 2008. Come si studiano le parole nuove. In Maurizio Dardano & Gianluca Frenguelli (eds,), *L'italiano di oggi. Fenomeni, problemi, prospettive*, 99–120. Roma: Aracne.
Furiassi, Cristiano. 2008. Non-adapted Anglicisms in Italian: Attitudes, Frequency Counts, and Lexicographic Implications. In Roswitha Fischer & Hanna Pułaczewska (eds.), *Anglicisms in Europe. Linguistic Diversity in a Global Context*, 313–327. Newcastle upon Tyne: Cambridge Scholars Publishing.
Furiassi, Cristiano. 2010. *False Anglicisms in Italian*. Monza: Polimetrica.
Furiassi, Cristiano. 2017. Pragmatic borrowing: Phraseological Anglicisms in Italian. In Cecilia Boggio & Alessandra Molino (eds.), *English in Italy: Linguistic, educational and professional challenges*, 38–60. Milano: FrancoAngeli.
Furiassi, Cristiano. 2018. *Macaroni English* goes pragmatic: False phraseological Anglicisms in Italian as illocutionary acts. *Journal of Pragmatics* 133. 109–122.
Furiassi, Cristiano & Knut Hofland. 2007. The retrieval of false anglicisms in newspaper texts. In Roberta Facchinetti (ed.), *Corpus Linguistics 25 Years on*, 347–363. Amsterdam & New York: Rodopi.

Furiassi, Cristiano & Henrik Gottlieb (eds.). 2015. *Pseudo-English. Studies on False Anglicisms in Europe*. Berlin: Mouton De Gruyter.

Furiassi, Cristiano, Virginia Pulcini & Félix Rodríguez González (eds). 2012. *The Anglicization of European Lexis*. Amsterdam/Philadelphia: John Benjamins Publishing.

Garret, Peter. 2010. *Attitudes to Language*. Cambridge: Cambridge University Press.

Gaudio, Paola. 2012. Words Leading an Independent Life: Four Anglicisms in the Field of Economics. *International Journal of Linguistics, Literature and Translation* (IJLLT) 1(4). 104–110.

Geeraerts, Dirk. 1997. *Diachronic Prototype Semantics. A Contribution to Historical Lexicology*. Oxford: Clarendon Press.

Geeraerts, Dirk. 2003. Meaning and definition. In Piet Van Sterkenburg (ed.), *A Practical Guide to Lexicography*, 83–93. Amsterdam/Philadelphia: John Benjamins.

Gianni, Michele. 1994. Influenze dell'inglese sulla terminologia informatica italiana. *Studi di lessicografia italiana* XII. 273–299.

Giovanardi, Claudio, Riccardo Gualdo & Alessandra Coco. 2008. 2nd edn. [2005]. *Inglese-Italiano 1 a 1. Tradurre o non tradurre le parole inglesi?* Lecce: Manni.

Gnutzmann, Claus & Frauke Intemann (eds). 2008. 2nd edn. *The Globalisation of English and the English Language Classroom*. Tübingen: Gunter Narr Verlag.

Görlach, Manfred. 1994. A Usage Dictionary of Anglicisms in Selected European Languages, *International Journal of Lexicography* 7(3). 223–46.

Görlach, Manfred. 1997. Usage in the Usage Dictionary of Anglicisms in Selected European Languages. *Studia Anglica Posnaniensia* XXXI. 67–77.

Görlach, Manfred (ed.). 2001. *A Dictionary of European Anglicisms*. Oxford: Oxford University Press.

Görlach, Manfred (ed.). 2002a. *English in Europe*. Oxford: Oxford University Press.

Görlach, Manfred (ed.). 2002b. *An Annotated Bibliography of European Anglicisms*. Oxford: Oxford University Press.

Görlach, Manfred. 2003. *English Words Abroad*. Amsterdam: John Benjamins.

Gorter, Durk. 2007. The linguistic landscape in Rome: aspects of multilingualism and diversity. Working paper of the IPRS (Istituto Psicoanalitico per le Ricerche Sociali) https://pure.knaw.nl/ws/portalfiles/portal/593367/21757.pdf (November, 2022).

Gottlieb, Henrik, Gisle Andersen, Ulrich Busse, Elzbieta Mańczak-Wohlfeld, Elizabeth Peterson & Virginia Pulcini. 2018. Introducing and developing GLAD – The Global Anglicism Database Network. *The European English Messenger* 27(2). 4–38.

Gottlieb, Henrik. 2020. *Echoes of English. Anglicisms in Minor Speech Communities – with Special Focus on Danish and Afrikaans*. Bern: Peter Lang.

Gove, Philip B. (ed.) 2022. *Merriam-Webster's Unabridged Dictionary*. 3rd edn. Springfield, Massachusetts: Merriam-Webster. merriam-webster.com (November, 2022).

Graddol, David. 2006. *English Next: Why Global English May Mean 'the End of English as a Foreign Language'*. London: British Council.

Graziano, Alba. 1984. Uso e diffusione dell'inglese. In Lia Formigari (ed.), *Teorie e pratiche linguistiche nell'Italia del Settecento*, 373–394. Bologna: Il Mulino.

Graf, Arturo. 1911. *L'Anglomania e l'influsso inglese in Italia nel secolo XVIII*. Torino: Loescher.

Granger, Sylviane & Magali Paquot. 2008. Disentangling the phraseological web. In Sylviane Granger & Fanny Meunier (eds.), *Phraseology. An Interdisciplinary Perspective*, 27–49. Amsterdam/Philadelphia: John Benjamins.

Griffin, Jeffrey L. 2004. The presence of English in the streets of Rome. *English Today* 78(20). 3–8.

Grossmann, Maria & Franz Rainer (eds.). 2004. *La formazione delle parole in italiano*. Tübingen: Max Niemeyer.

Gualdo, Riccardo & Stefano Telve. 2011. Il linguaggio dell'economia. In Riccardo Gualdo & Stefano Telve (eds.), *Linguaggi specialistici dell'italiano*, 357–410. Roma: Carocci.

Gualdo, Riccardo & Cristina Scarpino. 2007. Quanto pesa l'inglese? Anglicismi nella vita quotidiana e proposte per la coabitazione. In Serge Vanvolsem, Stefania Marzo, Manuela Caniato & Gigliola Mavolo (eds.), *Identità e diversità nella lingua e nella letteratura italiana*, Vol. 1, 257–281. Firenze: Franco Cesati Editore.

Guarda, Marta. 2018. 'I just sometimes forget that I'm actually studying in English': Exploring student perceptions on English-Medium Instruction at an Italian university. *RILA: Rassegna Italiana di Linguistica Applicata* 2(3). 129–143.

Gusmani, Roberto. 1981. [1973]. *Aspetti del prestito linguistico*. Firenze: Le Lettere.

Gusmani, Roberto. 1986. *Saggi sull'interferenza linguistica*. Firenze: Le Lettere.

Guția, Ioan, Grazia M. Senes, Marcella Zappieri & Francesca Cabasino. 1981. *Contatti interlinguistici e mass media*. Roma: La Goliardica.

Hagège, Claude. 2000. *Halte à la mort des langues*. Paris: Édition Odile Jacob. [It. tr. *Morte e rinascita delle lingue*, Feltrinelli, Milano, 2002].

Haller, Hermann W. 1993. *Una lingua perduta e ritrovata. L'italiano degli italo-americani* [*A Language Lost and Found: The Italian of Italo-Americans*]. Florence: La Nuova Italia.

Hartmann, Reinhard (ed.). 1996. *The English Language in Europe*. Oxford: Intellect.

Haspelmath, Martin. 2009. Lexical borrowing: Concepts and issues. In Martin Haspelmath & Uri Tadmor (eds.), *Loanwords in the World's Languages: A Comparative Handbook*, 35–54. Berlin: Mouton de Gruyter.

Haugen, Einar. 1950. The analysis of linguistic borrowing. *Language* 26. 210–231.

Hope, Thomas E. 1971. *Lexical borrowing in the Romance languages: A critical study of Italianisms in French and Gallicisms in Italian from 1100 to 1900*. Oxford: B. Blackwell.

Hornikx, Jos & Frank van Meurs. 2019. *Foreign Languages in Advertising: Linguistics and Marketing Perspectives*. Cham, Switzerland: Palgrave.

Humbley, John. 2008. Anglicisms in French: Is French still a case apart? In Roswitha Fischer & Hanna Pułaczewska (eds.), *Anglicisms in Europe. Linguistic Diversity in a Global Context*, 85–105. Newcastle upon Tyne: Cambridge Scholars Publishing.

Humbley, John. 2015. Allogenisms: The major category of 'true' false loans. In Cristiano Furiassi & Henrik Gottlieb (eds.), *Pseudo-English: Studies on False Anglicisms in Europe*, 35–58. Berlin: Mouton De Gruyter.

Iacobini, Claudio. 2003. Due casi di interferenza dell'inglese sulla morfologia derivazionale dell'italiano. In Anna-Vera Sullam Calimani (ed.), *Italiano e Inglese a confronto*, 43–56. Firenze: Franco Cesati Editore.

Iacobini, Claudio. 2015. Foreign word-formation in Italian. In Peter O. Müller, Ingeborg Ohnheiser, Susan Olsen & Franz Rainer (eds.), *Word-Formation. An International Handbook of the Languages of Europe*, vol. 3, 1660–1679. Berlin/New York: De Gruyter.

Iacobini, Claudio & Anna Maria Thornton. 1992. Tendenze nella formazione delle parole nell'italiano del ventesimo secolo. In Bruno Moretti, Dario Petrini & Sandro Bianconi (eds.), *Linee di tendenza dell'italiano contemporaneo, Atti del XXV Congresso della Società di Linguistica Italiana*, 25–55. Roma: Bulzoni.

Iamartino, Giovanni. 2001. La contrastività italiano-inglese in prospettiva storica. *Rassegna Italiana di Linguistica Applicata* (RILA) 2-3. 7–130.

Incelli, Ersilia. 2013. Managing discourse in intercultural business email interactions: a case study of a British and Italian business transaction. *Journal of Multilingual and Multicultural Development* 34(6). 515–532.

Inglese, Giorgio (ed.). 1997. *Niccolò Machiavelli. Clizia-Andria-Dialogo intorno alla nostra lingua*. Milano: Rizzoli.

Istat. 2020. *Livelli di Istruzione e Ritorni Occupazionali. Anno 2019* [Levels of Education and Occupational Outcomes]. Retrieved from https://www.istat.it/it/files/2020/07/Livelli-di-istruzione-e-ritorni-occupazionali.pdf (November, 2022).

*Italian Web 2020* (itTenTen2020). www.sketchengine.eu (November, 2022).

Klajn, Ivan. 1972. *Influssi inglesi nella lingua italiana*. Firenze: Olschki.

Klein, Gabriella. 1986. *La politica linguistica del fascismo*. Bologna: il Mulino.

Kowner, Rotem & Judith Rosenhouse. 2008. The hegemony of English and determinants of borrowing from its vocabulary. In Judith Rosenhouse & Rotem Kowner (eds.), *Globally speaking: Motives for adopting English vocabulary in other languages*, 4–19. Clevedon, England: Multilingual Matters.

Lanzarone, Marco. 1997. Note sulla terminologia informatica. *Studi di lessicografia italiana* XIV. 427–507.

Laviosa, Sara. 2007. Studying Anglicisms with Comparable and Parallel Corpora. In Willy Vandeweghe, Sonia Vandepitte & Marc Van de Velde (eds.), *The Study of Language and Translation. Belgian Journal of Linguistics*. Special Issue 21(1). 123–135.

Laviosa, Sara. 2012. Lexical primings of Anglicisms across English and Italian. In Vito Cavone (ed.), *Aspetti del Moderno*, 223–234. Napoli: Liguori.

Leonardi, Vanessa. 2010. The Effects of Globalization on Italian Specialized Language: The Case of Anglicisms in Job Advertisements. In Maria Georgieva & Allan James (eds.), *Globalization in English Studies*, 157–177. Newcastle Upon Tyne: Cambridge Scholars Publishing.

Leopardi, Giacomo. 1921. *Zibaldone di pensieri*. Firenze: Le Monnier.http://www.letteraturaitaliana.net/pdf/Volume_8/t226.pdf (November, 2022).

Linn, Andrew (ed.). 2016. *Investigating English in Europe: Contexts and Agendas*. Boston/Berlin: De Gruyter Mouton.

Linn, Andrew, Neil Bermel & Gibson Ferguson (eds.). 2015. *Attitudes towards English in Europe*. Berlin/Boston: De Gruyter Mouton.

Luján García, Carmen & Virginia Pulcini (eds.). 2018. Anglicisms in domain-specific discourse: Fashion, leisure and entertainment, Special Issue, *Revista de Lengua para Fines Específicos* (LFE) 24(1).

Lukasik, Marek & Virginia Pulcini. 2021. New Anglicisms in Italian corpora: A comparison between CORIS and Italian Web 2016. In Ramón Martí Solano & Pablo Ruano San Segundo (eds.), *Anglicisms and Corpus Linguistics: Corpus-Aided Research into the Influence of English on European Languages*, 159–176. Bern: Peter Lang.

Lurati, Ottavio. 1990. *3000 parole nuove. La neologia negli anni 1980–1990*. Bologna: Zanichelli.

Macaro, Ernesto, Samantha Curle, Jack Pun, Jiangshan An & Julie Dearden. 2018. A systematic review of English medium instruction in higher education. *Language Teaching* 51(1). 36–76.

Mac Kenzie, Ian. 2012. Fair play to them: Proficiency in English and types of borrowing. In Cristiano Furiassi, Virginia Pulcini & Félix Rodríguez González (eds.), *The Anglicization of European Lexis*, 27–42. Amsterdam/Philadelphia: John Benjamins.

Maiden, Martin. 2013. *A Linguistic History of Italian*. London: Routledge.

Maraschio, Nicoletta & Domenico De Martino (eds.). 2013. *Fuori l'italiano dall'università? Inglese, internazionalizzazione, politica linguistica*. Roma/Bari: Laterza.

Marazzini, Claudio. 2015. *La lingua italiana. Storia, testi, strumenti*. Bologna: Il Mulino.

Marazzini, Claudio. 2018. *L'italiano è meraviglioso. Come e perché dobbiamo salvare la nostra lingua*. Milano: Rizzoli.

Marazzini, Claudio & Alessio Petralli. 2015. *La lingua italiana e le lingue romanze di fronte agli anglicismi*. Firenze: goWare.

Marello, Carla. 2020. New Words and New Forms of Linguistic Purism in the 21st Century: The Italian Debate. *International Journal of Lexicography* 33(2). 168–186.

Marri, Fabio. 1992. Tendenze della varietà informatica nell'arco di mezzo secolo. In Bruno Moretti, Dario Petrini & Sandro Bianconi (eds.), *Linee di tendenza dell'italiano contemporaneo, Atti del XXV congresso della Società di Linguistica Italiana*, 225–253. Roma: Bulzoni.

Marri, Fabio. 1994. La lingua dell'informatica. In Luca Serianni & Pietro Trifone (eds.), *Storia della lingua italiana*, Volume II, 617–633. Torino: Einaudi.

Marri, Fabio. 2003. La lingua dell'informatica e lingua comune. *Plurilinguismo. Contatti di lingue e culture* 10. 181–195.

Martí-Solano, Ramón. 2012. Multi-word loan translations and semantic borrowings from English in French journalistic discourse. In Cristiano Furiassi, Virginia Pulcini & Félix Rodríguez González (eds.), *The Anglicization of European Lexis*, 199–215. Amsterdam/Philadelphia: John Benjamins.

Martí Solano, Ramón & Pablo Ruano San Segundo (eds.). 2021. *Anglicisms and Corpus Linguistics: Corpus-Aided Research into the Influence of English on European Languages*. Bern: Peter Lang.

Mastellotto, Lynn & Renata Zanin. 2021. *EMI and Beyond: Internationalising Higher Education Curricula in Italy*. Bozen-Bolzano University Press.

Matras, Yaron. 2009. *Language Contact*. Cambridge: Cambridge University Press.

Matras, Yaron. 2019. Borrowing. In Jeroen Darquennes, Joseph C. Salmons & Wim Vandenbussche (eds.), *Language Contact: An International Handbook*, 148–158. Berlin: Mouton de Gruyter.

Mautner, Gerlinde. 2005. The entrepreneurial University. A discursive profile of a higher education buzzword. *Critical Discourse Studies* 2(2). 95–120.

Messeri, Anna Maria. 1957. Anglicismi nel linguaggio politico italiano nel '700 e nell' '800. *Lingua Nostra* XVIII(4). 100–8.

Migliorini, Bruno. 1963. *Parole nuove: Appendice di dodicimila voci al "Dizionario moderno" di Alfredo Panzini*. Hoepli: Milano.

Migliorini, Bruno. 2019. 11th edn. [1960]. *Storia della lingua italiana*. Milano: Bompiani.

Migliorini, Bruno & Gwynfor T. Griffith. 1984. [1966]. *The Italian Language*. London: Faber and Faber.

Minutella, Vincenza. 2009 [2007]. *Translating for Dubbing from English into Italian*. Torino: CELID.

Minutella, Vincenza & Virginia Pulcini. 2014. Cross-Linguistic Interference into the Italian Dubbing of TV Series: The Cases of Realize, Impressive and Excited. In Alessandra Molino & Serenella Zanotti, *Observing Norms, Observing Usage: Lexis in Dictionaries and the Media*, 331–348. Bern: Peter Lang.

Molino, Alessandra, Slobodanka Dimova, Sanne Larsen & Joyce Kling. 2022. *The Evolution of EMI Research in European Higher Education*. London: Routledge.

Molino, Alessandra & Sandra Campagna. 2014. English-mediated instruction in Italian universities: conflicting views. *Sociolinguistica, Internationales Jahrbuch für europäische Soziolinguistik* 28. 156–171.

Monelli, Paolo. 1943. [1933] *Barbaro dominio. Seicentocinquanta esotismi esaminati, combattuti e banditi dalla lingua con antichi e nuovi argomenti. Storia ed etimologia delle parole e aneddoti per svagare il lettore*. Milano: Hoepli.

Myers-Scotton, Carol. 2002. *Contact Linguistics. Bilingual Encounters and Grammatical Outcomes*. Oxford: Oxford University Press.

Nocentini, Alberto. 2010. *L'Etimologico. Vocabolario della lingua italiana* (EVLI) (with Alessandro Parenti). Le Monnier: Firenze.

Oncins-Martínez, José. 2012. Newly-coined Anglicisms in contemporary Spanish: A corpus-based approach. In Cristiano Furiassi, Virginia Pulcini & Félix Rodríguez González (eds.), *The Anglicization of European Lexis*, 217–238. Amsterdam/Philadelphia: John Benjamins.

Onysko, Alexander. 2007. *Anglicisms in German: Borrowing, Lexical Productivity, and Written Codeswitching*. Berlin: Mouton De Gruyter.

Onysko, Alexander & Esme Winter-Froemel. 2011. Necessary loans – luxury loans? Exploring the pragmatic dimension of borrowing. *Journal of Pragmatics* 43. 1550–1567.

Onysko, Alexander & Esme Winter-Froemel. 2012. Proposing a pragmatic distinction for lexical Anglicisms. In Cristiano Furiassi, Virginia Pulcini & Félix Rodríguez González. *The Anglicization of European Lexis*, 43–64. Amsterdam/Philadelphia: John Benjamins.

Onysko, Alexander, Esme Winter-Froemel & Andreea Calude. 2014. Why some non-catachrestic borrowings are more successful than others: A case study of English loans in German. In Amei Koll-Stobbe & Sebastian Knospe (eds.), *Language Contact in Times of Globalization*, 119–144. Frankfurt am Main: Peter Lang.

Panzini, Alfredo. 1963. 10$^{th}$ edn. [1905]. *Dizionario Moderno. Supplemento ai dizionari italiani*. Milano: Hoepli.

Pecorari, Diane & Hans Malmström. 2018. At the Crossroads of TESOL and English Medium Instruction. *TESOL Quarterly* 52(3). 497–515.

Petralli, Alessio. 1992. Tendenze europee nel lessico italiano. Internazionalismi: problemi di metodo e nuove parole d'Europa. In Bruno Moretti, Dario Petrini & Sandro Bianconi (eds.), *Linee di tendenza dell'italiano contemporaneo*, 119–134. Roma: Bulzoni.

Petralli, Alessio. 1996. *Anglicismi e nuovi media. Verso la "globalizzazione multimediale" della comunicazione?* Bologna: Clueb.

Pfister, Max & Wolfgang Schweickard (eds.) (1979–2012). LEI: *Lessico etimologico italiano*. Wiesbaden: Reichert.

Picchi, Fernando. 2017. *Economics & Business. Dizionario enciclopedico economico e commerciale*. Bologna: Zanichelli.

Phillipson, Robert. 1992. *Linguistic Imperialism*. Oxford: Oxford University Press.

Phillipson, Robert. 2003. *English-Only Europe? Challenging Language Policy*. London: Routledge.

Phillipson, Robert. 2006. Figuring out the Englishisation of Europe. In Constant Leung & Jennifer Jenkins (eds.), *Reconfiguring Europe: The Contribution of Applied Linguistics*, 65–85. London and Oakville: Equinox.

Phillipson, Robert. 2008. Lingua franca or lingua frankensteinia? English in European integration and globalization. *World Englishes* 27(2). 250–267.

Phillipson, Robert. 2010. *Linguistic Imperialism Continued*. London: Routledge.

Pinnavaia, Laura. 2001. *The Italian Borrowings in the Oxford English Dictionary: A Lexicographical, Linguistic and Cultural Analysis*. Roma: Bulzoni.

Pinnavaia, Laura. 2005. I prestiti inglesi nella stampa italiana: una riflessione semantico-testuale. *Mots Palabras Words* 6. 47–48.

Pinnavaia, Laura. 2019. Italianisms in US English: Past and Present. In Guido Bonsaver, Alessandro Carlucci & Matthew Reza (eds.), *Understanding Cultural Change: Language and Narrative between Italy and the USA*, 216–231. Oxford: Legenda.

Plo Alastrué, Ramón & Pérez-Llantada Carmen (ed.). 2015. *English as a Scientific and Research Language: Debates and Discourses*. Berlin: de Gruyter Mouton.

Prat Zagrebelsky, Maria Teresa (ed.). 1991. *The Study of English in Italian Universities: Papers of the national conference* (Turin, 17–20 January 1990). Alessandria: Edizioni dell'Orso.

Prifti, Elton. 2013. *Italoamericano. Italiano e inglese in contatto negli USA*. Berlin: De Gruyter.

Pulcini, Virginia. 1997. Attitudes toward the spread of English in Italy. *World Englishes* 16(1). 77–85.
Pulcini, Virginia. 2002a. Italian. In Manfred Görlach (ed.), *English in Europe*, 151–167. Oxford: Oxford University Press.
Pulcini, Virginia. 2002b. Italian. In Manfred Görlach (ed.), *An Annotated Bibliography of European Anglicisms*, 147–163. Oxford: Oxford University Press.
Pulcini, Virginia. 2006. A New Dictionary of Italian Anglicisms: The Aid of Corpora. In Elisa Corino, Carla Marello & Cristina Onesti (eds.), *Proceedings XII EURALEX International Congress*, Vol. I, 313–22. Alessandria: Edizioni dell'Orso.
Pulcini, Virginia. 2007. Gli Anglicismi nella lingua italiana: aspetti lessicografici. In Serge Vanvolsem, Stefania Marzo, Manuela Caniato & Gigliola Mavolo (eds.), *Identità e diversità nella lingua e nella letteratura italiana*, Volume I: *L'italiano oggi e domani*, 283–299. Firenze: Franco Cesati Editore.
Pulcini, Virginia. 2008a. Corpora and Lexicography: The case of a Dictionary of Anglicisms. In Aurelia Martelli & Virginia Pulcini (eds.), *Investigating English with Corpora. Studies in Honour of Maria Teresa Prat*, 189–203. Monza: Polimetrica.
Pulcini, Virginia. 2008b. Anglicisms in the 2006 Olympic Winter Games. In Roswitha Fischer & Hanna Pułaczewska (eds.), *Anglicisms in Europe. Linguistic Diversity in a Global Context*, 140–158. Newcastle upon Tyne: Cambridge Scholars Publishing.
Pulcini, Virginia. 2008c. Lexical Obsolescence among Italian Anglicisms. In Giovanni Iamartino, Roberta Facchinetti & Maria Luisa Maggioni, *Thou sittest at another boke . . . Studies in Honour of Domenico Pezzini*, 471–488. Monza: Polimetrica.
Pulcini, Virginia. 2010. A Dictionary of Italian Anglicisms: criteria of inclusion and exclusion. In Laura Pinnavaia and Nicholas Brownlees (eds.), *Insights into English and Germanic Lexicology and Lexicography: Past and Present Perspectives*, 319–334. Monza: Polimetrica.
Pulcini, Virginia. 2011. Much the same meaning: semantic integration of Anglicisms in Italian. In Gabriella Di Martino, Linda Lombardo & Stefania Nuccorini (eds.), *Challenges for the 21$^{st}$ Century: Dilemmas, Ambiguities, Direction. Papers from the 24$^{th}$ AIA Conference* (October 1–3 2009, Roma), Vol. II: *Language Studies*, 437–445. Roma: Edizioni Q.
Pulcini, Virginia. 2011. Die Anglisierung des europäischen Wortschatzes: semantische Aspekte von Anglizismen im Italienischen und Deutschen. In Sandra Bosco, Marcella Costa & Ludwig Eichinger (eds.), *Deutsch-Italienisch Sprachvergleiche/Tedesco-italiano: confronti linguistici* (Turin, 2–3 October 2009), 29–43. Heidelberg: Universitätsverlag Winter.
Pulcini, Virginia. 2012a. Register variation in tourism terminology. In Roberta Facchinetti (ed.), *A Cultural Journey through the English Lexicon*, 109–131. Newcastle Upon Tyne: Cambridge Scholars Publishing.
Pulcini, Virginia. 2012b. L'anglicizzazione del lessico europeo: aspetti semantici di anglicismi in italiano e tedesco. In Luca Bellone, Giulio Cura Curà, Mauro Cursietti & Matteo Milani (eds.), *Filologia e Linguistica. Studi in onore di Anna Cornagliotti*, 855–869. Alessandria: Edizioni dell'Orso.
Pulcini, Virginia. 2017. Anglicisms in Italian: moving on into the third millennium. In Cecilia Boggio & Alessandra Molino (eds), *English in Italy: Linguistic, Educational and Professional Challenges*, 13–35. Milano: FrancoAngeli.
Pulcini, Virginia. 2019a. Internationalisms, Anglo-Latinisms and other kinship ties between Italian and English. In Elżbieta Mańczak-Wohlfeld (ed.), *Special issue on Anglicisms. Studia Linguistica Universitatis Iagellonicae Cracoviensis* 136. 121–141.
Pulcini, Virginia. 2019b. The English language and Anglo-American culture in Twentieth-Century Italy. In Guido Bonsaver, Alessandro Carlucci & Matthew Reza (eds.), *Understanding Cultural Change: Language and Narrative between Italy and the USA*, 31–46. Oxford: Legenda.

Pulcini, Virginia. 2020a. English-derived Multi-word and Phraseological Units across Languages in the Global Anglicism Database. *Textus. English Studies in Italy* 1. 127–143.

Pulcini, Virginia. 2020b. English Cyber- Words Across European Languages. In Magdalena Szczyrbak & Anna Teresziewicz (eds.), *Language in Contact and Contrast. A Festschrift for Professor Elżbieta Mańczak-Wohlfeld on the Occasion of Her 70$^{th}$ Birthday*, 349–365. Kraków: Jagellonian University Press.

Pulcini, Virginia. 2022. *La seconda montagna più alta del mondo*. Il superlativo relativo ordinale in inglese e in italiano. In Anthony Mollica & Cristina Onesti (eds.), *Studi in onore di Carla Marello*, 225–238. Welland, Ontario: éditions Soleil publishing, inc.

Pulcini, Virginia & Angela Andreani. 2014. Job-hunting in Italy: Building a glossary of "English-inspired" job titles. In Andrea Abel, Chiara Vettori & Natascia Ralli (eds.), *Proceedings of the XVI EURALEX International Congress: The User in Focus* (Bolzano/Bozen 15–19 July 2014), part 3, 1187–1201. Bolzano/Bozen: EURAC.

Pulcini, Virginia & Sandra Campagna. 2015. Internationalisation and the EMI controversy in Italian higher education. In Slobodanka Dimova, Anna Kristina Hultgren & Christian Jensen (eds.), *English-Medium Instruction in European Higher Education*, 65–87. Berlin: Mouton De Gruyter.

Pulcini, Virginia & Matteo Milani. 2017. Neo-classical combining Forms in English loanwords: Evidence from Italian. *ESP Across Cultures* 14. 175–196.

Pulcini, Virginia & Cristina Scarpino. 2017. The treatment of grammatical information on Anglicisms in some Italian dictionaries. *International Journal of Lexicography* 30(4). 504–519. (Advance article August 2016: https://doi.org/10.1093/ijl/ecw034).

Pulcini, Virginia, Cristiano Furiassi & Félix Rodríguez González. 2012. The lexical influence of English on European languages: from words to phraseology. In Cristiano Furiassi, Virginia Pulcini & Félix Rodríguez González (eds.), *The Anglicization of European Lexis*, 1–24. Amsterdam/Philadelphia: John Benjamins.

Quarantotto, Claudio. 1987. *Dizionario del nuovo italiano. 8000 neologismi della nostra lingua e del nostro parlare quotidiano dal dopoguerra ad oggi*. Roma: Newton Compton.

Quarantotto, Claudio. 2001. *Dizionario delle parole nuovissime*. Roma: Newton Compton.

Raffaelli, Sergio. 1983. *Le Parole Proibite, Purismo di Stato e Regolamentazione della Pubblicità in Italia (1812–1945)*. Bologna: Il Mulino.

Raffaelli, Alberto. 2010. *Le parole straniere sostituite dall'Accademia d'Italia (1941–43)*. Roma: Aracne.

Rando, Gaetano. 1967. Italiano e inglese in Australia. *Lingua Nostra* XXVIII. 115–18.

Rando, Gaetano. 1969. Anglicismi nel *Dizionario moderno* dalla quarta alla decima edizione. *Lingua Nostra* XXX. 107–112.

Rando, Gaetano. 1970. Voci inglesi nelle "Relazioni" cinquecentesche degli ambasciatori veneti in Inghilterra (1498–1557), *Lingua Nostra* XXI. 104–9.

Rando, Gaetano. 1973a. A Quantitative Analysis of the Use of Anglicisms in Written Standard Italian during the 1960's. *Italica* 50(1). 73–82.

Rando, Gaetano. 1973b. Influssi inglesi nel lessico italiano contemporaneo. *Lingua Nostra* XXXIV. 111–120.

Rando, Gaetano. 1987. *Dizionario degli Anglicismi nell'italiano postunitario*. Firenze: Leo S. Olschki.

Rando Gaetano. 1990. Capital gain, lunedì nero, money manager e altri anglicismi recentissimi nel linguaggio economico-borsistico-commerciale. *Lingua Nostra* LI(2–3). 50–66.

Renner, Vincent & Jesús Fernández-Domínguez. 2015. False Anglicization in the Romance languages: A contrastive analysis of French, Spanish and Italian. In Cristiano Furiassi & Henrik Gottlieb *Pseudo- English: Studies on False Anglicisms in Europe*, 147–157. Berlin/ Boston: Mouton de Gruyter.

Rodriguez Gonzalez, Félix & Sebastian Knospe. 2019. The variation of calques in European languages, with particular reference to Spanish and German: Main patterns and trends. *Folia Linguistica* 53(1). 233–276.

Rogato, Gilda. 2008. Anglicismi nella stampa italiana. *Italica* 85(1). 27–43.

Rogerson-Revell, Pamela. 2007. Using English for International Business: A European case study. *English for Specific Purposes* 26(1). 103–120.

Rosati, Francesca. 2004. *Gli anglicismi nel lessico economico e finanziario italiano*. Roma: Aracne.

Rosenhouse, Judith & Rotem Kowner (eds.). 2008. *Globally Speaking. Motives for Adopting English Vocabulary in Other Languages*. Clevedon: Multilingual Matters.

Rugge, Fabio (ed.). 2018. *L'internazionalizzazione della formazione superiore in Italia. Le università*. Roma: Fondazione CRUI. https://www2.crui.it/crui/crui-rapporto-inter-digitale.pdf (November, 2022).

Rugge, Fabio (ed.). 2019. *L'internazionalizzazione della formazione superiore in Italia. Le università*. Roma: Fondazione CRUI. https://www.crui.it/images/crui-rapporto-inter-digitale.pdf (November, 2022).

Sabatini, Francesco. 2008. L'italiano, lingua permissiva? Proposte per una strategia comune delle lingue europee verso l'anglicismo. In Sandro M. Moraldo (ed.), *Sprachkontakt und Mehrsprachigkeit*, 267–275. Heidelberg: Universität Winter.

Sabatini, Francesco & Vittorio Coletti. 2004. *Il Sabatini Coletti. Dizionario della Lingua Italiana*. Milano: Rizzoli Larousse.

Salomone, Rosemary. 2022. *The rise of English*. Oxford: Oxford University Press.

Salvi, Rita (ed.). 2009. *L'insegnamento delle lingue in Italia in relazione alla politica linguistica dell'Unione Europea*: Working Paper 59/2009. 7–14.

Santulli, Francesca. 2015. English in Italian universities: The language policy of PoliMi from theory to practice. In Slobodanka Dimova, Anna Kristina Hultgren & Christian Jensen (eds.), *English-medium Instruction in European Higher Education*, 269–290. Berlin: Mouton De Gruyter.

Saugera, Valérie. 2017. *Remade in France: Anglicisms in the Lexicon and morphology of French*. Oxford: Oxford University Press.

Scarpa, Federica. 2008 [2001]. *La traduzione specializzata – Un approccio didattico professionale*. Milano: Ulrico Hoepli.

Scarpa, Federica. 2014. L'influsso dell'inglese sulle lingue speciali dell'italiano. *Rivista internazionale di tecnica della traduzione-International Journal of Translation* 16. 225–243. Trieste: EUT.

Scarpa, Federica. 2020. *Research and Professional Practice in Specialised Translation*. London: Palgrave Macmillan.

Schirru, Giancarlo. 2019. English in Italian Education. In Guido Bonsaver, Alessandro Carlucci & Matthew Reza (eds.), *Understanding Cultural Change: Language and Narrative between Italy and the USA*, 47–58. Oxford: Legenda.

Serafini, Francesca. 2001. Italiano e inglese. In Luca Serianni (ed.), *La lingua nella storia d'Italia*, 597–609. Roma: Dante Alighieri.

Serianni, Luca (ed.) 2001. *La lingua nella storia d'Italia*. Roma: Dante Alighieri.

Shohamy, Elana & Durk Gorter (eds.). 2009. *Linguistic landscape. Expanding the scenery*. Oxon: Routledge.

Simpson, John A. & Edmund S.C. Weiner. 1989. 2nd edn. [1928]. *Oxford English Dictionary*. Oxford: Oxford University Press. www.oed.com (November, 2022).

Sketch Engine. http://www.sketchengine.eu (November, 2022).

Smith, John C. 2020. 2nd edn.*The Handbook of Language Contact*. London: Wiley-Blackwell.

Solly, Martin. 2010. Italy. In Barend Vlaardingerbroek & Neil Taylor (eds.), *Getting into Varsity. Comparability, Convergence and Congruence*, 27–41. Amherst, NY: Cambria Press.
Special Eurobarometer 386: Europeans and their Languages, version v1.00, European Commission, Directorate-General for Communication, 2014, accessed 2022-03-26, http://data.europa.eu/88u/dataset/S1049_77_1_EBS386
Stammerjohann, Harro. 2003. L'italiano e altre lingue di fronte all'anglicizzazione. In Nicoletta Maraschio & Teresa Poggi-Salani (eds.), *Italia linguistica anno Mille. Italia linguistica anno Duemila, Atti del XXXIV Congresso internazionale di studi della Società di Linguistica Italiana (SLI)* (Firenze, 19–21 ottobre 2000), 77–101. Roma: Bulzoni.
Stammerjohann, Harro. 2008. Introduzione. In Harro Stammerjohann, Enrico Arcaini, Gabriella Cartago, Pia Galetto, Matthias Heinz, Maurice Mayer, Giovanni Rovere & Gesine Seymer (eds.), *Dizionario di italianismi in francese, inglese, tedesco*, xi–xviii. Firenze: Accademia della Crusca.
Stead, William. 1902. *The Americanization of the World: Or, The Trend of the Twentieth Century*. New York: Horace Markley.
Sullam Calimani, Anna-Vera. 1995. *Il primo dei Mohicani. L'elemento americano nelle traduzioni dei romanzi di J.F. Cooper*. Pisa: Ist. Editoriali e Poligrafici.
Tappolet, Ernst. 1913. *Die alemannischen Lehnwörter in den Mundarten der französischen Schweiz. Kulturhistorisch-linguistische Untersuchung. Programm zur Rektoratsfeier der Universität Basel*. Basel: Universitäts-Buchdruckerei Friedrich Reinhardt.
Thomason, Sarah G. 2001. *Language Contact: An Introduction*. Edinburgh: Edinburgh University Press.
Tognini-Bonelli, Elena. 2001. *Corpus Linguistics at Work*. Amsterdam/Philadelphia: John Benjamins.
Tosi, Arturo. 1991. *Italian Overseas: The Language of Italian Communities in the English-Speaking World/ L'italiano d'Oltremare: La Lingua delle Comunità Italiane nei Paesi Anglofoni*. Florence: Giunti.
Tosi, Arturo. 2001. *Language and Society in a Changing Italy*. Clevedon: Multilingual Matters.
Tosi, Arturo. 2006. Languages in Contact with and without Speaker Interaction. In Anna Laura Lepsky & Arturo Tosi (eds.), *Rethinking Languages in Contact: The Case of Italian*, 160–172. London: Legenda.
Tosi, Arturo. 2008. The Language Situation in Italy. In Robert B. Kaplan & Richard B. Baldauf Jr. (eds.), *Language Planning & Policy, Europe*, Vol. 3. The Baltic States, Ireland and Italy, 262–350. Clevedon: Multilingual Matters.
Tosi, Arturo. 2020. *Language and the Grand Tour. Linguistic Experiences of Travelling in Early Modern Europe*. Cambridge: Cambridge University Press.
Truchot, Claude. 2002. *Key Aspects of the Use of English in Europe. Directorate of School* (Council of Europe Conference Paper). Strasbourg: Council of Europe. https://rm.coe.int/key-aspects-of-the-use-of-english-in-europe/1680887835 (November, 2022).
Universitaly. https://www.universitaly.it/ (November, 2022).
Van Meurs, Frank. 2006. *English job advertisements in the Netherlands: Reasons, use and effects*. Utrecht: LOT.
Ventura, Emanuele. 2020. Anglicismi recenti del lessico economico-finanziario italiano. *La Lingua Italiana. Storia, strutture, testi* XVI. 143–166
Venuta, Fabrizia. 2004. *E-finance e dintorni: il lessico dell'economia e dell'informatica: inglese e italiano a confronto*. Napoli: ESI.
Vettorel, Paola. 2013. English in Italian advertising. *World Englishes* 32(2). 261–78.
Vettorel, Paola & Valeria Franceschi. 2013. English and lexical inventiveness in the Italian language landscape. *English Text Construction* 6(2). 238–270.
Vettorel, Paola & Valeria Franceschi. 2019. English and other languages in Italian advertising. *World Englishes* 38. 417–434.

Viereck, Wolfgang & Wolf-Dieter Bald (eds.). 1986. *English in Contact with Other Languages. Studies in Honour of Broder Carstensen on the Occasion of his 60<sup>th</sup> Birthday*. Budapest: Akadémiai Kiadó.

*Vocabolario Treccani*. 2018. Roma: Istituto della Enciclopedia italiana. www.treccani.it (November, 2022).

Weinreich, Uriel. 1953. *Languages in Contact. Findings and Problems*. The Hague: Mouton.

Wexler, Paul. 1969. Towards a structural definition of 'internationalisms'. *Linguistics* 48: 77–92.

Wilkinson, Robert & René Gabriëls. 2021. *The Englishization of higher education in Europe*. Amsterdam: Amsterdam University Press.

Winford, Donald. 2003. *An Introduction to Contact Linguistics*. Oxford: Blackwell.

Winter-Froemel, Esme & Alexander Onysko. 2012. Proposing a pragmatic distinction for lexical Anglicisms. In Cristiano Furiassi, Virginia Pulcini & Félix Rodríguez González (eds.), *The Anglicization of European Lexis*, 43–64. Amsterdam/Philadelphia: John Benjamins.

Zenner, Eline, Dirk Speelman & Dirk Geeraerts. 2012. Cognitive Sociolinguistics meets loanword research: Measuring variation in the success of anglicisms in Dutch. *Cognitive Linguistics* 23(4). 749–792.

Zenner, Eline & Gitte Kristiansen (eds). 2014. *New Perspectives on Lexical Borrowing. Onomasiological, Methodological and Phraseological Innovations*. Berlin: De Gruyter Mouton.

Zolli, Paolo. 1991 [1976]. *Le parole straniere*. Bologna: Zanichelli.

Zoppetti, Antono. 2017. *Diciamolo in italiano. Gli abusi dell'inglese nel lessico* dell'Italia *e incolla*. Milano: Hoepli.

Zoppetti, Antonio. 2022. *Dizionario delle Alternative Agli Anglicismi*. https://aaa.italofonia.info/ (November, 2022).

Zuckermann, Ghil'ad. 2003. Language Contact and Globalisation: The camouflaged influence of English on the world's languages – with special attention to Israeli (sic) and Mandarin. *Cambridge Review of International Affairs* 16(2). 287–307.

# Index of names / subjects

abbreviation  13, 33, 73, 78–79, 99, 106, 107, 143, 145, 148, 149, 150, 177, 182
– *see* acronym
– *see* clipping
– *see* blend
*Accademia della Crusca*  15, 22, 39, 179, 224, 227, 233
acclimatization  8, 58
– *see* assimilation
acronym  62, 78–79, 99, 106–107, 110, 116, 122, 143, 147, 159, 164
– *see* abbreviation
adaptation  7, 14, 27, 29, 32, 54, 57, 64, 73, 83, 85, 89, 101, 128, 137, 203, 230, 231
– orthographic (adaptation)  11, 14, 34, 54, 57, 63, 64, 73, 92, 94, 95, 99, 101–103, 109, 110, 148, 161, 174, 230, 231, 238, 240
– morpho-syntactic (adaptation)  14, 57, 101, 107, 117, 137, 182, 230, 238
– phonological (adaptation)  10, 14, 54, 101, 104–107, 117, 238
– *see* integration
– *see* semantic integration
adoptability  53, 54, 107
– *see* borrowability
adoption  18, 33, 51, 58, 84, 92, 96, 115, 116, 124, 130, 131, 132, 144, 145, 146, 147, 148, 149, 181, 194
adstratum  4, 237
allogenism  86
Altieri, F.  25
Americanization  13, 41
Angela, P.  232
Anglicism  23, 43, 55–57, 101, 113, 124, 130, 131, 132, 136, 137, 143, 164
– direct Anglicism  13, 138, 140, 150
– indirect Anglicism  65, 143, 149
– adapted Anglicism  14, 56, 85, 101, 104, 143, 147, 187
– non-adapted Anglicism  14, 34, 37, 55, 64, 65, 73, 74, 92, 100, 101, 104, 143, 147, 174, 179, 184, 232
– primary Anglicism  54
– secondary Anglicism  54, 86

– *see* false Anglicism
– *see* pseudo-Anglicism
Anglicization  1, 4, 12, 43, 137, 139, 174, 184, 186, 207, 217, 225, 238
Anglo-Latinism  39, 85
– *see* Latinism
Anglomania  5, 13, 23–26, 30, 50, 225–226
archaism  14, 62, 73, 81, 100, 164
assimilation  14, 36, 52, 58, 81, 82, 83, 94, 101, 116, 132, 137, 139, 163, 189, 206, 227, 230, 231, 237
– *see* acclimatization
ATE (Academic Teaching Excellence)  222

Baretti, G.  23, 24, 25
Baudelaire, C.  70, 203
Beau Brummel  31
Beecher-Stowe, H.  35
bilingualism  1, 13, 35, 237
binomial  94, 95
blend  59, 73, 77, 99, 113, 116, 177, 181, 182, 186
– *see* abbreviation
Boccaccio, G.  20
borrowability  53
– *see* adoptability
borrowing  1–2, 9–10, 20, 33, 51–54, 56
– lexical borrowing  3, 4, 6, 8, 10, 13, 17, 51, 54, 58, 60, 99, 128, 142, 180, 232, 237, 241
– language borrowing  13, 17, 21, 229
– direct borrowing  52, 57, 64, 125, 147, 165
– indirect borrowing  14, 52, 53, 104, 111, 120, 121, 124, 125, 137, 150, 180, 182
– pragmatic borrowing  83, 98
– 'camouflage' borrowing  127
– cultural borrowing  21, 27
– 'intimate' borrowing  53
– nonce borrowing  58  *see* casual
– typology of borrowing  7, 8, 12, 13, 14, 58, 111, 121, 238, 239
Botero, G.  20
Boycott, C. C.  29
brand name  62, 159, 164, 206, 232
– *see* eponym
Buffalo Bill  35

calque 121–122, 123, 124, 125, 126, 127, 128, 132, 133, 135, 138, 139, 143, 147, 148, 165, 178, 179, 184, 204, 232, 239
– syntagmatic calque 122
– compositional calque 123
– derivational calque 111, 123
– 'camouflage' calque 113
– structural calque 182
– semantic calque *see* semantic loan
– *see* loan translation
– *see* loan rendition
– *see* loan creation
Castellani, A. 229–230
casual 9, 58, 144, 204, 240
CEFR (Common European Framework of Reference for Languages) 211
Chambers, E. 23, 25
CLIL (Content and Language Integrated Learning) 211, 222
clipping 73, 75, 77, 88, 89, 91, 99, 116
– *see* abbreviation
code-switching 58, 97, 98, 100, 205, 240
collocation 11, 53, 64, 73, 91, 93, 94, 95, 163, 164
combining form 73, 75, 76, 92, 93, 99, 102, 115, 123, 132, 134, 138, 182
compound 8, 13, 53, 64, 73, 75, 82, 83, 86, 92, 93, 94, 95, 99, 102, 103, 109, 116, 123, 132, 134, 177, 188, 203
contact linguistics 4, 13, 51, 56, 121
Cooper, J. F. 28
cultural borrowing 21, 27
cultural contact 4, 12, 13, 17, 18, 29
currency 8, 9, 11, 13, 14, 58, 62, 91, 141, 159, 161, 163, 164, 204, 239, 240, 241

Dante 19, 20
Darwin, C. 28
derivation 14, 52, 111, 113, 121, 138, 232
Dickens, C. 28
donor culture 17, 132
donor language 5, 9, 17, 24, 50, 51, 52, 54, 64, 85, 86, 92, 98, 118, 124, 125, 140, 237
Draghi, M. 205
Dryden, J. 25

EEA (European Education Area) 214
EFL (English as a Foreign Language) 1, 2, 209, 210, 212
Elizabeth I 22
EMI (English-Medium Instruction) 216–225
eponym 8, 14, 33, 40, 61, 73, 79, 80, 91, 100, 148
– *see* brand name
– *see* proper name
– *see* trademark
ESL (English as a Second Language) 1
etymology 26, 55, 64, 75, 84, 133, 134, 135, 136, 138, 148, 149, 239
– primary 55
– secondary 55
Europeanization 47
exoticism 8, 14, 62, 73, 81, 99, 100, 139, 140, 164

false Anglicism 8, 14, 30, 52, 54, 57, 62, 75, 76, 80, 85–91, 100, 131, 171, 188, 194, 232
– autonomous compound 86
– compound ellipsis 86
– semantic shift 86, 87, 88, 89
– autonomous derivative 90
– *see* clipping
– *see* eponym
– *see* pseudo-Anglicism
false friend 36, 113, 128, 133
Florio, J. 22
foreignism 58, 85, 195
Foscolo, U. 28

Galileo Galilei 22
Gallicism 3, 59, 136, 144
Gallicization 27
Gallomania 24
Garibaldi, G. 28
gender 11, 54, 57, 83, 101, 107, 108, 109, 110, 187, 188
genetic similarity 9, 14, 60
Gentile, G. 210
Germanism 136, 144
Giotto 19
Goethe, J. W. 26
Graf, A. 24
Grand Tour 24, 28

## Index of names / subjects

Hitler, A. 37
hybrid 14, 75, 88, 91–94, 99, 100, 182, 206
– *see* loanblend

ICLHE (Integrating Content and Language in Higher Education) 222
importation 51, 52, 116
inkhorn debate 22
integration 8, 9, 10, 14, 29, 57, 83, 84, 98, 101, 107
– *see* adaptation
interjection 73, 76, 83, 94, 98, 107, 108
interlexeme 135
interlingual identification 56
internationalism 8, 14, 28, 56, 62, 85, 133, 134, 136, 138, 143, 145, 180, 239
internationalization 3, 48, 184, 186, 187, 216, 217, 218, 220, 221, 224
Italianism 22, 52, 136, 183, 187
itangliano 233

Johnson, S. 24

language contact 1, 5, 6, 8, 12, 13, 14, 17, 36, 43, 51, 52, 53, 56, 57, 75, 99, 116, 121, 133, 136, 205, 237, 241
Latinism 13, 73, 82, 138, 151, 173
– *see* Anglo-Latinism
Lehnwort 51
Leonardo da Vinci 22
Leopardi, G. 28
lexical borrowing 4, 6, 7, 8, 10, 13, 17, 50, 51, 54, 55, 56, 58, 60, 99, 128, 142, 180, 232, 237
linguistic imperialism 2, 43, 218
linguistic landscape 15, 58, 204, 206, 208
neo-purism 7, 13, 34, 35, 39
loan 51
– necessary loan 54, 124, 130, 131
– luxury loan 124, 130, 131, 194
– catachrestic loan 54, 131
– non-catachrestic loan 54, 131
– *see* semantic loan
loan creation 121
loan homonym 121
loan rendition 121
loan synonym 121
loan translation 51, 59, 110, 121, 186

loanblend 91, 92
– *see* hybrid
loanword 9, 10, 51, 52, 54, 57, 83, 86, 92, 99, 101, 106, 124, 125, 130, 133, 136, 143, 150, 175, 184, 194, 204, 228, 229, 230, 237, 238
– adapted loanword 64, 84, 85, 111, 137
– non-adapted loanword 29, 64, 99, 125, 137, 230
loanword lexicography 8, 10, 12, 13, 61, 145, 240
Lord Byron 28

Machiavelli, N. 20
macrostructure 9, 56, 94, 109, 142, 146, 150
Marchionne, S. 43
Mazzini, G. 28
mediation 22, 24, 26, 34, 58, 60, 70, 81, 102, 104, 123, 133, 135, 204
Michelangelo Buonarroti 22
Migliorini, B. 39
Milton, J. 25
Monelli P. 39, 226
Montanelli, I. 232
multilingualism 47, 217, 228
Mussolini, B. 37

naturalization 57
neologism 7, 9, 11, 17, 38, 46, 47, 48, 50, 63, 73, 75, 78, 86, 91, 121, 124, 128, 135, 136, 142, 148, 149, 161, 171, 172, 175, 178, 179, 193, 204, 205, 207, 238, 240
Neologisers 22
neo-purism 7, 13, 34, 35, 39
number 11, 54, 57, 107, 108, 110, 137

obsolescence 15, 17, 30, 32, 70, 141, 193–195, 203, 207, 240

Panzini, A. 33, 38, 39, 226
Petrarca, F. (Petrarch) 20
phono-semantic matching 61
phraseologism 40, 73, 83, 94, 95, 98, 99, 100, 147
polygenesis 124, 180
Pope, A. 25, 26
proper name 61, 62, 74, 79, 80, 102, 143, 150, 159, 161, 164, 173, 189, 232
– *see* eponym

pseudo-Anglicism  61, 62, 143, 192
– *see* false Anglicism
Pullman, A.G.  33
pun  204, 205
purism  5, 37, 38, 50, 234
Purists  22

reborrowing  52, 90, 129, 187, 190
receiving language  9, 10, 51, 52, 53, 54, 55, 56, 83, 101, 130, 132, 180
– *see* recipient language
recipient language  9, 18, 51, 52, 57, 58, 83, 85, 86, 89, 92, 98, 100, 101, 116, 117, 118, 119, 120, 121, 125, 126, 127, 130, 131, 194, 239, 240
– *see* receiving language
Reid, T. M.  35
replica  9, 51, 111, 116, 117, 121, 122, 127
replication  51
representativeness  8, 9, 11, 81, 163
resemanticization  87, 177, 182

Sacco, N.  35
Scott, W.  28, 29
semantic integration  101, 116, 117
– semantic narrowing  87, 119, 188
– semantic reduction  14, 118, 119
– semantic widening  52, 119
– semasiological approach  117
– onomasiological approach  10, 117
– *see* integration
semantic loan  9, 14, 52, 57, 61, 120, 125–129, 137, 165, 179, 182, 204, 239, 241
semi-calque  92
substitution  37, 53, 101, 104, 105, 121, 203, 230, 231
Swift, J.  25

terminologization  182
trademark  8, 79, 91, 143, 148, 195
– *see* eponym

underdifferentiation  104

Vanzetti, B.  35
Voltaire, F.  26

Weinreich, U.  56–57
Wilde, O.  31

Zingarelli, N.  147

# Index of borrowings and quoted words

abolizionismo  32, 147
(and) the winner is  96
(the) best of  96
. . . is beautiful  115
ABS  79, 118
access key  182
– see chiave d'accesso
access point  49
account  44
accountant  120
ace  133
acid house  46
acid jazz  46
acid rock  46
acquiring  177
acro  21
address  182
administrator  178
adrenalina  85
ADSL  78
advergame  177
aerobica  135
affidabile  124, 181
affidabilità  123, 124, 181
afro-beat  46
agenda  128
aggiornare  40
agility  46
agility dog  86
agnostico  134
AIDS  78, 79, 106, 110
airbag  46, 73, 116, 118
air-show  46
ala  21
album  82, 92
alchemico  135
aldrimani  21
alert  49
alfanumerico  181
alias  181
all in one  73
all inclusive  73, 103, 178
– see tutto compreso
all you can eat  95, 103

allenamento  39
allenatore  40, 190, 191
alta definizione  122
alta fedeltà  121, 122
alta società  122
alto tradimento  19
altoparlante  39, 123
ambient  46
anchor investor  177
anglicismo, anglismo  23, 57, 147
angolo  40, 126, 127, 190
– see corner
anti-age  91
– see anti-età
antibiotico  143
anti-età  123
– see anti-age
antitrust  40, 107, 108
app  49, 182
application, applicazione  128
applicazione web  93
approcciare  129
appuntamento al buio  121, 122
aquabike  192
aquagym  45, 192
aquarium  82
area manager  120, 188
area test  86
aria condizionata  122, 124
arrampicatore sociale  124
articolo  2, 3
artificial intelligence  182
–see intelligenza artificiale
assenteismo  29, 135
asset  45
assets  110
assistente di volo  188
assistente virtuale  122
Associated Press  143
assolutamente  62
assolutismo  29, 135
attitudine  128
audit  45
auditing  45

auditor  45
authority, autorità  127, 128
autobiografia  28
autobus  33
autocarro  59, 135
autocontrollo  76, 132
– see self-control
autogoverno  123
autogrill  91
automatizzare  112
automatizzazione  135
automazione  112, 121, 123
automotive  62
autoscatto  76
– see selfie

B&B  78
– see bed and breakfast
B2B  78, 95, 107
– see business to business
B2C  78, 95
– see business to consumer
baby  75, 104
baby boss  75
baby dance  75
baby gang  75
baby parking  75
baby pensionato  75
baby pensioni  75
baby pusher  75
baby sitter  8, 120, 187, 194, 230
baby star  73
baby-foot  86
babysitteraggio  112
backgammon  198, 202, 203
backup  44
baco  182
– see bug
badminton  80
bagpipe  198
bail-in  49, 185
bailout  185
banconota  32
bang  83
banking online  49, 86
bannare  108
banner  44

bar  34, 38, 58, 83, 147, 187, 230
barbie  80
barcamp  49
barista  187
barlady  187
barman  120, 187
baronetto  21
bartender  187
barwoman  187
base jumping  103, 172, 193
baseball  103
basket  182
– see cestino
basket, basketball  40, 123
– see pallacanestro
basso costo  178
– see low cost
BB cream  79
beach basket  193
beach movie  46
beach rugby  193
beach soccer  193
beach tennis  73, 193
beach volley  45, 193
beagle  41
beat  104
beauty  90
beauty-case  90
be-bop  46
bed and breakfast  62, 95
– see B&B
behaviorismo  124, 147
– see comportamentismo
benchmark  73, 103
benchmarking  45
bermuda  102
bestseller  230
bi-fuel  46
big bang  17
big data  49, 73
Big Pharma  50
bingo  83, 98
biopic  46, 77
bio-tech  77
birdie  81
bistecca  31, 85
bit  104

## Index of borrowings and quoted words — 267

bitcoin 49
black 94
black comedy 46
Black Friday 80
blackout 230
blazer 40
blob 89
blockbuster 80
blog 44, 77, 182, 231
blogger 44
blues 40, 94
bluff 104, 230
bluffare 108
BMX 79
bob 40, 191
bobby 82
bobsleigh 40
bobtail 46, 86
body building 192
bogey 81
boicottaggio 123
boicottare 29, 57, 135
bomber 91
bonus 82
boogie-woogie 46
bookmaker 230
boom 40, 83, 108
boomerang 60, 230
bordercross 193
boss 40, 119
Boston 195, 196, 198
bot 182
bovindo 85
box 87, 92
box auto 88, 92
box doccia 88, 91
brand manager 188
brandy 31
breadcrumbs 182
break 83, 98, 197, 203
break even point 95
breakbeat 46
Brexit 77
bridge 41
broker 32
brokeraggio 61, 112
brougham 32

browser 44
brunch 77
bruxismo 85
budget 27, 70, 230
budino 31, 59, 135
buffalo 81
bug 182
– see baco
bulldog 70
bulldozer 41
bungalow 8, 60, 118
bungee jumping 45, 172, 193
bunker 81
buone pratiche 48
burberry 40
burkini 77
bus 33, 104
business 32, 184
business angel 45
business is business 40, 97
business to business 45, 73, 95
– see B2B
business to consumer 95
– see B2C
businessman 40
bye 97
bye-bye 83, 97
by-pass 46, 73, 131
bypassare 108
byte 44, 181

c/o 79, 96
– see care of
cab 32, 197
caccia alle streghe 147
cacciatore di teste 122
cachemire 34, 102
– see cashmere
CAD 78, 106
caddie 81
cake 198, 202, 203
cake designer 73
cakewalk 62, 196
calcio d'angolo 126
calciomercato 116
calcolatore (elettronico) 44, 180
– see computer

calcolatrice 180
cambiamento climatico 122
cambric 22
camcorder 77
camera 52, 129
camera/casa 20
cameraman 129
camper 87
camping 91
campus 82
canadair 91
cancellare 129
cane lupo 147
canguro 27, 60
cannabis 81
canyon 62, 81
canyoning 81
capacitazione 85
capsule collection 73
captcha 49
cardigan 79
cardiofitness 192
care of 96
– see c/o
cargo 41
carote baby 75
carrello 182
– see shopping cart
carro 36
car-sharing 46
carta d'imbarco 122
carta di credito 122
cartonista 111
cartuccia 182
Casa Bianca 143
case study, studio di caso, caso di studio 122, 123
cash-and-carry 95
cashmere 34, 102, 143
– see cachemire
casimira 143
casual, casuale 127
caterpillar 41
cavallo vapore 33
CB 79
cc 78
CD 78, 106, 110, 116

CD-ROM 78
celebrity, celebrità 9
celluloide 59, 135
CEO 78,107
– see chief executive officer
certificate 177
cestino 182
– see basket
chairman 30
charleston 40, 79
chat 44
chatbot 49, 77
chattare 108
check-point 103
check-up 46
cheese 83, 98
cheesecake 203
chesterfield 196
Chi è chi? 116
– see Who's Who?
Chi fa cosa? 116
chiave d'accesso 182
– see access key
chiavetta 181
chief executive officer 95
– see CEO
chierico 19
chill out 46, 94
chintz 30
chiocciola 181
chip 44
chips 110
choc 34, 102
– see shock
chutney 81
cibernetica 180
ciclocross 8, 102
cinema 59
cinemascope 195, 198, 202
cip 85
cisgenico 177
city 17, 27
city airport 47
city car 230
city manager 188
citypass 131
clacson 41, 102

clan  27, 162
clap  83
Clarks  143
classe capovolta  122
claunesco  102
– see clownesco
clergyman  196, 202, 203
cliccare  108, 182
clickbaiting  49
client  44, 178
clinch  197
cloud  49
clown  34
clown terapia  61, 92
clownesco  102, 115
– see claunesco
club  27, 104, 106
CMC  182
coach  40, 190, 194
coalizione  26, 84, 135, 147
coast to coast  95
coating  196
cochetto  19
cocker  34
cockney  34
cockpit  46
cocktail  31, 54, 110
code sharing  46
codice a barre  122
codice QR  79
– see QR code
coffee break  120, 203
– see pausa caffé
cold cream  198
college  34, 105, 120
collie  34, 46
colossal  46
colt  80
comfort, confort  34, 102
comitato  26, 84, 135
commercio elettronico  231
– see e-commerce
commissione  26, 84, 135
commodity, commodities  45, 110
commodoro, comodoro  26
common law  29
community, comunità  182, 230

comorbidità  85
company  45
comportamentismo  123, 124
– see behaviorismo
compost  113
compostabile  113
compostaggio  112
compostare  108
computazionale  113
computer  44, 55, 180
– see calcolatore (elettronico)
– see elaboratore (elettronico)
– see ordinatore
computer baby  75
concept album  82, 92
condizionamento  40
conferenza al vertice  122, 126
– see summit
conferenza stampa  121, 122
conformista  26, 147
congresso  32
connection  119
consumerismo  112
contact tracing  48
contactless  49
container  41
conto alla rovescia  122
contraccezione  85
contraddanza  22, 196
– see country dance
convention, convenzione  26, 128, 135
cookie  44, 182, 231
cool  119
cool jazz  46
coolie  196
copyleft  177
copyright  34
core business  45
corn flakes  110
corner  40, 126, 127, 190
– see angolo
cosplay  77
costituzionale  26
costuma  19
cottage  117
country  94
country dance  22, 196

– *see* contraddanza
country-rock 46
cowboy 32
CPU 78
craccare 108
crash 83
credere in. . . 143
cricket 34
cromlech 198
cross 40
crossare 108
cross-country 40
crossfit 49, 192
crowdfunding 49, 73, 177, 185
crowdsourcing 49, 177, 185
cruise control 46, 118
curling 40, 191
curry 31, 60, 81
customer care 45
customizzare 109
customizzazione 109
cutter 26
cyber 75, 93, 182
cyberbullismo 93, 112
cybercafé, cibercafé 93
cybercrime, cybercrimine 93, 182
cybernauta, cibernauta 102, 112
cybersecurity, cybersicurezza 49, 93, 182
cyberspace, cyberspazio, ciberspazio 93, 182
cyberterrorismo 112

Dammi un cinque 97
dance 94
dancing 91
dandy 31, 82
dandyismo, dandismo 82, 112
dark web 49
dashboard 49
data 106
data entry 188
database 44
day by day 96
day hospital 46
day surgery 46
day-care 46
decoder 44
deejay 79, 187

deep learning 177
denim 79
depressurizzare 109
depressurizzazione 109
derby 34, 79, 190
designer 110
desktop 44, 182
– *see* scrivania
destroyer 40
detective 34
detector 40
deterrente 147
devolution, devoluzione 230
dialer 177
digital divide 49
digitale 181
dimmerabile 113
diorama 135
director's cut 96
directory 44, 182
direttore artistico 122
dirty dancing 196
disco 94
disco fisso 182
– *see* hard disk
disco volante 124
disposofobia 177
dissolvenza 39
distale 85
distanziamento sociale 48
– *see* social distancing
DJ 79
DNA 78, 106, 110
dock 26
docudrama 46
dodgeball 193
dogleg 81
dollaro 84, 85
doodle 49
door-to-door 95
– *see* porta a porta
dopare, doparsi 108
dopobarba 123
dot com 45
double dip 177
down 80
downhill 193

download  44
downloadare  108, 182
dread  87
dress code  50
dribblare  108
dribbling  40, 190
drink  120
drive  197, 203
drum 'n' bass  95
dry  119
dub  94
duty-free shop  73, 95
DVD  44, 78, 107, 116

eagle  81
easy listening  46
easy rider  197
e-banking  45
e-book  76
e-business  45
e-cig  72
e-cigarette  72
– see sigaretta elettronica
e-commerce  45, 76, 231
– see commercio elettronico
editore  113, 128
editorial, editoriale  113, 143, 147
edizione limitata  122
– see limited edition
edutainment  77
e-health  49
elaboratore elettronico  44, 180
– see computer
e-learning  49, 76, 182
election day  232
electroshock, elettroshock  38, 93
e-mail  44, 76, 110, 124, 132, 182, 231
– see posta elettronica
e-mobility  49
emoticon  44
enclosures  21
e-reader  49
escapismo  112
escort  119
e-ticket  49
eurobond  93
eurovisione  147

evidenza  128
e-work  182
exit poll  231
– see sondaggio a caldo
export  40
extension, estensione  119, 230
extra-extra-large  95
– see XXL
extra-extra-small  95
– see XXS
extra-time  49

fablab  177
faccia a faccia  95, 122
face lifting  90
fai da te  95, 122
fair play  34
fairway  81
fake news  49
fan  110
fantathriller  77
FAQ  78
Far West  31
farm  196
fashion  30, 91
fashion blog  50
fashion blogger  50
fashion system  30
fashion victim  30
fashion week  30
fattoria  36
feed  182
feo  19
ferry-boat  32
festival  59
file  181
file sharing  49, 177
film  8, 34, 38, 58, 74, 83, 104, 147, 230
film TV  86
filmabile  113
filmare  108
filmico  115
filmografia  115
filmologia  115
filmoteca  115
filobus  32, 197, 203
– see trolleybus

fine settimana 110, 122
– see weekend
finestra 182
– see window
finish 40
fintech 177
firewall 44
fitwalking 49, 193
five o'clock tea, five o'clock tè 31
flash mob 50
flashare, flasharsi 108
flashback 46
flat 119
flexicurity, flessicurezza 177, 186
flippare 108
flipper 87
flirt 34, 91, 104
flirtare 108
floppare 108
floppy 104
floppy disk 44
flower power 197
fly and drive 95
FM 79
folk 94
folk music 46
folklore, folclore 34, 102
follower 110, 119, 177
font 44
food blogger 50
food delivery 49
football 33, 34, 40, 190
footing 89
footvolley 193
foreign fighter 50
format 45, 232
formattare 108, 232
forno a microonde 124
forum 82, 181
fotoblog 93
fotofinish 93, 102
fotogallery, foto gallery 93, 102
fotoreporter 93
foxtrot 40, 196, 202
fracking 177
free climbing 45, 193
free trade 32

freemium 77, 177
freestyle 191, 193
freeware 182
friendzonare 108
frisbee 80
fuga dei cervelli 122
full 41, 104
full contact 192
full optional 46
full time 61, 127
– see tempo pieno
fumo di Londra 27
funky 46, 94
fuorilegge 123
fusion 94

gadget 115
gadgettistica 115
gallery 105
game 40
game over 97, 107
gang 34
gangsta-rap 46
gangsterismo 112
garden-party 31
gasp 83, 98
gay 130
Gay Pride 80
gentleman 27
gentleman's agreement 96
geotag 49, 177
geotaggare 108
ghinea 21
ghosting 176, 177
GIF 177
Gillette 143
gin 31
gin tonic 95, 102
gingerino 115
giobba 36
gip 147, 148
gippe 144
gippone 145, 147, 148
gipsy 94
giungla 34, 85, 159
– see jungle
glitterato 113

global warming  177
glocal  77, 116
GMT  79
goal line technology  95
goal, gol  40, 102, 104, 162, 190
golden gol  102
golf  34, 38, 40, 101
golfista  101, 111
gomma da masticare  122
goodbye  83, 97
googlare  108
gospel  40, 94
GPS  78, 106
gran cancelliere  19
grattacielo, grattanuvole  36, 123
green  81
green pass  131
grizzly  31
groom  196
ground zero  58
grunge  46
GSM  78
guancia a guancia  122
guardia del corpo  121, 122
guest  119
gulp  83, 98

hackathon  177
hacker  44
hackeraggio  112, 115
hackerare  108, 115
hacking  115
hamburgheria  115
handball  193
handbike  193
handicappare  108
handicappato  113
handy  89
handycam  44
hangout  49
happy end  89, 90
– see lieto fine
hard  119
hard disk  44
– see disco fisso
hardware  44, 181, 182
hashish  81

hashtag  49, 177
hater  49, 177
HD  78, 122
HDTV  78, 122
heavy metal  46
hello  83, 97
help  83, 98, 104
hesitation  196
hi-fi  77
high life  31
high school  122
highlander  87, 89, 122
highlight  122
hip hip hip urrà (urrah)  83, 97, 98, 102
hip hop  94, 105
HIV  78, 106
hobbista  111
hobby  230
hockeista  111
hockey  40, 191
holding  40, 110
holding company  45
home  182
home banking  45
Home soft home  205
Home sweet home  205
homepage  44, 230
hooligan  45
hooliganismo  112
horsepower  33
host  119, 182
hostess  188
hot jazz  46
hotel  59
hotspot  86
house  94
house music  46
HP  33, 79, 118
HTML  78, 106
HTTP  182
hub  46, 104, 177
humour  110
– see umorismo
husky  46
hydrobike  192
hydrofracking  177
hydrospeed  193

hydrospinning 192
hyperlink 182
hypertext 182
– see ipertesto

iarda 101
ice climbing 193
icona 182
igloo 60
immobilizer 118
immunoterapia 116
impatto 9, 147
impeachment 30
implementare 129
import 40
indirizzo web 93
influencer 106
infopoint 86
informatica 59, 180, 181
infotainment 77
intelligence 119
intelligenza artificiale 122
– see artificial intelligence
interattoma 177
intercity 80
interfaccia web 93
interferenza 39
internauta 112
internet 44
internet mania 92
interrail 80
intervista 34
introdurre 129
IoT 78
iPad 62
ipertesto 182
– see hypertext
IQ 79
ISBN 79
ISO 78, 107
IT 79

jab 160, 161
jabber 160
jack 159, 160, 161, 164, 165
jack dempsey 159, 160
jack fruit 159, 160

jack rabbit 159, 160
jack russell 46, 160, 162, 171
jackass 160
jacket 160
jackpot 61, 62, 160
Jacuzzi® 159, 160
JAL 159, 160
jam 160
jam session 105, 160
jamboree 158, 159, 160
jambul 159, 160
jamming 160, 173
jangar 159, 160
jansky 159, 160
JATO 143, 159, 160
Java 159, 160
jay 159, 160
jazz 17, 40, 94, 106, 153, 158, 160, 165, 169, 170, 172
jazz-band 158, 160
jazzista 111, 158, 160, 171
jazzistico 158, 160
jazzman 111, 158, 160, 170, 171
jazz-rap 160, 171
jazz-rock 160, 171
jazzy 160
jean 160
jeans 158, 160, 170, 172
jeanseria 160, 162
jeep 8, 41, 79, 142, 144–150, 153, 158, 159, 160, 165, 172
jeep-girl 145
jeeppone 147
jenny 159, 160
jep 144
jequirity 160
jersey 30, 79, 153, 160, 166
Jesus revolution 159, 160
jet 160
jet executive 160
jet lag 160, 232
jet liner 158, 159, 160
jet set 158, 160
jet society 158, 160
jet stream 159, 160
jewel box 160
jigger 159, 173

jigsaw  160
jingle  158, 160
jitter  160
jitterbug  160
jive  160
job  36, 158, 159, 165, 172, 173
job center / centre  160, 162, 164, 172
job creation  160
job description  160, 174
job evaluation  160
job on call  49, 160, 164, 171, 172, 174
job placement  160, 162, 172, 173, 174
job rotation  160
job sharing  160, 172, 174
jobber  160
jobs act  49, 160, 161, 162, 172
jockey  173
jockey cap  160
jodhpurs  160, 174, 196
jogger  160
jogging  45, 156, 160, 230
John Bull  159, 160
Johnny  159, 160
join  160
joint  158, 159, 160
joint venture  45, 160
joker  160
jolly  41, 158, 160, 172
jorkyball  159, 160
joule  8, 159, 160
journal  106
joypad  160
joystick  160
JPY  159, 160
judo  60
jug  160
juggernaut  159, 160
juggling  160, 171
juju  160
jukebox  160
jumbo  160
jumbo jet  158, 160
jump  160
jumper  160
jumping  160, 172
jumpsuit  50, 160, 162, 272
jungle  160

– *see* giungla
jungle style  160
junior  106, 160, 165, 172, 173
junior suite  160, 162, 173
junk bond  160
junk food  160
junk mail  160
junkie  158, 159, 160
jupiter  159, 160
just in time  160
Just Pump®  159, 160
justiciar, justiciary  159, 160
jute  160

kamikaze  60
kayak  81
kayaking  81
Keep calm and. . .  97
ketchup  27, 55, 67, 70, 81
kick-boxing  45, 192
killer instinct  63
kilt  30
kiteboard  49
kite-surfing  45, 193
kleenex  61, 80
knickerbockers  31
knock out  40
knock down  103
KO  79, 106
k-way  91

L (large)  79
labrador retriever  46
laburismo  112
lad  196
Ladies and Gentlemen  9
lady  17, 21
LAN  78
laptop  17, 44
laser  79
laserterapia  92
last but not least  96, 107
lavaggio del cervello  147
lavoro agile  90
– *see* smart working
LCD  78
leader  30, 110, 111

leaderismo 111, 112
leadership 30
LED 78, 107
legislatura 26
liberty 80
lieto fine 89
– *see* happy end
liftare 108
lifting 91
like 49
lillipuziano 26
lime 81
limerick 79
limited edition 63
– *see* edizione limitata
linciaggio 123
link 182
linkare 108
Lions Club 143
living 91
loading 177
lobbista 111
location 46
lockdown 48
locomotiva 33, 59, 135
log 26
loggare 108
login 44
logout 44
LOL 79, 107
Lombard 19
look 120
lord 8, 21
lounge 46
lounge bar 63
low cost 178
– *see* basso costo
LP 79
LSD 198, 202, 203
luetico 85

M (medium) 79
mackintosh 30, 31
made in Italy 96
made in. . . 96
madison 195, 196
maggioranza 26

mail 91
mail box 44
malware 49, 182
management 106
management buy-out 95
manager 32, 55, 184, 188
manageriale 113, 115, 147
managerialismo 112
managerialità 115
marchio di fabbrica 32
– *see* trademark
marijuana 55, 81
market leader 45
marketing manager 45
mass media 82, 106
masterizzare 109
masterizzazione 109
match 34, 40, 190
mayor 21
media 82, 128
mediale 113, 128
memory 182
memristore 177
menu 182
microblog 49
microblogging 177
microchippare 109
microfono 8, 147
microonde 123
migration, migrazione 128, 182
milady 82
miledi 21
millennial 50
millennium bug 205
milord 82
milordo 21
minibar 86
minigonna 123
minimale 113
minimalismo 112
minimalista 111
miss 27, 67, 70
missaggio, mixaggio 112
mission 119
mission impossible 97, 119
mister 89, 105, 194
mixare 108

MMS  78
mobbizzare  113
mobbizzato  113
mobile banking  49
moblog  177
mod  197
moda baby  75
modem  44, 77, 181, 182
mogano  27
money transfer  45
monitoraggio  112
monitorare, monitorizzare  109
monitorizzazione  109
monorotaia  123
motilità  85
motocrossista  111
motorcaravan  102
motorhome  102
motoryacht  102
motoscooter  102
mountain bike  45, 193
mouse  44, 54, 181, 182
mozione  26
MP3  78
MP4  78
multijet  46, 118
multitouch  49, 177
mystery shopper  189

nanopublishing  177
nativo digitale  122, 135
navetta  126, 127, 132
– see shuttle
navetta spaziale  126
navigator  50, 189
naziskin  92
net  40, 177
net company  49
net economy  49
netiquette  182
neutracetico  85
new age  46
new economy  45
news  110
newsgroup  44
next opening  207
nickname  44

night  87
nimby  79
no comment  83, 97, 107
no global  49, 76
no problem  8, 97
no smoking  91, 97
no tax area  49
no vax  76
nobel  80
nomofobia  78, 102
non profit, no profit  45, 76, 102
non stop, no stop  76
nordic walking  49, 177
no-tax area  49
nurse  196
nursery  40
nylon, nailon  102

off-line  44
offside  40
OK, o.k., O.K.  58, 79, 83, 108
– see okay
okay  9, 58, 98, 162, 239
– see OK
omosessuale  130, 147
on the road  95
on the rocks  95
on-demand  45, 108
one-man band  95
one-man show  95
one-step  196
one-to-one  95
one-woman show  95
online  44, 108
online dating  50
op art  77
open access  50, 73
open source  106
open-toe  50
operatore turistico  9, 178
– see tour operator
opossum  27, 60, 81
opposizione  26
ordinatore  44, 180
– see computer
ordine della calattiarra/giarrettiera  19
oscar  80

ostruzionismo  29, 112, 123, 135, 239
out  76, 83, 98
outing  91
outlet  76
output  76
outsider  40, 76
oxford  79

pacchetto  182
pacemaker  46
paesi terzi  48
pagina web  93
palla break  203
pallacanestro  40, 123
– see basket, basketball
pallanuoto  121
pamphlet  59, 195, 198, 203, 204
pantaloni alla zuava  30
par  81
parasailing  193
pari opportunità  48
parking  91
parlamento  20
parola chiave  182
parola d'ordine  132
– see password
part time  132
– see tempo parziale
partenariato  59, 85, 113, 123
partnership  40
pass, passi  131
passo dopo passo  132
– see step by step
password  44, 132
– see parola d'ordine
pausa caffé  120, 122
– see coffee break
pay per use  95
pay per view  95
pay-tv  45, 107, 132
– see tv a pagamento
paywall  177
PC  44, 78, 106, 182
peep-toe  50
pellerossa  32
pemmican  81, 198

pen drive  49
penalty  40
pennicillina  143
penny  27
perdere l'autobus  143
performance  34, 106
performante  113
performare  108
performativo  115
performer  110
permalink  177
personal shopper  50
pet therapy  46, 92
petizione  26
petrello  143
phishing  49, 102
phone banking  102
phone center  102
photofit, fotofit  93, 102
photokit, fotokit  93
piattaforma  32
piattaforma web  93
piccio  143
pick and roll  95
picnic  31, 38
pigiama  40, 81
pilates  45
PIN  78, 106
ping-pong  40
pit bull  46
pit stop  45
pittografia  59, 135
placebo  147
plaid  27, 67
plug and play  95
plug-in  50
plumcake  203
podcast  49
pogare  108
pointer  34
poker  38, 41, 87
pole  87
pole position  45, 87, 118
politically correct, politicamente corretto  48, 120, 122
polo  34

pony  21
pony express  189
pop  46, 94
populismo  112
pornoshop  86
pornostar  102
porta a porta  122
– see door-to-door
portale  182
portale web  93
portfolio  52, 129
posta elettronica  124, 132, 231
– see e-mail
postare  108
post-it  232
post-verità  123
power walking  193
power yoga  49, 192
PR  78
pragmatismo  112
preistorico  34, 147
premier  30
premium  82
prequel  46
pressing  190
pressurizzare  40
print on-demand  95
privacy  106
private banking  49
processare  109, 129, 182
processore  85
proibizionismo  32, 112
project leader  49
project manager  120, 188
promoter, promotore  187
propriocettore  85
prosumer  77
provider  44
proxy  62
psichedelico  135
public company  45
public school  82
pullman  33
pullover  40
puritani  20
puzzle  41, 106

Q&A  79
QR code  49, 78, 79
– see codice QR
quacchero  147
quantitative easing  177
quantum bit  177
quiz  104
quotare  109, 129, 182

racer  40
racketeer  196
radiomica  177
ragtime  40
raid  199, 203
rallista  111
rally  40
RAM  78
ranch  36
rap  94
rappare  108
ready-to-wear  95
realista  147
reality show  45
realizzare  127
realtà aumentata  122
recital  34
record  34, 40, 89
recordman  86
red carpet  50
redingote, redingotto  26, 197, 203, 204
– see riding coat
reggae  94
relax  91, 106, 108
REM  79
Remington  195, 198, 199
remixare  108
report  106, 115
reporter  34
reportistica  115
resettare  108
retriever  34
retweet  49
retwittare  108
revenge porn  50
revolver  34
rhythm and blues  95

rianimatologia 85
rider 189
riding coat 197, 204
– *see* redingote
ring 34
riserva 32
ristopub 206
roast beef, rosbif 17, 31
rock 94
rock and roll 46, 95
rock duro 92
rockettaro 111
Rolls Royce 143
romantico 34, 59, 135, 147
Rome by night 143
rooftop 50
rough 81
round 118
router 44
routine 59
royalties 110
rugbista 111
rugby 106
rum 26
run 196
rush 34

S (small) 79
safety car 45
sales engineer 188
sales manager 188
sandwich 31
scanner 44, 181
scannerizzare 108, 109
scannerizzazione 109
scatola nera 122
scellino 21, 84
sceriffo 84
schooner 26, 32
sci-fi 77
scioccante 113
scioccare 109
sciuscià 36
scooter 41
scooterista 111
scooterone 115
score 40

scottex 91
scoutismo 112
screening 46
scrivania 182
– *see* desktop
scrollare 108
scull 197
sculler 197
sealskin 30, 197
security manager 49, 109
segnalibro 182
segnorina 143
self-acting 195, 196
self-control 105, 106, 109, 132
– *see* autocontrollo
selfie 50, 72, 76, 110
– *see* autoscatto
selfie stick 103
self-made man 32, 95
self-made woman 95
self-service 77, 94
sense of humour 95
sensore 85
sequel 46
sequoia 31, 60
serendipità 83
serial killer 109
serifo 20
server 44
servicer 177
servizio clienti 122
servizio in camera 122
servizio web 93
set 40
settare 109, 182
setter 34
set-top-box 95
set-up 44
sex-appeal 39
sexting 50, 78
sfidante 48
shake 196, 202
shakerare 109
shakespeariano, scespiriano 62, 102
shareware 44, 182
sharing economy 49
sherpa 55, 81

Index of borrowings and quoted words — **281**

sherry 31
shimmy 196, 202
shirting 195, 197
shock 34, 102, 119
– *see* choc
shock anafilattico 119
shock culturale 119
shock nervoso 119
shock termico 119
shopping 8, 120
shopping cart 182
– *see* carrello
shopping center / centre 125
short track 45, 191
shorts 30
show cooking 50
showbiz 77
shuttle 127
– *see* navetta
sigaretta elettronica 72
– *see* e-cigarette
sigh 83
Signore e Signori 9
silfide 26
SIM 78, 106
sincrotrone 143
sindaco baby 75
single, singolo 128
Sir 31, 82
sit-com 116
sito web, sito 91, 92, 122, 182
– *see* website
ska 94
skeleton 191
ski pass 131
skicross 193
skincare 50
skipper 40
sky-diving 45, 193
slam 41, 83
slideshow 182
slip 40
slogan 40
sloop 26
slow food 90, 232
slowfox 196
slurp 83, 98

smalto 21
smart city 50
smartwatch 50, 72
smart working 50, 90, 194
– *see* lavoro agile
smash 40
smog 105, 230
smoking 30
SMS 62, 78, 106
snackeria 206
sneakers 110
sniff 83
sniffare 108
snob 31, 52, 91, 108, 194
snobbare 52, 108, 109, 113
snobbato 113
snobbismo 112
snow tubing 177, 193
snowboard 191, 193
snowboard cross 49, 193
sob 83, 98
social card 233
social distancing 48
– *see* distanziamento sociale
social media 49, 103
social media manager 49, 95
social media marketing 95
soft skill 50
software 44, 181, 182
solarium 82
sondaggio a caldo 231
– *see* exit poll
soul 46, 94
sound engineer 188
– *see* tecnico del suono
spam 182
spam 44, 182
spammare 108
spazio web 93
speaker 27, 67, 70
speakeraggio 112
speed date 50
spencer 30, 197, 201
spending review 233
spider 41
spin 40
spinning 45, 192

spintronica 177
spiritual 40
splash 83
spleen 70, 199, 202, 203
spoilerare 109
sponsor 113, 115
sponsorizzare 109, 112, 113
sponsorizzato 115
sponsorizzazione 109, 112, 115
sport 33, 38, 40, 58, 83, 147, 190, 230
sportivamente 40
sportività 40
sportivo 40, 115
spread 183
sprint 40
sprintare 108
spyware 49, 182
squaw 32, 82
stage 106
stagflazione 113
stakeholder 45
stalking 105
standard 27, 68, 70, 71, 105
standardizzare 109, 113
standardizzazione 109, 113
standista 111
stanforte 19
star 125, 126, 127, 148
– *see* stella
start up 45
startupper 49
status symbol 82, 92
steamer 32, 198, 203
stella 61, 120, 125, 126, 127
– *see* star
step by step 96, 132
– *see* passo dopo passo
stepchild adoption 50
sterlina 84
sterlino 19
stilista 111, 123
stoccaggio 111, 112
stoccare 109
stock 27, 70
stop 38, 83, 98
stop-and-go 95
stoppare 108

stoppata 115
stopper 91, 115
stressante 113, 115
stressare 109
stressato 113
studio 52, 129
subliminale 85
subprime 49, 186
summit 106, 127, 132
– *see* conferenza al vertice
– *see* vertice
superman 125
supermarket, supermercato 121, 132
super-spreader, super diffusore 48
supervisore 85
supportare 59, 109, 129
supporto 59
surf 94
surfare 108
surfista 111
survival 130
sushi 62
SUV 79
sweater 40, 197
sweating system 195, 196
sweepstake 197
swing 94

tablet 44, 182
tabloide 147
tag 231
taggare 108, 182
talent show 109
talk show 105
tampax 80
tandoori 81
tank 195, 196, 198, 202, 203
tanker 197, 202, 203
tartan 27
tax day 232
taxi 32
teach-in 198
team 40, 190
tearoom, tea room 40, 198, 202, 203
techno 46, 94
tecnico del suono 121, 188
– *see* sound engineer

tecnostress 102
Teddy boy 197, 202
tee 81
telefilm 8
telefono 8, 62, 84, 134, 147, 239
telepass 131
telepatico 40
telettrofono 134
tempo parziale 132
– see part time
tempo pieno 9, 61, 122, 127
– see full time
tempo reale 122, 182
tender 26, 32, 70, 195, 197, 198, 202
tennis 34, 38, 110, 162
tennis tavolo 92
tennista 111, 115
tennistico 115
termoscanner 93
terrier 34, 70
test 27, 71
testare 109
tetto di cristallo 48
Tex-mex 77
The show must go on 97
think tank 232
thriller 105
ticket 87, 88
ticket restaurant 88
tight 30
tights 30
tilbury 32
timer 40
tisi galoppante 143
toast 27
toddy 199
tolleranza zero 122
tomahawk 32, 82
Tommy 198
Tory 27
total body 49, 192
totem 32, 82
touch 49
touch screen 44, 182
tour 59, 135
tour operator 9, 178
– see operatore turistico

trade union 32
trademark 32
– see marchio di fabbrica
trainer 40
tram 32, 38, 85, 162, 197, 202, 203
tramvai, tranvai, tranvia 32, 85, 197, 203
tramway (car) 32, 85, 197, 203
transistor 44
trash 104
trekking 45
trench 40
tribute band 63
troll 72
trollare 72, 108
trolley 32, 232
trolleybus 32, 197, 203
– see filobus
truck (system) 195, 196
tunnel 104
turf 199
turismo 39, 57, 59, 135
turista 34, 39, 59, 85, 101, 135
turnover 40, 106
tutor 106
tutoraggio 112
tutorial 44
tutto compreso 178
– see all inclusive
tuxedo 30, 41
TV 107
tv a pagamento 132
– see pay-tv
tv color 92
tweed 30, 79
tweet 49
twist 196, 202
twittare 108
two-step 196, 202

UFO 79
ulster 197
ultimatum 39
umorismo 112
– see humour
umorista 111, 115
umoristico 111, 115
uozze mera 36

up to date 95
upgrade 44
upload 44
urban 106
URL 78
USB 78
user ID 78
username 44

vagone 102
vamp 39
VAR 79, 106
veejay 77
veganismo 112
vegano 85
vegetarianismo 112
vegetariano 40, 85
vertice 126, 127
– *see* summit
video 75
video art, video arte 75, 76
video on-demand 95
videoblog 49
videoblogger 177
videocassetta 123
videochat 49
videoclip 75
videogallery 49
videogame, video gioco 76, 123
viral marketing 49
virale 128
virtuale 128
virus 182
vlog 77
voluntary disclosure 49
vonga-vonga 143
vs, versus 82

W (west) 79
wakeboard 193
walkman 80
WASP 79
waterproof 31
watt 34
way of life 95
WC 79
web 9, 44, 93, 177

web agency 49
web app 49
web community 49
web design 64
web designer 64, 187
web marketing 64
web radio 49, 64, 92
web tax 49
webcam 44, 77
webchat 74
webcomic 74
webconference 75
webdoc 75
webform 75
webhosting 75
webinar 49, 77
weblink 75
weblog 49
webmail 74
webmaster 64
webmistress 75
webpage 74
webpart 75
webquest 74
webring 75
webseminar 75
webserver 74
webservice 74
website 91
– *see* sito web
webstore 74
websurfer 177
web-tv 49, 64
webview 75
webwriter 74
wedding planner 50
weekend 110, 122, 230
– *see* fine settimana
welcome (to) 96
welfare state 40
wellington 197
west coast 94
Whatever it takes 205
Whig 27
whisky 31, 70, 110, 162
whistleblower 50
Who's Who? 116

– *see* Chi è chi?
wi-fi  49, 77
wiki  49
window  182
– *see* finestra
windsurf  45, 230
wine tasting  207
wireless  44
wow  83, 98
wrestling  192
WWW  78, 107

XL  79
XML  182
XS  79

XXL  79
– *see* extra-extra-large
XXS  79
– *see* extra-extra-small

yak  81
yettie  78
yorkshire  41
yorkshire terrier  79
youtuber  49, 80, 177
yuppy  78

zippare  108
zoomare  109

www.ingramcontent.com/pod-product-compliance
Lightning Source LLC
Chambersburg PA
CBHW050517170426
43201CB00013B/1984